GROWING INTO LOVE

Growing Into Love

*Teenagers Talk Candidly
About Sex in the 1980s*

Kathryn Watterson Burkhart

*G. P. Putnam's Sons
New York*

The author wishes to express appreciation for permission to quote from the following sources:
    The Johns Hopkins University Press and John Money for a selection from
Contemporary Sexual Behavior: Critical Issues in the 1970s edited by Joseph Zubin and John Money, copyright © 1973 by the Johns Hopkins University Press.
    Rightsong Music, Inc. for lines from "Hot Stuff" by Pete Bellotte/Harold Fal-
termeyer and Keith Forsey, copyright © 1979 by Rick's Music, Inc. & Revelation
Music.
    Warner Bros. Music for lines from "He's the Greatest Dancer" by Bernard
Edwards and Nile Rodgers, copyright © 1979 by Chic Music, Inc.; and for lines
from "As Time Goes By" by Herman Hupfeld, copyright © 1931 Warner Bros.
Inc.
    The Center for Population Options for use of the Rock Project Tapes with Loretta
Lynn and Charlie Daniels.

Library of Congress Cataloging in Publication Data

Burkhart, Kathryn Watterson.
    Growing into love.

    Includes index.
    1. Youth—United States—Sexual behavior.
2. Adolescent psychology—United States. I. Title.
HQ27.B87   1981   306.7'088055   81-5174
ISBN 0-399-12640-6   AACR2

PRINTED IN THE UNITED STATES OF AMERICA

Contents

Acknowledgments

I wish to thank Dr. Donald Nathanson, Ms. Marie Stoner, Dr. Winnifred Cutler, Dr. Judson T. Landis, Dr. Margaret Mandel, Ms. Pamela Mottley, Ms. Lee Gruzen and Dr. Diane Hatch for so generously giving their time in reading my manuscript as it developed and giving me the benefit of their professional insights and perspectives.

I especially want to thank Dianne Stern for her invaluable research assistance on this book. Her critical thinking, her creative contributions and her enthusiasm were vital to its development.

For their abundant help and hospitality on my journeys around the country, I would like to thank my friends Nancy and Wayne Fulcher; Linda and Merle Borg; Carol and Art Silbergeld; Valerie and John Stevenson; Bert and Janet Ahern; Peggy and Mickey Esmay; Glen and Mary Watterson; Mary Lou Duguid; Britt Louise Gilder; Michael Malone and Maureen Quilligan; Bob and Fay Kay; my sister, Alice Watterson; and my mother, Grace Watterson Landis.

For their help in arranging interviews, I am indebted to Robert C. Hanes, superintendent of Chapel Hill–Carrboro City Schools; Fred Lentz, director of the Alternative School at Lowell High School; David Fenwick, principal, East Los Angeles Light and Life Christian School; Ed Burlingham and Eta Mooser at Laguna Beach High School; Brent Beamish, principal, Columbia Central High School; Alta Landes, human relations teacher, Coronado High School; Frank Steinfeld at the Commonwealth School; Bill Abbott, assistant superintendent of schools in Boston; Martin Drapkin at the University of Wisconsin and the many other people who gave me introductions and shared their understanding of teenage development with me.

I also want to express my gratitude to the New York Public Library

7

for use of its research typing room; to Isabel Mora, who helped me so much in Los Angeles; to Joan Newsome, for early transcriptions; to Stephanie Croteau for so cheerfully taking on the typing of the final manuscript; to Elaine Markson, my agent, for her unfaltering enthusiasm and loyalty; to my very fine editor, Diane Reverand, who took on the project of shepherding this manuscript through its final revisions; and to Annmarie Dwyer, my loving friend and assistant, who took care of my son, Zachary, and the many details of our family life with tireless warmth, magnanimity and equanimity during the creation of this book.

To my husband, Jack David, I just want to say: Thank you for always being there for me, for sharing your time and your thoughts and your brilliant, but unquoted, quotes. Thank you for your generous love and involvement. You are the person, from start to finish, who's lived through this book with me, who's lived with my having a foot in each world and the echoes of my adolescence reverberating through our house.

Last but not least, I want to thank the many teenagers who shared so much of themselves with me—who instructed me about the meaning of adolescence and who told me firsthand about the nature of their intimate lives and fears and joys, growing up in America today.

Introduction

When I first began to think about writing a book on adolescent sexuality, I asked my stepdaughter, Jacqueline, then thirteen years old, what she thought about the idea.

"That's great!" she shouted, turning up the volume on "Saturday Night Fever" and continuing to dance. "Are you going to interview kids?"

Jacqueline's younger sister, Nicole, who had just turned eleven, was charitable but doubtful. "Well, it might be interesting to some people," she said, "but for someone my age, I think it would be, well, boring."

The idea for this book initially appealed to me because of my interest in my stepdaughters (my God, what do we do next?) and my son (who is still too little to know anything about hormones, although he certainly acts on them). I wanted to guide them in a healthy way through sexual issues that might confront them without repeating by rote what was taught me.

I began the project with very few prejudices or preconceptions. I didn't know what it would be like to be a teenager today, and I had no academic, social, psychological, sexual or cultural point of view to defend or postulate.

All I knew when I started was that for the people experiencing or observing it, adolescence is an absolutely magical, mysterious, maddening time of life. A child's small body suddenly changes, within a matter of weeks, it seems, into curves, muscles and movement. Suddenly your little boy or girl is all arms and legs, motion in front of your eyes, sneakers and moods laid on your coffee table, spilling over into your space. ("I saw my son this morning standing in the bathroom in his undershorts," one New Jersey mother of a fifteen-year-old told me. "I was shocked. I

9

couldn't believe my eyes. He's a man now. Overnight, he's a man!") It's hocus-pocus: instead of a ragged and out-of-breath ten-year-old asking for milk and cookies, a young adult stands in front of you snapping her fingers, radiating sexuality, asking for your deodorant.

Although our sexuality is integral to our identity and to our total being from the moment of birth (and now researchers tell us we exhibit sexual thrusting and lubricating even *in utero*), when puberty sets in, a switch flips into high gear. Music begins to throb, telephones become teenage property and food either disappears in gigantic quantities or remains untouched by these high-energy creatures who are sullen at one moment and ecstatically leaping into the air at another. These young people—and their parents, by association—have been swept into a growth that is at once biological, cultural, psychological, cognitive and spiritual; it is the one time in life, many authorities say, it's *normal* to be crazy.

Parents are often exceedingly anxious about how to deal with the onslaught of these "crazy" years. To make matters worse, they read alarming statistics about teenage suicide, drug usage and pregnancy. They hear that the number of teenagers having sex and getting venereal disease is increasing dramatically.

But what's behind the statistics? What do they mean?

When I first started working on this book, I thought briefly about surveying through questionnaires a "statistically significant" sample of the American teenage population to find the answers. The more literature I read, however, the more people I talked to, the more it became evident that a survey on sex-specific behavior and attitudes was not needed, unless such a survey was of the magnitude and quality of Alfred Kinsey's monumental work—a task that would require dozens of years, thousands of interviewers and a lifetime commitment. (Kinsey's work, by the way, was invaluable to me. Despite the passage of years since the books were published, the research remains thorough and unparalleled. I constantly learned from returning to *Sexual Behavior in the Human Male* and *Sexual Behavior in the Human Female* each time I probed a new idea.) On a more limited scale, Drs. Robert Sorenson, Aaron Hass, Anne C. Peterson, John F. Kantner and Melvin Zelnik and others had done or were doing quite thorough and interesting surveys by question-naire on the sexual behavior of teenagers. These researchers were find-ing what young people were doing sexually, with whom and how many times. Their surveys covered the attitudes and habits of adolescent mas-turbation, orgasm, contraception, premarital sex, pregnancy, and so on, as well as the influence of information and familial attitudes on behav-ior. I knew that we could learn a great deal about teenage sexual behav-ior from their research but that it would not necessarily help parents or teenagers understand the meaning of that behavior or their own reactions to it. It wouldn't help them comprehend the teenager's perspective, attitudes, dreams or desires.

What would help was parents hearing the voices of their teenagers talking about themselves. I thought that if parents could hear their teenagers saying what they were experiencing, and how they felt about it, their fears of parenting in the 1980s would be mitigated. They would have a new level of comfort and perspective on the subject of teenage sexuality. And if teenagers could hear their peers speak candidly on such personal topics, they would feel better about themselves and their own development. So I set out to listen and watch and learn.

I interviewed more than 250 young people from the ages of twelve to twenty. I also talked with many of their parents, teachers, counselors, social workers, doctors and relatives. I spoke informally with many other people about their own teenage experiences. This book is based on all of these interviews—concentrated chiefly on what the teenagers told me about themselves. Although I interviewed twelve-, thirteen-, and fourteen-year-olds, you may notice that many comments on early adolescence come from older teenagers—fifteen-, sixteen-, and seventeen-year-olds—who have begun thinking about their experience in a broader way, and who have begun to reflect on the effect of their early information and experience. Although I didn't plan a statistically representative sample, some of these teenagers come from wealthy families, others come from poor families, but most are middle income. About fifteen percent are black, another five percent Hispanic, Chicano and Oriental; the rest are white.

Some of their parents have been married up to thirty-five years in the same marriage; others had mothers or fathers who had been married as many as four or five times. Many came from homes with stepparents and siblings from combined marriages. Some were living with a parent who shared time or home with a male or female lover; a few lived with one parent and his or her homosexual partner.

These teenagers were urban and rural, religious and nonreligious, sexually sophisticated and sexually naive about themselves and others. Except where specifically noted, I'm reporting discussions about heterosexual interactions and interests. Their beliefs and activities and communities varied widely. Their parents were doctors, lawyers, truck drivers, construction workers, farmers, artists, teachers, clerks, accountants, college professors, unemployed actors, writers, photographers, maintenance men, stockbrokers and cooks. They lived in Brooklyn, New York, and Brooklyn, Michigan; Detroit, Beverly Hills, and a Spanish barrio in East Los Angeles. Others were from Chicago; Denver; Philadelphia; Washington, D.C.; Minneapolis; Fort Lauderdale; Phoenix; San Francisco; San Diego and Santa Monica. I interviewed more than two dozen teenagers in London, England. I talked to teenagers in beach towns and farm towns; big cities and summer resorts. They were optimistic, pessimistic, bored and exhilarated with life.

I found these young people in a variety of ways. For the most part, principals or teachers gave me permission to introduce myself to classrooms of students, tell them about the book and set up interviews. Sometimes friends or acquaintances of mine would arrange interviews with their teenage friends, and many times one session would lead to another. ("You've got to talk to Joyce; I know she'd want to talk to you.") I went to public and private schools, alternative schools, colleges and universities and places of employment. We had our interviews—which lasted anywhere from one hour to four or five hours—in homes, offices, school lounges, and coffee shops; on park benches, school lawns and beaches. The limits came from my time schedule more than theirs. In nearly every case, I had to end the interview before I wanted to. I felt I never had enough time to hear everything a teenager wanted to say. I could have stayed weeks and I don't think we would have run dry of conversation.

Although I didn't like doing it, I have changed most of the names of the teenagers. Where I used their real names, it's because they were legally adults and they wanted to take credit for what they had to say. Many more teenagers were willing for me to use their real names than I was able to do because of privacy laws applying to juveniles.

Some teenagers will recognize themselves speaking in an altered context or environment—in another city or state, with blond hair instead of red hair, with four brothers instead of three sisters and a brother. They should know I've had to change details to provide them with anonymity. Even in the altered context, however, they will see that their stories are faithful to their experiences and what they told me about them.

Certainly behavior is enormously complicated—and quite often, as a teenager talks, you will see contradictions, ambivalences and confusions that stem from conflicts I don't always spell out. My aim is to share with you the way they say it *feels* to be who they are at this point in their own development. My comments come from my observations and interactions with these teenagers and from my discussions with the adults around them.

From the moment I committed myself to writing this book, I began looking at teenagers through new eyes. My first look, unwittingly, was at a lineup outside *The Rocky Horror Picture Show,* which was playing at a movie house across the street from where I live. The white lips, grotesque costumes, mountains of frizzy hair and thick aroma of marijuana startled me. Other teenagers, without the makeup, looked equally unapproachable in their own way. What was behind those bland eyes, those smooth complexions? In the past, for newspaper and magazine articles on "juvenile delinquents" and status offenders, and in connection with research for my book *Women in Prison,* I'd interviewed literally hundreds of adolescents in turmoil—runaways, juveniles in trouble with the law and with their lives—so I knew what it was like to be on the bottom of the totem pole. But what was it like to be "normal" growing up today? Or is there such a thing as "normal"? Sixteen-year-old Vanessa, for one, says there is.

". . . My father calls me a lazy kid," says Vanessa, whose father is a college professor and mother a writer. "He says, you take, take, take. You don't give anything to anybody else. . . .

"My godmother is like my aunt and my dad. She always tells me what's wrong with me. She criticizes the way I dress . . . everything!

"The fact is that I'm a normal teenager with normal wants. I want to have clothes, and I want to go out with boyfriends and I want to stay in my room and think and have my privacy. I can't convince my dad that it's not only me. . . ."

When I scheduled my first interviews at the end of 1978, I panicked. What would I say? What did I really want to know? Here I was, a mother for the first time, in my thirties, approaching an alien population. I had spent my own adolescence struggling against the technical loss of my virginity, and now I was approaching youngsters (who could be my own children if I'd struggled less hard) about the intimate details of their sexual experiences and feelings. Tell me, how do you feel about premarital sex? About masturbation? Did your priest tell you that men have only a thousand orgasms to use in a lifetime, so they shouldn't use them up while they're young?

When I first interviewed several teenagers individually, they made *me* comfortable. They were seventeen and eighteen years old, and refreshingly open. After the interviews, they told me that they'd enjoyed talking and that they'd learned about themselves in the process.

Then it came to my first group interview. Five fourteen-and fifteen-year-old boys. Best friends. I drove my rented Thunderbird out to the suburban home of one of the boys, worried all the way about whether I had enough pens with me, enough gas, enough nerve to go through with this interview. They *all* met me at the door. Fresh, open faces, friendly and welcoming. To a boy, they were wearing T-shirts ("Jock" was written across one of them), gym shorts, sneakers and sweat socks rising up long, gangly legs. They had been playing basketball in the carport before I arrived.

I followed their sweaty backs through the kitchen, into the family room, where we all sat down. I got out my legal pad, and three felt-tip pens and started writing down names, ages, addresses, telephone numbers and brief family histories. By the time I'd finished, I felt at a loss about where to go next. I was quiet, and they were fidgeting in their chairs, giggling nervously, looking pale and expectant. I opened my mouth a couple of times and then heard myself say that this was the first time I'd interviewed more than one person at a time for this book, and I felt nervous about asking them personal questions and prying and "stealing their souls," as Studs Terkel would have put it. I said I didn't know where to start, but that I wanted to know what it was like being them, and I wanted them to tell me as best they could what it was like having their bodies change on them, their voices change, their interests change. How did they spend their days and what did they care about? From that point on, talking was easy. My confession made all of us comfortable.

At the end of our three-and-a-half-hour session, Jock asked, "Can you come back again tomorrow?" The same question repeated itself that evening and the next day with other teenagers. "Hey, let's have another interview tomorrow!" Although these remarks were made with laughter, they were genuine. The interviews provided an occasion for talking about issues that ran deep and were talked about too rarely. They were fun and cathartic.

As I continued my journey around the country, I realized that in these interviews, teenagers were discussing essential issues on a level of candor and directness few of them had experienced before, even with their peers.

After a joint interview with nineteen-year-old Denise and eighteen-year-old David in Boston, for instance, Denise pushed back her chair and looked at David. The two had been friends for three years and spent a great deal of time together. "It's like meeting a whole new person," she said. "It's this whole other world. . . ."

"It is," David agreed. "We've never talked about any of this before. It's not exactly the kind of thing you talk about in front of anybody else."

Over and over again, I felt surprised when teenagers said they had never before talked to any adult, least of all to their parents, about the intimate conflicts, experiences and ideas they had.

"I've *never* talked this way with an adult before," said seventeen-year-old Phillip. "We talk this way when we're by ourselves, the lot of us [friends], but not around anyone else. It's like you're one of us. We wouldn't talk this way to our parents."

At first, I felt that it was a terrible shame teenagers didn't talk to their parents "this way"—but eventually I came to believe that it was quite normal and natural they didn't. I realized that my being a stranger made it much easier for them. I also realized that in the process of growing into new relationships, in experiencing sexual excitement and new feelings within themselves, they needed some distance from their parents, room to make their own mistakes and form their own intimacies.

While talking about themselves so freely and informatively, some young people revealed old traumas for the first time. Sixteen-year-old Patricia, for instance, said that her parents were "pretty liberal" but that she'd never talked to them about her ideas or questions regarding sex. A heavy-set girl, Patricia bit her nails as she confided that she felt a lot of ambivalence about boys and dating and the mere idea of sex.

"The reason, I guess, is I have had some bad experiences as a child," she said at one point during our interview in San Diego. "I saw a couple of flashers. And I was sexually molested by a baby-sitter. I must have been about six years old then. I didn't know what I was doing. He said it was all right.

"That's left me really uptight about sex. I was six years old! It was really sick!

"That left scars. I never told anyone that before. No one. Not until now. I feel pretty bitter about it; it wasn't fair. I never told anyone anything about it—not my father or my mother or the psychologist I saw when I was in therapy. . . ."

Sometimes, I imagine, you will feel as if you are hearing your own child talking when you read some of these stories. Or you will hear yourself. As I worked on *Growing Into Love*, memories of my own teenage years were revived. I remembered being in cars parked by the railroad tracks, the thrill and deliciousness of a back rub or a hand on the knee, and many hot, wet nights when my body was still a vast mystery. I hope parents who read this book relive their youths as well. If you can remember your own feelings as well as listen to where your children are and what they're doing, then you may gain a new feeling of security about being a parent of teenagers in the 1980s.

After meeting and getting to know them, I am less sure that conventional generalizations about adolescent sexual behavior can be applied to individual teenagers, and I am absolutely confident that most parents don't have as much to worry about as they think they do. The teenagers I met are more capable of decision making than we give them credit for; they're more responsible, more caring and more substantial than we imagine them to be.

Decide if you agree, once you've listened. Often what they say seems simple, but it has to do with their feelings about themselves, about other people, about the intimate truth of their very human reality. This is as close to the skin, under it and inside it as I could get and relate to you how it feels to come of age in the 1980s.

For Jacqueline, Nicole and Zachary, with love.

PART I

Some things are better than sex, and some things are worse, but there's nothing exactly like it.

—W. C. Fields

I.

The Sexual Revolution

Yes, a sexual revolution is in progress. The climate we live in is more permissive, erotic and loose than it was fifteen and twenty years ago. The effect of this climate and the patterns coming from it have not fully emerged, but clearly it has had an impact on individual experience.

"I was a slow starter," says sixteen-year-old Marci in Westport, Connecticut. "In the eighth grade, all my friends had already been to third base, but I still hadn't had anybody even put his hand up my shirt. I never went to bed with anybody until I was fourteen and a half!"

Although we see some dramatic changes, we should recognize that just as it was before the 1960s, sexual behavior is still an individual matter, a personal exploration that is wrapped into the matrix of one's childhood, one's family and one's personal history.

It's true that the sexual revolution has sanctioned role changes and an active sexual life for the young, the old, the unmarried and the homosexual. But as Herbert Hendin, psychoanalyst and author of *The Age of Sensation*, suggests, what happens between two people in bed "is influenced less by sanction than by personality, by conflicts over involvement, intimacy, dependency and assertiveness and by fears of vulnerability that shape . . . the experience."

Young people today take in stride erotic literature and information that would have shocked their parents at the same age. Their familiarity with language and innuendo about sexual behavior precedes their actual experiences. Yet young people today are just as vulnerable as we were when we held hands for the first time, first kissed, first touched and made ourselves naked in front of another human being. When they first feel and first say I love you to another person, it's the earth-shaking event that it was to us. Just as we struggle with our self-esteem, our

19

fears of adequacy, intimacy, commitment and involvement, so do they. Sexual revolution or no, when it comes to our sexual interactions, we are all reduced to our common mortality—and to our sense of identity, security and personal worth.

In a large, carpeted room with a view of the Pacific Ocean in front of us, fifteen teenagers and I sat in a circle on the floor, sharing several large bowls of potato chips and popcorn. They were high-school sophomores, juniors and seniors from the area around Laguna Beach, California.

Fifteen-year-old Nancy sat to my right, munching popcorn and getting bits of it caught in her orthodontic paraphernalia. As she talked, she and every other teenager seemed quite oblivious to the fact that the neckline of her peasant-style blouse was draped so low over one bare shoulder that half of a breast and nipple were exposed.

"The main question I ask," sixteen-year-old Jamie was saying, "is do I feel that I have a good-enough relationship with the girl to have sex? That was the question I thought about when I decided to do it the first time. I concluded that we did, and she decided the same thing for herself. We both felt good about it."

Sitting in that living room, listening to those young people talking freely about orgasms, stress, drugs and parental divorce, I was awed by their candor and ease. What I perceived as changes in society's attitudes and expectations were taken for granted by these teenagers. Most dramatic to me was the openness they seemed to feel about revealing their own experiences and vulnerabilities.

"When I was in the fifth grade, I started smoking pot," said Rachel, a tousled blond who lives with her mother and two older sisters. "When I was smoking around people, I got really conscious of my boobs. I was afraid to move because I was so self-conscious about my boobs and my body. I was always that way, but when I was stoned, it was worse—I was paralyzed.

"When I got my first boyfriend, I was fourteen. He was the first boy I had sex with. It was pretty good, but he noticed that if we'd been smoking and then got into sex, I'd get all stiff and it was terrible. He got very confrontive about it, so after a while, I would never smoke pot when we were going to get into sex. Now I hardly ever smoke at all because I don't like the way I feel on it. . . ."

I tried to imagine a similar discussion twenty years ago, when I was in high school. It would have been comprised of extended silences or pontifications, theories and ideals. Only a rare group could have spontaneously and publicly talked about how "some kids actually don't know how to go about getting laid" or how they did or didn't like combining alcohol and sex, how they felt pushed about or fearful of intimacy and commitment.

Certainly in some areas of the United States and within different subgroups, I found views that more closely reflected the accepted mores of my adolescent years. In a small rural town in Minnesota, for instance, sex was not a topic of casual conversation. Several of the junior and senior football players, basketball players and other "stars" from the high school told me that they figured they wouldn't have intercourse until they were involved in a very close relationship when they were in college, or even until they were married. In the daily lives of those boys, sex was rarely mentioned.

"It's not an open subject," said Jud, a handsome seventeen-year-old who was captain of the football team. "Some people talk about it and say things, but you can't tell. Maybe one or two of the boys brag, but they're not too highly thought of. They're put down pretty low."

"Usually the ones who are involved sexually don't talk about it," said Aaron, a tall, gangly basketball player. "They've been going together a long time, so you usually don't know. It's the same for guys as it is for girls; they don't talk about it."

The California group was the most liberal of all those with whom I talked: the group in Minnesota, the most conservative. Regardless of differences in attitudes among individual teenagers about their own sexual behavior, I found an extraordinary level of tolerance for behavior and beliefs other than their own, especially among teenagers fifteen and older, who in general were more capable of abstract thinking, and were analyzing their own beliefs and values.

Teenagers of all ages were quite curious about the behavior of their geographically diverse contemporaries. Many times I found myself listening to their speculations. Boys in a farm town in Kansas, for instance, theorized that in big cities, sex probably wasn't as closely linked to reproduction as it was in their minds, and contraception was more easily available—"Your mother doesn't know the druggist and the doctor!" They figured that as a result of these two factors alone, teenagers from urban areas would be more likely to have sex as part of an intimate relationship than they would.

Teenagers from other parts of the country had their own theories. "In beach towns, kids are probably sexually active earlier," said Joe, a blond basketball player from Laguna Beach, "and they probably stay more tuned into sex because on the beach, all you think about is sex. There's so much skin showing.

"You see a lot of bodies and the bodies are almost naked, so not much is left to the imagination. I think we get sexual real young because of how body conscious everybody here is. You can't avoid seeing bodies."

"It's a stereotype—people want the thin butt and the tan body," said Annie, a seventeen-year-old who plans to become a doctor. "On the East Coast, you might have a really popular girl, but out here they'd say her hair is too kinky, or 'Look at that white skin!' or say 'Her thighs are too thick or something. Here it's more physical. That's too bad, maybe, but that's the way it is. A lot of people probably aren't appreciated as much as they should be."

Certainly the world of our teenagers reflects the world around them. If we notice that they are body conscious, we also have to notice that as a culture, we are obsessed with fitness, flat stomachs, firm thighs and muscle tone. Their narcissism reflects our own.

The ready availability of hard-core pornography and paraphernalia, X-rated movies and details of explicit sex in books and magazines is also part of a larger societal picture, is perhaps as symptomatic of our adult struggle against puritanism as it is symptomatic of liberation. We've created an atmosphere in which we can shout about sex in a way that seems to be in part our own delayed rebellion. However, what is deliciously new and forbidden to those of us who grew up in more repressive times is often old hat or even uninteresting to today's teenagers, who have been exposed to the complexities and contradictions of adult sexual life through television, books, movies and musical lyrics "for years." They have seen juicy, seductive scenes on television, where shows are rife with sexual themes and jokes. To learn about oral sex, rape, sodomy and incest, abortion and adoption, all they have to do is watch TV or go to normal, everyday movies.

I. W. Cole, dean of the Medill School of Journalism, remembers when *Life* Magazine ran a picture story of the birth of a baby. It was 1937 or 1938, and a lot of people were outraged. About the same time, he said, *Reader's Digest* created an uproar by publishing an article about venereal disease. Now everyone talks about toilet habits, sleeping habits, the body and sexual relationships—whether he or she is bisexual, homosexual, heterosexual or celibate.

Perhaps twenty years from now, many of these sexual themes in our popular entertainment media will be old hat.

"I would bet that sex is less powerful now than it was in the fifties," says Dr. Richard Friedman, assistant clinical professor of psychiatry at UCLA, and former director of the adolescent in-patient program at the UCLA School of Medicine. "Now it's something we know—we can have it. It's not out there, it's here, inside of us. New sexual freedom has meant demythicizing sex. It means that the sexual relationship becomes much less important and that the other issues become more important or equal in weight. In the fifties, the conflict and excitement came not from reality, but from fantasy. Now it comes from reality. Adolescent preoccupations in the fifties never got past that base of fantasy. Now other issues are just as important as sexuality. Like what do you know about your mate? What is the nature of relationships? What roles do you play—and what else are you interested in?"

Similarly, the widespread use of drugs is not unique to teenagers. It is part of a larger picture. As Dr. Elissa P. Benedek, director of training at the Center for Forensic Psychiatry at the University of Michigan Medical Center, points out, as a society, we are in the "midst of a pharmacological revolution" through which we have "discovered better living through chemistry." We expect drugs to give us a definite physical and psychological reaction such as "being healed, put to sleep, made alert, elated, relaxed, inebriated, and high." Most of the drugs we use to achieve these states are legal and are used by adults.

We are told by the National Institute on Drug Abuse that drug use among American teenagers is probably higher than in any other industrialized country. Overall, however, there has been a decrease in the level of illicit drug use among teenagers. Although 9.1 percent of high school seniors smoked marijuana daily in 1980, for instance, the year before, 10.3 percent used it daily. Although this shift may seem small, it represents a dramatic contrast to the rise in marijuana use that was occurring up until 1978. In addition, there has been a decline in the past two years in how "high" seniors get when they use marijuana and how long they stay high.[1] While the use of stimulants has increased and the prevalence of cocaine and heroin use has remained relatively stable, the use of hallucinogenics and inhalants has also declined.

According to the investigators and staff of the Monitoring the Future project at the Institute for Social Research at the University of Michigan, alchohol is the front runner among drug preferences. Their surveys show that some 60 percent of high school seniors have smoked marijuana at least once, while 93.2 percent have drunk alcohol at least once. On the average, female users take fewer types of illicit drugs and use them with less frequency than their male counterparts. The frequent use of alchohol and quantities of it consumed also tend to be disproportionately concentrated among males.[2]

Why do so many of today's teenagers drink alcohol and smoke dope? For the most part, like adults, they drink or smoke pot in social settings with friends. Regular drug usage or regular drinking, even in moderate amounts, often is used as a relaxant. Perhaps, to some extent, it is used as a means of reducing guilt and anxiety, which teenagers seem to have in abundance.

A minority of the young people I talked to had problems with drugs or alcohol use. Those with serious problems often recognized that their drug abuse was symptomatic of deeper issues. The one barbiturate addict with whom I spoke told me: "I think you should write about the loneliness of adolescence. In adolescence, everybody's not sure of what they are and who they are and why. I think of death every day. When I get up, I wonder, 'Am I going to live today?' "

Most of those teenagers who regularly or periodically smoked pot or drank alcohol did not view the habit as a problem or an issue to be resolved.

Although some people have equated increased sexual activity with increased drug use, there is no clear correlation. Some of the teenagers I talked to said they were "definitely stimulated" sexually by alcohol or pot, and others said it was a definite turn-off.

"I love it," said one seventeen-year-old in Santa Monica, speaking of pot. "It goes with sex. In fact, my best times are when I'm high."

"As far as I'm concerned, drugs increase my desire and decrease my performance," says eighteen-year-old Joseph. "I can't get into sex if I've been smoking. I pretty much stay away from pot, period."

"Boy, drinking or smoking a joint doesn't turn me on," said sixteen-year-old Annie. "It just makes me feel spacey."

"It increases intimacy," says Bill. "Sometimes you start talking to someone and you feel like you're lifelong friends. It transcends a lot of boundaries."

"If I've been smoking a joint, I just want to go crawl into a corner," says Kitty. "I don't want to talk to anybody. It doesn't have anything to do with sex!"

Feelings about combining either alcohol or drugs with sex were as variable as the individuals themselves. To most who did use them, neither was considered central to their sexual behavior. Rather, alcohol and marijuana were like minor characters on the stage of sexual interactions. They might change the scene or the perspective at the time, but they were not the main action or the stars of the show.

What's available to our teenagers at this time in their lives, when they are moving beyond our control, sometimes seems alarming. Teenagers have always been embroiled in struggles with their own power, but now they have access to tools that make a midnight ride on a stallion pale. Now they have cars and speedboats and LSD. They have empty houses in the afternoons, angel dust, the pill and legal abortion. We worry about their safety and about how they will manage a passage into adulthood that won't leave scars.

There is no question but that times have changed, and so have many of the pressures and expectations in an adolescent's life. As we know, life is quite different for a twelve-year-old than it is for an eighteen-year-old. They function on different cognitive levels. Their ability to know and understand themselves and others, to move from concrete to abstract thinking develops through adolescence—a process that normally spans the years from twelve to twenty. Today, however, ten- and eleven-year-olds seem to be entering the adolescent process, at least in appearance and awareness. Because they haven't been shielded from the harsher realities of adult life—the knotty issues of sex, drugs, divorce, suicide, war, hunger and politics—they grow up faster than many of their parents did. Their childhood is no longer sacrosanct.

It is very disturbing to know that younger teenagers and even pre-teens can and sometimes do conceive children when they're still not fully aware of the capabilities of their own bodies or behavior. Most of them are not cognitively able to understand what responsibility means. Nor are they able to support themselves or a child. Particularly disheartening is the number of teenagers who get pregnant when theoretically they did not want to—as indicated by the number who terminate their pregnancies by abortions. (In 1979, some 434,000 fifteen- to nineteen-year-olds and 16,500 girls fourteen and under had abortions.) On the other hand, if we acknowledge their adulthood, we also must note that the percentage of sexually active teenagers who had abortions corresponds with a similar percentage of sexually active adult women who terminated their pregnancies in the same way.

Early in 1981, parents read that of the 29 million thirteen- to nineteen-year-olds in the USA, 12 million had had sexual intercourse. They learned from a report entitled "Teenage Pregnancy: The Problem That Hasn't Gone Away" published by the Alan Guttmacher Institute, in New York, that despite racial, social, economic or religious differences, the average age at the time of first intercourse is sixteen, and that by age nineteen, four-fifths of boys and two-thirds of girls have had intercourse. From the same report they heard the projection based on today's statistics that four out of every ten girls aged fourteen will become pregnant at least once during their teenage years, two out of ten will give birth (accounting for one out of every five deliveries in the country) and slightly fewer than one in seven will have an abortion (accounting for three out of every ten abortions).

Although parental concern is not unwarranted, it's important to put these statistics into perspective. Teenagers having sex is no new phenomenon. Even in Kinsey's survey in the 1940s, one-half of the women interviewed had had intercourse before marriage, as had 90 percent of the men. Drs. Melvin Zelnik and John Kantner, at the Department of Population Dynamics, School of Hygiene and Public Health, at Johns Hopkins University, have documented the increased numbers of teenage girls having intercourse over the past ten years—but they point out that the age of first intercourse has remained stable, at 16.4 years of age for whites and 15.5 years for blacks, and that most girls report having had only one partner.[3]

Dr. Ellen Freeman, research assistant professor in the Department of Obstetrics and Gynecology at the School of Medicine, at the University of Pennsylvania, points out that part of why adolescent sexuality and pregnancy are making such an impact stems from the fact that we have an increased number of teenagers in our population. According to the U.S. Census Bureau, between 1950 and 1970, the adolescent population (aged 10 to 21) doubled from twenty million to forty million. Simultaneously, the proportion of adolescents who married declined. In 1970, slightly under 12 percent of the girls in this country age fifteen to nineteen were married, compared to just over 16 percent of girls the same age in 1960. In 1979, slightly more than 7.2 percent of all fourteen- to nineteen-year-old females and 2.2 percent of males in the same bracket were married. Dr. Freeman notes that the change in the age of marriage means that even if the proportion of sexually active adolescents remained constant, there would be greater numbers reported having premarital sexual activity.[4] Because of an earlier onset of sexual maturity (down from 13.54 in 1940 to 12.54 in 1968), which naturally raises the incidence of pregnancy where there is sexual activity, the likelihood of conception is also increased, even if the proportion of sexually active adolescents remained constant.[5]

As for the increase in teenage pregnancies, according to Drs. Kantner and Zelnik, teenagers are having sex more, but they are also trying harder to avoid pregnancy and childbirth outside marriage. Their ability to achieve the latter goal is complicated, these doctors say, by the fact that there has been a decline in the most effective form of birth control—the Pill—because of "nervousness" about the medical consequences of its use and by the substitution of one of the simplest methods, withdrawal. It's also complicated by a growing disinclination on the part of teenagers to marry early even when faced with premarital pregnancy.

Overall, fever teenagers today are choosing to marry—with or without a pregnancy, and a real decline is shown in teenagers marrying to legitimate a premaritally conceived birth. This may be due in part to the fact that the stigma against unwed mothers is not as strong today as it was thirty years ago. In many communities, in fact, "unweds" do in fact live with the fathers of their children or have regular contact with them, but do not feel any social pressure to marry legally.

Often the impression conveyed in articles about the "alarming" number of babies born to teenagers is that all of these babies are being born to young unwed mothers. In fact, of the 555,325 teenagers who gave birth last year, almost three-fifths (304,570) were married at the time of their child's birth. Of that number, nearly two-thirds (192, 360) were married *before* the conception of their child. The others married after conception, but before the birth.[6]

What is a matter of concern is that very few teenagers, married or unmarried, say they want to get pregnant or have babies *yet*. Eight in ten premarital teenage pregnancies and two-thirds of premarital teenage births are unintended, according to the Alan Guttmacher Institute. It's also a matter of concern that the prognosis for the teenage mother's future is particularly bleak economically, professionally and maritally.

Although there is much to be said for being older and more physically, financially and emotionally prepared for motherhood, many teenagers—married or unmarried—do a good job of raising their children, despite hardships. Last year in the United States, 250,755 unmarried teenage girls gave birth. Ninety-six percent of those girls kept their babies to raise—sometimes with the help of their families and/or the father of the child.

Certainly there is much that we don't understand about the trends in teenage sexual behavior. Dr. Phillip Cutright at Indiana University suggests that we adults talked so much about the sexual revolution when there wasn't one that finally teenagers started behaving to meet our expectations. They may, in fact, be acting more on our expectations than theirs. It also may be that some of the increased sexual activity has more to do with anxiety about the meaning of life and love during this personally disruptive, highly technological and scientific period of time than it does with erotic pleasure; more to do with searching for or avoiding intimacy that it does with establishing it. On the other hand, we may be shedding Victorian restraints and attitudes that are no longer needed. And perhaps, just as people did for hundreds of thousands of years before the twentieth century, teenagers are just doing what comes naturally at an age appropriate with the onset of enormous sexual drive.

Whatever it is, it doesn't seem to me that alarm is an appropriate response to teenage sexual behavior. Nor does it seem productive to jump to the conclusion that teenagers today are casual or promiscuous. Possibly one reason adults so readily buy this view stems from how we think we would have behaved as teenagers if we had been less restricted ourselves.

Another reason adults so readily assume that teenagers are sexually indiscriminate may be that what is commonplace to them is radical to many of us adults. Certainly, sex free from the threat of pregnancy is revolutionary in itself.

I found that although there are exceptions, most teenagers are just not as sexually sophisticated as adults tend to think they are. In fact, they don't know much. Myths and misinformation are still rampant among the young. For instance, in some neighborhoods, everyone knows you can't get pregnant if you're standing up when you do it and that you shouldn't use Tampax because that's a form of masturbation. This is not surprising. Misinformation and ignorance still exist for many adults—teachers, preachers and self-styled experts who give youngsters information about sex. At a large conference on teenage sexuality in Los Angeles, for instance, I heard an adult workshop leader tell teenagers in his group: "You shouldn't have sex when you're young because you'll burn yourself out; you'll use yourself up."

Although much has changed, much has stayed the same.

What has not stayed the same—what seems to be different—is the behavior of young women. The chief difference I observed is that girls today are competing more openly and aggressively in sports and academics than they ever used to. In the past, girls competed for marriageability, popularity and sexual appeal. They still do, but with a difference. There seems to be a drive toward individual and objective accomplishments among young women today. Many are no longer willing to be appendages who hide their own ambition and initiative. They openly strive to define themselves in their own right.

"There's no overall conspiracy anymore to keep quiet about aspirations or to be ladylike about wanting to win," says Pamela Mottley, a ninth-grade teacher at Dwight School in New York City. "The girls in my classes have no problems at all in wanting to be first in the class or to beat someone out. Nor do they have to let the boys be masterful. They throw themselves into competitive sports in a way that I find absolutely thrilling."

Girls today are also more aware of their sexual feelings and their sexual options than they used to be. The innovations of the Pill and the women's movement, it seems, have made a significant difference. Many expect that they will have intercourse before they are married and plan for it as they would any important stage of their development. In fact, surveys show that premarital intercourse among teenage girls in metropolitan areas has increased and, overall, their expectations about sex, love and marriage have also changed.

"The point is not that girls are having premarital sex," says Dr. Joan Morganthau, who has worked with adolescents for the past thirty years and is currently director of Adolescent Services at Mt. Sinai Hospital in New York City and professor of Clinical Pediatrics at the Mt. Sinai School of Medicine of the City University of New York. "They've always done that. It's that they had different expectations and feelings about it. It used to be that people had premarital sex, but usually it was with the person they planned to marry. Girls now feel equally free to admit that it doesn't have to be with someone to whom there's a marital commitment or with only one partner. So when a relationship ends, they know they will have sex with the next partner and perhaps more in the future."

According to many surveys on sexual behavior, there has been less of a change with boys. Boys have always had premarital sex and usually had it with more than one partner. The spillover from changes taking place with today's girls seems to be an easing of the double standard. The most obvious behavioral change is that today, compared with the days when Alfred Kinsey and his colleagues made their landmark studies, fewer boys—and fewer by a good margin—have their first experience of sexual intercourse with a prostitute.

Young men today also seem to feel that sex without affection is less acceptable than it was in the past. According to Dr. Elizabeth Wales at the University of California, males today are "less promiscuous than their fathers or grandfathers were [in that] they appear to be more concerned with the quality of a relationship as a prerequisite for sexual intercourse. The easement of the double standard which has permitted nice girls to participate in premarital sex and still be nice girls has also made it possible for men to combine love and sexual relationships."

On account of the sexual revolution, a wider range of behavior on the part of boys has been sanctioned. It used to be that boys were encouraged to compete in objective terms—to play ball and reach for the stars—but they weren't allowed to be emotional; they weren't allowed intimacy. Today's boys are often encouraged to explore their feelings and to talk with each other about their emotions. In many cases, I found boys more willing to make commitments than the girls with whom they were involved.

When I asked Evelyn Caskey, the principal of Scotsdale High School, in Scotsdale, Arizona, where I went to high school, how things have changed for today's teenagers, she sat back and thought for a few moments, moving her pencil through her fingers. A large, friendly woman and the first woman principal of the district, Ms. Caskey herself represents change.

"What I see from where I sit?" she asked. "I guess I compare it to when I was in high school. The main thing I see is that there's less stability in family life. I was raised in Chicago. It was a big city, yet I lived on one block, and probably at least eight of the families went to the same church. We lived in a house my father bought before he was married. I never lived anywhere else. I never heard of anyone going to bed with anyone else's husband or that sort of thing. There was a stability to life. There's a real difference in family life today."

The altered nature of the family seems to have had enormous impact on today's teenage girls and boys. The Census Bureau reports that nearly six million children under the age of eighteen live in a one-parent family. Besides experiencing the trauma of separation and divorce, nearly five million of these young people also have had to deal with the emotions and readjustments of their parents following the trauma of separation and divorce. Their view of the world is altered when they watch their parents dating and establishing new relationships. They often have to cope with taking the role of the missing parent in household duties until he or she is replaced. Also, with one or the other of their parents absent from home, the teenagers' sense of self-esteem, their understanding of what love and commitment is all about, go through an examination unknown to previous generations. For the most part, these teenagers don't have grandparents or aunts living close by to help them through periods of crisis.

Teenagers' developing identity also suffers additional problems as a result of divorce. As Georgia Anderson, director of Family Service of Pomona Valley in California, says, "The parent of the opposite sex gives them the consent to be a man or woman, and the parent of the same sex shows them how. It's a problem for children from divorced families. How does one learn to be a man if one relates only to the mother? How do you know how men and women relate to each other if you don't see models? How do you know how to behave as a man or a woman in relation to the opposite sex?"

While teenagers are trying to define their own values, determine the extent of their own attractiveness to the opposite sex and determine what behavior is appropriate for themselves, they often see their parents struggling with the same issues.

"The first time this guy slept with my mother, I came downstairs and saw his things hanging on the bed," said Austin, a sixteen-year-old boy who goes to high school in New Haven, Connecticut. "She has a four-poster bed, and his pants and jacket were on one of the posts and the door was open. It was a shock. It didn't fit. I saw it out of the corner of my eye and I just kept going. I was on my way to school so I didn't say anything. It takes time to get used to that sort of thing."

If it's not an easy time for being teenagers, it's not an easy time for being parents, either. Parents, too, are without support systems of parents, aunts, uncles and childhood friends who share burdens, allay fears and help us as parents by reminding us how we behaved in the process of growing up.

"I have a lot of sympathy for parents of teenagers today," says Sue Cohen, community coordinator at Mt. Sinai Hospital's Adolescent Health Center in New York City. "I think it's easy when your kids are little to be a parent. You can see other children that age, and it's reassuring to know what's going on with other two- and three-year-olds. You have the sandbox community. But parents of teenagers get isolated from other kids. If they could talk to other parents, they'd hear similar stories, like, 'Oh, you mean your kid's been staying out all night, too?' "

It strikes me that perhaps it never was easy to be a parent during a child's adolescent years. At a time when our own lives have begun to reach a state of equilibrium, at a time when we've begun to feel that we're fully functioning adults with some semblance of integration and control in our lives, we're thrown off balance by the eruption of moods, hormones and body changes in the small people we've grown to know through their childhood. These suddenly oversize children come barging into our lives with their massive energy and let it loose in our rooms, wreaking havoc on our calm. These high-powered creatures often look weird and insist on doing so. They impose their moods on our dinners, and they fling their emotions of fantastic proportions into our lives.

Why do so many parents find it difficult to live through the adolescent years of their children? Why do so many parents experience distress as a common denominator at least every other day in their disparate lives?

"I think I'd like to just put them in a deep freeze until they reach the age of twenty-one," I heard the father of two teenage girls say recently. "Then I'd let them out and they'd know how to behave." I've heard many parents applaud writer Fran Leibowitz's suggestion that all adolescents be rounded up and put into the state of Wyoming so they could wear sunglasses to breakfast and annoy each other.

I find many reasons for the difficulties confronting parents of adolescents. First of all, forces have been unleashed in adolescents that they understand no better than we do. Those forces frighten and enchant teenagers and cause reverberations in us. Sometimes it seems as if we don't speak the same language, but often what we're dealing with, it seems, are echoes and distances.

We know, for instance, that adolescence has to do with losing one identity and finding another. Our teenagers are teetering on the edge between doing and thinking in response to their impulses and anxieties. During this period of their lives, a tremendous amount of energy has been let loose that they're not used to.

That energy isn't just sexual. Sexual vitality is bubbling all over the place; there's no question about that. But there's also new aggressiveness, new hostility, new drives and ideas and feelings that are often overwhelming. It seems that all their powers are turned on at about the same time—which may have a great deal to do with why people so often go into high gear in sports and academics and social interactions during their teenage years. They have enormous amounts of personal power and drive at their disposal.

As adolescents, they are learning to develop controls on these new powers and drives. After they learn the controls, things seem to be pretty easy for them. But during the period when they are unsure of direction signals, lights, brakes and other mechanisms for exerting control, everything seems to be out of balance. They often feel crazy, and the adults around them feel crazy. It's during this time that parents feel the most alarm about their children and probably fight with them the most.

Part of our distress as parents, it seems, may stem from the fact that we were teenagers once, too. And unless we're quite unusual, we were mystified by some of our own feelings, conflicts and questions during these years. We did learn controls; we did solve a lot of issues for ourselves during that time; and we did manage to grow up in many ways—leaving the unsolved issues thinly covered or even comfortably forgotten. Then along comes this child-person of ours, bubbling over with newfound power, stirring forgotten memories and lobbing bombs into the most sensitive areas of our defenses.

That we have made peace with the unfinished business of our own adolescence is often of no use when our teenagers shout at us to examine ourselves, to recognize the contradictions in our own behavior. Their pursuit of identity, their intensity, confront us at every turn. When we see their struggles, listen to their turmoil and watch them try out various roles, our covers are often blown—and echoes of our own experience surface to haunt us. Whatever it is, there's a peculiar effect adolescents have in evoking certain reactions on the part of all adults.

It's also disturbing when teenagers start shutting off their receptivity to their parents, when they're making an effort not to be so dependent; to deny dependency. It's infuriating for us as parents to find that our teenagers often no longer want to receive the support, advice or even friendship we want to give them. For years, we have offered our time and interest; we have nurtured, fed and guided their growth. Suddenly the door to their dreams and their minds is shut on us; we are rarely if ever invited in.

When our children withdraw, which they need to do, at least to some extent, to define themselves as separate and apart from us, as individuals in their own right, we feel rejected, hurt, angry. And not without reason.

"I just want to be left alone!" Wendy complained. "She [Mother] wants to know *everything* about me. She wants to know how I'm feeling, if I had fun at the party, who I danced with—everything! When I come in, she's there, wanting to sit down and talk to me. I just want to go to my room. I don't even *know* what I think about everything, and I don't want to talk about it!"

Sometimes hostility becomes warfare. The adolescent, who isn't sure of her own perimeters, needs to define some territory as exclusively hers and within her control. A "prying parent" often doesn't realize he's treading on makeshift, tenuous boundaries that are all the adolescent has to hold onto. What feels like assault and rejection and hate (and is all of those things, too) is often the struggle of a person who feels as if she is drowning and barely holding onto a shred of identity.

"Mom, keep your fucking hands off this fucking journal!" one fourteen-year-old reported that she wrote on the front of her diary. *"Who the Fuck do you think you are anyway?"*

Parents sometimes feel they're not going to survive the upheavals to which they're subjected as all those hormones run amok in the blooming bodies of their children. The impudence or the outright repudiation feels terrible—there's no way around it. Parents find themselves furious at being put into the role of the enemy to this child they nurture, love and care for. It's quite easy—in the face of rejection—to overlook the fact that the child feels out of control and is aggressively defending himself against regressing into his childlike state, and that he is defining himself against the only backdrop he intimately knows—you. One mother of a thirteen-year-old from Great Neck, New York, said that even though she knows better, she's constantly enraged at her son. "It's just awful," she said of her two sons, thirteen and fifteen years old. "They're impossible. I go to bed at night and I'm angry, and I'm still angry when I wake up. I tell my husband, if I run away from home one of these days, you'll know why. Who ever heard of a mother running away from her children? I can't tell you how much I'd love to run away from home, especially to get away from the oldest one. He's terrible. I can't believe that my very own son would talk to me like he talks to me. I think 90 percent of it's his age."

"I hardly ever talk to Luke anymore," says his father. "Anything I bring up, he resists. Anything I offer, he has a need to reject. I see that in his interests even. He doesn't want to go fishing or camping with me anymore. He's created his own interests in activities totally foreign to me. I used to feel rejected by that, but I've learned to see it as a positive thing. He's establishing himself as a separate, independent person. He's found his own thing and has developed and grown in it. In another year or two, we'll probably get close again . . ."

Luke's father was right. We're not rendered unnecessary by our children's moves toward independence. We are merely being delegated to another space, another role. Our love and support are needed from a distance while they explore their own perceptions and discover, as well as integrate, the ideas they have about us, about themselves and about the directions they want to take in their own lives.

"There's no way to avoid this time of life," says Diane Hatch, a former college dean at the University of Michigan. "It's an awkward time; it's different from anything that preceded it. There are silences and differences and new distances. It's a necessary stage of transition that gives teens the boundaries from which to relate to their peers and eventually to be able to relate to their parents again from a new perspective."

While we feel great joy and confirmation of our own identity in seeing our children grow and develop, it is also painful to be confronted by their sexuality and emergence as fully functioning adults. Sometimes we find ourselves with feelings of attraction that not only startle us but make us uncomfortable. Unwittingly, our children of the opposite sex flirt with us and behave in seductive ways in their quest for approval and confirmation that they are attractive and appealing. They try out roles on us to see our response. Since they are usually unconscious or naive about what they are doing, it is incumbent on us to set limits, make them safe and, at the same time, reassure them that they are, in fact, pretty, clever, handsome and attractive.

Additionally, our roles are challenged. To the extent that we have defined ourselves as parents, we must begin to redefine ourselves in our own terms. If we are used to being the prettiest woman or the strongest man at the dinner table, we must sometimes reassess our other strengths—and must not take personal umbrage at the air of competition generated by our same-sex children.

One of the most difficult aspects of teenagers' transition into adulthood for their parents has to do with their biology and our own. When we see their reproductive capability developing, we are reminded that they can and will leave us someday to build their own nests. Our nests will be empty. Separate from us, they may have children. If so, their children will separate from them and build their own nests, and then, if not before, we will be bound by our biology. Our reproductive capabilities will wither, and eventually we will die just as naturally as we were born. Their pubertal growth, then, signals our own aging, our own mortality, our own death.

The signs are clear. As their muscles develop and grow firm and strong, ours are beginning to sag. As their sexual powers accelerate, ours begin to decline. As their energy increases dramatically, ours begins to decrease. We may still play a mean game of tennis or jog ten miles a day, but we tire more quickly; we don't have their resilience. Our staying power is not the same as it was twenty years earlier. We can't go to bed at three A.M., rise at seven A.M. and operate at top energy during the day.

Thus it's their adolescence, their energy, their potency, that confronts us with the reminder that we are actually mortal—that we must age and die. It's intolerable, unforgivable, but true.

"The growth at birth and in infancy is a pleasure," one mother said to me. "Isn't it interesting? It's the growth that takes the child away that we resist. That damned pubertal growth. It's the pits."

Because we have so many difficulties with ourselves and our teenagers during this period of time, we often feel we are rotten parents—or at the least, that they are rotten kids. Most parents, however, and most teenagers handle these years quite well. Parents, for the most part, do a better job than they think they do. And most teenagers, despite their wild swings and flings, manage to make the transition into adulthood without major problems. Joan Lipsitz, director of The Center for Early Adolescence in Chapel Hill, North Carolina, and author or *Growing Up Forgotten*, assures us that "more than 80 percent of American teenagers make their way through adolescence without unwanted pregnancies, running away, skirmishing with the law or suffering undue emotional stress. We can say no more about the adult years."

It's true that we live in a changing society and that many of our children are less protected by social customs than we were. Where we had pressure not to be sexually involved, they are sometimes encouraged to be experimental and experienced. They are not as restricted as we were by geography or social codes. The majority of the teenagers I met, however, impressed me with their ability to evaluate and analyze their options and make decisions based on respect for themselves and others.

They differ. Sometimes they make mistakes. And they almost always have conflicts. But it's all necessary in the process of growing up.

And no matter the similarities in external circumstances, the internal experience of each adolescent is unique. Some glide through their changes; others slip, fall, turn the world upside down. But for each, the response to adolescence is personal. And the way each teenager copes with the transition and the mysterious forces at work within seems to be the mark of his or her individuality. Although a new hormonal flow is let loose in all young teenagers, they do not come out as predictable little cell systems. They emerge as differently as do our fingerprints when pressed into ink and blotted onto paper.

Ultimately, the way we experience our adolescence is in many ways our psychological thumbprint. That print is the composite of the influence of our genes, childhood experiences, relationships and perhaps many other facts we still do not understand.

2.

Today's Girls: Choosing Their Way

When I tell some of today's young women about my attitudes and experiences when I was their age, they're appalled. "They asked you what birth control you used?" eighteen-year-old Elizabeth said incredulously when I told her that newspaper editors interviewing me in the mid-1960s routinely asked about contraception because they didn't want to hire a female reporter who would get pregnant and quit on them. "Did you sue?" she asked. "You should have sued! Even if you did go to work for them. That's discrimination!"

It's difficult for many of today's girls to imagine not feeling entitled to open athletic and academic competition or to their anger, their sexual feelings, their privacy and ability to control pregnancy. "No *Pill* when you were in high school? What did you *do*?" a high school senior in Queens exclaimed. "Oh, that's terrible!"

I found myself feeling like a historical relic when I told them that in college, we had curfews, weren't allowed apartments of our own and could be expelled for setting foot inside a boy's apartment! High school and college girls alike shrieked and hooted when I told them that girls in my high school were automatically suspended from school if they were pregnant, even if they got married. And they sobered when told that abortions were illegal and available only at great risk to a girl's life.

In many ways, life for females has changed enormously in the past twenty years, particularly in terms of their expectations. College and high-school counselors tell us that their female students worry about academic achievement, job prospects and career plans as much as they do about marriage. If they want to stay at home when their children are small, they usually plan to "interrupt" their careers to do so. Even for the girls whose chief goal in life is marriage, not a career, the environment is different. They usually expect to work, and they also expect to share domestic chores and child care with their husbands.

Clearly, girls today have more opportunities for growth—and possibly more opportunities for stress as well. They have seen more women with power outside the home who combine being feminine and sexy with making money and even having children. They see women as bank executives, doctors, lawyers, judges, teachers, stockbrokers and editors; women working alongside men as plumbers, carpenters, police officers, telephone line workers, pipe fitters and soldiers. They see many options open to women, and they know that if they choose, they can form for themselves a multilayered, fulfilling life.

How girls respond to the opportunities available to them, of course, is quite individual. But I talked to many who said they wanted to do well academically and go into the kind of work that would bring them pleasure as well as economic rewards. It seemed to me that economic changes and orientations of women professionally are interrelated with the new freedom girls have to assert themselves and to set their own goals sexually. The vast majority of girls I talked to said they would not rush into marriage but rather would consider their options and take their time when it came to making promises. They assumed rights and freedoms that belonged to a hidden minority when I was their age.

Winnifred, a freshman at Northwestern University, was one of several girls I talked to who said she planned to be "a grown-up" before she married. Her career and her own development would precede her commitment to a husband. As is often the case, her expectations were different from her boyfriend's.

"I believe that in life, you meet two or three people you could be happily married to," says Winnifred, a journalism major who asked me to use her real name. "I think [my high-school boyfriend] was one of them, but the timing was wrong. If we'd met eight years later, it might have been different.

"Before his freshman year of college—he was a year ahead of me—I'd said, 'I'm going to give you your freedom before you ask for it.' It was the beginning of the summer, and we were talking about having other relationships as a way of easing the pain of his departure, and then he was talking in a way that didn't make sense to me. So I said we should talk about how we feel and put it out on the table. It turned out that he was under the impression that we would get married, and that I would come back to that town every summer and vacation and that this relationship we had would hold on continuously. We'd get married after college and I would support him through graduate school. He had no doubt but that I'd be his wife.

"I told him I was planning to have many serious relationships before I got married, but that I'd look for many of his same virtues in people I was involved with. The whole summer was awful after that. He would come over, but we'd have a miserable time. He didn't like to spend money on me anymore—not that he'd ever spent a lot of money, but he didn't even want to go to the movies—he'd just want to sit around and mope. I started wondering about my source of attraction to him. I found myself thinking, grow up! You're acting like an infant!"

In many cases, I found that girls seemed more afraid of commitment than boys did and worried about being trapped in marriage before they had had a chance to see a variety of boys. Perhaps theirs is as much a reaction to being able to maximize their options as it is a healthy need to find out about the opposite sex without artificial or premature restrictions.

"I'd rather not be tied down," says sixteen-year-old Marci. "I'm too young. I'd like the opportunity to go to a party and if I meet someone, to go out with him. I don't want to have to say I can't because I'm going with someone.

"I'll probably be married in another seven or eight years, and now I want to be in a position where I can do what I want to do. I wouldn't want a boyfriend and go cheating on him. I figure I've gotta go out with a lot of people to see what I'd like."

In addition to having new role expectations for themselves, girls today have easier access to materials that will satisfy their curiosity about male-female relationships and sexual behavior in the "real" world. At the ages of ten, eleven and twelve, I read all of the books in the Young People's Section of my small-town library—everything about horses, war nurses, famous people and even infamous people. But I never found any books about suicide, sex, divorce, girls getting their periods or buying their first bras. Today's young girls by the hundreds of thousands read novels written for them by Judy Blume, Norma Klein and others about many complex real-life issues. Themes include their fellow adolescents making sexual decisions, running away from home, getting involved with drugs, prostitution or homosexual incidents. They have many nonfiction books available to them as well. Additionally, many girls have easy access to pictures of nude males in *Playgirl* magazine, *Viva* and others, not to mention even more graphic depictions of males and females in various positions of sexual contact. When I was in high school, most of the girls in my class had never seen pictures of male genitalia either in black and white *or* color. We could only guess, from lumpy shapes under swimming suits, what a penis and scrotum really looked like. The closest many of us got to male nudity was in books in our art classes or at the museum, gaping at marble reproductions of David or some other enthralling male body in a painting. By the time they graduate from high school, most of today's girls have a good idea of what a naked man looks like.

"When *Playgirl* came out, my friend and me were looking at it all the time," says Corina, a wiry, energetic eighteen-year-old with wide-set green eyes that seem not to miss anything. Her wavy black hair cascades down her back as she speaks. "I used to put it under my pillow so no one would find it, and then one time when I was at school, the painters came to paint our room and they had to move furniture. My mom went to move the pillows and there were those *Playgirl* magazines. The painters were looking at them, and my mom was really embarrassed.

"My sister thought in *Playboy* they make the girls look beautiful and in *Playgirl* the men are just out there. I think a lot of the men look pretty gross.

"I remember in the back of *Playgirl*, I saw ads for condoms. 'In all different colors,' it said. 'Surprise your man, choose your favorite color.' I learned a lot from the magazines."

Although we do not know in fact how *much* girls have changed or how drastically, I talked to a number of girls who felt quite comfortable about asking boys out and taking the lead sexually. Although some of the girls I interviewed wouldn't dream of calling up a boy and asking him out for a date, others felt no compunction about being the pursuer. June's attitude was, "If I'm interested, why not?"

Eighteen-year-old June, a loan servicer in a bank in Los Angeles, feels no hesitation about asking out a person she likes. The last person she asked out was twenty-five years old.

"I asked him if he'd take me to our Christmas banquet at the bank," she says, "and he said, 'Why?' I said, 'Cause you're the cutest guy around and I want to be seen with someone nice.' Then we went out a couple of other times, and then I got the old line that he is too old for me."

June, who was a cheerleader at her high school, and who is also asked out for many dates. She says, however, that she can't understand why a girl who likes a guy isn't direct and straight to the point. "I've asked a lot of guys out," she says. "My mother thinks it's great, and my father, who's an ex-navy man, doesn't understand it at all. He can't get over how outgoing I am. I'm different from my mother. She's a very quiet person."

Like June, seventeen-year-old Kathleen will not play a role of waiting and wondering. She takes responsibility for what she wants.

"One night I went into a liquor store to buy some wine," says the tall, lanky, high-school senior in Whittier, California, "and I met this guy who was a psychology major in college. I was fifteen and he was twenty. It was one of those things that goes *click!* He said he was hungry, so I went home and made him a steak and baked potato and got some wine and brought it back for him to eat. That was really jazzy. He was really knocked out by that. Nothing like making the first move. That was first-move city!"

Of course, when anyone asserts herself, when she makes the first move or acts as the initiator, she risks being rejected. Traditionally, males have had to run that perilous course and learn to handle rejection. Now young women seem to be assuming some of that load. In sexual relationships, sometimes the stakes are even higher.

"The first time I wanted to have sex, I was practically naked," says Barbara, an eighteen-year-old who lives in San Francisco, with her mother and four sisters. "I was loaded. We'd been drinking all evening and I knew what I was doing exactly. I wanted to make love and he wouldn't. I started saying, 'Well, I'm *not* a virgin, so you don't have to worry about that!'

"I was really curious, and I really wanted to do it to see what it was like. I wasn't in love with him at all. But there I am, practically naked, and he goes, 'I don't think you really care for me, and I care about you—that's why I won't.'

"I said, 'But I'm not a virgin, so it wouldn't matter.' We were in the back of a van at the park, and he goes, 'I *know* you're a virgin. Don't lie to me. I care about you, and that's why I won't.' I cried. I was ashamed of it in a way, but I'm lucky my curiosity point didn't come with another guy. I'd started seeing him in March, and that was in May.

"Finally, about four months later, after this dance one night, we were really tired, so we laid down in the back of the van to sleep for a while and we ended up making love. It was nice. We fell asleep afterward. I never bled, either. It was nice because by the time we did it, I really cared about him, so it meant more. I'm glad he wouldn't do it when I first wanted to."

Although Barbara's beliefs about premarital sex differ from her mother's, she accepts her own sexual views with quiet confidence. "My mom and all but one of my sisters have a different value system altogether from me. We were always taught that you have to wait to have sex until you get married or you go to hell. One of my sisters had premarital sex when she was twenty-four, and her and my mom cried for three days. She kept saying, 'What am I going to tell my husband?' At the time, I thought,'What a dumb thing to cry over!' She still feels guilty about it, even though she ended up marrying the same guy. She thinks she was wrong and weak for doing it. That's the way my mother feels, too, and I respect her value system. It's just different from mine, that's all."

Knowing about sex, being assertive, being aware, being interested, does not mean that most girls feel old enough or mature enough to engage in sex themselves. It means for many merely gaining comfort with the idea that sex can be a pleasurable and important part of life, not something evil or lurking.

"I've always been grown up, but now I'm growing into my body," says Louise, a large, wide-eyed girl with a somber expression on her face. She's wearing an army fatigue jacket over her V-neck velour shirt and army dungarees. "Lately I'm knowing my body is there and realizing I'm a physical entity. I'm beginning to learn what sexual pleasure is, and I'm getting used to myself. It's like you are here physically. I've always been sexually aware, but now I'm living inside myself and beginning to fit the body I live in."

Many teenage girls look at their sexuality as a process of getting to know themselves and their own responses, and at sexual experience as one part of that process. The actual act of sexual intercourse does not seem to be thought of as an act of rebellion anymore but rather as a normal part of life that comes either before marriage or with marriage, depending on one's beliefs.

Even girls who take their virginity very seriously and are committed to the belief that premarital sex is wrong seem able to visualize sexual relationships in an informed way, with comfortable humor and perspective on virginity itself.

"I'm going to hunt for a virgin to marry," says Maria, a sixteen-year-old at South Boston High School. "I want my old man to be a virgin. Girls can prove they're virgins, but guys can't. We have to find a way to prove they are. I guess you could tell by the way they're fumbling around. I want to fumble around together the first time."

"We used to think of sex as springing full grown, instead of as a process one learns by exploration and something one develops into," said Dr. Maj-Britt Rosenbaum, Associate Clinical Professor of Psychiatry at Albert Einstein College of Medicine in New York City and former director of the Human Sexuality Center at Long Island Jewish-Hillside Medical Center. "It's not like you turn on a switch and know how to operate sexually.

"I think it's a positive thing today—that kids have more time to learn in the sense of experientially learning, not just educationally learning.

"They can integrate their sexuality into the totality of who they are as a person and know that it's just one facet of them. *It's not separate and apart, some part of them that creeps out at night.* [My emphasis.] It's a very powerful impetus in them, and at the same time it's much less frightening than we used to think of it. We used to think of it as having a life of its own that was primitive and powerful that would take over if given free rein.

"They have the freedom to see its earlier, clumsier manifestation—somehow they have more play room right now, to make mistakes before it's fully developed."

The sense so many girls I talked to had of having that room to play in, of knowing that they had the control to make decisions and sexual explorations in a progressive, process-oriented way continually impressed me. Hearing them talk about the integration of their needs and their awareness of their own sexual levels of development was equally impressive.

"I've come really close to having sex with a few people," says Lucille, an eighteen-year-old who's planning on becoming a CPA and then going on for an M.A. and a job as a comptroller in a major company, "and it hasn't been right for me. A few times I felt pressured. Two different guys said to me, 'Everyone else is doing it, why not you?' If it's not right for me, and not the right time for me, I say no. It has to be right for me, and the right time for me.

"Sometimes I think, well, I'm an adult, so I should do adult things. But I do what I want when I want to, and nobody's going to make me do things when I don't want to, and that includes intercourse.

"I don't feel sex has to mean you love somebody. I think there should be a feeling of attraction, and that both people should know why you're in the relationship and what it means to you.

"When I have a relationship, I want to know the terms. If I have intercourse, is it going to be a commitment, a one-night thing or what? As long as I know the terms and the limits, it's okay with me. My fantasy is that it will be someone I've had a commitment with, and this will just be part of it, a growth part of it, but we'll see. I'm not waiting until I get married or anything like that. It just depends on my relationship and with the man. . . ."

Self-esteem seemed the most essential ingredient in each young woman's ability to choose whether she said yes or no to whatever it was she did or did not want to do. Self-esteem was very much involved with her sexuality and with the extent to which she valued herself and her own feelings, whether she saw herself as an object or a person. If she felt worthy, she knew she had the right to make choices and to assert her wishes.

Although I admired the confidence so many of the girls I talked to felt about deciding the if's, when's and who's of their sexual behavior, I was also struck by the realization that girls who do not have moral beliefs against premarital intercourse but who are not personally ready for it no longer have societal sanction to protect them. On the contrary, many of them feel pressure from their peers—and sometimes their parents—to be sexually knowledgeable before they're ready. From parents, the pressure often comes in subtle forms.

"My father had a big joke—that he didn't want me to get pregnant for a long time," says fourteen-year-old Allison. "And last year, my mother took me to Planned Parenthood to hear a lecture about all kinds of birth control. I didn't want to go, but she insisted.

"I'm not ready for it, though, even though they think maybe I am. I wouldn't want to go to bed with someone unless I felt very close to them.

I think that the first time will be something very special and will be with me for the rest of my life. I wouldn't want to be tricked into it or used. I would want it to be a genuine thing. I don't want it to have to be something I have to do to be accepted. I want it to be clean and pure and simple."

With peers, the pressure usually is not subtle.

"I'm still a virgin," says Caroline, a dark-haired high-school junior in Fort Lauderdale, Florida. "I never felt uncomfortable about being a virgin until three months ago, and that was because I got the feeling from some friends of mine who aren't virgins that they were saying, how can you relate to us when you haven't *done* anything? Like they didn't want me with them because like I couldn't know what they were talking about. And that's true. All I have is what I think about—fantasies and stuff.

"I'm really sentimental. Everything in that first experience is important to me. I'd like him to be a virgin, too. That's one of the things I'd like. My friends think that's crazy. They're saying oh, you're kidding. You'll be fumbling around and everything!"

Allison and Caroline seemed quite secure about their wishes for "the right time" for themselves, and most likely they will have the self-esteem and determination to set their own terms. Girls with strong religious convictions, likewise, usually have support for their views and an understanding of how sexual behavior does or doesn't fit in with the rest of their lives. Some of the girls I talked to, however, said that they had had sex because they felt a need to do what their friends were doing, to be part of the crowd.

"I told my mom when I was in the ninth grade that I wanted to go to the doctor and get a diaphragm," sixteen-year-old Susan said, laughing. "I said, 'I'm getting to that age, Mom, and I want to be prepared. All my friends have already done it, and I think I'm going to want to do it soon.' Finally she took me, but I'd already done it by then.

"I can't think of any of my friends who are still virgins," she said, pausing to think and shake her head. "It may be because of peer pressure—but we all like it. We're part of the cool group—that's how we're thought of. We don't look down on anybody who hasn't. But we're more, sort of, you know, wild.

"I knew this one girl, she was a year ahead of us, and she was still a virgin. One day we were sitting in the car, a bunch of us, and somebody said, 'Let's talk about sex.' We asked her what she thought about it, and she said her boyfriend wanted her to have sex, but she wouldn't have it until she was really in love. She said she respected herself too much for that. Then she asked what about us, and we said, 'Yeah, well, we all do it.'

"The very next week, she said, 'Hey, you'll never guess what. You'll never guess what Greg and I did last night.' Just the week before, she'd said she had too much respect for herself to do it. But I think she did it because we all had done it. I think she's a follower type person. She wants people to like her."

For girls who don't have an integrated sense of themselves, when they're emotionally not very secure, getting involved sexually before they're ready can be a real setback. Since they want the approval of their girl friends, and since they feel pressured to perform, they often can't do a good job of evaluating their own readiness or the feelings and intentions of the person with whom they're involved. Vanessa made a decision that ultimately led to her feeling very bad about herself. She says she made the decision because "all my friends had already done it" and "he wanted to." Her pleasure with her accomplishment was short-lived.

"The next day I went home and sat on her bed and said, 'Hi Mom!' I was all smiling," says Vanessa. "I couldn't stop smiling, and she says, 'What?' and I say, 'I slept with Jerry last night.' She goes, 'Oh, my little girl is growing up!' and hugs me really hard.

"That night he told me he thought we were getting too serious, and I said, 'What did I do wrong?' He could have said I want to see other people besides you or something like that, but he didn't. He just said he wanted to stop seeing me. It was my first time, so I thought it must have been something I did. For a long time, I went around thinking something must be the matter with me or he wouldn't have gone off like that. I was afraid to have sex again because I thought I must be so horrible. I'm insecure to start with and that just made it worse. . . ."

"A lot of girls around here get into sex before they even know what their bodies are about," said seventeen-year-old Helen, who lives in Malibu, California. "It gives them bad feelings about sex and makes it harder for them to learn to like it.

"I was thirteen when I first had intercourse and I didn't like it *at all.* I didn't know what I was getting into at all. I was a little bit drunk and one thing led to another.

"As soon as I got aware of my body and my sexuality, I stopped having sex. I wasn't interested in it again until I was almost fifteen. I wasn't inhibited at all in the fourth grade, for instance, but I got inhibited later because I was aware of my body in a different way. It was the same thing again when I got older. Like I saw other people seeing it and then I experienced myself differently."

Takey says her decision to have intercourse at fourteen didn't come from a desire to have an intimate relationship or express any feelings she had for the boys. Her sole motivation was to score points with her girl friends and to get them to stop harassing her about it.

"All my girl friends had told me about it," says Takey, who's now eighteen and has creamy light brown skin, dimples and warm brown eyes. They kept asking me, when are you going to do it, when are you going to do it?

"Finally I did it with Hugh Cummings. For a long time he had asked me to go out with him, but I didn't want to go because I knew if I did, I'd sleep with him. I knew what he was like . . . he was a real Casanova. He was fourteen, also. Finally I figured, oh well, I might as well get it over with, and I liked him well enough. That was the first time we got together.

"We did it at my girl friend's house. Everybody knew about it. They were all out in the other room waiting. It wasn't anything I was thrilled with 'cause I knew it was going to be painful. I can remember the next day taking a bath and feeling kind of dirty . . . knowing my mother and my family didn't know . . .

"I ended up going with him for seven months. The reason I stopped seeing him was 'cause he was seeing all these other girls, including my two best friends. I had an idea he was sleeping with them. At the time, I tricked Kay into telling me how they had done it. She told me and then she realized what she had said. I was mad at him, not at my girl friends. Everyone was in love with him because he was so cute."

According to Herbert Hendin, author of *The Age of Sensation*, a brilliant study of college students, the changes begun by the sexual revolution have "institutionalized" an escape from intimacy and love. Young women experience peer pressure to be sexually involved, he says. To be sexually experienced gives status, to live with a man is super status and to be casual, detached and experimental is supreme. "Virgins are without status," he says, "subjects of derision. The result is that women are now doing what men used to do; they lie about their sexual experiences."

The status that comes from sexual experience is almost humorous when contrasted with my high-school years. In those days, girls bragged about their chastity and denied their sexual experiments and pleasures. Now many girls deny their chastity and compete with one another verbally about sexual conquests. On a few occasions, I did hear girls talk about sex in the depersonalized way that used to be traditionally male— joking about who was the best lay—or speaking in a detached way about a boy's performance or feelings. "He was hung, but let's just say he couldn't dance," one girl laughingly describing a boy she had had sex with the week before. "When he called the next day, I told him I was sorry but I just didn't think it would work out. I didn't tell him that I kept thinking of fish lips when he kissed me!" Often such talk was just plain funny, but sometimes, particularly when I heard how much a boyfriend cared (and the girl didn't), I felt that an odd blend of anger and bravado was masking other fears—a dynamic not new to the 1980s.

"Ted's gotten so serious, it really bothers me," says Theresa, a college freshman at the University of Arizona, who has maintained a long-distance relationship with Ted, her high school boyfriend in Flagstaff.

"He called me before Christmas vacation and said he'd pick me up on the fourteenth and we could go out that night. I told him no, I wouldn't because I was going to go out and party that night . . .

" 'Does that mean you have another date?' he said.

" 'No, I don't have another date, but I want to be free to go out and talk to other people. I don't have a date now, but I might end up with one.'

" 'I don't go out like that because I think of you,' he said. 'I can't have fun with somebody else because I think about you.'

"I said, 'Well, I go out with other guys and I don't think about you.' I don't know why he has to make it so serious. If he *knew* how many other dates I had, he'd *die*."

Although many of the girls I talked to had reservations about making commitments and had fears of marriage, I didn't feel that many were casual about their relationships. Overall, they were very serious about their decisions, thoughtful about the outcome of their behavior and caring about the people with whom they were involved. Despite the measure of freedom they had, very few were involved in impersonal, frenetic sexual activity. Those who were, according to their friends, often had problems at home. Often I heard statements like "Her mother doesn't even know what she's doing; she can't be bothered if she does," or "Her parents are never home, what do you expect?"

"Some kids, though, I think they do it because it's their way of looking for love," said Ellen, a high-school junior from Bridgeport, Connecticut. "Like there was this one girl, she's a friend of ours, but her mother is dead and her father's getting remarried to a woman she doesn't like.

"One night we were at a party, and she pulled this guy into the bedroom. We were all drinking, so our defenses were down some, but she was pretty drunk, and she pulled this guy right into the bedroom—right off the room where we were all dancing. Everybody saw her do it, 'cause it was right there, and then she started taking his clothes off and then she like raped him right there in that room—like she made him make it with her. You could hear everything because she was really being loud. Then after that, they came out, and then this guy, Jim, he took her arm and pulled her into the bedroom and then they did it, too. I *know* she was looking for love. She always said it didn't bother her that her mother was dead, but I think it did. Now she has herself all straightened out and she doesn't act that way anymore, but for a while there, she was really off her rocker."

The minority of girls who try to take sex in a very casual way may not be reflecting liberated behavior or casualness as much as they're expressing confusion about themselves and who they are. "The problem of sleeping with a guy is that almost always afterwards, they don't call you back," said Janie, a seventeen-year-old who says she's slept with probably about thirteen guys over the past four years. "They don't speak to you again afterwards. Most guys are like that, or it usually turns out that way. It makes me feel funny, like you've done it with them and then nothing. Like something's wrong with what you did or something, I don't know. A couple of times last summer I slept with guys I met and then later I found out they knew each other. That made me feel cheap. Do you think they think it's cheap if you sleep with their friends?"

The confusion comes, more often than not, from the stress of increased opportunities and from not understanding their own motivations. They behave in an intimate way without an intimate relationship, and they understand the person they're with even less than they understand themselves.

Even girls who are older, more experienced and more aware of themselves, like nineteen-year-old Trisha, who lives in Minneapolis, are often confused by sexual behavior that doesn't quite fit their feelings.

"The first time I slept with Kenny, I had a crush on Ben," she says. "I had just gone on a ski trip with Ben, and when I got back, I was planning to see Kenny. Kenny and I had just made out up to that point, but that weekend we were driving to Chicago to stay in his brother's apartment for a couple of days. Kenny was very inexperienced sexually. He'd never slept with anyone, so this was going to be his first time.

"The first night we were really uptight. Besides Robert (who lost his virginity when Trisha lost hers), I'd never slept with a virgin, and I didn't want to teach him. We spent the night hugging and cuddling and rolling around. He couldn't get hard. And all night as we'd roll over, I'd blink and see Ben, and then I'd blink and see Kenny.

"I thought, *this is horrible!* Here I'm starting a relationship with Kenny and I'm having Ben on my mind. It was *very* confusing."

Despite birth control and the relative freedom it creates, the idea of reproduction is much more entangled with a girl's sense of her own sexuality than it is with a boy's. I met a number of young women who were virgins and quite comfortable with the idea of waiting for intercourse. For many of them, the possibility of getting pregnant was the main factor in their decision not to have intercourse. When asked about birth control, they said they had heard too many cases of it not being foolproof and too many bad stories about the side effects of the Pill and IUDs. They weren't taking any chances.

"I haven't had intercourse yet," says Terri. "I could see it happening with Bob, but I don't want to have a baby now. I have too many things I want to do. It probably won't happen until I'm assured I won't get pregnant. I don't think he'd want to be a father right now, either." Terri has long red hair pulled back from a mature, softly freckled face. She is a confident, comfortable young woman. "I heard someone say that if you don't do it before twenty, your skin gets wrinkled," she says. "But I don't want to tamper with my future for an immediate gratification."

Fear of pregnancy also makes many girls nervous about intercourse when they're having it and interferes with their ability to relax and fully enjoy the experience. Because of surveys conducted by Doctors Melvin Zelnick and John Kantner of Johns Hopkins University in metropolitan areas in 1971, 1976 and 1979, we know that the numbers of girls aged fifteen to nineteen having sexual intercourse increased by two-thirds in the 1970s. Their most recent survey showed that 50 percent of girls in metropolitan areas are having intercourse, but no studies have been made on whether enjoyment of sex has increased along with the contact. Many girls do have sex without birth control—and we'll discuss the many complicated reasons for that later. But even with the use of birth control, girls often fear the possibility of pregnancy. Many say they have reduced pleasure as a result of their fears or unresolved conflicts about intercourse.

"I never had an orgasm with a guy," says Lisa, an eighteen-year-old from Darien, Connecticut. "I always have this twinge of guilt or worry or something hanging over me like a cloud. I think about what I'd do if I got pregnant and it really makes me nervous. It's a hang-up I have, I guess, but it always takes away from the fun. When we start doing it, I just get worried about will he pull out in time, and even though I have a diaphragm, I think if he doesn't pull out in time, I could get pregnant."

One nurse-counselor told me that she often talks with girls who say they have trouble lubricating during sex, so she talks with them about how to relax and how to communicate with their boyfriends. "I try to help the girls get a feeling about what they want so they feel free to become more aggressive in their relationships," she says. "Once they feel free to be aggressive, they also become more orgasmic.

"One girl I saw this morning couldn't relax at all during sex and was quite upset about it," she said with a smile. "So I prescribed a little wine."

Despite the wine, sex researchers tell us that teenage girls are not as orgasmic as boys. Boys have an orgasm almost every time they have sex, but girls don't. Part of this may stem from worries about pregnancy. It may also have to do with biological differences in levels of drive. I suspect, however, that it has more to do with experience (lack of it) on the part of girls and their partners, conditions surrounding the interaction and a great deal of anxiety and ambivalence about their sexual excitement and the morality of premarital intercourse that stems from the teachings of the double standard (it's okay for them, but not for us). Whatever the reasons, not having orgasms doesn't seem to bother teenage girls as much as it does their boyfriends or adult women who still have not had orgasms.

"I still haven't had many orgasms," said Wendy. "I felt it would come with experience. I didn't feel I wouldn't be complete until I had an orgasm. I felt I didn't need it. I felt if I never had an orgasm in my life, I wouldn't be unhappy.

"I was really into *Cosmopolitan* at one time, and they wrote about orgasms. They said as you grow up, sex gets better and better, and that in your late twenties, a woman sexually blooms. I felt great, like why rush it? Knowing Gary, I was always worried he would say, 'You *are* having orgasms, you just don't know you're having them.' But he didn't, and I was glad for that. I always said, 'Look, don't feel bad. It's a beautiful experience for me.'

"Boys always want you to have an orgasm, and they want an orgasm themselves over almost anything else," says Melanie. "Manny is always saying, 'Did you come? Did you enjoy it?' I always enjoy it; I just wish he wouldn't ask me. He just feels like I had to come or he feels bad, like he didn't satisfy me. I tell him that to me, it doesn't matter if I come or not. Sometimes I do and sometimes I don't."

Generally, girls did not seem as concerned with their performance as boys. "Last year the captain of the football team kept asking me out," says Agatha, "and I'd go out, and then he'd try to get me to go to bed with him. We went out quite a few times and I kept saying no to him. Finally I said okay, and then afterwards he says to me, 'How was I?' I thought that was so weird. He was so self-centered. He kept asking me how he was, and I said, 'I don't know. I don't know how to scale those things.' He got really mad at me."

Many times girls have their first orgasm not when they're having intercourse but when they're petting, having oral sex or masturbating. Several told me that when it happened the first time, whether by themselves or with a boy, they were shocked at themselves and felt upset about what had happened to them. The rush, the loss of control, frightened them. Two or three girls said they felt bad, like they were doing something they shouldn't be doing; perhaps on some level, they were frightened to fall out of a role and into life.

"We were lying on the bed, and I didn't have all my clothes off, just my blouse, and we were lying together, with our front sides touching," say Claire, a seventeen-year-old in Boston. "Our rhythms were exactly together, and it came from a lot of foreplay, touching each other, kissing all over each other, and then lying together very hard. Then it surged up in me.

"I remember afterwards feeling cheap. Not guilty, but I felt bad. I had a bad taste in my mouth, like that was the only reason I was lying there to get the feeling that only lasted one minute anyway. It was like a cheap thrill. I was lying there for those few seconds of joy. I was disgusted. I got up and put on my clothes, and that made it worse—like, well, that's it. That's all there was to it!

"This summer it was different. There were no bad feelings in the air, and it came off with a whole different aura. I found out it can be beautiful. You don't have to live for the orgasm; it's nice, but you don't have to have it.

"The whole orgasm thing—sometimes I think I'd rather not have it because I find the lying together and touching, feeling so much more gratifying. But of course, right after orgasm starts, once you're intertwined, you can't stop it. . . ."

Although many girls today feel extraordinary freedom compared to girls twenty years ago, some girls still go through enormous personal conflict about having sexual desires and acting on them, even when they stop short of intercourse. They are unaware, as many of us were in the fifties, that Kinsey's studies showed quite clearly that petting definitely contributes to the effectiveness of sexual relations after marriage and that, depending on the attitudes of the people involved, premarital sex has no negative effects and often contributes to a more successful adjustment in sexual relations after marriage. Of course, a girl's conflicts and feelings of ambivalence depend greatly on where she is, what she believes and how she feels about herself.

More often than boys, girls feel conflict about their behavior because they have been taught by their parents that sex is wrong for good girls. Jennifer, for instance, has been told that if she "comes home pregnant, she's out of the house." She lives in a small town in Illinois and feels great anguish about what she and her boyfriend Michael have done when they've been petting. Although she doesn't seem to understand why, she feels that her sexual behavior is bad and something that would disappoint her parents and mean she's an unworthy person.

"I feel like a slut," she says. "I really do. We've talked about having sex, but he's the shy type. I want to but I don't want to. I wasn't positive I was going to marry him, and I wanted it left for my husband. I haven't done anything but kiss him for the last two weeks."

Jennifer puts her face in her hands, and when her head comes up again, her face is covered with tears and her eyes are red. "We were so close to making love," she says. "We didn't, but I feel like I have. We were only this far from it. [She holds up her thumb and forefinger together.] I feel like I have. Oh, I feel so ashamed. . . ."

Although seventeen-year-old Connie lived in a California beach town, and although she had had sexual intercourse, her feelings about her behavior seemed to be much the same as Jennifer's. Her more worldly experiences didn't abate her anxiety. I met Connie at Palisades High School, shortly after I had interviewed four boys, when she came running up to me with her face flushed and tears rolling out of her large blue eyes.

"Scott told you, didn't he," she said, biting her lip in a vain effort to stop the tears. "He told you in front of those other boys. I'm going to kill him!" She burst into sobs.

"I wouldn't mind him telling *you*," she said. "But that boy Jim, he's so *evil!*" She turned around and nodded toward Jim, who was standing by a door, talking and laughing with two other boys. "Look at the way he's looking at me. He'll tell everybody. Oh, I could die. I could just kill Scott!"

Connie's reaction is what I would have expected when I was in high school. It wasn't the offhand attitude of sixteen-year-old Mattie, who'd said after she had sex with Raymond: "I knew he'd talk about it and he did. Some girl said to me, 'I heard what happened to you prom night!' I tried to deny it, but it's something a lot of people do, so I don't mind. I wasn't mad at him for telling. I was glad I'd experienced it."

Connie's reaction reflected the norm of the fifties—all the shame and guilt of "it" being known. As she continued to talk, we walked out to a patch of grass in front of the school and sat down. She began pulling blades of grass out of the lawn where we were sitting and stopped crying, gulping big breaths of air in an attempt to calm herself and regain her composure.

"The first time I did it was at my house," she said. "It was a Sunday and everybody else was at church. I felt really bad. I felt like, God, am I a whore because I did this before I was married? I don't think it's anybody else's business, but I was really scared. I had always told myself, I'll never do that! Not before I'm married! That's what I thought.

"The guy I did it with was the guy I went with before I started going with Scott. Recently he called me up and asked me to go out, and I told him I couldn't go out with him because I was going steady with Scott. He says to me, 'Whatever you're doing with Scott is wrong.'

" 'You talk!', I said.

" 'You know no other man's going to want you 'cause you're *used*,' he said.

" 'Then how come you're asking me out?', I said. He says, 'Well, that's different.' "

Connie pulls more grass. "A lot of guys say they want to marry a lady that's a virgin," she says. "I asked Scott how he felt and he said, 'Sure I would, but there's none left.'

"I take it for something meaningful, but I'm afraid guys just take it for what they can get and it doesn't mean anything to 'em. The guy I get married to, I'll be with him for a while beforehand, so he'll know about me and he'll know about my past. I doubt if it'll bother him if he accepts it as part of who I am . . .

"I'd die if my mom ever found out. She'd kill me. She got mad because I had a hickey on my neck. She gave me a big lecture about it. I don't think she has any idea about me. . . ."

"Guys are supposed to have sex and girls aren't!" said Connie's friend Sarah, who had come up and sat down while Connie was talking.

"Yeah, we're supposed to *save* ourselves while they go out and get experience!" says Connie, bitterness edging her words. "Oh, I hate Scott. I really could kill him."

Although a great deal has changed, perhaps even more has stayed the same. "People are going to do what they want to when they're damn well ready," said one young doctor at New York Hospital. "Just like in the past, when the pressure was not to have sex, girls still had it. They just weren't free to talk about it. Now, when there's pressure to have sex, a lot of girls aren't having it. People choose for themselves no matter who's pushing."

It will be a long time before we know how much of what we see that's "revolutionary" is experimental—and how much is actual change. In the meantime, we can only hope that what is happening is a move toward a natural and healthy self-expression that incorporates the idea that females are at once sexual, emotional, intellectual and spiritual. Perhaps the pathway to an even more emancipated future for the daughters of these young women may lead all of us into a fuller view of our own humanity.

3.

Today's Boys:
The Myth of the Macho Male

In recent months, I've heard many adult men talk about what it would be like growing up today. They can't imagine the effect of living in an environment that's so sexually permissive and free in contrast to when they were teenagers. The mere idea of having their sexual peak coincide with the Pill, co-ed dorms, and easy access to sexual intercourse with peers instead of prostitutes makes some men of the fifties nearly dizzy.

"The differences must be dynamite, absolutely dynamite," said one New York businessman. "The other day my son was thumbing through *Club* magazine, and I was trying to tell him how extraordinary it was that he could be so casual about seeing pictures of naked women in all these provocative poses. We never saw anything like that when I was in school. He thinks it's normal to see pictures like that."

In fact, as Gay Talese points out in his book, *Thy Neighbor's Wife*, prior to the publication of *Playboy* magazine in 1953, very few men in this country had ever seen a color photograph of a nude, let alone the graphic pictures they can now study at their leisure of a penis entering a vagina, a woman touching her clitoris, men and women intertwined in any number of sexual positions.

"Spring in New York, when you see all these beautiful women on Fifth Avenue walking around with their breasts loose and free, it's *incredible*," he said. "There's nothing like it. When I was a kid, the closest I got to breasts like that was in the underwear section of the Sears, Roebuck catalog. I still can't get over seeing all those breasts; every spring is like a fantasy come true."

Although teenage boys do have freer visual access to female anatomy and freer contact with it than their fathers had, they have not lost the sense of mystery, fantasy and romance that men of the fifties experi-

enced. It may be that the male response to spring in New York or any
other part of the country is more universal than one would expect—
unrestricted by age or access.

"Spring's the problem for me," says Bruce, a seventeen-year-old from
outside Detroit. "That's when I start seeing the girls again, and my
blood begins to boil. I don't have sports and I have a lot more time on my
hands. It's just like a clock. In the spring and summer, I need the attention of somebody. When school starts, I have footfall, then in the winter
I have wrestling, and I get through that, but by the end of track, I want
to start seeing girls again.

"If I was reading a book like yours, I'd like to know from other kids
what they think is a moral standpoint. What is a moral standpoint? I
believe masturbation and sexual intercourse before marriage is wrong.
But is it a necessity? I'd like to know I'm not the only one who's against
it but ends up doing it anyway.

"Sometimes I can turn down the volume a little bit, but at times like
this, in springtime, the blood's beginning to boil again. Lately I feel like
having a little romance—not the I-love-you part, but some romance."

Bruce studied his arms. "Really, I don't like being so free," he says.
"It's kind of fun having someone you can go talk to and share your
feelings with. Mom and Dad and the guys don't help all the time."

"Springtime drives me crazy," says Wells, a college freshman at the
University of Pennsylvania who comes from New Orleans. "I feel kind
of high about seeing everybody take off their coats—seeing the buds
come out and the girls walking around. My girl friend said maybe she
ought to go on vacation for a couple of weeks. I never let her get any
sleep."

It may be that boys today have more realistic expectations about sex
and about sexual and marital relationships than did their fathers. Certainly many expect to behave somewhat differently within their roles as
husbands and fathers. According to the Institute for Social Research at
the University of Michigan, the majority of high-school seniors in this
country, for instance, assume that their wives will work at least until
children are born and that they will share household duties and child
care. Many of today's boys seem to have an easier time expressing fears,
crying, showing physical affection and softness to one another than did
their fathers. Their dreams and desires, however, often sound quite like
those of older men.

"I think I'd enjoy teaching geography and being a sports instructor in
a private school," said Graham, whose father owns a carpentry shop and
whose mother is a lab technician. "I definitely want to get married and I
definitely want to have kids. The woman I want to marry, first of all, she
has to have a sense of humor and big breasts. . . ."

Although boys today may appear to be more sexually mature and
sophisticated, in the privacy of their own rooms, they still have adoles-

cent worries. They worry about the size and shape and adequacy of their sexual equipment, muscles, stamina and experience. They still fret about being old enough to get their driver's licenses and suffer agonies over pimples and popularity. The boys I talked to seemed to feel more anxiety about their attractiveness, about making contact with girls and negotiating dates and social situations, than I expected they would. I had forgotten the chasms they had to bridge.

"Half of the kids have a problem, including me, just talking with girls or vice versa," says sixteen-year-old Eric, a soccer player in his California high school. "There's a group of school swingers, but it's a pretty small group. With them, outsiders are not welcome. People who belong to that group are popular. They're just naturally outgoing and friendly, and they're more open and loose.

"What it boils down to is either you have it or you don't. You can tell right away if a guy is loose and can talk with people, if he has a smile on his face, or if he's uptight. It's an age and experience problem."

Another age and experience problem for boys is that they are confronted daily by genital equipment with a life of its own. To complicate the matter, they have enormous sexual drive, which is in itself complicated by continuing mores against casual sex and the fact that the average adolescent girl seems to get along well enough with less sexual activity than boys. (Kinsey's Studies showed that girls managed with one-fifth as much sexual activity as boys, but I suspect that if current research were conducted on this topic, it would show a narrowing of that gap.)

As Dave said, sipping his beer: "When you're about fourteen or fifteen, everything starts getting complicated. At least that's so for guys. You discover you've got a cock, and you expect people will say, 'Oh, you've only used it once?'

"Most people at school say, 'Who have you screwed?'

" 'Oh, I've screwed so and so,' you say, and he says, 'I've screwed more than you have,' And in fact you both want to but neither one of you has screwed anyone!"

One of the greatest revelations to me in the process of researching and writing this book was how misunderstood boys and men are. I was absolutely awed by the depth of their feelings, their tears and their pain. Since males are so strong and powerful physically, since they're often quite aggressive, competitive and assertive, we lose sight of their vulnerability and tenderness. We forget that warm, sensitive and loving feelings can be encased in such hard, strong young bodies.

I talked to one young woman, for instance, who couldn't figure out why two different boys she had had sex with on two different occasions hadn't called her again afterward. She was an unusually beautiful young woman, and it didn't seem that their disappearance would have stemmed from any lack of her appeal or attractiveness.

"Maybe they were embarrassed," I said. "Maybe they didn't know how to handle what happened, or maybe they felt guilty. Maybe they just didn't know what to say."

"Hey!" she said, her eyes widening. "Wow, that *could* be! I never thought of that. *They* might not know what to say. They might feel guilty . . . *Wow!*"

Although this young woman was intelligent and articulate, she was astonished at the suggestion that *boys* might feel even more anxiety about their behavior than she felt about hers.

The popular assumption is that teenage boys, like the engines of shiny, brand-new cars, are revved up and ready for sex. By a certain age, regardless of what they know, how they feel or what they want, they're expected to be sexually confident, knowledgeable and ready to leap into bed with anyone who taps them on the shoulder. In fact, most boys *are* horny a great deal of time, and they are potentially more capable and more active sexually than their fathers. But the expectations do not take into account individual differences. If confronted by a girl who is ready to go "all the way" before he's ready, for instance, a boy who's a virgin is usually expected to perform as well as lead the way in the sexual exchange. And as the sensibilities of boys are being bombarded with erotic stimuli, millions are living in female-headed homes with an absentee father as a role model. Perhaps I shouldn't have been surprised when a number of boys expressed their disaffection for the "sexual revolution" and the supposition that they're always ready, willing and able to screw on signal.

"I resent the fact that there's a sexual revolution and I'm supposed to go out and get my share," says Kim, walking at a fast clip across the frozen ground at Northwestern University, where he's a junior. I keep pace with him, watching his intense expression as he speaks. He's short and solid, with his black hair parted in the center and slicked down, thirties style, his bright brown eyes topping a royal blue parka with red shoulder stripes.

"I have very personal views of sex," he says. "I don't think it's right if someone has a sexual desire to go out and find an opening to satisfy it. I think too much of myself to sell myself short."

We continue walking until we reach the cafeteria. I have clamored and made great noise for a cup of coffee and getting warm; Kim seems free of such immediate needs but indulges me. Once seated, we are joined by Kim's friends Britt, George and John and continue the discussion.

"If someone made a pass at me, I'd be very infuriated," Kim says. "The way I see it, if you find love, forget about the biological element. We shouldn't be dictated to by our biological desires. If there has to be sex, it shouldn't be out of proving one's love. It should be out of the mass of energy and feelings that you have for one another. . . ."

In light of what we hear about the sexual revolution and about boys being out to get what they can when they can sexually, what Kim's saying may seem quite unusual. It's not. It's just that we don't often hear such a conservative view. Perhaps we don't hear it because it's not popular; perhaps we don't want to hear it; perhaps we don't hear it because boys don't normally say it or especially want to distinguish themselves with what may seem an odd perspective.

"Being a virgin," says Kim, "I think you're more careful about yourself. If you're going to give yourself, you question, am I getting someone on the same plane? I wouldn't want to be taken casually. If I was taken lightly, I think it would be devastating.

"Society today tells us love is superficial, and all the Beautiful People seem to be leading decadent lives, setting an example . . . for all the people who want to be beautiful, too. It's the Studio 54 scene. You go to the disco, man, and what do you hear?" Kim sings and beats out the rhythm to "The World's Greatest Dancer" on the floor:

"He has the kind of body that would shame Adonis,
He never leaves the disco floor alone
He wears the finest clothes,
The best designers, heaven knows,
Halston, Gucci, Fiorucci . . ."

"This is the middle-American role model," interjects George, a freshman from Fort Lauderdale, Florida. "The macho guy going to disco with his wife in the golden chains, going upstairs afterward to snort cocaine and have an orgy. These are the people trying to be cool and beautiful."

"Love's not superficial; caring for and relating to another person is not superficial," says Kim. "It should be whole and full and spiritual. In Bali, lovemaking averages six hours. In the U.S., it averages five minutes. That says all the differences in our cultures.

"I guess the best person for me hopefully would be a virgin, and then hopefully after we got married, where we'd have our own private space . . . then, we'd unite. I hope it would be whole and loving . . . a spiritual union. . . ."

In addition to resenting pressure to prove themselves sexually, many young men seem either to resent or to be unnerved by increasing aggressiveness of young women. They feel depersonalized when they're treated as if they're undiscriminating sexual performers. In fantasy, it may be stimulating; in reality, the reaction can be quite upsetting.

"Girls have come up to me and wanted to go home with me," says Jon, a tall blond at Yale University who went to a Catholic high school in Queens, New York. "First of all, it was an automatic turnoff for me. It just doesn't fit my expectations or ways of thinking about things. I wondered what they really wanted.

"It happened to me several times last year, and it just struck me as not being right."

"Why?" Jon's friend Rick asked.

"Maybe fifteen years of Catholic school," Jon said after considering the question for a moment. "But the abruptness of it really got to me. They didn't know me, but they wanted me to take them home.

"I wouldn't do that to a girl. I'm not against two people really knowing each other and talking that way to each other, but I think that's really aggressive."

"I don't give a shit if two people don't know each other and sleep together," says Ronald, who came to Yale from York, Pennsylvania. "That doesn't bother me at all. What I don't like when someone tries to pick me up is the manipulation of it all. I hate the feeling of being manipulated. For instance, if someone calls and asks me to go out and get a cup of coffee with her, and then as soon as I get there immediately gets sexually aggressive with me, then that offends me because it's not straight. It'd be a lot more honest to just call up and say 'Let's fuck. I want to fuck.' "

Another Yale student felt that the apple-barrel upset wouldn't be so bad if women were more tuned in to the possibility of being refused. As a graduate of a prep school, he said, he was used to the games and the manipulation from his side of things, but he thought he was more sensitive to subtleties than women. Their lack of sophistication in playing the game of aggressor was what bothered him the most.

"The fact that women can come up and say what they think is especially confusing for guys," says David, who went to prep school in Massachusetts before going to Yale. "Especially if they're [the guys] used to being aggressive themselves. For me, it depends on whether the girl is attractive or not. I tend to romanticize things a lot . . . I think of wine and music and romance, and it usually doesn't exactly fit that image.

"It's an ego thing for me. When I grew up, with dances and things, both girls and boys wanted the same thing, but it was all cute and coy. All the tactics were manipulative. None of it was straight—and that doesn't bother me. But what bothers me here is when people [women] are trying to *exert* themselves. I get irritated when people are trying to persuade you and they don't pick up on the signs when you're saying no, I don't want to have sex with you, I'm not for it. They can be more inexperienced at the games, so they don't pick up on the subtleties, and that bothers me."

Of course, role reversals that do occur can be very rewarding. Like Rick, many young men said they were quite happy with women doing the asking—and as far as they were concerned, they wouldn't mind being spoiled by it.

"I like women being aggressive," says Eric, also a Yale student. "It removes responsibility from the guys, and that's good. But I think it's still very much that the male is the aggressor and the woman is passive. I think the big difference is that women are more receptive than before. To the extent that women are aggressive, it's good. There's no reason for it all being one-sided."

"I don't like it much," said Tom, a University of Florida sophomore who had suffered repercussions of a girl friend's "macho" behavior. "In high school, I wasn't exposed to games," he says, "maybe because I was in sports. But I think the games here at college sometimes border on viciousness. For instance, when you're sleeping with someone and she gets up and leaves in the middle of the night, and in the morning you see her coming out of someone else's room. That happened to me last year. We didn't have that kind of casual agreement. I'd been seeing her for eight months. My first reaction was that I felt sorry for her. Then for the next few days I felt sorry for myself. Then I just let it go."

As Tom sees it now, he says, it's better not to have a full-time girl friend at college anyway. "There's just too much pressure," he says. "Commitment takes time. I've realized lately that I'm very selfish with my own time. It's easier to be just friends or sexual partners—but it's harder to have a real commitment or to have to see each other every day. I know a lot of guys would resent the time being taken away from being with the guys. There's still a macho thing—a lingering of the separation of the world of women and men."

Although young men obviously focus a great deal of attention on the response of their own genitalia to the breasts and buttocks of the opposite sex, it also seems clear that boys are just as concerned about sharing, being cared for and being loved as are girls. While boys like and respond to a nice body, survey after survey shows that other things are more important to them. Aaron Hass, Ph.D. and author of *Teenage Sexuality,* found that teenage boys, for instance, ranked "doing well in school" number one on their list of priorities, "having friendships with members of your same sex" number two and "athletics" number three. Having sex was ranked next to last in six items of importance.

In a survey commissioned by *Seventeen* magazine in March, 1978, boys admitted to being drawn initially to a girl because of physical attraction. The vast majority of 1,039 sixteen- to twenty-one-year-olds said that they considered *personality* (not sex appeal or attractiveness) a girl's most important quality. The most important reason they chose for asking a girl out on a second date was her *sense of humor.*

"Awhile back, I hoarded all the *Playboys* I could find, and my mom pointed out that even though those girls have such great bodies, they're not necessarily very smart," says seventeen-year-old Frank, a muscular, high school junior in Chicago who has a poised, thoughtful manner. "Well, my mom's proven right. I've taken out that kind of girl, but it's all show. The cover looks great, but there's nothing inside. Girls like that, they'll get someone just like them—a Mr. America—and neither one of them will be willing to compromise. They never get much in the end.

"My ideal woman is my best friend's older sister. She's in sports— she's real athletic and hardworking. Her sense of humor is the biggest thing. I kind of fell in love with her last year. I love when she comes home because then I get to kiss her. I love kissing her and putting my arms around her. She's just perfect."

When boys do get involved in an intimate relationship, they're rarely as casual about it as the media might lead us to believe. In interview after interview with teenagers about their relationships, I found that the boy, not the girl, was more deeply invested, the one who got dumped and hurt. Although boys cover their hurt feelings with more aggressive behavior, I found that in some ways, the boys seemed much more at risk than the girls.

"In the tenth grade, I fell in love with a dancer, Sally," says Dennis, shaking his head as he sips his hot coffee in downtown Madison. "We were in a show together and we fell in love. We had marvelous sex. It was always marvelous. We always came together. We didn't have a real high-powered intellectual relationship. She thought she was smart, and I thought I was smarter. I took pleasure in showing her in little ways that I was smarter . . . I still do, I just can't help it.

"With her, I was so in love, and then I was jealous. I found out she was sleeping around with a lot of people, and that really hurt me. When we talked about it, she said she thought we should stop seeing each other. She said, 'I don't think I can grow anymore with you,' which was ridiculous because we'd never grown together in the first place.

"But that didn't matter. I was crushed. I cried all day. I cried for days."

"It's tough to be a male adolescent and to know how to act," says Dr. Maj-Britt Rosenbaum, associate clinical professor of psychiatry at Albert Einstein College of Medicine in New York. "There's pressure on them to be macho, but often they're still quite lost and don't know how to handle their own sexuality.

"They're just as concerned about being cared for and loved as girls— it's just a different manifestation of the same concerns.

"They're much more vulnerable in a strange way. Just the same way that their genitalia are out there, they're more vulnerable and more easily rejected. Boys put themselves out there. They can't hide behind anything.

"They're also handicapped because of their unequal growth. How they often lag behind girls a year or two adds to their sense of not being quite with it. They feel out of control—they're constantly having hard-ons from so little stimulation. Just touching or having clothes rubbing on them can give them a hard-on, and that makes them feel even more vulnerable. . . .

"They move from castration anxiety to fear of not being manly enough to easing off into am I a homosexual? Girls have such an easier identification. It's so rare to hear a girl saying she's afraid she's a homosexual. They sometimes have hair on their arms, but they're not as disturbed about their sexuality because of it.

"The boys have much more vulnerability in gender identity as well. There are many more disturbances with males in terms of their sexuality. Boys have to fight against regressive identification with their mothers—I'm *not* a girl!

"If you scratch that exterior, you get to the fear—like, if I'm not making out with the girls, I'm homosexual. You can tie that in with the unpredictable and vulnerable genitalia. They don't function when you want them to and do when you don't.

"Then they have the added burden creeping in of girls knowing more and being sexual. Now they have to wonder, will I live up to it? There's a real switch from I know it all and the girls are still out there. . . . But at the same time, there's still the expectation from girls that boys should know more and be stronger and more knowledgeable and be the dominant male. That's tough on boys."

"Guys have to prove their masculinity," observed Molly, a college freshman at the University of Wisconsin. "Think about it. Women know from having their period that they're feminine. Men know only from having sex that they're masculine. A lot of them feel it's necessary not to be a virgin to prove to themselves that they're masculine. One guy told me that he felt like he had to get over being a virgin so that when he meets someone special, he'll have had some experience so he'll know what to do."

I met many boys who expressed insecurity about being capable and adequate sexually. Their anxiety was often compounded by their awareness of girls being more sexually experienced and expectant. An attitude I thought was particularly reflective of their insecurity was that so many of them said they would prefer marrying a virgin to a nonvirgin.

"It feels like a girl has lost something if she's not a virgin," one high-school junior told me right after he had been talking about his sexual relationship with his girl friend. "I'd definitely want to marry a virgin. I'd want to know she was all mine."

In their 1978 survey, *Seventeen* magazine found that 60 percent of the sixteen- to twenty-one-year-old boys in this country preferred to marry a virgin. Half of the college students felt the same way. Two-thirds of the Southerners, the most traditional group, wanted sexually uninitiated brides, as opposed to less than half of the Northeasterners. More than two-thirds of the nonwhites, against 56.8 percent of the whites, favored virgin brides.

"I want a wife that hasn't been with every guy in town, but who has been experienced," says Jim, a slightly more "open minded" high-school sophomore. "I don't want to go to a ten-year reunion of my high-school class and have said to me, 'I was with her, man, and she really whips it on!' "

At first, I was bewildered (and disgusted) by hearing such comments. I categorized them as the old double standard, rehashed once again. The more I listened to what the boys were actually saying, however, I also heard a less obvious message. That message was that these boys want to be special; they want to be unique; they want to know that they can't be replaced in the eyes of a lover or spouse. If they make a commitment, they want to know they're number one. Since they do feel so vulnerable, one way of ensuring that they are irreplaceable is literally *being* number one, the first and only man on the scene. The magical thinking involved seems to be that if she can't compare you, she won't reject you; you will be the best.

Another reason for the desire to have a virgin wife may stem directly from the fact that many young men have little sexual experience themselves, and want an equal match. We tend to forget that there are many sexually inexperienced young men. Nearly half of the young men in their mid to late teens are still virgins, as are more than a quarter of the men in college.

Since it's often assumed that they've had intercourse, a lot of uninitiated boys begin to wonder about their own virility and to doubt the validity of their own pace.

Gabriel, for instance, laughed when he told me about watching the TV movie "James at Sixteen," about James losing his virginity. and then another such show called "Sooner Or Later."

"Here I was, sitting there watching," he said, "seventeen years old and still a virgin, saying, 'Hey, I'm seventeen! What's the matter with me?' "

Underneath the laughter was concern. With so much public emphasis on pubic regions, it can be disconcerting to feel you are one of the only teenagers who doesn't feel comfortable about or ready for sexual intercourse.

When fathers put pressure on their sons to "prove themselves" sexually before they're ready, they can add to their sons' concerns and undermine their self-esteem.

"When I was in seventh grade, my dad started making comments about how hot this or that girl looked and what I should do to turn her on and pump her up," said Mickey. "I think he was kind of worried about me being normal. I sort of appreciated it, but I thought it was pretty disgusting, too. It was like he wanted me to do it real bad. I'm eighteen and I still haven't done it. I'll do it when it's the right time for me, not before."

"Every time I go out the door on a date, my dad says, 'Keep the barn door open!' " says Randy, a senior at a Minnesota high school. Randy, who plans to remain a virgin because he's "not ready for a kid," says, "Sometimes when I'm getting dressed, he'll say, 'I hope that gun is loaded with blanks.' "

When youngsters were pushed into action before they were ready by the expectations of their peers or parents, they usually said the resulting encounters were not particularly satisfying sexually because they had no idea what they were doing. Most of these experiences were reported to be terrifying, exciting, chaotic and clumsy. Chad's experience seems typical of very young boys who first have intercourse as a way of gaining approval and proving their masculinity.

Chad was twelve years old and in the seventh grade when he first had intercourse. He had never had a girl friend. "I had a lot of older friends in my neighborhood," he says. "They all hung out together and they sort of took me in. They had told me what to do. Then they set me up with this girl a grade older than I was. They told her it was a party for a few people at this house, and in fact it was sort of a party, but there were only six people there. Then the other two couples left, so I was left alone with her. They had a couch there, and we were sitting on the couch.

"It happened fast. I took off my pants, and she took off her pants and just unbuttoned her shirt.

"For me, it was like, God, then I'll be one of the gang, if I show them I can do it. If I don't do it, they won't like me. That's what was in my mind.

"I didn't do it longer than I had to. I pulled out just before I came. It was kind of scary because I knew what could happen. . . .

"Later these older guys, fifteen and sixteen, bought a condom and showed me how to use it. I was twelve, and I think they thought it was funny, but they were good friends of mine."

The girl in this ritual also lived in the neighborhood and, according to Chad, didn't seem adversely affected. "I didn't know her that well," he says, "but after that we kinda went out. We went to a couple of dances together and went together a few months. I liked the feeling of doing it with a condom. I thought it was pretty neat."

In Bart's case, it was also an older girl who initiated him. He was twelve; she was fourteen.

"In 1973, we moved into these apartments downtown," said Bart Campanelli, an eighteen-year-old from Glendale, Arizona. "There were two girls there who were pretty loose. My friends, a couple of guys, and I used to pull their pants off in the swimming pool and stuff. We'd mess around with them.

"Well, there was this one girl, Linda, who liked me. She'd had intercourse before. When we'd rip down her pants in the pool, she never cared. She'd turn around and pull 'em up slow.

"We both (she and I) wanted to do it, and we decided we were going to go all the way. I didn't care where or when. Anyway, this one night we decided we would do it. We walked out of this old lot out in the desert where there was this nice soft dirt underneath a tree. She had her pants off and I took off my pants and my shoes. I had my shirt and my socks on. I was real nervous, but I wanted to. (This was even before my first wet dream.) She had this tank top on, and that was exciting.

"I kind of liked it. She was teaching me, though. That much was clear. I was listening to what she said. She was telling me what to do and I was doing it. When people ask me how you do it, I always say it's sort of a natural instinct.

"I had the feeling she wanted more of me. I was glad she was the one—somebody had to know what they were doing!

"My brother and our friends were in the apartment with her sister and this other girl. When we came back in, they all started laughing. We had dirt all over us. We didn't realize that."

More and more, young men seem to have the opportunity—as well as the stress—of giving up their virginity before they're the initiators.

"I did it once before with someone and I never told my girl friend," says sixteen-year old Carey, shaking his blond head and plucking several blades of grass from the ground outside Hoover High School in San Diego. "I felt really bad about it at the time, too. It was somebody I'd known for a long time. We were at her house, and I didn't want to and she wanted to and so I did it anyway. She was eighteen, and she'd had intercourse before. I went to lay on the couch and she came over and she just forced me into it. I couldn't say no.

"My girl friend and I have done it three times now, and it's really different. It's totally different when you do it with someone you love a lot. It's not just physical, it's a lot more."

When boys have decided that they want their first sexual intercourse to be with someone they love or with the person they marry, they find themselves in the sometimes awkward position of being the one to set limits. It's difficult for them because often, they say, their intellect is saying no but their bodies are saying yes. A biological drive seems to be pushing them, like it or not, making it particularly difficult to say no both gracefully and comfortably.

"There was a twenty-six-year-old woman who was very interested in me," says nineteen-year-old Harvey, a college sophomore from El Paso, Texas. "She was married and getting a divorce, so I wasn't breaking anything up. Anyway, this one time we were making out, and she was the antagonist . . . She wanted to have sex, and she was reaching down, ready to get into heavier things. Totally unlike the seventies male, I removed her hand and refused to have sex with her.

"Sometimes I toyed around in my mind . . . I'd get up in the morning and think, this is the day I'm going to have sexual intercourse. I knew I could have sex with her, and I'm not sure what stopped me except some fear and some guilt about her being married. Even though she was going to get divorced, she still was married, and I didn't want to play any role in their break-up—or be used in any way for the breaking up of it.

"I had fun making out with her, though. It was a very enjoyable experience, and it was natural, so I did it. I think I should be natural sometimes and not just be intellectual about sexual activity. . . ."

Certainly there are rewards in being selective. Boys like Harvey seem to feel very good about themselves and about setting limits that fit their own development. David, a sophomore at Harvard College in Cambridge, explained the decisions he's made about his own sexual behavior.

"When I was a senior in high school, I was going out with a person in my class," he says. "Our relationship was growing physically, but not as much emotionally as physically.

"I was trying to figure out whether the relationship we were having was really right. I was asking myself, do I love her enough to express it physically and sexually?

"When I thought about it, I felt the relationship wasn't good because it didn't reflect those feelings. I realized she felt more for me than I did for her, so I broke off with her. She was really hurt, but I decided that breaking up was more honest because she was expecting more and hoping more for the future than I was, and that would have been worse for her in the long run."

It may be that the encouragement for boys as well as girls to leave the role playing behind allows a wider variety of options that will eventually be considered quite normal.

David, for one, came to the conclusion that he wanted to postpone sexual intercourse until he marries. "It's a symbol of the unity of two people who've grown together," he says. "It's an expression of love. It's a commitment and responsibility.

"I would degrade myself if it was less," he says. "My body's important to me. It's a two-way thing. It's knowing another person—and without that, it's a limited thing, just a physical or emotional thing.

"I think about what I do. And I like to be aware of what I'm doing even if I don't like what it is I'm doing. A lot of people don't look at all the pieces of their behavior, and say: how do they fit into my life? I think people are afraid to risk being vulnerable and being hurt.

"They want intimacy quickly without the process of getting there. Like with fast food—you get it quick and then complain about the quality. With a relationship, it's like becoming a butterfly. It takes time."

"With me, it's okay as long as I know the terms," said Jack, a freshman majoring in business at the University of Arizona. "Like, if we both agree, hey, this is strictly physical, we're not going to get involved, then I can enjoy myself and not worry. But if I think I'm like taking advantage, or like she's going to get all involved and I'm not really interested, then I don't enjoy myself very much—or I just back out of it altogether."

Many boys I talked to had a lot of sex with the one particular girl with whom they were going and felt very positive and secure about the relationship. Boys who had frequent sex with many different girls quite often seemed to express much more anxiety, conflict and insecurity about their behavior.

"I've only had a few really serious girl friends, but I do a lot of fooling around on the side," said eighteen-year-old Jonathan, the son of a dentist and a teacher in San Diego. "I seem to get involved with everybody, though—and I feel really guilty about ripping people off emotionally. I don't really know why I keep doing it all the time."

"Personally, I don't know why a lot of people even go through all the hassle," said eighteen-year-old Curtis in Los Angeles. "I mean, even kissing, they always pull the bottom of your tongue out. And it hurts, man! I been hurtin' my tongue. I mean, I could even do without the kissing for a while!"

Sometimes the boys involved in frenetic sexual activity that doesn't involve real emotional intimacy feel a great deal of confusion about *why* they're leaping from bed to bed. Like girls in the same situations, their "sexually liberated" behavior often masks immaturity or fears of intimacy.

"I'm getting it on with lots of women and letting them tear me apart," says Wayne, trying to wake up from a drunk the night before with a cup of coffee. "I'm searching for some kind of quintessential relationship and I'm not finding it.

"I commented to my older sister that I'd had sex with more people in my first three months of college than I'd had in my whole life. She smiled and said, 'Don't worry about it. It gets better.'

"I think I'm looking for a really perfect relationship. In the meantime, I just keep creating messes for myself. I get a lot of things like 'I don't have time to put in on a relationship' or 'I already have a boyfriend.' " He smiles. "Let them sleep on the wet spot!"

More often than not boys who mainly have one-night stands wish for something more substantive, where they could explore their own feelings and their own sexuality.

"That's one attraction for a serious relationship," said Ev, when I asked about a feeling of pressure to satisfy a woman sexually. "The one-night stands have rarely gone to the full extent sexually. . . . Usually it's late and after a mixer. I'm drunk and it's not that much fun. In fact, it's not fun at all. You just do it and afterwards you say, 'oh well, that was interesting.' And the next morning you smile, and then you try to be the same the next time you see her.

"The one-night stands act as a common denominator. There's the old view of things that if the guy goes sleeping around with different women, he's a stud, and if a girl does, she's a slut. If I'm sleeping once with a girl, my main concern is not to make her feel bad or like it's just a one-night thing, but on the other hand not to be too friendly or to promise more if it's not there. But it becomes confusing. There's a fine line between making them feel okay and not going overboard."

Some boys, of course, are not so considerate of a girl's feelings, and some still hold the view that a girl who sleeps around is a "slut"—even when they behave in exactly the same fashion.

"I think that she was just a whore," sixteen-year-old Bret said, talking about a classmate he had had sex with when he was fourteen. "It was so long ago that I can't remember her name. I don't remember whether it was Tracy or Lisa, but it was that kind of name. I know she'd done it before, but I don't know how much. She didn't seduce me. It was pretty mutual, but I don't know really, it was so long ago. I've been with a lot of girls since then."

Around their female peers, however, most boys can't get away with articulating these sorts of views without being chastised. Sometimes, they say, they're scolded for chauvinist behavior toward females long before they feel like men and certainly before they feel as if they have perpetrated any abuse. They're caught in a new level of anger in women and harangued for crimes they haven't personally committed.

"This summer I saw an old friend and we went to a movie," said Eric, a quiet, friendly nineteen-year-old. "When we came out, she said she thought it was sexist. I said I thought it was sexist, too, but that wasn't a very important part of the film. She started screaming at me that I'd made her have a baby and put her in the hospital. People gathered around us and I said, 'She's speaking metaphorically,' but there wasn't anything I could do.

"When the subject of women's liberation comes up, I feel hated and like I haven't done anything to deserve that hate."

"People tend to confuse gender differentiation with discrimination," says Eric's classmate, Raman. "If you say there are differences between men and women, they call you a male chauvinist pig."

While many dynamics remain the same, the effect of the women's liberation movement can be seen—and heard. I was amused when I heard the following exchange.

Raman: "I'm curious to what extent the barefoot, pregnant and in-the-kitchen attitude prevails."
Dennis: "What attitude is that?"

In the extreme, some of the real horrors in the adult male-female world are quite frightening to teenage boys. Although they personally may have had no exposure to experiences of men battering their wives and children, of men raping or sexually abusing women, stories about these sorts of incidents can be quite appalling to boys who are worried about finding the balance in their own sets of controls. Being both enraptured and intimidated by their own anger and power is not new to adolescent males in the 1980s. But the specter of their own potential for destruction can be overwhelming.

"I get worried to the degree that I worry about anyone having sex being abusive," said John, a tall, angular, eighteen-year-old college student who's still a virgin. "I've asked a lot of people if they think of a woman's orgasm when they have sex. They say no or, 'Well, I've never waited,' or, 'Why bother—it takes too long.' That's abusive to me. Then I think of what if that happened to my sister?! What if she was with a person like that!"

John's face as he talks reflects his humor and thoughtfulness. I tell him that I think much of what boys say to one another is talk that masks their feelings of vulnerability or the sense that they don't perform well.

"For me, it's strange because I went to a private school before this," he says, "and there wasn't any promiscuity there. There were close relationships and relationships that meant a lot to the people involved in them.

"I find it very upsetting when people are measuring how good a man or woman you are by who you screw—or the idea of measuring one's character by the number of dates you have in a week, or who is attracted to you.

"Like that woman who slept with over three hundred people in three days at [a midwestern university]. People were lining up outside her room. She had to have gone nuts. . . . But that people would even take advantage of a person like that! It's sickening! I'm sure she had a nervous breakdown afterwards." John shook his head soberly.

"It's abusive to me to hear someone say he has fucked his brains out but he had never made love to someone. . . .

"I think a relationship between a man and a woman can be a marvelous thing, but it has to be mutual. The thing I object to is when it excludes any intellectual level or pleasure in that person at all beyond a pumping love machine."

Earlier, when we had been in the cafeteria, a girl with long brown hair and an enormous bust lay down on her back on the cafeteria table next to ours. She was wearing a thick-knit white sweater and very tight blue jeans. After lounging on the table and talking to a friend, she stood up and walked past our table to get another glass of milk, and then walked past us again, her pendulous breasts leading the way. John's face screwed itself into a prolonged look of agony.

"She looks like she's got a lot to push!" he exclaimed dramatically. When she walked by the table yet another time, he slumped down in his chair, his head lowered. "Oh, she leads from the chest!" he proclaimed. "Like the maiden on the front of a boat." He held his lean arms at his side and thrust his chest forward. "Like a mast!"

"You may think I have a breast fixation," he joked. "But sitting at eye level, with all these clinging shirts walking by. . . ." Another girl, with no bra and breasts jiggling under a silken shirt, walked by John at that moment as if to illustrate his point. He followed the breasts with his eyes bounding up and down, and then put his head on the table again. "Oh dear!"

"Most people probably think I'm a perverse Casanova from the way I joke and speak," he said, "but I like to shock people out of their stupor, wake them up, make them question their existence. . . ."

"It's also just plain fun, isn't it?" I said.

"Yes," he admitted. "It's not altogether altruistic. But I could never have sex as the center of my relationship—and I couldn't be promiscuous ever. . . . I prefer to think of myself as a thinking being. At this point, I don't know if I ever want to lose my virginity. It's one last vestige of beauty and innocence. I've read too many books, seen too many ugly things. I know it will take me years. I'd have to find someone I love *very much*. . . ."

Yes, things have changed for today's teenage boys. They have most of the old pressures and some new ones—like the pressure to be the sexual aggressor before they're ready or to be casual about their eroticism when they don't feel like it. But they also may have more freedom to say what they think, a freedom to make their own way and to design their own plans. While "everything" has changed, more hasn't changed, when it comes to the individual who is making decisions about his own life and moving toward other human beings. I felt that most of the boys with whom I talked had great potential, perhaps more than their fathers had, to form close relationships with other boys, to achieve a full awareness of themselves and the girls with whom they're intimately involved.

Certainly from my conversations with these young men, I discovered that it's not easy to be an adolescent male today. I suspect it never was.

4.
Today's Parents:
Effects of the Parental Bedroom

"I still get nervous when I think about my parents in bed," said Delia, recalling when she was a sixteen-year-old in Boston, ten years ago. "It's like sometimes at night, I'd be listening, but I didn't want to hear. I remember so well . . . I'd sort of have my ear to the wall, but then when their bed started to squeak, I'd cover my ears. I still don't like it when my parents tell dirty jokes or my mother looks too sexy. I think they have a pretty good sexual relationship, but it still sort of embarrasses me."

If teenagers ever thought that the only reason their parents slept in the same room was because it happened to be Their Room, that time passed long ago. Surely, with the advent of parents who dress in younger, sexier clothes, when so much talk about sex is in the air and when their own antennas are primed to sexual innuendo and electricity, today's teenagers are almost always more alert to the sexual interactions of their parents than their parents realize.

"I can always tell, I think, when they made love the night before," says Caroline, a seventeen-year-old in Madison, Wisconsin. "In the morning, you can tell because they get up and they're singing around and then they go out for breakfast together. That's the dead giveaway. And then they go to bed at eight o'clock that night." Caroline laughs. "My mom's pretty. She's got a good figure and she dresses real young. Dad's jealous, you can tell. Sometimes when she's getting ready for work in the morning and she looks really good, he'll say, 'Isn't that a little dressy for work?' Or, 'That's too sexy to wear into the office.'"

Relationships between parents and children are complex in the first place. We bring many expectations and fantasies to our interactions with one another that have a great deal to do with the molding of private character. Within the traditional family setting, these interactions often lie at the very root of our sexual excitement, and are a gold mine of psychoanalytic material. When we add the changing social environment, the changes in family structures, homes where parents have been divorced and remarried or reattached to another person, the web of complexities—of fantasies, conflicts, scripts—becomes even more dense.

Certainly, in the 1980s, the "normal" family is not necessarily the nuclear family. A wide variety of new kinds of families are evolving these days, and each has some stresses and some advantages peculiar to it. Each family constellation highlights certain aspects of negotiating everything from division of labor within the home to the handling of sexual feelings and behavior.

Although many negative assumptions are associated with the single-parent home, for instance, it's clear that living in a single-parent home can contribute in many ways to a teenager's sense of himself or herself in ways unique to that kind of family.

According to Dr. Phyllis Clay, who directed a national survey of single parents for the National Committee for Citizens in Education, research shows clearly that one parent in the home is more healthy than a home where two parents are constantly hostile and angry toward one another. "Another advantage," she says, "is closer communication between the one parent and the child so that there's a feeling of closeness and a desire to pull together." Perhaps the biggest advantage to the teenager is the increased sense of both rights and responsibilities, because the situation necessitates more freedom and independence on the part of the teenagers.

It seems clear that there are no "right" or "wrong" kinds of families. There are different kinds of families. There aren't right or wrong things for teenagers to know about their parents' sexual lives. There is information that is helpful and unhelpful, positive or negative in each situation with which teenagers learn to cope.

Certainly from all kinds of homes, teenagers I talked to were aware of the adult conflicts and pleasures, financial pressures, work pressures and realities of adult life.

Teenagers often talked about how their parents felt about themselves and each other—whether or not they were single, married, remarried or never married. Over and again, I could hear a correlation between what teenagers told me about their parents' feelings about themselves and the way those particular teenagers felt about themselves. For whatever reasons, much of the adolescent's own identity is interwoven with the same-sex parent's feelings about himself or herself and with the opposite-sex parent's response to her or his spouse.

"My mom likes herself," says Heather, a confident, comfortable seventeen-year-old who says she is close to both of her parents. "I know they probably do it all the time. I know they really love each other. They're always holding hands, and he opens the car door for her. He's always telling her how much he loves her. They disagree, and sometimes they argue, but they never have real bad fights."

Sonya, an energetic basketball player, reflected the way her mother felt about herself. Sonya is a college freshman who has a very full and rich relationship with a law-school student she's gone with on and off since she was a freshman in high school.

"My parents were a high-school romance, too," says Sonya, who plans to be a veterinarian. "I think my mother feels very good about herself and her body. She also has never slept with anyone but my father, but she doesn't condemn me for what I've done. My parents have their ups and downs, but they have a great relationship. In the past few years, my father's also gotten more romantic. He used to buy her impersonal presents. Now he buys her jewelry and clothes and that sort of thing."

Chip, confident about himself and his future, attributes his inner assurance to his father and mother.

"I'm sure my father thinks my mother is the best thing that ever happened to him," he says. "He thinks she's wonderful and she thinks he's wonderful. They have what I consider a good marriage, and I think they really love each other. I hope I can have the kind of relationship they have when I get married. I think I will. . . ."

Teenagers aren't usually consciously aware of how they project themselves into the role of their same-sex parent and identify directly with whatever treatment is accorded that parent by the spouse or partner. When a mother or father is complimented—or struck with a blow—the same-sex child often feels the impact quite directly. When adults are at odds, their simple interactions are often fraught with double entendres as a result. Inevitably, parents should remember, when they attack the other parent in front of the teenager, they're indirectly (and inadvertently) attacking a part of their child.

"My father is always telling me I'm just like my mother," says Brook, whose parents had a bitter separation and divorce three years earlier. "So if he calls her a whore, then he's calling me a whore, too. If he calls her a stupid cunt, he's calling me a stupid cunt, too. It's not direct, but he's always telling me I'm like her, so it's the same difference."

The identification makes it that much more difficult for teenagers who feel that one parent doesn't love the other—or that one is "unfaithful." Perhaps as traumatic for many teenagers as any other is the discovery that one of their parents is involved in an extramarital affair. Although the fathers or mothers involved may try to be discreet, their teenage children don't miss much. What's going on under the surface is often quite clear to the adolescent observer, who is already in the business of figuring out what goes on in this interesting world of sexual relations between men and women. He's looking for meanings, analyzing data, intuiting problems. The reporter, philosopher, detective and judge in residence often knows, without knowing why, that something is wrong.

"Sometimes I wonder," says fourteen-year-old Bernard Jablonski. "Like my mom sees a good-looking guy and she says to her friend, 'He's really a hunk,' and she wonders out loud if he's messing around or if he fools around with other women. One time she said something to a guy and I was embarrassed. I don't like that very much. It makes me wonder if my mom's messing around behind my dad's back. I don't think she would, but I don't know. The way she acts, it makes me wonder. . . ."

I found that young people are usually quite aware of the state of their parents' sexual relationship, even if they don't know the details. They know if their parents are happy or unhappy—and if they're unhappy, the teenager often takes sides.

"My mom and dad haven't done it in two years," said Michelle. "My mom hates her body. She has lots of trouble with her period. . . . I know he goes out with other women. He came home at four A.M. Friday. I despise him for it. My mom's been hurt, but she always talks about how she'd like to be skinny and how my dad would worry if she walked out the door.

"Somebody called my mother once. The person said, 'Tracy, your husband's at the gas station with another woman.' We went over there and we saw this woman sitting next to my dad. He saw that we saw them. When my dad came home that night drunk, my mom asked him about it and he said, 'Oh, it was nothing. She just ran out of gas.' My mom said, 'Oh yes, that looked just like a gas can sitting there beside you in the car.' "

Autumn sat, watching her hands, lost in her own thoughts. "My mom and dad haven't done it for seven years," she said. "They aren't like that. But then she's fifty-four; what do you expect? He kisses her every night before they go to bed, and that's it. He saves it for his girl friend. I've told him I hated him before."

Autumn is a large girl with short, wavy hair. She's heavyset, wearing faded overalls over a white T-shirt. Her parents have been married thirty-two years, she says, and she has two sisters and three brothers older than she is. Autumn's parents are Presbyterians in Columbus, Ohio. Her father works in a lumberyard; her mother keeps house.

"My mom had an operation this winter," said Autumn, "and she was in the hospital for a long time. She almost died, and he was out having a good old time. Then she came home, and now they're going to get a divorce. They should have gotten a divorce thirty years ago.

"When she was in the hospital, my dad asked if I wanted to go skiing with 'them'—him and his mistress—in Vail, Colorado. I told him not to ever ask me to go anywhere with them again."

"My mom is basically a cold person," said Steven, a seventeen-year-old in Los Angeles. "She doesn't mean to be, but that's the way she is—that's the way she was brought up. She never had enough love, so she didn't learn how to give it. I can't blame my dad for leaving her. I wouldn't want to be married to her, either."

More than one out of four teenagers today have seen their parents separate and divorce. They have watched the effect of the breakup on at least one, but usually both of their parents. They have then had to cope with the realities of their parents beginning to date other people, struggle with their own identity crises and desire to make commitments. Teenagers are forced into an exposure and an examination of the fabric of assumptions that make up their parents' lives as well as their own. There is no question about the pain these experiences cause children. Recently on a plane ride back to New York from Boston, I sat next to a redheaded eight-year-old girl who had just visited her maternal grandparents. She told me her parents were divorced. "I feel like there's a line drawn down the middle of me," she said, illustrating her statement with her hands. "This half belongs to my mother, this half belongs to my father."

"I'll never forget the night they told me they were going to separate," said sixteen-year-old Scott in San Diego. "I started crying. I hardly ever cried before that, but I couldn't help it. My dad was hugging me, and he and my mom tried to explain that they weren't happy and that they hadn't found a way to make things better between them. They said I'd live with my mom, but I'd still get to see my dad. He drives a truck, so he's gone a lot, but I still see him about once a month. Now it's okay, but it was pretty rough for a while there. . . ."

Often, the trauma of a divorce brings out in adults conflicts from their own adolescence that they haven't resolved. In addition to the divided loyalties they feel, the teenagers then must also cope with their parents' emotional upheavals, crises in identity and personal preoccupations. Sometimes the roles of parent and child seem to reverse themselves. One time, for instance, when I was visiting in the home of seventeen-year-old Bernice, her mother came swinging across the room in her narrow-hipped Gloria Vanderbilt jeans and snug T-shirt. She wore no bra and her hair hung loosely on her thin shoulders. She ruffled Bernice's hair and flipped her third finger at her twelve-year-old son, who was standing by the fish tank next to the couch.

"Hey, Mom," Glenn said, "I wish you'd stop doing that."

"He nags me," the mother said in a stage whisper to Bernice and to me. "He's always nagging me. He was put on this earth to nag me."

"Well, it isn't very nice to greet someone by flipping them the bird," said Bernice.

When I witnessed this interaction, I remembered what Dr. John O'Brien, a psychoanalyst of the William Alanson White Institute, and Director of Child and Adolescent Services at St. Vincent's Hospital in New York, had said during our interview. "We've gone into an era that idealized the young," he'd said. "The coming of wisdom in older age is in many ways lost—and this is very disturbing. I've had adolescents say to me, 'My parents have robbed me of my own thing. They dress like me, they talk like me, they're interested in the same things I'm interested in.'"

I was also reminded that many of us don't solve all the questions of adolescence when we are adolescents. Some we never resolve. So many of our teenagers are living with the issues and conflicts we didn't unravel when we were teenagers—and thus are growing up with either our same problems and misconceptions or the opposite ones for various reasons.

Bernice's mother, for instance, married her husband when she was a twenty-year-old virgin. After twenty-three years, she and her husband separated. Bernice's father, Glenn, had gotten deeply involved in an extramarital affair, which eventually led to the breakup. He never went out to explore new relationships because he was locked into a second monogamous living arrangement before his first was legally ended by divorce.

Bernice's mother, Helen, fell in love very quickly with the first man she slept with after her husband, had an intense relationship that lasted three months and then, when that didn't work out, went on to the next one and the one after that with the same fervor and preoccupation that had characterized the first. At this point in her life, her fantasies are still very adolescent. She wants to be a sex object, she wants to have a daddy and she wants to be eighteen years old instead of forty-five.

In the meantime, through her romances, she confided in Bernice, who was going to high school, living with her father and new stepmother, and struggling to get a toehold on herself. When I spoke with Bernice, she surprised me with her level of understanding and insight into her mother's behavior.

"My mother was recently living with someone and then they split up and got back together again and then split up again," said Bernice. "It was a terrible relationship, and I became her mother for a while. She didn't ask me as much about my life as she told me about hers. She tells me everything. I hear about her sex life and everything else. Sometimes it's too much, but I know she needs to get it out. Sometimes, though, I'd just as soon not know."

While their parents were initially preoccupied with their own emotional upheavals and preoccupations, Bernice said it was "perfect hell" for herself and her brother.

"It still causes me a lot of problems," she says. "But I'm glad I didn't latch onto one guy as an escape from an unhappy life during that time. Some people do that, but I'm glad I didn't."

Currently Bernice is a college freshman and just beginning to unwind emotionally. Not surprisingly, she hasn't had any intimate relationship with a boy. She hasn't even started dating anyone on a regular basis.

"I've never had a relationship with a boy for more than a month," she said the last time I talked to her. "I'd like to have a serious relationship and know what that's like. Some people can't believe I haven't had a serious involvement because I seem to know so much—but that's just because so many people have confided in me, and I read and think a lot and have an understanding that's beyond my experiences. . . .

"I know that my time will come. In high school, I said, just wait until I get to college. The guys will be more mature then. Now I'm thinking that in my career I'll meet someone. Lately I've been hearing about people meeting men on the job. Who knows?" She laughs at herself and ruffles her hair. "My time will come. It *has* to! I'm just a late bloomer, that's all!"

Many of the teenagers I talked to felt that they had matured and had gained personal strength from what they had witnessed and experienced because of their parents' divorce. They feel that the insight into themselves helped them have a better understanding of what they want in their own lives.

"The roughest time of my life was when I was little," says Lanie, a sixteen-year-old from Englewood, New Jersey. "I feel like if I could handle that, I could handle anything that comes up. . . .

"My parents got divorced when I was three," she says, "and then my mother married Tony when I was four. He had four children who lived with us in the summer, and then they were married about two years and got a divorce when I was almost six, just after my father married Judy.

"During all the time my mother was married to Tony, I would see my father on weekends. They had a country house and I'd go up there with them. My dad and Judy had my little brother Jacob when I was ten and their second son, Artie, when I was thirteen. Now they live out in Seattle, and I spend a lot of time with them. I really love them. I spend every summer with them. They're the greatest little brothers. . . ." Lanie shows me pictures of Jacob and Artie, cards from her stepmother and father and brothers that adorn her dresser tops.

"I never knew what it was like to have real parents," she says. "Mom and Tony were the closest to that I knew when I was really little. I saw Tony like you would see a regular father for a while after they split up. I called him Dad for a little while, and I think that was sort of hard on my real dad. But he felt like my father, and for a while, I had had constant playmates—brothers and sisters—and then all of a sudden, I was separated from all that. For a while it felt like I didn't have anybody. . . ."

Some of the teenagers I talked to had already been through multiple losses with divorces, remarriages and more divorces. Although many felt cynical about romantic love lasting and expressed anxiety about making the right choice when they married, many had a good sense of what had caused the marriages to fall apart. They said they still wanted to get married and have families of their own. Most said they would live with someone before they married, however, to test the strength and workability of the relationship.

"I've never seen what a good marriage is," says Brigit. "But I believe that a good marriage is possible. I know that someday I will try to have one—but I'm going to spend a lot of time ahead of time making *sure* I really want to spend a lifetime with this guy."

"I'll get married someday, but not until I'm older," says Adele, a high-school senior whose mother has been divorced three times in the last ten years. "When she started going through the divorce with my stepdad, I told her I'd never accept anyone else.

"She has a boyfriend now she sees regularly. I didn't really approve of her staying at her boyfriend's house, but I wouldn't really try to stop her. He is really good to her. He does everything for her. He opens her car door and picks up things for her when she needs them. He's always calling and is very thoughtful of her. Maybe it would be good for her to marry him eventually. I don't know."

"There's a whole social dilemma for teenagers when they have sexually active single parents," says Rayetta Krall, a nurse-practitioner in the adolescent program at the University of California at San Francisco. Ms. Krall, who was also a school nurse for four years, points out that teenagers who see adults coping with anxieties by acting out sexually often think that behaving in a similar way is the best, or only, way of coping.

"What do they do when they have a one-bedroom house?" says Ms. Krall. "When Mom brings home a boyfriend, where do they go? There's a lot of exposure. A lot of parents are going through a sexual identity crisis of their own, and their teenagers are exposed to all of it."

Ms. Krall points out that this exposure is particularly hard on the younger teenager who has no concept of his or her own body. Cognitively, she points out, twelve- or thirteen-year-olds can't think abstractly about issues. "They can't think about things like a man putting his penis into a woman's vagina happening to them. They can't imagine it happening to their bodies; they're still so concrete. But when they learn from their parents that sex is the way to cope, they often get into sexual situations before they're ready for them."

Such was the case for Maureen, who learned from her mother how to use sex as a way of acting out her loneliness and alienation. Maureen's mother, who also was an alcoholic, had four children in rapid succession, beginning when she was nineteen years old. When Maureen was growing up in Baltimore, Maryland, she rarely saw her father. Her parents had separated shortly after she was born.

"I was really young when I had my first sexual experience," she says, "and I blame it on my mother a lot." Maureen, who has a round face, wide eyes and light brown hair, is pretty and poised. Her fingernails, however, are bitten below the quick. Occasionally as she speaks, she puts a finger into her mouth and chews it.

"I blame it on my mother because when I was growing up, in the years from ten to thirteen, we lived with my grandmother, and my mother and grandmother, they'd get into fights. When they'd fight, my grandmother would kick us out, and we'd have to rent a motel room. We'd all four kids be in one bed, and she'd be in the other bed with a man. She worked at a bar then, so it would be different men all the time. We'd be right there with them. So I saw and heard a lot of things for someone my age. I saw too much in a way for being that age.

"I think it's why I had sex so early. I was too young, really, and I don't like that about me. I wish I could change it.

"The first time it was with a boy from around the corner. He'd lived on the block a lot of years. I was living with my grandmother at the time. My grandfather had just died. That sounds sort of morbid, but anyway, Marty told me he wanted to go to bed with me. I didn't know how to say no, so I did. I don't remember feeling hardly anything at the time, but now I feel hatred towards him. I feel bitter towards him 'cause I was so young. I was only twelve years old. The summer after sixth grade.

"Afterwards, I was uncomfortable around him. He hardly talked to me afterwards. He had a sister I loved and looked up to, who he told. She said he was an asshole. I had sex with him twice. We didn't use anything, but I didn't worry about getting pregnant.

"My next boyfriend was Don—the stud around the apartments. We had sex, but it wasn't anything big. It was nothing to me really. I didn't feel anything.

"Then there was this guy Mauri. I was thirteen and he was eighteen. He wanted to get married and everything. He was head over heels with me. He thought he was really in love and that this was big stuff. We had fun; we went to Disney World together. But I didn't want to get married. Thirteen was still too young."

Maureen's situation was extreme. Her mother was blatant, and unable or too immature herself to consider her children's feelings. But even when parents make every effort to be discreet and protective, teenagers still "catch" their parents being sexual—or inadvertently unearth clues as to their parents' private behavior.

Jeanie, for instance, said that one day when she went home early from school to pick up her sheet music for piano lessons, she assumed no one was home. She wasn't expected, but she had forgotten the music, so she talked her friend Maria into going back to her house with her. "I was on my way to my room, and when I passed by my mother's bedroom, I saw this form under the sheet. I just about froze in my tracks.

"I said, 'Mom? Mom, is that you?' Then this man's voice came out from under the sheets. 'She's in the bathroom.'

"I'd never met him," says Jeanie, who's thirteen. "I knew she was seeing somebody new, I mean, she'd mentioned him, but I didn't know she was seeing him *that* way."

"Our house is pretty small," said Don, an eighteen-year-old in Baltimore. "And so you can't help but notice when my folks shut the door to the bedroom. Lately I just holler when I see it shut, 'Oh, no! They're at it again!' For all I know they might be brushing their teeth, but I doubt it. I just like to tease them."

Sometimes teenagers, who are deeply involved in analyzing their own values and priorities, are not pleased with how their parents behave and are "revolted" or "grossed out" by any evidence of their parents' less-than-perfect attitudes. It's difficult for them to deal with their parents' conflicts and imperfections—and the way they reflect on them. It's also difficult to witness their parents in a nonparental role.

"I was staying at my mother's apartment one vacation, and when I answered the phone once, this man asked for her," said Lillian, a seventeen-year-old who had stayed with her father after her parents' divorce. "She talked to him in a strange way, laughing and giddy and flirtatious. After she hung up, I asked her who it was. 'Oh, it was this man I had in Athens,' she said flippantly. She was just so offhand, like it didn't mean anything. 'This man I had in Athens!' I was absolutely repulsed at my mother having this flippant attitude towards an affair. Athens was also where she had gone after my parents split up—leaving me to do all the housework and the taking care of my father and our family.

"I was so disgusted with her. I smashed my plate down on the floor and ran out of the house. I ran away for three days. I didn't go home and I didn't call. I made it very clear how I felt.

"When I came back, she was very guilty, so I ended up dealing with her guilt and just like always, she was the problem again. I ended up feeling guilty and sorry that I'd make her feel bad. Now, even though I love her, I try to keep my distance. Her love life is just too crazy and too painful for me."

Many teenagers' response to knowing about their parents' sexual relationships—even realizing that they actually have intercourse—is a mixture of excitement and revulsion. Their own sexual feelings are stirred, and the reactions are intense.

Austin says he's never quite gotten used to his father's sexual relationship. "I have a kind of cynical feeling about it," he says. "I don't allow myself to think about it too much, but this woman he's seeing is very insecure and very self-conscious. She doesn't like her job and she is always complaining about it. At the same time, she's pretty. She reminds me of that actress Diane Keaton. As soon as I begin to think about my father having sex with her, I think of that being their bond. I try not to think about it, though, or I feel contempt for them, and I can't allow that because I live with them half of the time."

Austin got out of his chair and stretched out on the floor. He put his hat over his face and then sat it on the top of his head. "I have a very strong relationship with her [my mother]," he said. "We talk a lot. I spend a lot of time with her. I'm her son, but sometimes it's like we're in love. It's remote. It's on a different plane, though. I think of her as a sexual being. I can only imagine her as a girl friend of mine would feel. It's sacrilegious to think of her in a sexual way, so I don't do that. I love her, but it's on a different level, like a spiritual level."

Just as parents often find themselves feeling jealous or competitive about their sons' girl friends or daughters' boyfriends, children also feel the same emotions when their parents are the ones dating or establishing new relationships. It's a normal response, one that should be expected.

"I remember when my mother went out on her first date," said fourteen-year-old Manuel, in East Los Angeles. "This guy had been coming around, and then they started going out together. I wasn't too thrilled. All this time she'd been with me, and I don't want to lose her. I just wasn't happy. She said I wasn't happy because I wanted her all to myself. I guess that was true. She was upset with me, but I couldn't help it."

When Manuel's mother remarried, he said he felt both relieved (of the responsibility of taking care of her) and grieved (at losing her). Ultimately, when the new marriage started falling apart, however, he became angry.

"My stepfather is not so hot," says Manuel. 'Some of my aunts say he used my mother for food and a home, that's all. I don't know. But he went back down to Mexico a couple of months ago, and he hasn't come back. He has a ranch down there. Now she wants to get a divorce. She's all sad and everything."

Manuel pulls one chubby hand with the other hand, looks away, looks up at me and looks down again. "I didn't like him that much. He was a creep. I never went anywhere with him or had a conversation with him."

Manuel's contact with his real father is also limited. His father has remarried and has a baby boy with his new wife. "I don't like my stepmother that much because I don't think she likes me that much," he says. "I still love my dad. I could go to him and talk, probably. They say I look like my dad. I'll probably be taller than him, though. He's in the marine reserves. I'd like to go into the coast guard or something like that.

"Some people say my father insults people a lot, and that his attitude is bad. My mom says I do it the same as him. Sometimes I guess I do." Manuel, who hasn't started dating but goes out in groups, says he would like to stay a virgin until he gets married, and then that he'd like to adopt two children—two boys about twelve or fourteen years old.

Unlike Manuel, some young people find themselves in the position of being the ones to encourage their mothers or fathers to date and get romantically involved. The only thing worse than losing one's mother or father to another adult, of course, is having to keep the parent for yourself. Also, despite feelings of jealousy, teenagers usually want to see their parents happy. So sometimes they are the ones who try to push their parents out of the nest instead of vice versa.

"I never minded my mom dating," says Bart Campanelli, in Phoenix, Arizona. "In fact, I kind of fixed her up. We were living in these apartments and I was friends with these two guys, Bill and Bert, who lived with their dad. My mom thought their dad was kind of good-looking. She'd seen him one day and she joked to us that she'd send the dog down to his apartment and then go back and pick him up. Like, 'Excuse me, have you seen my dog?' I told him the joke, and he went up and met her. They got married a year later. She might have dated before that, but I don't remember it if she did. I think she only brought one guy home to meet us kids before that, and she didn't get too close to him. She was always thinking about us kids first."

A lot of complexities arise for teenagers when their parents remarry. Often the teenager feels replaced—and in fact, after a remarriage, and in the face of a new romance, the teenager does have to compete for the parent's time and attention. Even if he likes the new stepparent, he often feels that there's only room emotionally for loving one mother—and one father. Many childhood fantasies still continue even after we are grown—and the fantasy that Mommy and Daddy will get back together again is often harbored even by grown children whose parents have divorced. The presence of the stepparent interferes with those hopes and threatens the possibility of reunification as well. Additionally, the stepchild's loyalty to the original parent often feels in jeopardy. Jealousy, resentment, anxiety, conflict are mixed into every package of remarriage, no matter how terrific or loved the stepparent is. The mix is complicated by the parent's feeling of guilt and wanting to satisfy the children as well as the new spouse, and by the new spouse's conflicting feelings. All of this is further complicated by feelings and messages from the other parent who is being replaced.

Sometimes the response of teenagers to their parent's remarriage must be extremely painful for the parent. Maggie epitomized the negative reaction to her father's new, and probably improved, life.

When I asked eighteen-year-old Maggie if she liked her stepmother—after she had told me that her father, a doctor, and her mother, a nurse, had divorced when she was thirteen—she said brusquely: "I don't know."

"How could you not know?"

"I've never met her."

"Don't you see your father?"

"Yes, but she leaves when I visit."

"Why?"

"Because I don't like her."

"How many times have you visited him?"

"Often. I go to visit him often."

"And each time she goes away?"

"Yes. I won't come to visit him if she's there."

"How do you know you don't like her if you never met her?" I persisted, feeling sympathy for a fellow stepmother and for a father so intimidated by his daughter.

"Well, I saw her once. My sister stayed with them one Christmas and then my father drove her home afterwards. He had taken my sister's suitcase into the house, and a friend dropped me off in front of my house. *She* was sitting in his car and she introduced herself. That's the only time I ever talked to her."

"From that you decided you don't like her?"

"Well, to me and my mom and my sisters, she's not a good person. We moved away from a small town because people were talking about us so bad. And it was because of her. He was seeing her before my folks were divorced, and she got him to leave my mom."

Teenagers who find themselves with a stepparent not that much older than they are often say that they have "odd" feelings about the parent's motivation in marrying a person so young. Sometimes they feel competitive; sometimes they find themselves relating to a peer as a parent or a stepparent as a peer. Often they have to explain to people outside the family that "this is my stepparent—not my sibling."

Signe, her two sisters and brother were surprised when their sixty-year-old father married a woman twenty-two years old, the age of his oldest daughter. "In the beginning, he'd be entertaining, and people would say, 'Oh, here are your five lovely children!' " said Signe. "They didn't know she was his wife, and she was our same age. He would say, 'Excuse me, this is my wife, and they are my children.' We four would sit there and smile, saying to ourselves, 'You got yourself into this, you old bugger.' All of us find it absolutely impossible to talk to either one of them. Every meeting is a performance. We all pretend to have a good time."

For Daphne, there's less distance and even more discomfort.

"My stepfather, James, he's only twenty-nine, and my mother's forty-two," says Daphne, a high-school senior in San Francisco. "When she first got together with him, I had a strange feeling he was going to attack me because he was looking at me all the time. He moved in with us for a while, and so I went and lived with my father because I was scared of him. I just told my mom I didn't like the way things were handled at home. I didn't want to say anything to jeopardize their relationship because I knew it was important to her at the time, but I thought it wouldn't last at all. When she told me she was going to marry him, I was furious."

Daphne, whose honey blond hair is neatly bobbed, looks like the All-American cheerleader who should decorate the cover of *Seventeen* magazine. When she smiles, her teeth are perfect and her face lights up. From her wholesome, well-groomed appearance, my guess would have been that her father was a well-to-do businessman and her mother played tennis three times a week. In fact, Daphne's mother and father were divorced when she was four; her mother remarried and Daphne acquired two stepsisters and a stepbrother. Then Daphne's mother and new father were divorced when she was ten, and her mother remarried again when Daphne was thirteen and divorced that man when Daphne was fifteen. She married James when Daphne was seventeen. Daphne didn't start menstruating until she was almost seventeen years old.

"My boyfriend still thinks that James will try to do something to me. He gives me weird eyes all the time. My mom and I used to think it was our house and we could go around without clothes on, but I don't do it anymore because of him. I could walk around with my bra and panties on, but I don't because of him. He's young. I've always thought that maybe my mother doesn't please him with sexual pleasures, and I'm afraid he'll come for more, but to me, not to her."

In many cases, once the dust has settled and a sense of some sanity is regained, teenagers find themselves feeling fortunate that their parents have formed new bonds that make them happy.

"I think I have the best of all worlds," said fifteen-year-old Karen. "I have three great parents in my life who care about me. They all have different points of view, and I learn from all of them. I spend the weeks with my mom and the weekends with my stepmom and dad, so if I have a problem, I go to all three of them for advice to get different perspectives. Besides that, I think they're all fun—and smart and interesting people."

Teenagers who have come to terms with their feelings of divided loyalties also seem to feel strengthened by the experience and more able to overcome other obstacles.

"When my mom fell in love with Keith, all I could think about was how lonesome my dad must be and what a pisser it was that they'd ever split up," said sixteen-year-old David. "I sort of blamed myself for their breakup and I was really confused about it. I sort of liked Keith's sense of humor, but I kept my distance from him for quite a while. I'm not sure exactly when it all changed, but one day we were making breakfast together and he said, 'Hey, I like you, David'—and I said, 'Hey, Keith, I like you, too.' Now I feel really close to him, too. I'm close to my dad—and he's my dad and always will be my dad. But to me, Keith's a good friend and somebody I care about."

Sometimes, when the stepparent acts on the fantasy that he or she is the original parent, a strain is put on the teenager. Even though the stepparent can be very maternal or paternal—and dearly loved—he or she is not the natural parent. Often, requiring stepchildren to call the acquired parent Mom or Dad when such is not the case, makes teenagers feel an internal pressure on their loyalties and gives them the feeling that a lie is being told. For Martine, a dark-skinned, lively high-school junior in Atlanta, Georgia, the contradiction is obvious. Both Martine's natural parents were black, and until the year before our interview, Martine had lived with her mother, a psychologist in New York. Martine's mother had died of cancer, however, and she had gone to live with her father, a city administrator, and her stepmother, a psychiatric social worker, who was white.

"My stepmother introduces me as her daugher all the time," says Martine, "and it makes me feel so odd. She's white, and her skin is very white, and she's all white, and she stands there beside me and says, 'This is my daughter Martine.' People have to think 'What?' because I'm so black, so very black right there beside her. She has a ball introducing me that way. People just about fall over. Sure, it bothers me. It's crazy. But I've never said anything to her about it. She's a good person, and I figure it's her thing, not mine. I don't want to get into it with her, but I sort of feel she's cutting out my mom, which I don't like."

Today's teenagers have learned to cope with a wide variety of sexual behavior on the part of their parents. They've moved into different family structures and accepted new roles for themselves and their parents. At a time when they are questioning their own sexual identity and learning about their own attractions, some teenagers find their parents coming to terms with being homosexual. Some wind up living with a parent and that parent's homosexual partner.

"Mom started going with women when I was about eight years old," says Dierdre, a sixteen-year-old from Boston. "For a while, she went out with men and women. Now she lives with another woman, Florence.

"About a year ago, it started to bug me that Mom was a lesbian," she says. "I started being bitchy around the house, and I'd get mad at both of them. I didn't talk to Florence at all. That was when I was fifteen.

"I didn't want my friends to know. I still don't. I was embarrassed. Then I confronted her and told her I hated it, and I sort of hated her for doing it. She said, 'Remember it's me, not you.' She said, 'Don't worry. You don't have to be a lesbian.' I said, 'Don't worry, I won't!'

"Then I started realizing I was being stupid, and I accepted it and that was that. I'm still not crazy about Florence. But I never was crazy about her. If I liked her a whole lot, it'd be different, maybe. She's okay, but she's not fantastic to me. She's always been nice to me. But, of course, she jumped into my life and took over my mother—and I'm sure in some unconscious way I hated her for that."

Dierdre says she never tells her friends that her mother is in love with another woman. As far as her friends know, her mother is heterosexual and is divorced, and they share a house with another woman. That's all.

"I always wonder about the questions they might ask," says Dierdre, pushing a strand of her blond hair back over her ear. "Like, what if they say, 'Is your mother going to get married again?' I don't know what I'd say. But it's never come up.

"I wouldn't tell my friends, I guess, because I'm not proud of it and I don't like it. I'm so proud of my mother as a person, and I'm afraid if they knew, they would judge her. They probably wouldn't, but there might be something in their mind. Some attitudes are so stupid. It seems easier not to deal with them at all."

Dierdre says she doesn't worry about her own sexual orientation. She's attracted to men and always has been. Her relationship with her father, whom she lives with half of the year, remains central to her life.

I asked her if she thought she'd tell any man she got involved with about her mother's relationship with Florence.

"I would probably tell Louis," she said, speaking of her current boyfriend. "I don't know about anyone else. I'd tell him if it ever came up, that is. I wouldn't bring it up. I wouldn't just tell him. I'm sure if I did, he probably wouldn't mind. He's pretty open-minded.

"There's so much talk about it—and most people just don't want to deal with it," said Dierdre. "They think it won't ever happen to them and it does. They think it's so far away. I know this sixth grader. His father is gay, and he hates his father for it. He has an ulcer. In sixth grade, with an ulcer. He goes to a psychiatrist because he's so upset about it. I really feel for him."

Allison moved out of her mother's house when she was eleven years old to move in with her father and stepmother. Now she visits her thrice-divorced mother, who lives with a woman who became her lover during her second marriage. Both women are attractive, professional women who share a house in suburban Chicago. Both were married before. Allison's two brothers live with her mother, as does the daughter of her mother's lover.

"I moved out because I just didn't get along with her or her roommate or their system of life," says Allison, who's dressed in painter's pants and a pretty paisley Indian blouse. She looks much older than her fourteen years. "My mother and Meg were together for a long time off and on from when I was about age seven. I didn't know they were lovers or that they were lesbians. It was a feeling I had about their relationship that they loved each other, but I didn't really discover what that was for a long time. My mother, she's one of the neatest people I ever met. I didn't see anything strange at all about her relationship with Meg until later, when I was confronted by other kids about it. I felt resentful at first, when I knew. I felt I was obviously different from the normal trend of kids who went to school every day. Then I decided to turn it to my advantage. I prided myself in being different and I thought it was great. I decided I might as well enjoy being different.

"I didn't really have any good friends until three years ago. Most of the friends I had were Mom's friends who weren't really kids.

"Kathy was my first real friend. All of a sudden, about three years ago, I bloomed, and everybody liked me. I became really popular, and Kathy was part of it all. She became the best friend I'd ever had before and ever since. We're still best friends. I've talked to her a few times deeply about our lives. She's upset with me and my mom's differences and the hurting we've done to each other. I don't think there's any attitude on her part because my mother's gay.

"My urge to get away from my mom comes from my desire to be independent, and probably from my dislike of her handling of children. She's always had a strange way of dealing with kids. She's a really strong person and she's overpowering. Like she's always pulling rank and putting you in your place. She's very bright, so she's pretty successful professionally.

"My stepmom, she's somebody I really respect. She's almost an idol for me. The problems we do have are usually not us—it's outside pressures or tensions we feel. Like one of us had a really hard day at school or work or we both did or something like that.

"My dad is the only person I've ever been able to talk to. He's probably the closest person inside my family right now. Him and my brother, who still lives with my mother.

"Every three of four weekends, I go and see my mother now. I go by bus, and she picks me up at the bus stop. She was really hurt about my leaving. It made her look for a lot of faults in herself. When a petty fight comes up, when not a lot of controls are operating, she'll yell at me, 'You had to leave, you had to run away!'

"It was a big decision at age eleven. She knew I wasn't too happy with her and that I'd probably be happier with my father and stepmother. But she said I'd have to make up my own mind.

"I'd defend them both very strongly. Recently they had an argument over money for me, and they fell into old times and old ways. I found myself defending my father to my mother and my mother to my father.

"My father had had a very wicked family life. He hadn't seen his father until he was twenty-six years old. He was brought up by his grandmother after his mother abandoned him. The grandmother was harsh and resentful, and he never had a man in his life except his uncle.

"My mother came from the All-American family, but she had a lot of problems. She was told that she was bad and that something was wrong with her because she didn't do well in school, and they made her feel guilty and bad about everything she did. So, anyway, they both have reasons for why they act the way they do sometimes."

"It's just amazing some of the things our children are dealing with," a school psychologist said to me. "For example, I had a sixth grader say to me, 'I was very lucky I had both parents until I was ten years old. My younger brother and sisters never had parents.' "

Certainly teenagers today are dealing with a great deal of adult reality. They don't have to have their ears to the wall of their parents' bedroom to learn about sex or relationships or what the world of adulthood is all about. But maybe that's not so bad. Maybe they'll be better equipped for living fuller, more integrated lives themselves. And knowing about adult sexuality, about the intrigues and mistakes and joys people experience, at the least is interesting. Sometimes it's even quite promising.

PART II

5.

Hormonal Happenings

"My son has the best definition of puberty I know," says Joan Lipsitz, director of The Center for Early Adolescence in Chapel Hill, North Carolina. "He gave it when he was thirteen. He had said something to me about puberty, and I asked him what he meant by puberty. He said, 'You know what puberty is, Mom! It's when you grow hair and you stink!'

"His most prized possessions during that time of his life were a comb and his antiperspirant. I called it deodorant. He called it antiperspirant."

In case we forget how bound we are to our biology, all we have to do is look at a young adolescent. In every one of them, some sooner, some later, we can observe the incredibly rapid growth of the human animal in height and weight. We can witness attendant bodily changes in contour, characteristics, size and smell that represent the development of sexual maturity and serve to attract the opposite sex. Before our eyes, often before we have fully realized the phenomenon we are witnessing, the young adolescent becomes a physiologically mature human being, as capable as any adult of mating and reproducing the species.

Puberty is a natural, biological process. Natural as it is, however, every individual case still seems to come as a shock, even if the child has been "prepared" for it and even though mothers and fathers themselves have been through it.

"I was expecting my period for a year before I got it," says Sarah, a fourteen-year-old in Brooklyn, New York. "I had pains once a month for a year before I got it. Each time, my mother said it was my period. I'd run to the bathroom, but nothing happened. I finally got it just after I turned thirteen. I couldn't believe my eyes; I couldn't believe it had actually happened. When I got it, my friends—the people upstairs from us on Flatbush Avenue—came over to me on the street and started congratulating me. My mother must have told their mother, but I didn't know it. It was awful!"

Each major event of puberty, each signpost—from having a few straight, thin pubic hairs suddenly appear to buying a bra, from having a wet dream to starting your period—is a significant happening. In the life of the "recipient," it's surprising, personal, unique and often cataclysmic.

"I started my period at eleven and sprouted up around the same time," says Signe, an elegant sixteen-year-old who's wearing Gloria Vanderbilt jeans and a Halston blazer on this particular fall morning in Manhattan. "It was when I was about thirteen that I started developing. I only really noticed it when we went down to the south of France. I was tall. I was developing, but I hadn't really noticed it so much. Well, they have topless bathing there, you know, and so my sister and I were without our tops. Suddenly my mother noticed that I was getting a lot of attention for my age. She said, 'What's going on?' She sat there looking at me and saying, 'You're only thirteen!' "

As teenagers talked to me about their development, I remembered how thrilled I was buying my first bra, getting my period. I also remembered how I awoke one morning on my side and discovered that one of my newly grown breasts—the one closest to the bed—had shrunk into nothing and the other had grown. The horror of this lopsided deformity kept me frozen in position. When I finally stood up, I found, of course, that my breasts resumed their normal shape again. It was a hazard of tissue flexibility I'd never before witnessed. I didn't know anything like *that* happened to anyone else. In accordance with the laws of adolescence, my anatomy was distinct, my experience unique.

Anyone who has gone through the changes of puberty will recall, at least dimly, how it felt to be waiting on the brink of adulthood for the mysteries of your reproductive system to begin functioning; watching for your penis to grow or your nipples to bud; watching as your older brother or sister or boyfriend began to fill out and look like a woman or a man and then not quite believing it when the same thing happened to you. You'll remember how jokes about the bathroom and the body began to travel the school, how tempers flared at home when you wanted privacy, how people patted you on the back to see if you were wearing a bra—or how boys down the line in the locker room checked to see if you were wearing a jock strap or if you had the imprint of an unused condom marking your wallet.

No matter what you thought of the changes happening to yourself and your body, they happened anyway. One summer your pants started getting shorter and shorter until they didn't fit at all. One summer you said, "Yuk, I wouldn't want hair down there," and the next summer you were secretly admiring the hair growing "down there." Other things happened, often before you were ready for them or much later than you thought appropriate.

"I used to cry because I was the only one having a period," says Shyrell, who started menstruating when she was eleven years old and in the fifth grade in Phoenix, Arizona. "I felt odd. When I mentioned it to other kids, they'd say, 'What?' At first, it kind of scared me. I didn't have any idea what it was. I thought it was something wrong with my body."

Shyrell's friend, Megan, didn't start her period until she was fourteen and well into the eighth grade. "I was really relieved," Megan says. "I was embarrassed because I hadn't started yet. Everybody else had started before me. I called Shyrell and told her, and we celebrated the next night. I always thought something was wrong with me. My mom would always say, 'Nothing's wrong with you!' I'd ask her when she thought I'd start and she'd always say, 'Oh, soon!' I'd ask her if she thought something was wrong with me and she'd say, 'Nothing's wrong with you! It's normal to start late. You'll start soon!' And then I wouldn't start and it seemed like it would never come. When it did come, I was scared."

For boys, the first emission of semen is just as much a shock as the first sight of blood is for girls. Although most boys have had erections from the time they were infants, and an increased number of erections as pre-teens, ejaculation is a new experience.

"I couldn't believe it when I saw the stuff come out," said fifteen-year-old Shawn, the son of a construction foreman in Cleveland, Ohio. "At first, I thought I'd gone to the rest room or something, but then I wasn't sure what it was. It was so differently."

"When you can, you know, make it happen, everything changes," said Roger, seventeen, a junior at Bronx Science High School in New York. "It's like this new power in you. It just makes you see everything differently."

Although the majority of boys first ejaculate while masturbating, many others have their first emission of semen when they are sleeping. This is called a nocturnal emission, or a wet dream.

"I had my first wet dream when I was about twelve and a half," says thirteen-year-old F.G. in Los Angeles. "I didn't know what was happening when I had it. I woke up and the bed was kind of wet. I thought I had wet my bed or something—I didn't know what! I was curious about it, but I kept it to myself. I didn't really know what it was until I came to this school in the seventh grade and learned about it in the sex-education class."

"I started puberty when I was in the sixth grade," says Nathan, in Paradise Valley, Arizona. "I got hair down there and under my arms. Then in the seventh grade, I thought I had wet the bed. I wake up and my underwear's wet but my sheets aren't and I can't figure out what's going on. In the eighth grade, I found out what they were, so I didn't worry about it anymore."

"I thought maybe I had a leak in my bed," thirteen-year-old Dallas explained. "Awhile later, I figured from what I heard that it was normal." I figured from his face that he had just then figured it was normal. His expressions when his two friends had talked to me about their wet dreams had moved from alarm to relief.

Feelings about growing into a woman's or a man's body from the childhood body you "always knew" vary enormously. Quite often, the way girls or boys feel about these changes echo their core feelings and fears about themselves and their own worth.

A total lack of information from their parents on what is happening to them often causes additional and sometimes acute discomfort, particularly if young people have no one they feel they can talk to.

"The first time I got my period was in seventh grade," says Vanessa, shaking her straight brown bangs out of her large brown eyes. "I was the first one to get it. I got it at school. All my friends had been lying about it. They were saying they'd gotten it but they hadn't. I asked this one girl what to do and she didn't know, so that's how I knew she'd been lying. She was so jealous that I'd started first. I didn't know what to do, either. I was embarrassed to tell my mother. She'd never talked to me about it and I was frightened to death. I used tissues because I didn't know what to use. For a whole week I bled and used tissues and didn't tell anyone. It was awful. The second time, I told her and she got me pads. . . ."

"Puberty's not only a group of facts you're relating to," says Dr. John O'Brien, psychoanalyst and director of Child and Adolescent Services at St. Vincent's Hospital in New York. "It's a very emotional subject. It's not neutral. It's value issues, moral issues—not just issues of fact. For instance, a girl's attitude towards menstruation makes all the difference to a girl. You can talk to the girl about the facts, the biology is there. But then the mother says, 'Ah, the curse!' and there's a value judgment, a moral judgment that is also handed to the girl.

"You have very little control, if you're a girl, over when you're going to menstruate, or if you're a boy, of when you're going to have nocturnal emissions or erections from all sorts of stimuli. A boy is always having erections whether or not he wants them; he can't do anything about it. Also, you may have little control over the physiology of your voice cracking, of acne, or of your height or weight distribution. A lot of adolescents gain weight and this creates problems for them. For girls, there's a curving of the hips, and breast development. All of a sudden, an eleven- or twelve-year-old girl has developed breasts. There's all sorts of reactions to her physiology.

"With all of these things happening to their bodies and feeling out of control, adolescents get scared. They look to other people to find out what's happening to them. If their parents respond with 'These are the things we went through,' and they empathize and tell their children about their own experiences and how they felt about them—like 'I was excited' or 'It was scary' or whatever—it makes life much easier for the children."

The young people who had talked to their parents about pubertal changes and received positive input from them or from close siblings often reacted with confidence and happy feelings to the events that heralded their adult sexuality.

"I remember I started my period on the Fourth of July, when I was twelve," says Corina Egurrola, a wiry, energetic eighteen-year-old in Whittier, California. "I thought I had peed in my pants. Then I thought I had diarrhea. Then I realized what it was. As my older sisters—all seven of them—came home, I told them. I thought I'd be a part of them then. It did kind of change things, too. I was so excited! My sister two years older said, 'Wait awhile, then you won't be so excited.' But that didn't stop me. I told everybody I'd started my period. I told my brother, and he said, 'You're not supposed to tell boys!' "

"In the filmstrip they showed us in the sixth grade, there was a little bit about wet dreams," said Dick Roberts, a fourteen-year-old in Seattle, Washington. "But it wasn't clear. So I asked my dad and he told me about it, so I sort of knew it was coming. I knew what it was going to be. When you start to get hair under your lip up here, and under your arms, and down there, you know you're starting to grow up. Then when *it* happens, you think, well, I'm *really* starting to grow up now."

"It gives you a good feeling," says Nathan. "It's not a good feeling that you had an orgasm 'cause it's kind of gross and sticky, but it's a good feeling that you're growing up. You know that you're getting mature and becoming a man and all that. . . ."

For boys, the signposts of puberty aren't as public as they are for girls. Girls can use menstruation as an excuse to get out of gym classes or swimming or as an effective way to intimidate male teachers. ("I can't tell *you* why, but I could tell Miss Jones!"). Girls often told me of friends and parents congratulating them for starting their periods (while they said they died of embarrassment, of course). Boys didn't have parallel stories. What happens to them is more often than not never talked about by family members. When a boy's penis and scrotum begin to grow, when he begins to have more erections and new sensations associated with his gentials, it's enormously significant to him personally. But his passage into manhood is nearly always surrounded by silence. I talked to very few boys who were told ahead of time what would be happening to them physiologically.

Few are prepared for the constant erections they begin to have with the onset of puberty. Their erections often occur from the slightest physical stimulation of the penis, from general body tensions and from generalized emotional situations even when there's nothing specifically sexual involved. Catching a pass during a game of football, feeling scared, feeling angry, sitting in a movie—anything can stimulate an erection in a boy. Boys are often confused and embarrassed by this phenomenon that is entirely out of their control.

Alfred Kinsey wrote some thirty years ago in *Sexual Behavior in the Human Male* that it's "impossible for a majority of women who care for these boys and control moral codes to understand the problem that the boys face in being constantly aroused and regularly involved with their normal biologic reactions."

It's also a difficult problem for boys to understand and accept. Some feel sabotaged by their own physiology. Author Julius Lester, for instance, says there was a period of time in his life when he wished passionately he was a girl named Julie instead of a boy called Julius, for no other reason than not to be bothered by that thing that kept popping up between his legs. In an essay for *Ms.* magazine called "Being a Boy," he wrote:

> That thing was always there. Every time we went to the john, there it was, twitching around like a fat little worm on a fishing hook. When we took baths it floated in water like a lazy fish and God forbid we should touch it! It sprang to life like lightning leaping from a cloud. I wished I could cut it off or at least keep it tucked between my legs. . . . But I was helpless. It was there, with a life and mind of its own, having no other function than to embarrass me.

Though actual experience is the best teacher, boys who had discussed puberty and its significance with their parents or other adults seemed to manage with less anxiety and guilt than did boys who had never discussed these events. They also seemed to have easier access to their dreams and fantasies and were more articulate about their feelings. Duncan, for instance, said he felt comfortable talking about puberty with me because he had always talked about it with his folks.

"When I was about twelve, I started getting hairy," says fourteen-year-old Duncan. "We're a real hairy family. I had my first wet dream just around my thirteenth birthday. It was a funny dream. I was into Roman history, so there were all these Romans walking around down the street.

"This one Roman, a woman, said, 'Do you want to hear a Mickey Mouse story?' She takes me into this room, and she was reading me a Mickey Mouse story. I remember the book was red. Inside the Mickey Mouse book, all the people were Romans. They were all women, of course, and they were taking off their clothes. Then that was it. It didn't take me very long."

Duncan said he knew about wet dreams from the first grade and had discussed puberty with his older brother and his parents. "If my mother reads this book," he said to me later, "she'll know it's me because I told her that dream. It's okay. It wouldn't matter 'cause I tell her everything anyway. . . ."

One of the difficulties youngsters have in coming to terms with what is happening to their bodies involves timing. On the average, girls' spurt in height takes place between the ages of eleven and twelve, and boys begin two years later, between the ages of thirteen and fourteen. At age twelve, girls are usually bigger and sometimes stronger than their male counterparts, but by the age of fifteen, boys have usually passed them by.

"Part of the difficulty of puberty is that these kids don't go through it together," says a social studies teacher who has taught junior high school students in San Francisco for the past ten years. "The seventh-grade boys and girls are cultures apart. At the precise time girls are getting interested in boys, boys their age are still playing tag.

"Chronological age isn't any measure of development at this age, but it's how they're grouped. You can be quite certain that in any class of eighth graders, 1 percent of the boys or less will be up to the girls in that class emotionally. That's just the way it is."

The fact that boys and girls don't seem to have any real understanding of what is happening to each other physically compounds the distance and discrepancies between them at this age. Most of the boys I talked to said they didn't understand exactly how a girl had a period, but they knew that girls had learned about them in a film *they* weren't shown. Girls said they had been shown films of the sperm and the egg and the shedding of the uterine lining, but that they learned nothing of the mysteries of the male. In addition to general ignorance about what is happening to their own bodies, they don't understand what is happening to the opposite sex.

"The neighborhood I used to live in, there are a lot of older kids," says fourteen-year-old Nathan. "This one guy in particular, I learned mostly everything off of him. The way I learned about girls having their period was my sister had this stuff in a wastepaper basket, and I used to throw it out and everything. I didn't really understand what it was, so I, you know, made a lot of noise about it. And then my parents sat me down and they told me about it. And they said, you know, my sister was doing this, and that it was from when women had their periods. Well, I didn't know what they were, periods. I wasn't very comfortable in that conversation. I wanted to get out of that conversation quick. So I just sat there and nodded my head. I didn't really understand what it was they were saying or what it meant. I didn't really understand how a period worked. I still don't, but now that I know what those things [Kotex] are,

I don't even look in the cupboard. I don't go near 'em. I don't do that sort of thing anymore."

"It embarrasses me to remember it," says Rachel, an eighteen-year-old freshman at Barnard College, "but when I was fourteen, one time I was sitting on this boy's lap at a party, and he got hard, you know, under my leg. I got really angry at him. I said, 'Johnny Davis, you stop that!' I thought he was doing it on purpose, and I was so angry at him. I didn't know anything. . . ."

Since I didn't understand the processes of puberty very well, and since boys and girls started asking me questions about themselves and each other, I asked several scientists and doctors to explain to me exactly what puberty is and what triggers it. Their response was that puberty is extremely complex, and many pieces of the whole picture still remain a mystery. There's a tremendous amount that we still don't know about the forces set loose during adolescence.

They explained that puberty is not a single event, even though many of the changes involved in it are so rapid that it might seem so. It is, rather, part of a complex process that may be triggered by a critical metabolic rate or a number of other factors scientists still do not agree upon.[1] Exactly at what time puberty begins is difficult to pinpoint. At that unknown point, and for unknown reasons, the brain gives a signal to the gonadatropin (i.e., the ovaries of the female and the testicles of the male) to produce estrogen, progesterin and testosterone in much higher amounts than they have been producing in middle childhood. The released hormones travel in the bloodstream, find receptive cells and enter them. They get inside the DNA center of a cell and make things happen. For instance, estrogens find receptive places in the cells of the breast and proceed to make the breast soft and round. They find other receptive homes in the hips and pelvis, which become larger as a result; in the skin; in the uterus; in the clitoris and vulva. Testosterone acts on receptors in the cells of the penis and scrotum, the skin of the face, the cartilages of the shoulders and ribcage, which expand, and certain parts of the brain.

Until this time, the bodies of our children have looked like they did the day before the day before that, which has given them a sense of competence and control. The processes of bodily change that begin with puberty are predictable and well defined—although they come as a surprise to the individual child and often upset his or her sense of control in the universe.

There is no predicting the exact age at which puberty will begin for any individual, but once it starts, the sequence is quite the same for everyone. According to the noted British pediatrician and professor of child health and growth at the University of London, James M. Tanner, the *sequence* of pubertal changes in an adolescent's body has not altered in the last ten years or the last fifty thousand. Girls always develop two years earlier than boys, and some boys have completed their whole physiological development—their spurts in height and penis development—before other boys of the same chronological age have begun theirs. The sequence of events occurs now at an earlier age than it used to, however, for both boys and girls.[2]

The average age of first menstruation is now about 12.45 years, which is down from an average of 16.5 a century ago in England. In the United States, the average age has declined from 14.2 in 1900 to about 12.45. A similar trend in male sexual development has occurred. Like girls, boys of today are considerably better developed physically than in the past. For example, a nine-year-old boy today is 3.8 inches taller and nearly nineteen pounds heavier than a boy that age living in 1881. For the average boy of thirteen or fourteen, ejaculation is now possible. Also, a change in voice occurs about the fourteenth or fifteenth year, whereas at the time of the eighteenth-century Bach Boys' Choir in Leipzig, the average age of voice change was eighteen.[3]

For girls, the first sign of puberty is usually the softening of the tissue in the breast and the enlargement of the areola around the nipple. The appearance of pubic hair sometimes precedes the "breast bud" or coincides with it. The clitoris, labia, uterus and vagina grow and develop simultaneously with the breasts. In a way that's similar to the boy's focus on his penis as a measure of his masculinity, the development of the girl's breasts is often the way in which she becomes conscious of her own femininity and measures her sex appeal. The growth of her breasts contributes to her awareness of becoming a woman and her new feelings of increased sexual excitement. Since the uterus and vagina are internal and the clitoris is not as visible as a boy's penis, girls usually focus more on their breasts than their genitals as their way of defining their femininity.

Sensations in the breasts and genitals seem to develop during their growth. Some girls do begin to have orgasms during this time without genital manipulation. Others begin to have orgasms during nocturnal dreams, not unlike the male.

The first menstruation, called menarche, is quite often thought of as the signal event for the onset of puberty in girls, but, in fact, according to Tanner, it occurs late in a girl's pubertal development, *after* the peak of a girl's spurt in height has passed. Although menarche does indicate that her uterus is maturing, it doesn't necessarily mean that a girl has attained her full reproductive capacity. Frequently, but not always, girls have menstrual periods for over a year or more before their periods are accompanied by ovulation. Some young girls who have had intercourse but have not used birth control during this time have come to the false conclusion that because they didn't get pregnant, they can't get pregnant.

Despite the fact that menarche is not the signal event of puberty, it usually represents for each girl her transition into womanhood.

"I was ready to start my period," said Liz McClendon from Fullerton, California. "I was so excited about it. All the girls said, 'Have you started yet? Have you started yet?' It's such a big mystery. It's like you're complete when you start your period."

In boys, the first sign of puberty is the accelerated growth of the testes and scrotum. The scrotum skin reddens and wrinkles. Sometimes there is a slight growth of pubic hair at the base of the penis. Next comes a growth spurt in height and in penis circumference. The acceleration of the penis growth in circumference and length, according to Tanner, begins on the average at about twelve and a half, but sometimes as early as ten and as late as fourteen and a half. Between the ages of nine and fifteen, the boy's penis and scrotum nearly doubles in size. The completion of penis development usually occurs at about age fourteen and half, but in some boys at twelve and a half and in other boys at sixteen and a half or seventeen.[4]

At the same time that the boy is growing in height, his prostate and bulbourethral glands enlarge and develop. The prostate gland then begins to produce fluid that can be ejaculated during orgasm, but this fluid will probably not contain mature sperm. The time of the first ejaculation of seminal fluid usually happens about a year after the beginning of the accelerated penis growth.

At some point after boys have begun their spurts in height and penis growth, and after the prostate gland, seminal vesicles and scrotal sac have enlarged, germ cells in the lining of the seminiferous tubules of the testes begin to divide and differentiate into mature sperm. Mature sperm are first present in the ejaculatory fluid at the age of fifteen, on the average, but for some boys they are present as early as age eleven or as late as age seventeen.[5]

According to Kinsey's studies, 90 percent of males ejaculate for the first time between the age of eleven and fifteen. The mean age is thirteen years and eleven months.

The first ejaculation derived from nocturnal dreams usually occurs a year or more after the onset of other adolescent characteristics occur and after ejaculation would have been possible by other means (like masturbation or intercourse).[6]

The breaking of the voice and a change of voice pitch is due to the enlargement of the larynx and usually occurs relatively late in puberty, along with the growth of facial and auxiliary hair. Often family members kid a boy whose voice is changing, telling him that he's starting to grow up. Or they'll see hair on his chin and tell him that soon he'll be a man. In terms of his biological transition, he's already past the midpoint of his development into manhood.

The sebaceous and apocrine sweat glands, particularly of the axillae, genital and anal regions, develop rapidly during puberty and give rise to characteristic odors. This change occurs in both sexes but is usually more marked in boys than it is in girls.[7]

One mother told me that when her son started going through puberty, she kept smelling "the weirdest smell. It wasn't just sweat or semen," she said. "It was just a bizarre body odor. Before I figured it out, I kept going around and saying, 'What *smells?*' Then I realized it was Matthew!"

Teenage acne—the enlargement of the pores and the appearance of blackheads and pimples, is more common in boys than it is in girls. For both sexes, however, it's a common biological aspect of pubertal development. For best prevention, doctors recommend soap and water. But even with soap and water and an effort to keep the skin clean, the oil glands of some teenagers get out of hand, and the resulting pimples or sometimes more severe acne can become an obsession as well as a humiliation.

Some boys worry about an increase in the diameter of the areola around their nipples. For that increase to be considerable is perfectly normal. Many boys also have a distinct enlargement of the breast area about midway through adolescence, which can alarm them considerably. This usually regresses again after about a year.

Before adolescence, girls and boys are similar in strength for a given body size and shape. Afterward, boys are much stronger, since they develop more force per gram of muscle as well as greater muscle mass. Boys also develop larger hearts and lungs relative to their size, a higher systolic blood pressure, a lower resting heart rate, a greater capacity for carrying oxygen in the blood and a greater power for neutralizing the chemical products of muscular exercise such as lactic acid.[8] In short, the male is becoming biologically prepared for the primal, age old tasks of hunting, fishing and manipulating heavy objects.[9]

All of the sex-differentiated developments arising at puberty are caused by hormones that serve the reproductive capacity of each person. The penis is directly used for copulation. The uterus is the home for the fetus, the vagina becomes the birth canal and the mammary glands can be used for lactation. The secondary sexual characteristics—the wide shoulders on men, the particular scents of women and the wide shape of their hips—all of these things biologically attract the opposite sex.

Since their bodies become the focus of their sexual self-awareness, their source of appeal and their self-image, young people often worry a great deal about the "normalcy" of all their parts. They wonder if their genitals and the secondary sexual aspects of their bodies are also acceptable and appealing. Their feelings of self-esteem, competence and personal dignity are rooted in their bodies, so it becomes extremely important that their physical selves are properly put together.

Obviously boys focus a great deal of attention on the normalcy of the

penis and testicles, and girls on their breasts. Girls study the curve of
their hips; boys, the width of their shoulders. Both trace the line of their
legs, the hair under their arms. Some girls worry about the appearance
of their genitals as well. Among girls, the early developers seem to worry the most. Among boys, the late developers are equally anxious.

Some develop physically long before they begin to grow up emotionally. Fifteen-year-old Melanie, the daughter of a building contractor
and bookkeeper in northern California, for instance, talked about how
large her breasts got when she was in the sixth grade and how she tried
to hide them with thick sweaters and rounded shoulders. She said that
one day in gym class, while she was cowering in a corner, changing
clothes in a hurry, another girl yelled at her: "You don't wear a bras-
siere yet, Melanie Frasier? How disgusting!"

"I was so ashamed," says Melanie. "Here I'd been ashamed of having
breasts and then I was suddenly ashamed for *not* wearing a bra. Oh, it
was horrible. I was so miserable then."

"I hated being developed so early," says my friend Linda, recalling
"the most painful time of her life"—age eleven. "These two girls in my
class used to follow me into the bathroom so they could see what boobs
looked like. I wore blouses under my sweaters to give me more bulk so
no one would notice."

Dr. Barbara Otto at the Adolescent Health Center of Mt. Sinai Hospital in New York often has questions from boys and girls about sexual
adequacy of their bodies. "I got into a conversation last week with a
boy," says the slim, dark-haired doctor, "and we spent a half-hour on
penis size and what's normal. I asked him if he had any questions about
sexual activity or his body and then he asked me what was normal size
for a penis.

"I told him that there is an average size, but that many men are on
both sides of that average. There are men with penises larger than average and men with penises smaller than average, and they're all normal.
I also told him that studies have shown that penis size has nothing what-
soever to do with successful sexual performance or with satisfying a
woman. I told him that whether a woman has an orgasm or doesn't have
an orgasm doesn't have anything to do with penis size. I'm not sure he
believed me at first, but I think he did after we'd talked awhile, and he
felt a lot better about himself."

Sixteen-year-old Lauri told me that she had been quite upset at the
age of fourteen, when she looked in the mirror at her labia. "The lips of
my vagina were all wrinkled up," she said, "And I thought, oh, my God,
they're so *ugly*! I thought it was my fault for having played with myself
when I was younger. I thought I'd stretched the lips out of shape and no
man would ever want me. For at least two years I thought they were a
mark of shame. Then I saw some magazines and I realized that most
women have wrinkled lips down there."

Sometimes teenagers allay their fears about their own sexual equipment by comparing apparatus. Young boys sometimes see who can pee the farthest, and adolescent boys sometimes see who can ejaculate the farthest. Girls often study the size and shape of their friends' breasts. And although a great deal of comparing goes on at a distance, sometimes young teenagers give closer examination to the bodies of their good friends in an attempt to confirm their own body and its normalcy.

"I used to play football and tag with the guy who was my best friend," says Dennis, a strong eighteen-year-old from Vermont. "One time I remember spending the night at his house, and we both ended in the bathtub with all our clothes off. We ended up jerking each other off and we tried everything—penis in the bellybutton, you name it. It was pretty innocent, really, even though it doesn't sound like it. There didn't seem anything wrong with what we were doing."

Courtney, an eighteen-year-old who had graduated from high school in Cleveland, Ohio, the day before our interview, told of a similar experience when she was younger. "When I was eleven or twelve, with my female friends, I was discovering my own body and so were they," said Courtney. "I always wanted to feel out the body of another girl. I touched my breasts, but I wanted to know what their breasts felt like, too. When I was with my best friend one night, overnight at her house, it started with touching and sensual feelings and got very sexual. It was like feeling my own body, but hers, too. I felt really good about it."

While confirmation is found for oneself in looking at the bodies of same-sex peers, the opposite sex also begins to stir excitement and hitherto-unknown fantasies in most adolescents. Although each person's response varies, boys and girls alike find themselves with increased libido, with secret conscious and unconscious fantasies constantly stimulating them. Additionally, they respond to erotic stimuli that fit their fantasies. Boys have spontaneous erections more often, and with less provocation, than ever before in their lives. They say they constantly think about hard-ons, about girls and about sex. It's biology; whether boys want erections or not, they have them. As author Julius Lester said, there's no way not to think about sex when that thing is always popping up between your legs.

Girls have more diffuse erotic patterns than boys, but they, too, find themselves feeling a new level of excitement and mystery and erotic response to people and events around them. They have heightened sensations in their developing breasts and in the vaginal region. Most girls don't have orgasms from breast fondling alone. But touching their breasts, or having them touched, gives them a sense of beauty, femininity and erotic power unmatched by any earlier experiences.

"I'll never forget the first time a boy touched my breasts," recalls forty-year-old Nancy. "I was thirteen and it was the most sensational feeling, literally and figuratively, I had ever experienced. It was absolutely wonderful. I didn't ever want to stop. . . ."

Of course, with their bodies changing and their sensations, perceptions and explorations changing, not to mention the reactions of people around them, adolescents have to readjust themselves to new realities. Teenagers work out ways of dealing with the new emotions, impulses, fantasies, feelings and ideas that seem to arrive and distribute themselves along with the hormones. Teenagers learn to manage themselves, while the hormonal levels work themselves out in their bodies.

"At adolescence, it seems that the hormone levels fluctuate wildly," says Dr. Winnifred Cutler, a reproductive biologist at the University of Pennsylvania whose research includes studying hormones and behavior. "They surge around in fits and starts until the system gets calmed down and synchronized. It's like learning to drive a car when you put on the gas and lurch forward, and then drive around stopping and starting in jerks and fits. That's the way the body reacts when it has these great swings in hormonal levels."

Since hormones and behavior seem so closely related, it's not unusual for teenagers going through hormonal changes to experience vast emotional changes, says Dr. Cutler. "There are two times in life when the hormones seem to show wide swings and that's during adolescence and during menopause," she says. "That's the time people experience vast emotional changes. They have massive highs and lows—troubles at home, terrible depressions, tremendous excitements, and often experience extremes of moods. . . ." That's biology affecting behavior, and the body working out its own balance.

Although it's been well established by anthropologists that stress and erratic behavior are not a given for the adolescent years, it is clear, at least biologically, that mood swings are normal for a majority of adolescents. In our culture, for a variety of reasons, adolescents also often feel a great deal of vulnerability during this period of their lives. Their mood swings, along with their dating and mating habits and perhaps even their use of alcohol and drugs, may have a great deal to do with their hormones—more than we currently understand.

Sometimes parents feel the effect of the hormones almost as much as their children; they feel as if "teenage" hormones are controlling their lives.

"I can't *believe* how impossible he is," an attractive, thirty-eight-year-old mother said about her fourteen-year-old son. "He's always starting arguments! And he's rude! I don't understand it; I refuse to understand it. The hormones of his body must be driving him crazy or something. Sometimes I think adolescence is like a volcano—all these emotions welling up and flowing out."

Even for youngsters who seem to take their bodily changes and sensations in an easy, graceful stride straight from childhood to adulthood, hormones may play a role we don't understand. Donna, for instance, seemed to be one adolescent who breezed through her transitions with the even, happy confidence she displayed when she breezed into our interview in San Diego after a five-mile run.

"When I was about eight years old, I was worried because I hadn't started developing breasts," she said, taking off her sweat band and pushing her blond bangs behind her ears. "And so I asked my mom why men like breasts. She said, 'That's the way we were made, so we were attractive to men.' Then she told me about making love. I was kind of shocked by the whole thing. She was very basic that women had a special place for men's penises and there was a special sac for sperm. She told me about the uterus and that was where we were to bear children like the Bible said. She didn't make me frightened. She made it sound like a wonderful thing to be a woman.

"I got breasts a little before I got my period. I was happy about that. I've always wanted to be older, though some people want to be younger. I was so excited about my first bra. Unlike my mom, who never wanted to wear a bra!

"I was excited and happy about my period. I'd been waiting for it and I finally got in the summer before seventh grade, when I was eleven years old. I was running water to take a bath and I saw blood on my underwear. I ran and asked my mom what happened, and she said I'd started my period. When you start your period, you feel like you finally are a woman. I thought I *was* a woman. Later I found out it takes time."

It does take time to become a man or a woman. The instant our children are born, they begin the process that carries them into adulthood. They explore the world of men and women with new, fresh eyes. When they are adolescents, they develop the capacity themselves to reproduce our species. How they feel about themselves, what decisions they make for their lives, the way they will live as adults and the kind of relationships they will have with the people around them will reflect how they feel and live in their bodies.

6.

Measuring Up: Am I Okay?

"My nose!" says Margaret Ann, covering what seems a perfectly pretty nose with her hand. "I hate it! Everybody at school makes fun of it!" I imagine her, face to the mirror, studying her reflection intensely for hours. Finally the straight, freckled nose bends grotesquely in front of her eyes, turns blue, and she shrieks in horror, confirmed in her judgment.

Margaret Ann, at fourteen, has legs that remind me of a Harlem Globetrotter. Her brief yellow shorts sit at the top of them, and long white bobby socks rise up her straight calves out of red and white sneakers. Altogether, her legs must be at least two-thirds of her long, lanky frame.

"I think I would rather like to be a blond," she says, pushing her shiny brown hair back from her shoulders. Red barrettes hold a piece of her hair on each side of her pretty face. "Blond people, everybody looks at them more. Also, I'd like no freckles. If I could, I wouldn't want any freckles. I'd also like to be shorter. I'm five foot nine and three-quarters. Nadine's five ten and a half. I'm glad I'm not that tall, but I'd like to be a little shorter than I am now. Not as short as Noel, but in between Noel and me."

I haven't met Nadine, but Noel, who's five foot three, blond and without freckles, sits across a linoleum-top table from us. We are all drinking lemonade from jelly glasses in the kitchen of a modest row house in a working-class section of Brooklyn, New York.

"It's too bad Nadine isn't here," Noel says. "She always criticizes herself. Her hair and her height. Everybody likes her curly hair, and she's always trying to straighten it. She's always asking you, 'Do you think my pants look too short?' and that kind of thing. She didn't want to come to talk to you today. She's that way. She likes to go to movies."

106

"Nadine's our other best friend," says Noel, looking like an ad for Ivory soap. "We've been in the same home room for three years and best friends for four years."

"I'm as much best friends with Nadine as I am with Noel," Margaret Ann said. "And the same's for her. We do different things together, but we all get along really good."

As Noel and Margaret Ann talked about themselves, I was reminded that regardless of what children look like at the age of eight, nine or ten, in adolescence they find themselves in totally unpredictable new bodies. In most other areas of development, they know pretty much what's going to happen. Sixth grade follows fifth grade follows fourth grade. A soft ball is followed by a hard ball. Junior varsity basketball is followed by varsity basketball. But now they're in bodies that are changing daily along with their emotions. They don't know what they're going to look like and they don't even know when the process is going to stop. They have no road maps as to who they're going to be, so every change that occurs has to be studied. It's not unusual for adolescents to have the feeling that perhaps they've been sent to a new planet where their minds have been transferred to these larger, smelly bodies that are getting wet or having erections all the time.

Although most adolescents go through a period in which they feel bewildered by these new conditions and questions of who they are, there is tremendous variation in the way individuals go about trying to find out what their new bodies and energies do, and how they measure up.

Margaret Ann, for instance, seems to be enjoying the search for who she is. She's playful and experimental and seems to take her new attributes in stride and enjoy them. She tries on new roles and identities with cheerful abandon. "I've told all my classmates that [singer] Donnie Osmond is my boyfriend," she says. "So every time I get anything new, like a necklace or something, and somebody asks me where I got it, I say, 'Oh, Donnie gave it to me.' Now people say things like, 'Hey, I like your sweater. Did Donnie give it to you?' "

Noel is less articulate about her anxieties than Margaret Ann, and much less playful about the way she appears to others. She feels unsure of how boys find her looks—and doesn't have any idea whether she is a little bit attractive, not at all attractive, or very attractive.

Although her story will be different in two or three years, right now she's so different from what she was as a child that she has no way to measure herself. Like other adolescents, she's relentlessly comparing and contrasting herself to others—whether they're at school, in magazines, on the television or movie screen. She's acutely sensitive to reactions to her looks, clothes, habits and behavior. Because she's so out of step with herself and so unsure of who she is, she feels even more out of step with her peers.

During this time of development, when each change in one's body seems to reveal more secret flaws that could be detected, most adolescents feel extremely vulnerable to criticism. They feel uncertain, inadequate and incompetent. Often they focus all their conscious anxiety on their appearances.

"I got this dislike about my body," says Maria Cordero, a perfectly proportioned sixteen-year-old of Puerto Rican descent, who was wearing a crew-neck sweater tucked into the narrow waist of gray wool slacks. "I'm too fat. Oh, sometimes I like my body, too, but sometimes I think I'm too fat. I think I don't look so good . . ."

Girls have no monopoly on these concerns. "I don't like my hair, the way it sticks up here in the back," says thirteen-year-old Bob, in Phoenix. "Also, I'd like to put on some weight. I don't care how tall I am as long as I hit the golf ball straight through. There are small guys on the team that win just as much as tall guys. But it's not how far you hit the ball, it's how well you play the game and how accurate you are. Of course, I wouldn't really mind if I got taller. Five-three is pretty short. . . ."

"In high school, it's a self-conscious thing that will hit you all of a sudden," says Adam Newton, sixteen, a tall, muscular boy who's wearing faded jeans and a red T-shirt that complements his wide shoulders and strong arms. "Like you think your hair's messed up and you want to comb it. Or you want to wash your face because you think there's a zit on it. You're aware of yourself in a different way."

Resolving the dilemma of who we are to others, as well as to ourselves, is a mammoth and overlapping task—one often approached in our culture by spending a preponderance of time in front of the mirror. Adolescents ask the same questions we all ask, but more intently. Who is that looking back at me from the mirror? Is that *me?* Surely it's not the real me, the person I feel inside. Is what I see and feel visible to other people? Will they see that blackhead, that bend in my nose? And on a more secretive, worrisome level—will they be able to tell that one testicle hangs lower than the other or that my right breast is larger than my left? Because of the intensity of the feelings and sensations they are having in their bodies, many teenagers privately feel they must be insane, and thus focus all the more anxiety on external images.

Parents spend an enormous amount of time reassuring their daughters that their thighs are not too thick and their sons that their hair looks *fine* parted on the side. Teenagers grow sensitive if not morbid over any negative comments pertaining to moles, noses, legs, eyes, skin and other basically unchangeable aspects of their appearances. They internalize their parents' responses to their appearances, but they don't fully trust positive judgments from them. Such judgments from parents don't have the objectivity of the judgment of peers. Besides that, teenagers are concerned about the approval of their age mates, not their parents, at this point. Parents are often relegated to the observation decks while their teenagers are agonizing over the most minute details of their image and identity.

Peter Blos, a faculty member and supervising analyst at the New York Psychoanalytic Institute and the Columbia University Center for Psychoanalytic Training and Research, as well as the author of many major books and articles on adolescence, points out that the adolescents' drive to attach themselves to their peers serves as an important if not essential means of detaching from identification with the mother and father. It also serves as a new area for definition of one's self in the world outside the family.[1]

"Every day now there's a discussion about the skin," says the mother of twelve-year-old Kathryn in the Chicago suburb of Winnetka. "She'll say, 'Oh, look, I have a pimple here'—and I usually can't see a thing. And the hair! She gets up at seven and she's finished with breakfast at seven thirty. She has to be out to the bus by eight, so she spends twenty minutes on her hair and then walks out every morning saying, 'My hair looks terrible.' She wants approval of what's she's wearing, too, even though I know it doesn't matter what I say. She's very concerned that she's wearing what everybody else is wearing. . . ."

For boys, the ritual is quite similar. "Luke gets up at five o'clock every morning, showers before anybody else, and washes his hair," says his mother, Irene, a history teacher in Larchmont, New York. "Then he blow-dries it. He has thick, black hair that's curly, so he has to fluff it up. He tends to his toilette before he even goes in for breakfast. It takes him nearly two hours to get ready for school.

"Usually he's not very conscious of trying to keep up with any look or what everybody else is doing, but he did get overalls because the other kids are wearing them and because he wanted them, too. He also asked for a jock strap, which I got for him, but it's still sitting in his drawer unused. He's had it for six months—and I have the impression he wanted it because everybody else had one and he thought he should have one, too!"

To be accepted by others, adolescents seem to stretch themselves into a variety of different shapes and styles. It's impossible not to notice their terrible need for conformity—whether it means wearing skeletons painted on the backs of their jean jackets; boasting a daily uniform of jeans with holes worn in the knee; never being seen in a suit; or any number of details—from red twine in braids to silly-looking haircuts. The reason given rarely varies: that's the way everybody else does it. The "everybody else" being a person or persons to whom approval has been granted. As Philadelphia psychiatrist Dr. Donald Nathanson points out, the need for conformity comes from the sense that "If I'm so different from what I was, I'd better at least be like somebody or something else.

"For instance, if everybody knows that Mick Jagger is okay, and I look like him, then I'm okay, too," says Dr. Nathanson. "It doesn't matter if Mick Jagger has thick lips and slouches when he walks. It is that he is approved of, and by analogy, then I too am approved.

"In early adolescence particularly, the push behind the attempt to be the same is magnified by our own terror at being different. As adolescents, we know that's we're really different because of the pimple on our face or because of the size of our earlobes."

Any deviation from the standard approved by peers, then, becomes mortifying because it implies inferiority. Even a deviation in awareness, knowledge or experience cannot be tolerated by a group consisting of members desperate about their own adequacy. They displace their own terror at being different onto the scapegoat—which none of them wants to be. In Jason's case, what he didn't know kept him out of a group, unconfirmed.

"When we went to visit Jason at camp last summer, when he was eleven, he saw us and broke into tears," said Jason's mother, Jane, from Englewood, New Jersey. "He was sobbing and sobbing. Joe finally got him to calm down and tell us what was the matter, and he said, 'How could you send me to camp without telling me what a blow-job was? How could you do that to me?'

"Apparently the other boys had been teasing him for a week because he didn't know what a blow-job was. Probably half of them didn't know what it was, either, but they weren't about to let on, and he wasn't cunning enough to act like he knew."

"Well, we sent him with a sleeping bag and mosquito repellent and four towels and twelve pairs of socks and shorts and shirts and sneakers and a flashlight and soap," said his father, Joe Maloney. "But we left out the most important thing."

Part of the game of pretending you're the same, of course, is trying to hide what's different. For very young adolescents, bodily processes are still painfully new—and different. They're distressed by anyone knowing what is happening to them (unless they choose to share it themselves). They may know that other people are going through the same experiences, such as menstruating, getting turned on, masturbating or having wet dreams, but their experience still seems unique.

To the extent that adolescents find confirmation of their own adequacy by excluding others or punishing nonconformists for the anxiety they have "produced," they feel they have an advantage and try to hold on to it in any way possible. They often seize on what makes them feel strong or superior and safe from their own fears, and they'll milk these methods dry. In the process, they're desperately trying to find out more about the extent and effect of their personal power. Often the conscious search is extremely primitive.

"I used to be a nice sweet little kid," says thirteen-year-old Johnny in Dallas, Texas. We're sitting in the elegant living room of Johnny's home. "Now I'm big and I have to be tough. I'm one of the two biggest kids in my class. I've five-four. So if I want a milk, I say, 'Go get me a milk.' Sometimes they say no. If they do that, you just punch 'em on the arm and the next time they'll go get you the milk. Usually, though, they're good friends, and they say, 'Sure, I'll get you the milk.' I'm a faster grower than people in my class—that's why I'm bigger.

"Then there's Charlie. He's five-ten and in the eighth grade. I'll do anything for him. If he says something and I say 'What?' he'll say, 'Are you questioning me?' If I say no, he'll hit me on the knuckles with a screwdriver. If I say yes, he'll hit me, too. I never get mad at him. He's the boss. I respect him. When somebody over here is bigger than you, you respect him.

"Then there's this guy Vincent. He's the natural violent guy. . . . He's had troubles with his parents and the police. And then there's Patrick—the guy who picks you up by the ears. He's a nice guy, but he's just dumb. . . .

"I hate violence myself. If someone picks a fight with me, I wouldn't try to hurt them back. If someone hit Patrick, he'd probably kill them. There's no point trying to hurt him."

As Johnny talked, I wondered what his father, an international businessman, and his mother, a nurse, think when or if they hear their son talk about these matters. It might be hard for them to believe this was normal talk for a thirteen-year-old in Johnny's school, but it was.

Earlier in the month, another thirteen-year-old, this one from San Francisco, had said to me, "I'm not going to get pressured into anything by anyone because I'm a leader. I'm popular. Nobody tells me what to do. I tell them what to do. I don't order people around exactly—I'm nice about it—but I call the shots in my class and nobody really questions it. It's mainly because I'm bigger and pretty good looking, and, well, I'm just a natural leader type."

Sometimes to the adult eye, the proving ground on which teenagers do battle seems brutal. Tensions, conflicts and anxieties seem out of proportion to the stakes. The boy who cries nightly because the mole on his neck looms so large in his mind that he wants to have plastic surgery, and the straight-A student who suddenly wants to drop out of school because her "mind has changed" and she can no longer "concentrate" are telling us something important. They're literally yelling that the stress of all these new attributes and feelings and interactions is too much for them. They're having trouble managing the accelerated changes altering their experience. Too much is happening at once.

Much of the cruelty of adolescents, it seems, could be measured in direct proportion to their levels of anxiety. Sometimes we hear about vicious behavior on the part of juveniles toward people who are old, crippled or deformed and we wonder what makes them attack someone unable to defend themselves. I suspect that these particular teenagers feel such enormous insecurity and inadequacy about their own differences that the more strange the other guy, the more their tension and rage is provoked. By focusing on the victim and punishing him for his differentness, these teenagers distract the focus from themselves. In a similar way, common jealousy is also a function of adolescent insecurity. The adolescent who is always complaining that "If it weren't for Roger, I would have been captain of the soccer team" is attempting to focus the cause of his difficulties on others, not on himself. It seems that the greater a teenager's self-doubts, the greater the morbidity of his or her jealousy and the greater the attack.

"When I walk up to a girl, I don't look at her," says Amy, an attractive sixteen-year-old from the High School of Performing Arts, New York. "I look at what she's wearing and how good she looks. You can tell when people are going over your clothes and sizing you up.

"Girls can be really evil towards each other. They'll talk about you behind your back and cut you down to boys they think like you.

"I'm the kind of girl a lot of girls are jealous of because I make a good impression. I look good and the boys see me and are interested in getting to know me. Some girls see this and they won't invite me places or to parties because they want the boys there to be interested in them, not in me. . . ."

"Gossip is vicious," says Johanna Markson, sixteen, also from the High School of Performing Arts. "It's usually the result of vying for popularity, but it can destroy you—you can lose your friends and your position. It can be fake, too—something made up so the other person can get on top. . . ."

Of course, after these initial and often brutal contacts in early adolescence (whether it's happening at age twelve or age eighteen developmentally), friendships are often formed that contribute enormously to a teenager's self-discovery. Through a friend, a teenager can discover how he is different as well as similar. He sees responses and reflections of himself. Often teenage friendships seem quite incongruous to parents. An eighth-grade drummer, Marylou, for instance, is best friends with a tenth-grader, Bobbie, who is half a foot taller and three years older. At first glance, the two are an odd match, but it doesn't take long to see that they are at a similar level in their development. The two share intimacies and humor and space. They play tennis together and talk for hours. They help each other define who they are and what they care about.

Exercising loyalty to friends also helps teenagers learn about their own values. Just as personal boundaries are often clarified through friendship, adolescents strengthen bonds and learn what it means to support one another.

"We're a group," Phillip explained as I sat with six members of a rugby team in London. We sat on couches around a comfortable living room, wearing extra sweaters to keep out the cold. "We go places together—to the local disco to dance, and to films and parties. . . ."

"None of us goes out looking for a fight," says Ian. "If anything we avoid fighting; we'd sooner resolve it. But if we're pushed, then we fight."

"We're linked just like brothers," says Ray, a dark-haired eighteen-year-old. "We stick up for each other off the field as well as on. And because you are a kind of brotherhood, because you play in the field together, you make special concessions for each other you wouldn't make for other people—like with Graham's temper; you wouldn't let someone from the street shout and yell like that—"

"I don't shout and yell!"

"Another thing that keeps us together is our humor. It's zany. It's sarcastic, too, but we all laugh together all the time."

For acceptance in some groups, it's important *not* to make good grades, get along with popular kids or have any friendly interactions with teachers or other authorities.

Because subjective ways of defining oneself are so cloudy, and because friendships are sometimes mercurial, adolescents tend to move into objective areas of competition that help them integrate and recognize themselves as individuals. Through new friendships, through sports or academics or school politics, teenagers begin to figure out who they are and to put that knowledge into context. While one may dance four hours a day, another may debate, work out programs on the school computer or write poetry, each is in the process of carving out a personal identity.

"Competition is another way we reassure ourselves that we have metamorphosed properly," says Dr. Donald Nathanson. "We fit into some well understood order of rightness, giving us an identity, a sense of self in this new body. The obsessive need to compete, that is, to find a self by constant measuring against others rather than from within, probably implies psychopathology in adult life. But not in adolescence."

As Marylou Davies, the eighth-grader from Lawrence, Kansas, says: "You get a good view of everybody else from where you sit when you play the drums. Playing the drums is a great way to see the world."

Whether a teenager perpetually bounces a basketball, or, like Marylou, plays the drums four hours a day doesn't matter, what counts is that the activity gives her a sense of competence and achievement and it helps her to view the world and herself from a different perspective.

Peter Blos points out that ego growth is particularly evident in the area of social competence, in building physical prowess in team-oriented combat, in competition and "in awareness of tested body skills which allow freedom in action, inventiveness and playful adventure, in short, in the emancipation of the body from parental, especially maternal, control, care and protection. From these various sources accrues a sense of total ownership of his (or her) body . . .[2]

As they're growing them, adolescents wonder whether their bodies are Masaratis, Volkswagens, MGs or Cadillacs. In the same way they rank cars, they learn how bodies work through physical play and competitive athletics. The endeavors help them build muscles, move into and control their bodies, and develop a sense of community and good relationships with peers. In a very tangible way, the rules and regulations of tennis or football, baseball or basketball, track or field hockey, to name a few, give them firm and objective boundaries and a security from which they can play a game and reduce their feelings of not knowing the rules during the rest of their waking moments. Competition simply helps them figure out who they are and how to measure their strengths.

For Wendell, a tall, muscular seventeen-year-old at Trinity High School in New York, group sports was the avenue to self-esteem during a time in his life when he felt out of control and somewhat ineffectual in the rest of his life. His parents had just gone through a divorce and each was involved in new relationships when he started playing basketball.

"I guess you could call me a jock," Wendell said during an interview that followed a soccer game. "I consider that a degrading term—like 'He's a dumb jock,' but at Trinity, that 'dumb jock' doesn't apply since the academic standards are so high. Anyway, now I play soccer in the fall, basketball in the winter and track in the spring.

"I played my first team sport in the eighth grade when I started playing basketball. It was so good for my head . . . Before that, I used to be into swimming and scuba diving, and I'd ride horseback.

"At this point, I could not imagine *not* being on a team. My friendships with my teammates are really important to me. Our soccer team won an archrivalry and it was so beautiful afterwards. When I'm in college and I'm working, I'm not going to remember my Ones (A grades) from Trinity. I'm going to remember my sports experiences and my teammates."

Although being a jock makes being accepted automatically easier for boys, it's also true that athletic achievements are a great outlet for girls and serve much of the same purpose to the individuals involved.

For thirteen-year-old Julie, for instance, basketball has been a way of "testing my strength" and "learning what my arms can do." At five-foot-eight inches tall, she has been the lead offensive player on her junior high school basketball team in Philadelphia for the past two years. A pretty girl who is often mistaken for an eighteen-year-old by boys, Julie said, "What does basketball mean to me? It's strength. It's when you move your arm and it's effortless. It's like after a basketball game, when I stand up, and walk home, I feel more alive and happy. I feel better about myself.

"I really like basketball because it challenges me but I don't have to think too much," she said. "When I play, I don't feel psychologically pressured like I do a lot of other times. Afterwards, when I walk back home, I feel not so heavy. It's like one time when I was in the fifth grade, this other girl and I ran up and down the stairs for fifteen minutes for this math experiment—and then afterwards, when I went down to lunch, I felt like I was hardly walking. It's the same in a way, after a basketball game. I feel better about myself.

"Like, this morning, before I was talking to you, I was having a good time reading *Shogun*—but it's different from playing a game. After I've played really hard, it's a feeling like after you've had a good night's sleep, if you have a shower and walk outside and it's a really nice day. . . . It makes me feel good. That's especially true when it's fun, and if you're playing with people you like.

"It's also a great feeling during a game to know that with the other team, you're going to try to spill their guts, and then afterwards that you'll go to each other's house and have fun talking and laughing," she said.

"Like, I can say to Christie, who's on my team, 'Hey, Christie, move your ass!' or 'Get to the back of the court!' I'm really aggressive or competitive, and they know that I mean it—and that's it's not only okay, but that it's really a good thing 'cause we're all in it together to win.'"

Because teenagers have such enormous physical energy, along with the tension of new drives and feelings, physical activity and hard-driving games are a wonderful outlet. But at the same time that their aggressive and sexual energies seem to have been turned on full blast, so have their mental powers. They can think in more abstract and analytical ways. They find new perceptions of their parents and of the world. They search for new meanings and new understandings—and many, in the process, find essential means of defining and confirming themselves through intellectual challenges. Academic competition often becomes a driving force during this time of their lives. Doing well in school, conquering new information, learning about the way the larger world works, gives them knowledge of how their own minds function and how they stack up against other minds—adding to their sense of control, validity and self-esteem.

"On Sundays I start my homework at twelve and finish about ten at night," says Hamilton, with an apologetic smile. "I'm a perfectionist. Sometimes I'd rather not hand in anything than hand in a bad essay. I'd rather talk to my teacher and say that I'd rather get a lower grade by turning in my paper three days late than turn it in before I'm satisfied with it.

"This last semester, I got two *A*'s and two *B*'s in math and science. I want to go to Harvard or Princeton. I'll graduate with five years of math

116   GROWING INTO LOVE

and five of science. I know my major's going to be in science. I'm going to take courses in all kinds of things.

"In my spare time, if there's a party, I get there . . . but because of homework, I don't go out much.

"Math has always been my number-one subject. I've always been a whiz. People are always calling me for help; I'm like the Sears diehard ad. There are points where I have no contact with anyone, so it's nice to get some attention, even if it is taking advantage of me, so to speak, for math."

"I really enjoy my studies," says Chris Figuorea, a seventeen-year-old junior at South Boston High School. "I've always made good grades naturally—and it's mainly because I'm so interested in learning about the way things work and the relationships one thing or one person has to another. . . ." Chris, a large-framed, comfortable girl, has dark Dominican eyes that dominate a round, friendly and animated face.

"There's one problem with competing in school, though," she says. "When a girl does really good in school, other people can't stand it. A lot of people don't like me, for instance. I like to get involved in everything I can. I'm in student government, and I work on the newspaper and that sort of thing, so when I've gotten publicity—like a story about student leaders or something, some of the girls just don't like it. They want the publicity, but they won't go out and work for anything. They don't understand that I get involved in doing things because they're interesting to me, not for the publicity."

For Hamilton, Chris and for a young man named Martin Ashley, intellectual achievement provides great confirmation for the person inside. Hamilton, however, has the advantage of also playing basketball, whereas in Martin's case, his body betrays him. At seventeen, Martin is no more than five foot four, and he wears thick, black-rimmed glasses. Watching him devour a Big Mac, french fries, a Coke, a cup of coffee and three doughnuts, I think that he may be one of those teenage boys who has a growth spurt during his eighteenth year.

Since he's a late developer and nonathletic, Martin defines himself through an antimacho stance, straight *A*'s and a great deal of work in citywide student government.

"I'm not very competitive," he said. "Guys are so competitive in physical build. There's always situations where I'm shorter than someone else. And to compete, you have to be stronger and better built. There's pressure on guys to have large biceps and big shoulders—and here's me being short and not very strong and muscle-y.

"I always wish I was taller and that I spent more time exercising. I'd like to be stronger looking," he said. "I don't like the pressure to have sex or to be going with someone. . . .

"Most of my friends have been girls, but people don't really accept that, either. Not just as friends. One of my best friends since sixth grade has been a girl. We talk about private things and secrets. Everyone thought I was weird because we were friends. Boys then, at that age, didn't like girls. They only thought of them as physical objects, so they assumed if I was talking with her, I was going with her. . . ."

During adolescence, however, the more areas within which a teenager gains competence and discovers new abilities, the more his overall sense of achievement and self-esteem grows. If a teenager doesn't succeed in any areas during this time, he can, in reverse, acquire feelings of inadequacy and incompetence that make him less sure of himself and more uncomfortable in his own body.

"These are such formative years," says Dianne Stern, a mother of two teenage sons in Scarsdale, New York. "You worry about it if they're not successful in every part of their lives. Will they turn in another direction out of defeat? I think that parents feel the pain of their children intensely. If your children are feeling rejected, you feel rejected. . . ."

Some adolescents do turn other directions out of defeat. If they can't find out who they are and integrate all those feelings in successful or positive ways, they sometimes choose a group where it's important not to make good grades, not to get along with "popular kids" or not to have friendly interactions with teachers or other authorities. Depending upon the group, it may be more prestigious to strip a hubcap from a car in record time than to run hurdles or make the dean's list. Many teenagers, but a minority of the total, are competitive in destructive ways. The thrust of their behavior is negative rather than positive, against authorities rather than for themselves, rejecting rather than accepting, and ultimately, self-defeating. This behavior, however, is often just another form of the same adolescent attempt to measure, define and understand themselves and their place in life. Some will pass by this time as a stage in their development. For others, it will become a way of life.

"Our lot has been rejected by our own age group," says nineteen-year-old Toby, sitting in a bare, bleak pub in a working-class section of London. As Toby speaks, he holds his shaggy, thick blond hair at a tilt to the right, over his shoulder, and his brown eyes are alert. His mouth is held tight in a long, thin line and his narrow lips open slightly as he speaks.

"At most parties, we don't get let in because they think we're going to wreck the place. They think we're junkies and weirdos. And that's true. We are.

"I don't mind because I reject them, too. They're narrow-minded. They're not prepared to accept individuality. I reject them just as much as they reject me. They're stereotyped; they come out by the thousands. In fact, I'd worry if they accepted me. I'd figure I was doing something wrong."

"If I could be anything, I'd be Iggy Pop of the Stooges," says Toby's friend, a short, brown-haired teenager who has asked me to use Iggy as his fictitious name. "I'd love to be him because he hates everything. I'd get the excitement of being up on the stage and telling everyone to fuck off." Iggy's face shines as he says this, and shows, for the first time since our interview began, excitement and life. "I'd stand up there and tell everyone to *piss off!* He can tell everyone what he wants to do; he can tell 'em he hates them and to go fuck themselves. I hate everyone, too, and I'd love to stand up there and tell them to piss off.

"Even the rich so-called pop stars, I'd like to tell them, too. Fuck off, piss off! I hate you!"

Iggy's eyes glaze, and his small face seems to sag. "I'd like not to need anybody," he says, "Because I hate 'em. I like my friends, but I don't particularly like anyone else. I find life a big bore. When I'm up on that stage, I still find life a bore."

Iggy is a loner with friends. He feels blocked off from his own life and his own body, and he says he's not sure he'll even live much longer. He's been dead three times from drug overdoses, he says, and he thinks he liked it better that way.

His case is extreme. And I think because his ambition, underneath the pretense of boredom, is so great, his response to his sense of failure is even greater than it would be if he truly didn't care.

Some young people, unlike Iggy, are not in a group where they at least feel the comfort of like-minded views. Although I felt that Iggy and his friends lived a pretty bleak life, those teenagers who sit on the sidelines and never get into any trouble, who never disagree with their parents or struggle with the conflicts and anxieties of their age, worry me more than the teenagers who are rather tyrannical or even antisocial during their adolescent years.

Often these youngsters appear to be perfect from their parents' perspective because they aren't defiant. They don't run with a wild or unruly crowd. The problem is, they don't do anything. They are so terrified of their own feelings and the issues confronting them that they repress them and close down shop. They don't play with their bodies, they don't have fun; and they don't grow up. As Peter Blos points out in *The Adolescent Passage*, maturing, finding a sense of well-being and the assurance within oneself that a course of self-realization is possible, involves internal and external struggles, which by their very nature promote a process of development.[3]

Sixteen-year-old Toni, a high-school junior in Detroit, Michigan, is a fat and bulging youngster, who remains uninvolved in the world outside her family.

"When I have a problem, there's nobody I can talk to," said Toni during an interview at her high school. "Nobody!" Her short hair and glasses did nothing to complement her figure. Toni said her parents had been together for twenty-one years. Her dad works for the telephone company and her mother runs the lingerie department at a woman's store in Denver, Colorado.

"I don't talk to anybody because some people just don't care. Other people you just can't talk to because they've got enough problems of their own. If I have a problem, I keep it. I swallow it.

"I don't talk to anybody much. I just go home and watch TV and go to bed after I do my homework. I'm not close to my brothers or sisters, either. I'm a loner. My youngest brother would rather wait and tell my sister whatever it is he has to say; he doesn't talk to me. I don't like myself, really. I could change it, I just don't. Things get in the way. . . ."

A young woman like Toni doesn't worry her parents with late-night hours. She makes good grades and does her jobs at home without complaint. Although she's a model child except for her weight problem, she's paying the price of her own growth by not engaging in important developmental tasks and by becoming increasingly alienated from her peers.

Heidi, now a freshman in college, feels she is still paying socially and emotionally for the many years she withdrew and refused to compete with her peers. "I'm still trying to make up for lost time," she says. The year before, during her senior year in high school, she told me, "I'm a solitary person, and sometimes that's because I want to be, and sometimes that's because I'm forced to be. I'm just not around my age group that much—partly because I'm working and partly because I don't know how to take friends home. . . ."

There are reasons people don't let themselves grow up. Those reasons can usually be found in their personal histories.

Take Heidi's case, when she was in third grade, her father moved his family seventy miles north of their home town and then took off and left them. She was in a new school where the other kids were already doing cursive writing, which she didn't know how to do, and life didn't seem quite right again for years.

"I was never good athletically, either," she says, "and I had one leg shorter than the other one, so to begin with, I wasn't good. Also, my mother had sheltered me, and none of it added up to me getting along with other kids.

"About the eighth grade, you started to see overt sexual interactions in our school. It was a Catholic school, and after lunch, our two eighth-grade classrooms would sneak back up to our rooms. A couple of kids would always kiss. They had parties, but I only heard rumors about them. I was never invited.

"Looking back, all the ugliness my family was going through left emotional scars that led to overeating, that led to me getting fat, that led to kids making fun of me and ostracizing me. They have to have a scapegoat and I was convenient for it.

"I *felt* very ostracized, too. Partly because of my looks and partly because of my behavior, so I didn't do well academically, either. The other kids hated me."

Toward the end of eighth grade, however, Heidi joined Weight Watchers with a neighbor and lost twenty-five pounds. In ninth grade, she went to a new school that was public. "I decided then," she says, "okay, I've lost weight. I'm a new person. I saw myself as a new body, and I would be at a new school. I figured most of the kids won't know me and it can be a fresh start. I can try to be more popular with the kids. I can try. A guiding factor for me was not to be like my mother. She was an underpaid, overworked housekeeper. I said what does she lack? Education! So I started focusing on academics, and I did really well. I still wasn't Miss Popularity, but I wasn't ostracized, either. I hooked onto the scholastic, academic part of my life, and I saw success. I've continued to do well scholastically, and now I'm very much accepted by my peers in school, but I'm still learning how to bring my friendships home. It takes a long time. . . . I used to think that there was something wrong with me, but now I believe that people do like me. I also realize that they'd be willing to come over or get to be better friends, but I don't know how to reach out. I'm learning, though—and I'll get there."

Deciding that you are okay, that you are competent and valuable, knowing your own boundaries and capabilities as a person and a body, takes time and testing. There are many starts and stops along the way.

"I like the way I look at the way I am," says Ronald, a tall, strong fifteen-year-old. "People are always saying things about my red hair, but I like it. I think it's pretty neat. I think I'm probably also going to be about six feet tall—another inch or two, and six feet's fine with me.

"The best thing is if you can just be yourself and accept yourself," he says, swinging his leg over the chair. And you gotta make your own decisions. You gotta do things that you know are right for you. Not when everybody else tells you you should. You gotta do what you think is right for you. . . ."

At fifteen, Ronald knows something that many of us take a long time to learn. Some of us don't accomplish the adolescent task of "resolving body image" until we're in our twenties or thirties. But to get to the place where we accept ourselves, we have to have selves that are stable in some way. We have to have passed through the time of feeling "If I'm not me, then who am I?" to one of self-acceptance and discovery. This integration, whether it happens when we're eighteen or twenty-eight, it moves us into a brand new game.

7.

Solo Explorations

"One problem boys my age really have is getting a *Playboy* magazine," said fourteen-year-old Lennie, crossing his legs on top of the table and leaning back in his chair. "It's really difficult. You have to go to a store, and they're usually behind the counter and you have to ask for one, and the man will peer over the counter and ask, 'How old are you, sonny?' "

"Have you really had that happen to you?" I asked, startled. "Do they really ask you your age before they sell you the magazine?"

"I haven't had the nerve to ask," he said, reddening. "Fortunately I have an older brother who gets *Playboy*s from a friend of his and I know where he keeps them." He smiled.

"When boys are between thirteen and sixteen, all they can think about is sex," he said. "That's it. You can't help it. It's your age. It's a new experience to deal with. When you play spin the bottle, that's one thing. But it's totally different when you can, you know, *make it happen.*"

"Making it happen"—masturbating to effect erotic arousal and orgasm—is often one of the most thrilling and confusing experiences of adolescence. As younger children, most teenagers touched or stimulated their genitals and many had orgasms. But as teenagers, they have new sexual equipment, new sexual energy and excitement. For the first time, boys can ejaculate. And for both boys and girls, bringing themselves to orgasm with the private and powerful fantasies and feelings involved is a new experience, an intense, personal and compelling pleasure. The pleasure, however, is often accompanied afterwards by feelings of guilt and shame.

Boys particularly suffer conflict about masturbating. Because of the enormous drive they have to ejaculate once they have begun to do so, 99 percent continue once they've started, according to Alfred Kinsey's unparalleled research. As Kinsey found, masturbation is a common, natural and convenient outlet, and nearly all boys do it. If they feel they should not be masturbating, they can be thrown into a great deal of turmoil about it.

"I'm against masturbating, but I do it anyway," said seventeen-year-old Bruce, in Detroit, Michigan. "I wonder if other people do the same thing. I don't think it's right, but sometimes it just feels necessary. When I do it, I feel bad afterwards. But then I do it again the next time. About once every two weeks, usually on Sunday nights, I say, 'Starting tomorrow, I'm never going to do this again.' But then I just get this feeling. . . ."

Although fewer girls than boys reportedly masturbate, those who do often feel guilty about their behavior. Although many have overcome internalized restrictions to experiment in the first place, which perhaps reduces their anxiety, many girls who masturbate say they still feel conflict about "doing something" to themselves sexually.

"I never had fulfillment when I was young," said nineteen-year-old Marti, who first had intercourse when she was a thirteen-year-old ninth grader in the Bronx. "We didn't do it very often. He was afraid I'd get pregnant, so we only did it once every three or four months. I'd get all hot, but then it would be over and I'd just lay there saying, 'That's all?' I just wasn't fulfilled. It took me a long time to discover I could give it to myself if I didn't get it from a guy. I didn't have to go to anybody else to get it. But before, I'd never touch myself down there. I felt so guilty the first time I did it. I thought I'd die, I was so ashamed. But I talked to a friend, and she said it was a normal thing for people to do in private. She said a lot of people did it and it was normal. That made me feel better. But I had to accept myself first before I could do it. I had to love myself more."

Neither Bruce nor Marti was aware that throughout history, men and women have struggled within themselves about masturbating. Nor did they know that moral arguments against masturbation have been promulgated for centuries by the churches and by "scientific evidence" that it's harmful as well as sinful. Bruce asked me if any other kids I'd talked to ever "did it when they didn't think they should." He seemed comforted when I told him, "Millions." I explained to him and to Marti that Alfred Kinsey spelled out years ago the mental conflict that literally millions of people had lived through in attempts to stop masturbating. Kinsey said they suffered through cyclical efforts to stop the habit, failures to stop, remorse and the making of new resolutions. He said that what was harmful was the mental anguish, not the masturbation.

Despite the fact that Kinsey and his colleagues interviewed thousands of people and proved that masturbation does not cause warts, blindness, genital cancer, fatigue or insanity, and does not make hands fall off or hair fall out, the taboos against it are still strong. Even though many churches have revised their stand against it, and though doctors and health officials and researchers tell us that it is considered a healthy form of self-expression that enhances self-confidence, sexual adjustment and good overall social adjustment, many people are still disturbed by simply hearing or saying the word *masturbation*.

Researchers have found through the years that the vast majority of the population masturbates. At the same time, many people refuse to answer anonymous questionnaires about their masturbatory behavior, even when they have been forthcoming with answers to other questions about their sexual behavior. Robert Sorenson in his national survey of teenagers found only 17 percent who said they "never felt guilty, anxious or concerned about masturbation."[1] He said that "self-exteem, embarrassment and personal disgust seemed to be the major inhibiting factors against it."[2]

When I talked to teenagers, I found that most were uncomfortable with the subject. While many swallowed their initial embarrassment and talked quite freely, others seemed mortified when I raised the question. Some chose to answer in generalized ways by talking about the attitudes of their peers.

"Attitudes are against it at school," said seventeen-year-old Jud, in Morris, Minnesota. "Like if somebody is into jerking off and other people know it, they'll say things like, 'Stay away from that guy. He's a fruitcake.' It's an embarrassing subject."

Others revealed some anxiety and ambivalence when they made brief comments on the subject. "It's up to him, the person doing it," said sixteen-year-old Jonathan from Aurora, Illinois. "I think it depends on how much you do it. If a guy does it all the time, he must like doing it, but I suppose if you don't get carried away, it's okay. I think it might be real bad if you did it too much or you did it all the time."

Once, ten years ago, when I was a newspaper reporter at the *Philadelphia Evening Bulletin*, I wrote a sentence in an article on the women's movement that said some of the more militant women's groups advocated masturbation as a substitute for sexual contact with men. The morning the article came out, one male editor shouted, "Isn't this supposed to be a *family* newspaper?" about the same time another reporter in the back of the room stood up and ripped his paper to shreds. Another yelled that he wouldn't take the paper home to let his "wife and children see this trash!"

Although part of the reaction may have been stimulated by the suggestion of the expendability of men, the focus of anger was on the use of the word *masturbation* in the newspaper. The switchboard put through dozens of calls to me for more than three days afterwards, and the following day, the newspaper's librarian announced that I'd "made history" at the *Bulletin*. "I've just opened a file on Masturbation," he said, holding up the envelope. "This newspaper is 119 years old, and that's the first time that the word *masturbation* has ever appeared in print."

Why do people have such strong reactions to the subject and to the behavior itself? I assumed that the embarrasent and the internalized prohibitions must stem from experiences in infancy and early childhood, when parents display obvious displeasure or discomfort when their children fondle their genitals.

When the baby's hand goes to the genitals and is quickly removed, and the action is repeated, guilt and fear become a conditioned response to any touching, sensation or pleasure from "down there." The negative message from parents often gives the child the impression that her vagina or his penis or the good feeling itself is what is bad, and that badness is what is causing the anger or distress on the part of the parent.

A less obvious reason has been explored by Dr. Robert Stoller in his most recent book on the nature of sexuality, *Sexual Excitement: The Dynamics of Erotic Life*. Dr. Stoller points out that although we know very little about sexual excitement, we do know that it's a very primary state, and that when we are sexually excited, we are in an altered state of consciousness.

In that altered state of consciousness, Dr. Stoller says, we release in a playful way many conflicts, oedipal fantasies and feelings of hostility that we don't deal with consciously. By and large, our feelings are contained in "playlets"—sexual fantasies that involve our deepest unconscious concerns.

The exact details of the script underlying an individual's sexual excitement, Stoller says, are meant to "reproduce and repair the precise traumas and frustrations—debasements—of childhood; and so we can expect to find hidden in the script," or playlet, the history of a person's psychic life.[3]

It makes sense, then, that once we end a masturbatory experience—during which we have been privately ensconced in an altered state, dealing with unconscious material that we usually are not at all aware of in our daily, awakened states—we feel somewhat guilty because of the "experiences" we have had. There are reasons we don't deal with this sort of material in our waking lives, one being that it is just too threatening, particularly if it involves hostile or sexual interaction with our own parents. We come out of our waking dream state, in which we have passionately thrown ourselves into our subconscious and private scenarios, and of course we carry with us a residue of anxiety.

Stoller points out another reason for the anxiety. He says that even the nonreligious believe on some level that "sex is sin—and not just because of society's rules but because our consciences know how 'bad' these forbidden desires are. So erotic pleasure is preserved by secrets.

These are secrets operating between ourselves and the outside world."

Secondly, he says, secrecy is built into the sexual playlets and story lines people use consciously and preconsciously for ensuring their excitement. He says secrets in this category operate as barriers between one part of oneself and another part, serving especially to provoke or heighten excitement.[4] In adolescence, because the experience of masturbating is new and fresh, because the passion is so great, because the child is in the parents' home and oedipal issues are close at hand, the conflicts and the energy needed to keep out the awareness of the conflicts are more intense, adding an extra flavor of guilt and excitement to the experience.

When I asked one New York psychologist why she thought people so often felt guilty and upset about masturbation, she said our confusion may have something to do with learning that goes on during toilet training about the vicinity called "down there."

"Masturbating is doing something 'down there,'" said Dr. Margaret Mandel, a private practitioner who has worked with adolescents and adults. "In some ways, I think people feel that it's like playing with feces. It's a part of yourself, and it gets mixed up with the dirtiness people ascribe to bowels and feces and toilet training.

"If it's 'down there,' you're not supposed to touch it. It's dirty. The products of the body are very confusing. They're valued, but at the same time, they're demeaned. This is compounded by the parental reaction and the fact that masturbation is a secret pleasure; completely private. The fact that secrets are invested with significance in the first place makes such an experience special and unique."

Most of the young people with whom I talked either had no conscious awareness of the altered states of sexual excitement they were in while masturbating, or were unable or unwilling to articulate their private scenarios. Nor did they remember reprimands for touching their genitals during infancy, and most did not recall anything about their toilet training. They did recall more conscious fantasies and more current interactions that reflected parents' historical and sometimes hysterical attitudes on the subject. Samantha, for instance, doesn't have any doubts about the messages conveyed during her early childhood, even though she doesn't remember them. Her mother's attitudes, she says, are pretty much the same as her grandmother's and probably her great-grandmother's.

"I always sleep in funny positions," says Samantha, a high-school sophomore at Friend's Central in Philadelphia. "And for one period of time, I used to sleep with my feet up and my head down. Well, this one time, I had my feet up on the wall and I had my hands low on my stomach, like this. [She folds her hands together on her stomach.] I was almost asleep when my mother woke me up. She was yelling and hollering at me and she made me get up and wash my hands.

"She thought I'd been touching myself down there, and she was all upset. She was saying, 'It's dirty, it's dirty!' I kept saying, 'But Ma, I was just sleeping!'

"My mother's funny. She is very clean and she has a lot of funny ideas. She was upset that we talked about oral sex in our class in human sexuality, for instance. She said, "Anybody who does that, there's got to be something wrong with them. It stinks down there!'

"She feels genitals are a dirty part of the body, and that they stink and carry disease. She said, 'You wait. Fifteen years from now, they'll get throat cancer.'

"She says if a woman has sex and doesn't get up and wash right after sex, you can smell it. I told her there's no reason for women to use vaginal deodorant and douche after sex, and she said, 'Funk is funk!' "

Coleman, the third of six children, talked with me three days after his parents had gotten divorced. A high-school junior in Fullerton, California, Coleman seemed deeply depressed, even worn. His fifteen-year-old face had the lines of an old man. The subject of sex was depressing and evocative for him. He said he didn't feel good about himself or his body, he didn't have a girl friend right then and he felt crummy about masturbating, though he did it, and frequently. It seemed his attitudes and experiences could be traced directly to his father, who worked on a construction crew in the area.

"He's an asshole," Coleman said of his father. "He never laughs or has a good time with us. He used to hit us over stupid things. He was really very strict, very old-fashioned. One time when we were about ten, me and my brother, we were looking at this little book. It was a little book actually put out by the Catholic church on questions about sex. It told how people have babies and just basic questions for little kids. He grabbed the book out of my brother's hand and ripped it up and said he wouldn't have us reading that sort of trash. Then he started hitting us and told us he'd teach us not to sneak books like that behind his back. I still think he's an asshole."

Despite the inhibitions, despite conditioning, masturbation seems to evolve as naturally for most children and young adults as does the biology of their bodies. Apparently up to the age of about ten, boys and girls masturbate and have sex play at about equal rates. But at about that age, girls begin to suppress this kind of activity and boys increase it. With the changes of puberty, spontaneous erections direct a boy's attention to his genitals, and because of the sensations involved, boys are motivated to experiment further. Slightly more than two-thirds of all boys ejaculate for the first time when they are masturbating. For most of the other boys, the source of their first ejaculation is a nocturnal emission or heterosexual intercourse.[5] Alfred Kinsey's study of more than twelve thousand men showed that after the initial experience in ejaculation, no matter the source, practically all males (99%) become regular in their sexual activity. This involves monthly, weekly or daily ejaculations. (The major outlets for these ejaculations are masturbation and heterosexual intercourse.) Kinsey wrote:

"There are a few males who masturbate only once or twice in their lives. And there are others who have frequencies that may average seven to fourteen or twenty or more per week for long periods of years. There are males whose high frequencies extend from preadolescence through all of the premarital years and males who may maintain average frequencies of three or four a week through the marital years into old age."[6]

In his recent survey of six hundred teenagers, Aaron Hass found that 75 to 80 percent of the fifteen- to eighteen-year-old boys he surveyed masturbated, as did 52 to 59 percent of the girls.[7] Although the incidence of masturbation for males has remained fairly stable over the past thirty years, the incidence for females has reportedly doubled since Kinsey's study in the late 1940s and early 1950s.

Despite the increase in masturbatory behavior reported by females in the past thirty years, however, the research shows that boys begin to masturbate earlier than girls, more of them masturbate and do so more often. This may have something to do with sex-role stereotyping, parental conditioning and simple anatomy. It may also have to do with sex drives and genetic programs we don't fully understand.

Parents have been found to be more in favor of their sons masturbating, having erotic fantasies and making sexual explorations than they are in favor of their daughters' similar behavior. It may be that this implicit parental acceptance of male experimentation has to do with the fact that the boys don't get pregnant, as well as the fact that a boy's sexual anatomy and excitement is so obvious.

If it's obvious to no one else, it's obvious to the boys themselves. An erection is their unsolicited response to visual stimuli, to movement or to erotic thought, let alone any other number of factors. Even if a boy hasn't heard about masturbation from friends or hasn't read about it in books or magazines, he still discovers it quite easily on his own. Most boys I talked to about masturbation said that the first time it happened, they were surprised by the ejaculation itself. Usually they had been stroking an erect penis when it happened. After the first ejaculation, however, they repeated and refined the experience.

"The first time I was just rubbing my dick because it was so hard, and then I got so excited I thought I was peeing, but I couldn't stop it," said Carey, a sixteen-year-old in Whittier, California. "I was surprised by the white gooey stuff. I wasn't sure what it was then or afterwards, but later I found out what it was because I overheard some guys talking about it."

"I guess I was about fourteen and a half when it started getting stiff every morning and I'd say, 'Damn, what is this thing?' said Clifford, a nineteen-year-old from a working-class area outside Boston. He had light brown hair, hazel eyes and very fair skin. "So when I woke up, I'd start rubbing it and it feels good. I knew something because of my older brothers and sisters, but not any detail. I just knew it felt good to rub it. That's how I started it. Then I started using slippery stuff, like shampoo, when I was in the shower, and I found I could get off quicker.

"When I started masturbating, I liked that feeling. That feeling got ferocious. I wanted to do it twenty-four hours a day, but I couldn't so I did it once a day. It felt wonderful, and I wanted to feel wonderful.

"I looked at it as when you have sex with a girl, you have to be married to her. So I said to myself, it looks like I'm not going to get sex with a girl because I'm only going to be making $100 a week when I'm seventeen. And I couldn't when I was fourteen because I was only making $30 a week, and that wouldn't support a wife, so I gotta get off in the shower.

"When I was older, I always tried to get away from jacking off. I didn't want to do it. I'd think, I might meet a girl tonight, and if she wants to do it, I won't have enough left. . . ."

Some boys don't masturbate until nature has taken responsibility for the first ejaculation through a nighttime emission.

"Masturbation doesn't happen until a long time after your first wet dream," fourteen-year-old Jimmy explained, leaning back in his chair as if to remove himself from the subject. "You have to really desire sex to masturbate. With a wet dream, it just happens. If you don't know what you're missing, you don't miss it. A wet dream is like a warning of what's coming. Your glands aren't fully developed when you have your first wet dream, but they are after that."

I asked if he felt any conflict about masturbating.

"I should take the fifth," he said, blushing. "Really, though, I have no problems with it or about it. I'd say it was an evolutionary process with me, so I never feel guilty or conflicted about it."

Some boys don't begin to masturbate until after they've had intercourse. For most boys who have this experience, the intercourse is the source of their first ejaculation. However, Joseph, a sixteen-year-old at a private school in Boston, said he was so frightened the first time he had intercourse that he didn't ejaculate.

"The girl I was with was a good friend of mine," he said, "and we knew each other very well. But I'd never masturbated before that, and so I didn't know what it was like. The whole thing filled me with fear. I was so scared that I couldn't come. That first time was between eighth and ninth grades.

"I did start masturbating after that, and that helped, but it wasn't until I was in the tenth grade that I had intercourse again and had an orgasm."

As we talked, Joseph remembered a time when he was in the fifth or sixth grade and his mother came into his room while he was reading a *Playboy* magazine. "I remember her scolding me for having the magazine," he said. "She asked me why I had them, and I remember not being able to answer why I had them. She took the magazines away from me and said, 'If you want to find out what women are like, I'll get you books.' She did go out and get me some books to read. . . . But that might have had something to do with why I felt so guilty and scared and why I didn't masturbate. . . ."

The only boys I spoke with who said they had not or would not masturbate were members of religious groups that had strong taboos and religious mandates against masturbation and premarital sex. Two of these young men played football, basketball, and baseball at a high school in Santa Ana, California, were handsome, healthy and robust— the stereotype of the kind of boys who kayak down rivers or toss the volleyball on television commercials. Douglas was tall, blond and tan. Tim, a year younger at fifteen, was brown-haired, shorter and more muscular than Douglas. Somehow I didn't expect to hear what I heard from them.

"Last year, I wasn't as strong in my faith as I am now," said Tim. "During the summer, I was up in the mountains with my dad, and I had this one-day deal with a girl from school. We went for a walk, and we were kissing and all, and I ended up putting my hand up her blouse. We didn't even like each other. It was just for pleasure. Then my friend's girl friend's cousin and I went up to Disneyland one day and the same thing happened. We were necking and petting and I was doing it for pleasure. My views on it now are different.

"I think masturbation is just as bad as actual intercourse. There's a verse in the Bible that says if you look at a woman and feel lust for her, it's the same as intercourse. That's Matthew 5:28."

At this point in our interview, Tim pulled a Bible out of his pocket and looked up the verse. "Here it is," he said. " 'Matthew 5:28. 'But I say unto you, That whosoever looketh on a woman to lust after her hath committed adultery with her already in his heart.' " I asked them about their church, and they told me that it was a Fundamentalist Protestant church that was "fully scriptural and Pentacostal."

"I try to stay away from *Playboy* magazines and anything like that," said Douglas. "In the last six months, I've committed myself deeper [to Christ and the church's philosophy]. I try to stay away from anything like that because I don't think that's what I should do. I don't avoid temptation. Temptation is always there. I just avoid yielding to the temptation."

"I've discussed it with friends of mine," said Douglas. "I tell them I'm against nonprocreative sex of any kind. Sometimes they think I'm a Holy Joe, but a lot of people have beliefs of their own. They're not going to cut me down for what I believe."

"I used to enjoy looking at *Playboy* when I wasn't strong in my commitment to Christ," said Tim. "I know Satan has it there to get people away from the Lord. So now even if there's one lying around, I'm not tempted to look at it."

Some boys who belong to religious groups that strongly condemn masturbation don't personally live by the taboos of their religion.

"It took me a long time not to feel guilty when I masturbated," said Nicholas, a college sophomore. "I still feel a twinge sometimes, but then it was a pretty strong thing we were taught. The nuns told us from the time we were in sixth grade that you shouldn't masturbate. They said it was sinful because it wasn't sharing your love. You shouldn't have premarital sex because it's not procreative. All sex is supposed to be procreative. Another reason masturbation is bad is because it's not procreative."

For girls, the act of masturbating is not as widespread or as accepted as it is for boys. Girls did not have to be religious to not "believe" in masturbating. As discussed earlier, the lower incidence of masturbation for girls may have to do with their anatomy, their conforming to sex-role stereotypes and their conditioning from parents who don't approve of their daughters masturbating, having erotic fantasies or sexually experimenting. Additionally, girls are not as apt to have masturbation forced upon them by their own physiology in the same way it's forced upon boys. While a boy who hasn't masturbated will often experience ejaculation through a wet dream and then be motivated to experiment further, girls apparently generally don't have orgasmic sleep experiences until *after* they've developed a pattern of orgasmic response through masturbation or heterosexual contact.[8] Whatever their individual reasons, many of the girls I talked to seemed more upset by the topic than did boys. Many told me that they had never tried it.

"I wouldn't do it," said Lisa, a fifteen-year-old from Jackson, Michigan. "The idea doesn't really turn me on. But if that's what makes somebody's crank turn and their boat float, then I suppose it's up to them!"

"Oh, God! I'd never do that!" said another young woman with horror on her face. "That's disgusting! That's only for perverts!"

Having information about masturbation, knowing it's all right, seems to have less to do with whether a girl masturbates than with her own internal set of values, expectations and inhibitions.

"Masturbation was discussed in this class I took on human relations and human sexuality," said nineteen-year-old Polly, a freshman at Yale University in New Haven, Connecticut. "Nobody was offended by the fact that everyone thought premarital sex was fine.

"But when the professor asked about masturbation, nobody really said yes, they thought it was fine. Everyone was very nervous about the subject, including me." Polly shook her long blond hair back from her face and shrugged her narrow shoulders.

"I don't think there's anything shocking about it. It's not going to make people mentally retarded or anything. I just wouldn't feel comfortable doing it. I haven't tried it. Not myself. I guess I feel nervous or uncomfortable with myself about it."

Sometimes even when girls had had sexual intercourse, they still were quite inhibited at the idea of masturbating. Even when they were curious, they were unwilling or felt it wasn't right.

"I've never had an orgasm," said Jenny, a short girl with a full head of long, curly, brown hair framing her small face and wide-set green eyes. "At some point, I'd like to, but I don't feel constantly frustrated by it. I haven't tried to give myself an orgasm . . . I think I'm afraid to masturbate. I really don't think about it that much, but when I do think about it, I don't want to. It's not a moral thing. I feel like if I can get that pleasure with someone else, I'd rather do it. If I was masturbating, by definition, I'd think something was missing. . . ."

"I don't think I'm afraid to masturbate, but given the chance—like when you're lying in bed in the morning and feeling good—I'd rather not," says sixteen-year-old Claire, in Boston. "I've thought about it, but I don't think I've ever done anything to provoke it. I've done things to make my body feel good—like letting the shower pound on my body— but nothing *to* myself.

"Weston [Claire's boyfriend] used to say I wasn't a very sexy person. I turned him on, but he meant in myself I wasn't very sexy. It was like when he was up for something, I wouldn't be—and whenever I was, I wouldn't say anything about it. I could influence him if I wanted to because he was always up for it, he always responded. Anyway, maybe that's part of why I don't masturbate—maybe it's just that I'm not that sexy on my own. . . ."

Perhaps one reason that girls are so hesitant about exploring their own anatomy has to do with the anatomy itself. Despite the sexual revolution, despite the fact that this generation of young women can see full-page color pictures of a female's legs spread wide, showing the clitoris, urethra, labia, vagina and anus, many of them have never looked at their own genitals with a mirror to see what they look like. Even more have never touched or explored their genitals to find out how they are constructed or what sensations their own touch would evoke.

"In high-school classes, when I've suggested that they get a mirror and look at themselves, they go *arrgghhh*—I wouldn't do *that!*" says Marcie Brensilver, a Planned Parenthood counselor from Stonington, Connecticut, who speaks to many students throughout the state. "I say to them, a guy can look down and see himself. You may as well see what you can, even though you can't see it all. . . ."

Another Planned Parenthood counselor said, "I tell girls the tip of their cervix feels like their nose—and you'd be *surprised*. Hardly any of them have stuck their finger all the way up inside their vagina."

Dr. Maj-Britt Rosenbaum, associate clinical professor of psychiatry at Albert Einstein College of Medicine in New York and former director of the Human Sexuality Center at Long Island Jewish–Hillside Medical Center, points out that boy's genitalia are right out there for them to see, as is their sexual response. Masturbation and genital focus, then, are naturally straightforward propositions for boys.

Girls, on the other hand, have a "hidden anatomy," and so to masturbate, they must make a search for "hidden areas," and one doesn't necessarily go and search for hidden areas. Inhibitions thus may spring from the anatomy itself. "Because of the nature of their anatomy, girls also have more confusion with urinary and bowel training," she says. "A lot of girls don't even know where their vagina is. Unfortunately, many of them grow up and still don't know where it is."

At various times during her many years of clinical and educational work in sexuality, Dr. Rosenbaum has asked young women to try to visualize their uterus and to tell her how large it is.

"It's difficult for them to visualize," she says. "There's a great deal of confusion about inner anatomy. In many ways, the focus on a woman's inner anatomy has become a hygienic question that has more to do with tampons and keeping clean than anything else. . . . On the other hand, there's more exploration with girls than people tend to think."

Most of the girls who told me they had masturbated said that the first time it happened, it was an accident or was not entirely volitional. They didn't know about self-stimulation from their peers, and few of them had heard about it from any other source. For them, masturbation was a unique discovery, and quite often, the method was indirect—not hand to genitals, but more likely rubbing up and down on the bed or letting warm water run on the clitoris from the bathtub spout.

"The first time it happened to me," said Shelly, a seventeen-year-old from Coronado High School in Scottsdale, Arizona, "I was lying on the bed thinking about my boyfriend. He had moved to California, and I was really missing him. I was imagining kissing him and I started moving up and down on the bed. All of a sudden, there was this incredible sensation that just seemed to take me over and carry me into heaven. I couldn't believe it afterwards. It sort of scared me, and at the same time, I thought it was great."

Shelly said that after the first experience, she did it again and always enjoyed it. Many girls, like Shelly, however, report that even though they masturbated indirectly, they hadn't explored the sensations by using their fingers or hands.

When they had used their hands, it had also evolved "by accident"— or in other words, without conscious intent.

"The first time I did it, I was just loosening the elastic around the leg of my underpants and my hand went over myself, you know, and it felt good," said eighteen-year-old Janie, a high-school senior in Philadelphia. "So I kept doing it and then I got flooded with all these wonderful feelings I never had before. I love it. I don't do it very often, but I think it feels so good and I just feel all warm and velvety afterwards.

"Sometimes when I'm laying on my bed at night, I rub my breasts too, or lay a pillow on them, and I get some of the same feelings. . . . Then it's like one thing leads to another. . . . I like it, I don't feel bad about it."

Other girls said they had never touched themselves until after they had had a boy touch or fondle their genitals or until after they had had sexual intercourse. In his survey, Aaron Hass found that nonvirgins generally tended to masturbate more than virgins. He also found that teenage boys involved in relationships tend to forego masturbation, but the same was not true for girls. If girls were involved in a sexual relationship, they tended to masturbate more, theoretically to relieve heightened tension and frustration from sexual encounters which are not culminating in orgasm.[9] Once they have "broken the barrier," girls often seem to be more open to exploring their own bodies and to feel freer with their fantasies and sexual excitation.

"I don't think I've ever had an incredible orgasm with a person," says Brigit, a throaty-voiced seventeen-year-old who started having intercourse when she was in the ninth grade. "When it's happened, it's only been a little bit, but it's like it almost happens, not quite. When Danny finds the spot, it's like a little bit of one comes, and I'm on the verge of it happening. I think it's going to, but then it sort of dies off or it never really happens big.

"I'd never really had it happen at all, and then last year sometime, I had one in the bathtub and I knew what it was. See, I have this little hose in the bathtub, and I spray the water all over me, and this one time, I found the right spot and I discovered that when I put it there, I'd come. That's the only way I've really come. . . ."

In addition to their hidden anatomy, the source of sexual excitation seems to be less direct and perhaps more complex for girls than it is for boys. Researchers tell us that girls more often respond to a more complicated set of stimuli, such as a story or romance or even an abstract, unspecified feeling, unaccompanied by specific fantasies, than do boys.

Whereas a boy can be sexually excited by looking at a picture of a naked woman, a girl may be aroused by reading a historical romance—a much more diffuse experience.

"The evidence as of the present time, and it does indeed seem to be evidence that can be repeated in many different ethnic societies," says Dr. John Money, professor of medical psychology and pediatrics at the Johns Hopkins Hospital, "is that the male is the one who is more responsive to visual and narrative stimulation, and the female is more responsive to the sentimental and romantic type of stimulation, perhaps incorporating some visual stimulation, that leads rather rapidly to the importance of tactile and close body contact stimulation. I can illustrate this by saying that many women with whom I've talked . . . have consistently agreed on one issue; it is that if a woman sees a sexy picture, for instance, even an advertisement for Coca-Cola, she tends to project herself up onto the screen, onto the picture, and to imagine what it would be like to be that woman. Or, if she's seeing a sexy film, or a romantic film, to project herself into the story and perhaps change it a little to suit certain circumstances or her own existence, and also to feel that she's learning a few good lessons from the woman up there. She will then be able to put the lessons into practice in her own romantic and sexual life.

"As for the male viewer, his reaction is rather different, for he does not project himself up into the picture of a male on the screen and imagine what it would be like to be that lucky one with that good-looking girl. He objectifies. He takes that girl down off the screen and has sex with her on the spot."[10]

The subjective aspect of sexual stimulation for women is one of the factors that make romantic novels so popular with women. Barbara Cartland and many others write historical romances that provide the stories into which women of all ages can project themselves. John Money says that the pornographic material for women has a story line and always has a romantic and sentimental aspect but does not necessarily "go into minute details about nudity and the sexual act itself."

"All the pornography laws have been made by men," he says. "They have never caught on to the fact that *True Confessions* and *True Love* magazine stories are, in fact, the genuine pornography of women."[11]

Everything that teenage girls told me about their fantasies and sexual excitement supported this theory of rather diffuse stimulation. One seventeen-year-old, Kerry, told me that the only time she "got the feeling" of an orgasm was "when I've been by myself reading a book or something."

Another seventeen-year-old who lived across the country from Kerry told me that "the only time I come seems to be in my English class or my history class.

"It's really embarrassing," she says, "but in both those classes, I start daydreaming about this great love affair and I just seem to lose myself. I don't think anybody notices, but I can't seem to control it. I'll be sitting there, lost in my fantasies, which are just full of warm feelings— I don't even know what they are, but suddenly, I'll have these waves of sensation run through me and then I'll realize I've been sitting there with my legs crossed really tight and stiff and lord, it's ridiculous. I feel so embarrassed!"

While boys said they often visualized the bodies of their partners and had specific sexual fantasies, girls more often told me that they had feelings or scenes in their minds and felt close and loving with a person, but didn't have detailed erotic images. Certainly there are differences in male and female responses to erotic stimuli, and there are differences person to person. It seems to me, however, that we have only begun to tap the edges of the female psyche when it comes to sexuality. In the next thirty and forty years, researchers will find out more about what comes naturally to women and to girls. I suspect that along with what comes naturally, a "peaking" of sexual drive for girls in adolescence will be found that parallels the "peaking" in boys, in addition to the "peak" that has been found in women in their late thirties.

For both girls and boys, masturbation can be a constructive way to explore one's sexual response and to prepare for a sexual relationship that may come sometime in the future. Many of the teenagers I talked to who were virgins said that they felt masturbation was a good substitute for sexual intercourse. They also felt that once they had a sexual relationship or were married, they wouldn't need or want to masturbate anymore. At this point in time, they imagined that masturbation would only be a prelude to intercourse, not a supplement.

"I can see masturbating when you're a virgin," said thirteen-year-old Patty. "But once you get married, I can't see any reason for it."

"I had one college retreat that was a time of intense Bible teaching," said Cathy, a member of a Pentacostal church in San Diego. "There was this one minister who brought up masturbation. He was really refreshing and open. He said that a lot of people go through it growing up, and not to feel guilty. He said it's something you go through in younger years and then you grow out of it after you get married and have a satisfying sex life.

"I don't feel that it's really bad if that's your only release of your sexual drive. But when you have any other release, it should be with your husband or your wife, not with anyone else or before marriage."

"I think masturbation is good preparation for a marital relationship," said Kim, who describes himself as "basically a Calvinist." "I think to love someone else, you have to love yourself first. I see masturbation as self-love, and positive, not as self-abuse. That's where I find total fulfillment. It's an opinion of yourself."

Several young people said that they felt masturbation was a normal, healthy and satisfying experience that gave them a chance to have real sexual release, afforded a general release of their tensions and an opportunity to explore their sexual responses and feelings without the worry or the possibility of pregnancy. Several said that it also served as an outlet for some of the sexual fantasies they otherwise might not allow themselves. One girl told me that her fantasies would be "dangerous" in "real life" but would not elaborate beyond saying it was not a rape fantasy but had to do with "strangers." Several older teenagers said they wished they had been told when they were younger that it's natural to masturbate.

In East Los Angeles, Mrs. Raquel Espinosa says to her students that masturbation is natural. She tells her third and fourth graders at the Light and Life Christian School that masturbation is normal, but that there is a proper time and place for it.

According to Mrs. Espinosa, masturbation is normally discussed in her curriculum on human sexuality. "I had never had a problem with it right in my classroom before," she says. "But this year, there were three—and the one who was doing it constantly was a little girl who had real family problems.

"I knew I had to deal with it directly. . . . With this one girl, her masturbating was nearly constant. Her color would change right in the fourth-grade class, and you could see perspiration on her forehead. The two others were third graders, and they were bored; it happened once and it hasn't happened again. Anyway, with my fourth grader, I took her out of class during recess. I was hoping I could bring it up in a way so she wouldn't be ashamed.

"I said, 'X., I've noticed that you've been fondling yourself in class.' She turned red and she said, 'Yes.' When I know, I don't ask in such a way that they're going to say no. Anyway, I said, 'You've been fondling yourself in class when you should be doing other things. It concerns me because you've been getting behind in class.'

"Fortunately I was able to make her feel that what she was doing wasn't wrong—it was just the time and place. I asked her if she liked her body and she said she did like her body. Then I explained that in class, you don't excuse yourself to go and take a bath, and during reading time, you don't bring out your lunch bag and eat lunch. You don't get your friends together and talk in the middle of the church service. There's a right time and place to masturbate. She didn't know it was the wrong time and place.

"I think that I was able to make her feel that masturbating was fine as long as she did it at the right time and place, which was private time," said Mrs. Espinosa. "I think she felt accepted and ended up feeling much better about herself. I gave her the term so she'd know what she was doing. It also turned out that she was masturbating all the time because she was so disturbed about her parents splitting up. Our talk, and the fact that she felt understood and accepted by me, as well as things settling down at home, stopped the excessive masturbating."

"Imagine if pediatricians told parents, 'It's *normal* for your daughter to touch her vagina,' " says Michael Carrera, professor of Community Health Education at Hunter College in New York. "Imagine if they told parents, 'It's *normal* for your son to touch his scrotum or his penis. Let them touch and explore, and more than that, tell them that it's good, giving themselves pleasure from their own bodies.'

"Parents constitute a large part of the fabric of their children's identity," says Dr. Carrera, who is also chairman of the Sex Information and Education Council of America. "If that fabric can contain fibers that respect their child's sexuality, they will have more confidence in themselves.

"Everybody knows that it's okay to masturbate, so why is it such a dilemma in the United States today?" says Sol Gordon, director of the Institute for Family Research and Education in Syracuse, New York. "The average parent will say to the child, 'Honey, it's okay to masturbate . . . if you don't do it too much.' How much is too much? Once a year, twice a week, after every meal? That's the dilemma.

"What is this nonsense about masturbation? It's a normal expression of sexuality at any time, at any age; it's a problem only if it's guilt-ridden. Once is too much if you don't like it. If you don't like it, don't do it."

Alfred Kinsey and his colleagues found that there was no record of "disturbance of adjustment" from masturbating, even at the highest frequences, "except when parents discovered the activity, reprimanded or punished the youngster, made a public exhibition of the offense or upset the child's peace of mind in some other way."[12]

Of course, many parents do take the fact of their children's sexual drives in stride and show respect for their children's private and discreet masturbating experiences.

One such accepting mother of three in Croton-on-Hudson, New York, said with a chuckle about her fourteen-, fifteen- and seventeen-year-old sons: "I don't know how often they masturbate. All I know is that I do the laundry myself and they masturbate at least as often as they change pajamas, which is every day."

It's quite clear that masturbation is natural and healthy. It feels good and provides sexual and emotional release. Many more teenagers have gotten this message today than their parents did when they were teenagers. But it seems as if many more parents will have to internalize and believe that it's perfectly all right to touch, explore, and enjoy the human body and mind before their children can be taught the same message.

8.

Facts, Fears and Misconceptions

Sex is a wonderful capacity in people, like the ability to see, talk, walk and anything else that comes with being fully alive. I watch my two-year-old son begin to master the basics of speaking and moving, and I see in him the inherent joy of identifying feelings and sounds, objects and people. "That's the garbage truck, Mommy!" he says, his eyes widening. "Listen!" He leaps and jumps, runs and spins, obviously reveling in the wonder of being alive. He breaks into song in the middle of dinner. And he is as fascinated with his own body as he is with the world around him. "That's my elbow," he says, pointing. "That's my navel, that's my penis, that's my knee, that's my toe. . . ."

I watch him and I realize that his sex education has begun. When it's so comfortable and natural, I wonder why it is that from the time so many of us began to learn about our bodies, our education was so fraught with negatives, warnings and reprimands.

"Rarely, if a child points to his teeth, do parents say chomp chomps, says Barbara Whitney, director of the Sex Information and Education Council of the United States (SIECUS). "But if he points to his penis, parents say pee pee. We don't use pet names for any other part of the body, which reflects our discomfort with our sexual parts. I've run workshops in high schools and one classroom of teenagers can come up with lists of fifty or sixty names they have heard or used for sexual parts of the body."

"It's interesting," says Marsha Lawrence, senior communications consultant of Planned Parenthood in New York City. "We measure kids' heights. We put marks on the wall. We record you are this tall, you can do this or that. And we do this about every accomplishment. We look at their SAT scores, we praise them for getting on the basketball team, we are thrilled when they learn to read and write. But we do not treat sexual maturation in the same tone of voice as any other development.

"When we talk about sex, the voice tightens and the voice tenses, and our concern in acknowledging and explaining sex is that we always want to warn kids about sex. It's almost impossible to pick up any book about sex without finding a warning in it. You would never know from our middle-class agencies and our books about sex that it is supposed to be a pleasurable experience.

"On the other side of our official 'talks' with our children, of course, is the cultural mythology that says sex is the greatest thing in the world. There is nothing better. It is the A Number One of all things. What it boils down to is that two opposite things are being told to kids."

Maybe it's precisely *because* our sexuality is so implicitly part of our humanity that we fear it and either over or under emphasize it. Our reproductive urges, our reproductive systems, are fundamental to our being alive, to giving birth. As I have pointed out earlier, our reproductive urges underscore our physical limitations and impending death. If our own sexuality is threatening in this way, then our children's sexuality is all the more threatening.

Certainly there are also more obvious and immediate concerns as well. Parents often give warnings about sex because they don't want their child becoming a pregnancy statistic or getting venereal disease or being hurt. They're alarmed by the sexual stimuli their children are exposed to and unsure of how the children will process them.

Whatever the reasons, the two-step that people do around the subject of sex has left our teenagers sorely lacking information about their anatomy, their own sexual responses and their options in relationships and other decisions. People who work with teenagers in schools, clinics and hospitals find it remarkable that these young people who have been exposed to such open permissiveness regarding sex know so little about their own bodies and reproductive systems.

"I've been here three and a half months and I'm surprised at the teenagers," says Terry Scher, a young nurse with short brown hair and an abundance of energy, who works in an adolescent clinic in New York. "A lot of these kids are very smart but very undereducated about what's serious and not serious when it comes to their bodies. They'll walk around for months with a lump in a breast or a backache or a urinary infection, thinking it will all go away after a while. . . .

"As wise as they are in many ways, some girls don't even know they have three holes in their bodies. They think they urinate and have sex from the same place, and that at the most, they have one or two 'places.' One girl I saw thought that if she stopped taking the Pill, she couldn't get pregnant for six months."

A fifteen-year-old at a sophisticated private "preppy" school in New York City got very upset when her counselor cautioned her about being

reckless sexually. The counselor had become quite alarmed when she
found out that the girl was having sex but not using birth control. "Oh,
Mrs. S.," the girl said, "you *know* I can't get pregnant! I'm only in the
ninth grade."

During the course of my research, teenagers asked me many questions. From sex educators, health workers, doctors, clinicians, school
counselors, clergymen and the Ann Landers column, I heard even more
questions and misinterpretations. Overall, they reflected a quality similar to these questions collected from students by a ninth-grade teacher
in Gary, Indiana:

My boyfriend said if I drink some hot tea or some vinegar after sex, I
    would not get pregnant. Is this true?
If you clean yourself out after having sex, will you still get pregnant?
Is there any other way to get pregnant besides sexual intercourse?
Do you think sex is bad?
Why are parents always trying to hide sex?
What is orgasm?
Can a girl take birth-control pills when she is thirteen years old?
Why do people have sex? When a girl and boy have sex, can either the
    girl or boy catch a disease?
Will a girl get pregnant the first time she has sex with a boy?
How do you talk with someone about sex?
Do you bleed after sex? Or do the boys bleed?
Why do you have monthly menstruations? How long do you stay on it?
    Are you healthy if it's six days?
Is it true that if you do it alone, you would not get a good feeling?
Will a girl's breasts get bigger if she has sex before she turns six-
    teen?

As I heard these and similar questions, I remembered one of my own
early insights on the subject of sex. In my neighborhood, we had played
doctor from the time we could talk, and to us, as first and second graders, sex was literally kids' stuff. When one of the neighborhood boys
reported one day that he had seen the Smiths, a married couple on our
block, "doing it," I quizzed him thoroughly. Finally convinced that he
had seen them doing it, I was horrified. "You'd think they'd know better at their age!" I roared. "That's terrible."

Today's teenagers seem to have learned by similar method. Surveys
show that teenagers get most of their information from magazines,
friends, and gossip they hear on the playground or streets. Thus, from a
combination of myth, accumulated experience, fantasy and random
pieces of information, they come to their own conclusions about sex—
how it works and what it means.

"I remember seeing this book about animals and how they make babies," tow-headed Katherine said, "and it showed dogs and chickens all doing what they do, and then it showed a human couple under the covers in bed and said that's how human beings make babies. I thought that meant that if you got under the covers with a man, you would have a baby."

"I learned more about sex from friends than from anyone else," said Trisha, a nineteen-year-old who says that only now has she really begun understanding fundamentals about her own feelings. "My mother told me if I had any questions, to go ask my gym teacher or the school nurse. That's what she told me! I asked our girl friend, Judy Fuller, though, because she knew everything! But she told us all wrong. She told us about all the bases, but we got those all wrong. It took a long time to figure it all out right. First base is kissing, second base is touching your breast; third base is touching genitals and fourth base—a home run—is making love.

"I remember in seventh grade sitting on this guy's lap and I was so uptight. He kissed me on the cheek and I got up and got Judy and said, 'Come on, I've got to talk to you! That guy tried to . . .'

" 'To *what?*' she said. 'Go to second?'

" 'No! He tried to kiss me!'

" 'Is that *all?*' Oh, she was so mad at me! But I thought if you kissed someone, that was really serious. I didn't kiss anyone seriously until I was a junior in high school."

"For a long time, I thought a girl couldn't get pregnant unless she was married," said Eve, a West Philadelphia high-school junior. "I learned more about explicit sex from listening to the guys talk to each other after class than I learned anywhere else. I'd sit over at the side of the room working on a project and listen to them. The guys would pull out colored condoms and show them to each other. They talked about what they used, how to use it, how to do it and when to pull out. One guy'd say, 'Pop gave me these; he told me when to use the house. He said we could go over there this afternoon.'

"The conversation was always different with the girls, but I'd learn from them, too. I'd walk into the bathroom and they'd be saying things like, 'Mom better not find out I have these!' The girls, they can't go to their own houses."

"I remember when I started my period. My grandmother and my dad told me about menstruation and told me that now I could get pregnant," says Caprice, a junior at the Parkway School in Philadelphia. "They gave me this little pamphlet my father had found in the rain with dirt all over it. I read it backwards and forwards.

"I never knew anything about guys. I just knew they ran around the cloakroom pulling up girls' dresses. When I heard about sex, I thought, who'd want to to *that?* Oh, my goodness, not that! Later I got the book *Everything You Always Wanted to Know About Sex*, and my friend

Jerome would decipher words for me. I think he didn't know any more than I did, but he'd been around people more, so he'd heard more."

"I used to think sex was just for having babies, but now I know it's for having fun," one sixth grader told me.

"How'd you learn that?" I asked.

"Karen Riley told me. Sarah Ronstadt told her that's what her mother said."

Like many other people, I had assumed that sex education was widely available in schools throughout the United States. It isn't. I had also assumed that teenagers would know more than I did at their age about where to go for contraception if they wanted it, and whom to talk to about themselves and their behavior. I was wrong.

Most schools do not address the subject at all.

"The nurse at our school has pamphlets on the board that you can take," says Peggy, a junior at Paradise Valley High School in Paradise Valley, Arizona. "But it's in this small classroom off the nurse's room and people don't normally go to the nurse, let alone go into that room. You wouldn't know about the pamphlets being there unless you specifically asked or, like me, just happened to walk into that room. Sometimes the sociology teacher will talk to kids about it, and the human-relations teacher, too, but otherwise you wouldn't know there was any such thing as sex at our school."

The vast majority of youngsters in this country don't have sex education in school. Only three states—Kentucky, Maryland and New Jersey and the District of Columbia—require family life [sex education] as part of the public-school curriculum. Only six additional states—Pennsylvania, Illinois, Iowa, Kansas, Utah and Minnesota—encourage it. It appears that nationally, about one-third of the junior high and high schools offer family-life courses.

In an analysis of U.S. sex education programs, the Department of Health, Education and Welfare estimated that if approximately one-fourth of all students in each high school with sex education actually take that course, less than 10 percent of all students actually receive sex education.

As for the content and structure of the courses, the National Education Association reports that sex education is most frequently a brief unit within another course. The majority of units last less than ten hours. Of these, fewer than half of the teachers give their students information on sexual intercourse or contraception. Even fewer discuss masturbation or premarital sex or the questions teenagers have about the responsibilities and obligations one has in a sexual relationship with another person.

What passes for sex education in many of the schools that do teach it comes in cartoon form that stops just short of calling a penis a ding ding or a vagina a choo choo.

"Before, all I knew was what I'd seen in the sixth-grade films on reproduction," says fifteen-year-old Liz in Philadelphia. "They took all the girls into one room and all the boys into another. I don't know what the boys saw, but what we saw was little sperm in top hats dancing towards little eggs in negligees."

"In the sixth grade, we saw a film showing boys' anatomy and girls' anatomy," says Alynn, a ninth grader in Minnesota. "They showed how Sammy Sperm, with little eyes and a tail, swims up to Edith Egg. They just showed the travel, they didn't show intercourse. The boys saw that film, too, so they learned the same thing we did."

"We had sex education in the tenth grade as part of PE," says seventeen-year-old Wiley, in Minneapolis, St. Paul. "They told us a lot about VD—a lot about syphilis and the gonorrhea germ. He was an actor dressed up as a germ and he crawled around inside this guy. They talked about symptoms and treatment—what to do if you had it. They said to go see a doctor and don't be embarrassed to tell your contacts about it."

Sometimes, along with cursory information on sperm, eggs or the hazards of venereal disease, youngsters are also exposed to the prejudices, misconceptions or phobias of teachers. "When I was in the seventh grade," says Carl, from Villanova, Pennsylvania, "we had this John Bircher teacher. He was supposed to teach us sex education, but he told us sex was horrible and wrong and that sex education was horrible and wrong. He felt he shouldn't be teaching the subject and that the schools had no business teaching sex education. He told us that death occurs from syphilis and that you shouldn't have intercourse because then you could get syphilis and die. He also told us that older homosexual men would come to the school and molest us if we weren't careful. When he told us that, I said, 'Where can I find these men?' He threw me out of class."

"When I was a freshman in high school, the nun in our religion class told us that using Tampax was a form of self-masturbation, so of course we should never use it," says Theda Lloyd from Aurora, Illinois. "She said it was a sin. She also said that premarital sex was a mortal sin and anyone who did it wouldn't go to heaven."

"We have a Human Relations II class at this school that includes marriage, the family and some sex education," said a guidance counselor at a high school outside Denver, Colorado. "It used to be that *only* girls could take this class. Finally, two years ago, boys were allowed in the class and the guidance counselors handpicked the boys to be in the class. We wanted to make sure the boys would be sensitive because the teacher was so worried about it being co-ed. On the first day, the teacher—before she said anything—turned around and wrote on the board, 'This is NOT a sex class!' "

Of course, sex education is, at its best, an education about sexuality—which is much more than a focus on reproduction. It's what being a man or a woman in this society means and how one acts on it. That includes genital sex, but also much more than that.

"Our social-living class is the best class I've ever had," says Craig Mason, an eighth grader at King Junior High School in Berkeley, California. "It covers personality, sexuality, sex roles, sex, love, birth control and responsibilities. It is the perfect class for eighth grade. There was a lot of stuff I already know, but there was stuff I didn't know, too. The teacher was great. He wasn't embarrassed at all.

"You learn a lot about not to rush things, and you learn about birth control. You learn about how dangerous it is to get somebody pregnant. I never knew about percentages with birth control—how you can get somebody pregnant even if you use birth control!

"You also learn about relating with your parents. He says you should try to tell them things, not try to hide things. . . . We talked a lot about responsibility to other people and ourselves. It was a great class. Some of the people didn't know anything at all, so it was really valuable for everybody."

When sex education is thought out and taught in a coherent way, it can be extraordinarily constructive in helping young people think about their values and goals. It can be a setting for working out personal issues, clearing up myths and, ultimately, it can lead to making more responsible decisions regarding sexual behavior.

A recent Gallup poll showed that 77 percent of American adults favor sex education in the schools, and that of these, 69 percent favor teaching birth control. Another survey of citizens in a Midwest city found that 88 percent of the respondents agreed that sex education should be offered in schools, 85 percent would allow their own children to take such a course, and only 6 percent believed sex education was an invasion of family rights and privacy. Similarly, in a study by the widely respected Project for Human Sexual Development, some 80 percent of 1400 parents interviewed in Cleveland, Ohio, said they supported sex education. Moreover, more than a majority of them believed contraceptive information should be made available to pre-teenagers. So it would seem that a very vocal minority often lobbies to keep sex education out of the schools. One of the main reasons this minority gives in objection to the belief that if children are taught about sex, they'll lose their values and start having it sooner. In fact, research has shown just the opposite to be true. Children who have had sex education deter first intercourse and have lower rates of unwanted pregnancies and births. They tend to use contraception more once they have started having sex, and have reduced rates of venereal disease.

Another reason many people give for being against sex education is that it encourages abortion and undermines religious teachings. In a criticism of the Planned Parenthood film *About Sex* that caused great furor when shown in a classroom at Coronado High School in Scottsdale, Arizona, Phoenix *Gazette* Editor Loyal Meek wrote that the film mentioned "nothing about the evils of abortion, nothing about immorality or sin." Spiritual consequences are quite often evoked as a reason not to expose young people to factual information about their sexuality. Citizens opposed to sex education in the school often say it should be taught in the home or in a religious context. But more often than not, the same people never offer factual information about sex in either the church or the home.

Ironically, one of the finest and most thorough sex-education programs I found anywhere was in a fundamentalist Free Methodist church school in Los Angeles, California. For the past twenty-three years, the East Los Angeles Light and Life Christian School has included as part of its required curriculum a sex-education program that begins in the third grade and continues through the ninth grade. The curriculum is the work of the school's principal, David Fenwick, and his wife, Nellie Fenwick, a counselor and teacher at the school.

When I went to the Light and Life Christian School, I met David Fenwick—wiry and lean, in his fifties, with his shirtsleeves rolled above the elbows—and Nellie—a large woman with short, light brown hair, wearing slacks and a flowered blouse—on the school's hot, dusty playground. Over a lunch of Mexican food—cheese enchiladas and bean burritos—I asked the Fenwicks how a Christian-oriented church school came to have such a thorough sex education curriculum. It seemed so contrary to my stereotypes of conservative Protestant churches.

"David and I felt that the pressures young people faced were confused," said Nellie. "They weren't sure whether it was right or wrong to have babies when they were sixteen, and they didn't seem to have a sense of who they were in relation to their own bodies. . . .

"The first year we taught here, we had a seventh grader who was having intercourse with some guy in the balcony at the movie theater every Saturday. She came to talk to me about it because she didn't know what to do. I felt he was taking advantage of her and that he didn't really care about her. He'd made no effort to use birth control or protect her in any way."

Sex education at the Light and Life Christian School starts in the third grade. Raquel Espinosa, who teaches the seven- to nine-year-olds, says that the course begins by focusing on the correct terms for the body.

"At that age, they use all kinds of weird terms," says Raquel, a tall and attractive woman with an ease about the way she moves and speaks. "They say boobs for breasts and butt for bottom and all kinds of things they often make up. I make them repeat the correct words. I tell them, 'You're growing up now, and these are the correct words to use. The old ones are for little children to use. . . .

"My feeling is that when they continue to use these terms, they can't develop respect for their bodies. They seem less embarrassed when they use slang words than when they use the proper words. When I tell them the proper words—like I will say *penis* or *breasts* or *vagina*—they laugh. In their faces, you can see they're saying, *really?* They can't *believe* those are really words. It's a novelty when they find out there are acceptable and appropriate terms, so they begin to try them out.

"Would you believe some children don't even know mothers can breast-feed their babies?" she said. "The idea of a mother's milk is totally novel.

"They don't know there are acceptable ways of learning about sexuality besides in alleys or in whispers. I figure if they're old enough to ask questions, they're old enough to get answers. I don't tell them more than they ask for.

"They are confused the most at this age about how babies are born. Parents tell them that the doctor brought them in the doctor's bag, or they say, 'I found you in a basket at the front door.' They tell them all kinds of stories. They want to believe what their parents say, but they can't reconcile that kind of story with the shape of their mother's body when she's pregnant.

"They ask, 'How can the baby get out?' I say, 'What do you think?' They'll answer, 'She vomits it out,' or, 'It comes out through the navel.' They are really surprised when they learn that certain muscles of the body are made so the mother can give birth to the baby. Once we know how the baby grows and how the baby comes out, the next question is, 'How does the baby get in?'

"I explain to them about seeds and eggs, and how when the child is born, they're born with the seeds or the eggs they're going to need to reproduce a child when they're older. Then I explain how the penis deposits sperm in the vagina.

"The kids will say, 'That means a woman can have a baby every time they sleep together.' I tell them that *sleeping together* is not the right term. A woman and a man can sleep together without having sexual intercourse, which is what you meant when you said sleep together.

"That term causes no end of distress. It's very misleading for a child. You'll hear little girls saying, 'I'm going to tell my mother I can't take a nap with my little brother anymore!'

"I also tell them that little boys and girls don't have mature enough sperm and eggs to produce a baby. They'll say babies are so cute, why can't I have a baby? I try to explain to them that what makes a father and mother is not just making a baby. Being a father or mother takes responsibility. I tell them that even though teenagers can bear children, it's better to be more grown up so you can be more responsible about having children."

Raquel Espinosa talks to the children about menstruation, about keeping their bodies fresh and clean and taking responsibility for what happens to their own bodies. When they talk about parents being mean or parents who aren't nice to their children, she tells them *they* can't fix what their parents do because they're too young. They *can* do something for their own future, she says. They can make sure their own children don't go through the same things that made them unhappy.

With older students, the Fenwicks talk in more detail about the male and female bodies, about reproduction and responsibilities to yourself and others. They discuss oral sex, orgasms, masturbation. erections, ejaculation, menstruation, nocturnal emissions, pregnancy, menopause. They also talk about homosexuality, prostitution, rape, free love and sexual repression. Their point of view is that the human body is not dirty, that in fact it is "God's temple" and "the Creator's masterpiece— the earthly home of man and woman." The course for older students emphasizes the wholeness and joy of sexual pleasure *in* marriage, both for reproductive purposes and for purposes of mutual stimulation and pleasure. In fact, they say once you are married, "It is *wrong* not to fully enjoy your body and the body of your mate because God gave us these bodies for pleasure. They are part of the natural laws of God."

In presenting their view that premarital sex is wrong, the Fenwicks state: "Sexual intercourse is not a plaything to try out for selfish fun. It is rather a way for two people to show that they belong completely to each other by sharing a joy that means more than any other physical joy. . . ." Despite the bias against premarital sex, however, the course discusses progressive ways of showing affection and decision making about sexual issues in relationships. Light and Life students also receive very thorough information on birth control and venereal disease.

Against such a backdrop, students at this school have an opportunity to formulate their own opinions and make responsible decisions about their sexual behavior. Most young people are not so fortunate. The way they feel about their bodies, sensations, attractions and interests are confused with myths and warnings from their parents or other well-meaning adults who further compound conflicts by handing their children information based on generations of fears and phobias.

"My mom said you never had sex in the daytime," says Cordelia, a junior in Washington, D.C. "The room has to be dark. So I didn't know how the guy found the girl. I thought, well first of all it's dark, and then I thought, if the organs that merge are down there and your eyes are up here, how do they get together?

"Two months after my ninth birthday, I was taught the functions of a female body," she says, rolling her green eyes to the right side of her little olive-shaped face. "Not the male body. I didn't know where the sperm came from. I didn't think guys had anything to do with it.

"When I was in the ninth and tenth grades, I saw about ten girls who were pregnant at the school. This one girl, Sally Davis, took the sex-education course. I went home and said, 'Mom, the girl's pregnant— why should she want to take this course?' She said, 'It doesn't take brains to get pregnant. All you have to do is lie down.' She told me that my great-grandmother didn't know how she'd gotten pregnant. When she gave birth, she was trying to cover herself up so no one could see. My great-grandmother prided herself that neither one of her husbands had ever seen her naked.

"It was so long before I really understood anything. Until my Aunt April gave me a human biology book when I was fifteen, I had a hard time believing a woman had an opening. You don't see that, and it's just impossible to imagine a baby coming out of there. Or anything going in there. I thought the baby was just in the stomach and then was out. I couldn't imagine it coming out of any opening in *me!*"

"Really, I'm embarrassed to say how old I was before I really understood much at all about sex. It was last year, when I was in the tenth grade, that I saw the film *Developing Sexual Maturity.* Our teacher showed it to us and said not to tell anyone we saw this movie or he'd get into trouble. But it was good. The thing was, though, people were nude in this film, and I'd never seen a man naked before. I couldn't believe what I was seeing. It was so explicit. It showed erections and masturbation. I thought I would die."

Many parents find great difficulty talking to their children about sex. Some handle their difficulty by never mentioning the subject; they cannot bring themselves to utter words in that direction. Despite their reticence, however, many parents feel that when their children get to be teenagers, they are obligated to have "a talk." Often, valiant as the effort is, the one-shot talk is quite uncomfortable.

"I grew about five inches over the summer and my voice changed," said Hugh Green, whose mother and father were divorced when he was four years old. "I was visiting my dad that summer, and one time he said, 'Well, it's time for our talk. Is there anything you want to ask me about?' I said no. I felt a tiny bit embarrassed because I really didn't know what to say to him. If he had felt totally comfortable about it, I would have been comfortable, I think, but we weren't that close since we hadn't lived together."

The following year, Hugh said, his mother's boyfriend Jimmy, who had lived with Hugh, his mother and sister for four years, talked to him about sex. "That was real comfortable," Hugh said, "probably because we'd lived together. It wasn't as detailed. It was about morals, and at the end, we were laughing and he was cracking jokes.

"During that talk, he told me that when he was sixteen or seventeen, he got his girl friend pregnant. She couldn't have an abortion in those days, so she had the baby. They were both really frantic about it. Her parents took care of the baby and really raised it. He was saying you really have to be ready for it, and that he wasn't at all ready for it. He has a kid eleven years old and he's only twenty-six. So he talked to me about that a whole lot. He said that he was real ignorant, and that nobody had ever talked to him about it."

For the single parent of an opposite-sex child, talking about sexuality can be particularly difficult for both parties. "My mom came into my room the other day and said she wanted to talk to me," said Randy, a fourteen-year-old in Denver, whose mother works as a real-estate agent. "She said that she knew I was growing up, and that I might have questions come up from time to time about girls or sex, and she wanted me to know she was willing to answer any questions I had. It was pretty embarrassing. I said, 'Okay,' and that was pretty much the end of it."

Of course, it would be easier if parents had been answering questions about sexuality and sharing some of their own experiences growing up from the time their children were small—something some parents seem to do quite naturally—because then it's an ongoing conversation. But apparently not that many parents talk openly with their children, even when their children are young. In a study of the role parents play in the sexual learning of their children, for instance, the project on Human Sexual Development found that the majority of parents of children eleven years old and under had never discussed intercourse or contraception with their children. While they said they wanted their children to know about it by the time they were teenagers, between 85 and 95 percent of all the parents interviewed said they had *never* mentioned any aspect of erotic behavior or its social consequences to their children. Project Director Elizabeth J. Roberts points out that when parents have not mentioned these subjects, it might affect the child's willingness to ask parents for additional information as he or she grows older.

Their study, *Family Life and Sexual Learning: a Study of the Role of Parents in the Sexual Learning of Children*, published in 1978, found that many parents have difficulty talking about this subject with their children because they simply do not know what to say. Some of the parents hinted that they knew very little themselves and that this inhibited them from discussing the subject with their children. Sex was not discussed in their homes when they were growing up, and they received little information. They were recreating the same conditions for their own children.

In talks with teenagers and their parents, the influence of the grandparents (and probably the great-grandparents and on before them) still reigned throughout their households—even when circumstances were greatly different in the lives of their children. One time, for instance, when I met with a group of parents, the mother of an eighteen-year-old

daughter and sixteen- and thirteen-year-old sons said she hadn't told
her sixty-four-year-old mother the topic of my book. "I was embarrassed to tell my mother what we were doing here tonight," she said. "I
just told her it was something about teenagers, I didn't know exactly
what."

Marsha Lawrence, senior communications consultant for Planned
Parenthood in New York City and herself mother to three teenagers,
says it shouldn't be surprising that parents tell their children just what
they themselves were told. They're caught off guard, she says.

"It's not just that a sexual revolution has taken place," she says, "it's
that the different ideas and modes of behavior co-exist with the old
notions. They sit side by side within our brains, and when we're caught
off guard and expected to talk about sex to our children, we grab for the
old notions that are familiar to us; they're the ones we grew up
with."

Even when parents' behavior contradicts what they were taught, they
have the old set of rules and regulations easily at hand. Rather than
articulate the conflicts and confusions they themselves feel, they reach
for what's comfortable and known.

Another reason for the difficulty in talking about sex, says Father
John E. Forliti, director of religious education for the Archdiocese of St.
Paul and Minneapolis, Minnesota, "is that there's a natural hesitation
and reticence to discuss the reality of intimate sexual relationships with
one's children. It's too personal, too poetic, too spiritual, too sacred.
Like a friendship. It's like getting too close to the rose if you try to
explain it. That's one factor."

Father Forliti, designer of an area-wide sex-education course for
ninth and tenth graders *and* their parents, believes that another reason
parents feel so paralyzed discussing sex is that they don't have the same
kind of education as their children. They don't have the language or the
facility. "They haven't seen television as youngsters," he says. "It didn't
even exist when they were growing up. . . . Today you can talk about
homosexuality, incest, rape, because it's on the news. We're more open
to talk. But a lot of people in their middle age didn't really have training
in communications. They're much less adept at talking about personal
things. Everybody's a lot more personally oriented these days than they
used to be. . . .

"I don't think that kids know more about sex than their parents do,"
he said. "Some people say that, but it's just a put-down. It's very difficult to be a parent these days, partly because everybody's telling them
that they don't know how to do it."

At the time I spoke to Father Forliti in late 1979, some two thousand
young people were taking his sex-education course in the Minneapolis/
St. Paul area, and 60 percent of their parents were also taking the
course, ahead of their youngsters. As of this year, some six thousand

young people here have taken Father Forliti's sex-education course. Sixty percent of their parents have also taken this course.

"One of the reasons that the course is working very well is that it's helping parents *before* they talk to their kids," he says. "It gives them some vocabulary and it gives them some practice in talking to other parents. It's so good for them to know the parents of their kids' friends."

Although most parents have trouble talking about sex, some parents go to the other extreme in imparting their values and ideas about sex to their children. They say too much rather than too little.

In Joe's case, his father was overly interested in Joe's knowledge about sexual behavior and, it seems, was projecting himself beyond the bounds of fatherly interest.

"When I was about five years old, my dad told me, 'This is how you get the girl going, this is what you do to her,' " said Joe, a high-school junior in Santa Monica. "My parents got divorced when I was two years old, and then my dad remarried when I was seven. When I was in the seventh grade, he told me again about different techniques he used to get the girl going and how to make her come and all that sort of thing. . . ."

In Courtney's family, the parents went overboard in forcing their children into an awareness of a disturbing sexual relationship that reflected their deeper psychological problems. Certainly, the parent's attempts to "educate" their children were not made in the interest of their children's welfare.

"My parents would always say to us, 'We're going into the bedroom now to make love,' " says Courtney, a short, lively eighteen-year-old from Houston, Texas, whose face exudes vitality. I am surprised, when she begins to speak, at the shyness and softness in her voice, at the reticence and openness at odds within her. "Then they'd go in there and they'd start fighting and screaming. They'd push sex. They'd tell us, 'Sex is good! It's wonderful!' I'd say, 'Yeah, yeah, I like it, I like it. I don't know what it is.'

"When they'd go off to the bedroom to have intercourse, which they always announced first, my sister and I would say, 'Groovy.' I remember finding in the bottom of my father's drawer these weird magazines. Not just *Playboy* but weird ones with people doing things to each other and hurting each other. I thought that's what sex was. I withdrew into a fantasy world. Even when I was little, I had sexual dreams. I'd have this one dream where I was sliced up and parts of me were hung up. There was a breast here, a vagina there. It was very scary. There was always something very scary about sex to me."

"I'm of two minds in how much you should talk to your kids about sex," says Dr. Maj-Britt Rosenbaum at the Albert Einstein College of Medicine in New York. "Too much talking can be negative, because I think it can sometimes be too much intrusion into your child's privacy. It can also be a vicarious reexperiencing and living through one's kids, which is not good for the kids, even though it appears to be positive to sit down and talk with one's kids.

"It can maintain a tie that is sort of tricky for the adolescents. They have to wonder, should they report everything? And, of course, they should not, because it's the beginning of autonomy in their own lives. There's maybe a gap that's needed, where they have some privacy and autonomy and a confidence in making and managing their own decisions."

It seems clear that whether or not they strike a perfect balance, talk a lot or a little, too much or not enough, parents are their children's first sex educators.

"Children are sexual beings from birth," says Dr. Mary Calderone, founder and president of SIECUS, the Sex Information and Education Council of America. "And that's why sex education begins at home. Parents are sex educators whether they like it or not, whether they do it well or whether they do it badly or not at all. . . ." Dr. Calderone points out that silence and evasiveness are just as powerful teachers as openness and frank discussion—but that ignorance, not knowledge, is what leads young people into irresponsible sexual behavior.

Michael Carrera, chairman of SIECUS and professor of community health education at Hunter College in New York, insists that parents should become *consciously* responsible for the primary sex education of their children. It's equally important, he says, that parents not look at sexuality as a "narrow, episodic, event-oriented experience.

"It's a psychological, sociological, spiritual, cultural experience," he says. "It's not just genital, biological, sexual behavior. This is the basic stuff of life."

Carrera points out that parents often focus on the issue of unintended pregnancy. "This preoccupation is unfair to young people because it defines them in terms of their genital activity," he says. "It's unfair because they see themselves defined that way in school by people who zero in on birth control, and nothing else, and then again at home. It's unfair to millions of other adolescents who are negotiating adolescence with highs and lows, who are not exploiting others and who are not abusing their bodies. We take too few cases, generalize from pathology and forget the norm. We work with them in the narrow parameters of genital concepts and lose sight of the child in the process.

"I've heard people tell parents, you have to be together yourself about your own sexuality to be able to talk to your children about it. That reinforces the parents' fear that they don't know enough. They don't have to know more; they don't have to be in touch! They need to tell their children, 'You're beautiful and valued and valuable. Take care of yourself. Respect others.' This is the fundamental of family planning and sex education.

"If your child respects herself and feels that she's valuable, she won't let herself be abused," says Carerra. "If she respects and values other people, she won't abuse and exploit others."

Dr. Carrera says it doesn't matter if parents are not comfortable talking about sex. If you're not comfortable, he says, "Just say, 'Hey, I'm not comfortable about it, but I'll try.' The important thing is to be honest. Recognize and define your own feelings about sexuality, and then you can communicate what you feel to your children.

"When the preschooler asks, 'Why is the sky blue?' and then asks you about sex, it's on the same plane," he says. "They're not aware of the intimacy we feel. A rule of thumb is to answer simply and directly. If you don't know, say, 'I don't know.' "

Certainly parents don't have to be experts to share their values and ideas with their children; nor do they need to share information about their own sexual experiences. But they should recognize that their own development and their own experiences do influence their attitudes and the messages they give their children.

My paternal grandmother, for instance, apparently didn't know anything about her own body when she was a young woman. Even though she was a farm girl, she went into marriage totally unprepared for the shock of sexual intercourse. When her own sons and daughters were growing up, she was determined to tell them whatever they wanted to know. Her youngest daughter, my Aunt Helen Beth, says that when she was in the second grade, a classmate told her how babies were made. "Oh, you may have been made that way," she recalls saying, "but I was sent from heaven. My mother wanted me."

She went home from school and told her mother what the girl had said. "Then and there she told me that God had made a woman's body and a man's body different, and how with those bodies, a baby is made," Helen Beth said. "Before I got married, she took great care in explaining to me the duties a husband and wife have to one another sexually. . . ."

My grandmother wasn't an educated woman, but she shared with her children what she could of her views and values. She did what many teenagers say they want to do as parents.

"If I had children, whatever questions they asked, I would explain the best I knew," said seventeen-year-old Megan in Phoenix. "I think they deserve to know whatever I know that can help them."

With time, we'll learn if our teenagers do a better job with facts, fears and misconceptions about sexuality than we have done. If their children accept sex as a wonderful capacity in themselves, we'll know we're on the right track.

9.

Rules and Regulations:
Repressing the Irrepressible

"My mother's absolutely crazy," says Josie, a high-school junior in Fort Lauderdale, Florida. Josie, brown haired and fun loving, half-cries and half-shouts about her parents. "She really is crazy. She's *for* nude beaches, but *against* premarital sex. She's always talking about how beautiful the body is, how it's a sacred temple and nothing to be ashamed of, but she'd kill me if I used mine sexually.

"It's not at all the same for my brother as it is for me. I remember my mom found a bunch of rubbers in my brother's jacket pocket. She was mad, of course, but my dad says, 'He's a guy. . . .' and that was that. They wouldn't have reacted that way if they'd found a diaphragm in my purse!"

When children begin bringing home foreign legions of strange-looking adolescents to loll around in clusters eating potato chips, when the telephone is constantly in the grips of yon Romeo or Juliet or when hours or dates begin to become issues, many parents feel slightly disoriented. They find themselves saying inconsistent things and behaving in ways they wouldn't have expected. Even though they *know* better, they often shock themselves with jealous inclinations and a desire to interfere.

"Last month this girl started coming over to our house every day after school, and it drove me stark raving mad," said the mother of a sixteen-year-old boy in Clarke Lake, Michigan. "I found myself doing and saying incredible things. I didn't mean to talk against her; but I just couldn't stand her. I'd try to hold myself back and then bingo, there I'd go and say something again. Fortunately, he didn't like her that much, either, but it was my behavior that alarmed me, not his!"

"I'm almost embarrassed to say it," said a Great Neck, New York, mother of two. "But I'm thrilled when my son acts sexually experienced and macho. And I'd absolutely *kill* anyone who tried to touch my daughter. I know that's wrong and that it's unfair and outrageous—but that's my gut reaction."

How do parents cope with their child's sexual interests; with her desire to stay out until dawn and his request to have his girl friend sleep over—in his bed? How do parents react to the fact that their children might experiment with sex free of pregnancy—or with the possibility of pregnancy? How can they respect a child's privacy and still set limits, instill values and show that they care? In the old days, the job was easier in many respects.

"When I was a young girl, your parents had that kind of hold on you," says Jovina Hankins, supervisor of nurses in the Oakland, California public schools and mother of a teenage son and daughter. "I felt like my mother watched every move I made and knew every thought I was thinking. It was like her eyes were always on me even when she wasn't there, so, of course, how would I dare jump into bed with a boy when she'd be standing there looking at me? I was afraid to even *think* about it because I knew she knew what I was thinking. . . . Parents used to have that kind of hold on their kids, but they don't anymore.

"When my daughter asks me a question," she says, rolling her brown eyes, "sometimes I repeat the question just to give myself a little bit of time to get the answer together. I didn't even know enough to ask those questions when I was a girl."

Years ago, people also had neighborhood norms to follow. "People used to have standards in common because parents talked to each other," says Father John E. Forliti, director of Religious Education for the Archdiocese of St. Paul And Minneapolis, Minnesota. "They talked about things like when was the appropriate time to date, what hours their kids should get in, what to do if their kids drank. They'd talk to their kids at night and the next day they talked to each other on the phone or over the fence. Parents had that kind of support for each other. Today they're so dispersed and isolated. . . ."

Teenagers today often find themselves friendly with peers who come from backgrounds quite unlike their own. What may be a rule or a value in one household may be unheard of in another. Teenagers talked a great deal about how their parents responded, particularly with rules and regulations, to their dating and going out. Although it often wasn't acknowledged, it was clear that teenagers' involvements with boyfriends or girl friends marked a break with their parents, a transfer of love and attachment, investing the situation with emotionally charged feelings from the beginning. The parents' response to their choice of dates, their time away from home, their independent decisions, is important to teenagers. It's a measure of how much their parents care as well as how much they accept and respect the teenagers' growing separateness and individuality. Some ambivalence, conflict and misunderstanding in negotiating this new terrain are inevitable.

One of the first fertile fields of conflict is curfew. When is late enough but not too late? Some teenagers said that even though they'd been going out in groups or with friends of the same sex for quite some time, their parents became much stricter when they started dating. Some parents, of course, solve ambivalences by making blanket rules like no dating until age seventeen. Inflexible rules were often reported to have bred contempt or, at the least, dishonesty.

"My parents believe you're so-called Polly Pure until you get married," says Maryanne, a Born-Again Christian who lives in Santa Monica, California. "They say, if you have a relationship with anyone, it has to be approved by your father. If it's okay with your father, you proceed. If he doesn't meet up to your father's standard, you stop the relationship." Maryanne shifts to a more comfortable position, one knee under her chin, her tam-o'-shanter tilted over her left eye. She's lively and jaunty, with curly black hair bobbed short around her face.

"My father, he grew up in east Texas. He's a Mexican or Chicano or Spanish or whatever you want to call it. He came from a real hard-nosed family. He broke away from the image of being greasy and sloppy and bumming around. Now that he has his own business, he doesn't have much in common anymore with that background. He's interested in classical music and the good things in life and he doesn't want me 'slumming,' as he puts it. My mother's basically the same way, but she's more lenient.

"Last year the rule was that I couldn't date until I was eighteen. Now that I'm almost eighteen, they said I could have started dating when I was seventeen if I'd wanted to.

"They have all kinds of rules for me. Number one: No kissing on the first date. Number two: No holding hands." Maryanne counts the rules off on her fingers. "If he gets fresh, slap his face. He has to pay, and he has to open the car door for you. That should go on at least three months. After that, then you can kiss, I guess, and after that, whatever happens happens, but you have to wait for all the good stuff until you get married.

"I'm totally opposite of what they think. I think if there's a guy you're attracted to, you should do everything to get to know him inside and out. I think if the relationship is good and you know your feelings, then you should do whatever you're comfortable doing.

"Usually I tell them I'm going out with friends. I haven't told them I have gone out six or seven times with this one guy, for instance. They know about two or three of the times I went out with him. I haven't done anything sexwise—I'm too much into my own thing to be involved with any one particular guy—but I don't talk to my parents about the way I feel about things.

"If I had a real problem, I wouldn't tell anybody. There's nobody I would trust. Maybe a little conversation with God, but that's about it. . . ." She pushes her hat back on her hair and smiles.

Rosie, a thirteen-year-old from San Francisco, also sees her parents as being too restrictive. Wearing white jeans and a T-shirt, she shakes her head with anger as she speaks about her mother and father.

"Every party I go to, they call beforehand to make sure it's chaperoned," she says. "I have to give this big explanation about everything I do. It's embarrassing. I suppose it's because I'm a girl. But none of my friends' mothers call and ask questions about liquor and drugs and chaperones. Usually she'll call anyway, even if I tell her adults will be there and there's no liquor—she'll call anyway. That's why I like to go to big dances. They can't go there and they can't call."

Rosie, the youngest of four (the others are boys), says her parents don't believe in premarital sex, alcohol, smoking or television. She's a television fanatic—at her girl friend's house—and she assumes she'll have premarital sex, smoke and drink when she's ready. "They have a rule I can't go to R-rated movies unless they take me. That means no *Saturday Night Fever*, no *Omen I*, no *Damian* or *Warriors* unless I sneak out or go when I'm staying over at my girl friend's. I've seen all those movies.

"I seem to be in arguments with them a lot," she says. "I was going to run away one time, and she said, 'Oh, you're watching too much television.' She couldn't accept that it was her, not TV."

As a general rule, parents have far fewer do's and don'ts outlined for their sons than they do their daughters. They tend to be more controlling and protective of their daughters and more lenient with their sons. They still believe that their sons will sow their wild oats and girls will not, or, at least, should not. The study of parents in Cleveland by the Harvard project on Human Sexual Learning shows less than 30 percent of mothers want to convey to their daughters that premarital sex is permissible, while almost 60 percent of mothers want to communicate to their sons that it is all right. Less than 40 percent of fathers wanted their daughters to think it was all right; 70 percent wanted their sons to think it was all right.[1]

Of course, conflict around curfews and many other rules often stems directly from a collision of interests: "I don't want to stay up until four A.M. waiting for you" vs. "You don't have to wait up for me; I have to go!" Parents vs. children; "protection" vs. "independence." Sometimes the conflict and hostility become so intense that the parent is seen as the enemy. One time, in fact, when I was interviewing several boys who felt quite alienated from their parents, one of the group suddenly asked me,

"You're not a parent, are you?" We were sitting in a pub, and the conversation all around us hushed. "Yes," I confessed. "I have a son and two stepdaughters." One boy, Dave, looked at me and gasped. "You're a parent?" he said incredulously. "Don't you feel *guilty* being a parent?" They were stunned. It was as if they had just realized they had been divulging secrets to the enemy.

Often, the most difficult conflicts reflect as much the teenagers' ambivalence about their independence as the fact that they're striving for it. They often behave in a way that encourages parents to respond as if they are dealing with small children rather than teenagers capable of handling responsibilities. They fail to meet commitments, fail to make the telephone call that would assuage their parents' worry, cry independence and then throw a tantrum like a two-year-old. The result is often punishment that fits the crime—usually an earlier curfew or restrictions on activity for a limited period of time.

"One day my parents got pretty pissed with me because they heard rumors of me drinking at the disco," said Ryan, a seventeen-year-old from a small Wisconsin town. "I wasn't at the disco, but I was drunk. They put a curfew on me—ten P.M. on weekdays—but they're getting more lenient on me."

"Another time," says Ryan's friend Guy, "we got a little intoxicated. We went down to my old girl friend's house, and we'd been drinking and everything, and we were sick. We couldn't drive back. So we sort of passed out down there, and we took off to come home about seven A.M. They don't have a phone number down there, so there was no way they could get hold of us. Dad called the state police about a half-hour before we got home. We both got grounded."

"I got my privileges dropped," said Ryan. "I couldn't go to the disco for four weeks, and I couldn't go snow skiing for a month. . . ."

"I was grounded for life," says Joe. "I couldn't do anything for about a week and then she [his mom] dropped it. I had to ask her permission for everything for a while. . . ."

"With my parents, the rule is, don't come in drunk and smelling of beer," says JoAnne, a high-school senior in Chapel Hill, North Carolina. "But in some ways, everything's changed since I turned eighteen. I'm not going to get wild and crazy. I can choose my own time to come in and I can go out on school nights. Since I turned eighteen, it's a change. Just the attitude is different. They'll let me do more, and in a way, I'm more responsible about it. When you turn eighteen, you're not any older. One day you're not eighteen and one you are. You're not any older, it's just that, in this state, you're legal."

In some cultures, the transition from childhood to adulthood is relatively smooth and is often marked by ceremony. Through a symbolic ceremony—and there are many, ranging from having one's teeth filed to a period of isolation or fasting, from undergoing a sexual initiation to a tattooing or mutilation of some part of the body—the young person is granted full adult status and then assumes the responsibilities of an adult in the community.

Since, in our culture, we have a prolonged adolescence and there is no precise point at which a young person is automatically considered an adult, the move from child to adult often isn't smooth. With the delay of economic independence and the assumption of adult responsibilities, parents find themselves living with a semi-mature or mature person who has replaced their child in many ways but still resembles him. Often he's a philosopher-in-residence who questions the parents' values, actions, decisions and advice.

"It's like suddenly you're dealing with an adult in your house who you did not choose to live with," said the mother of a fifteen-year-old and a sixteen-year-old in Minneapolis. "It's a shock. Older kids have a profound impact on the family. In many ways, it's harder, because the problems get worse at just the time that the mothers tend to be busier and have less time to listen. . . ."

In days gone by, these same children would have married, started to work and begun their own families. Being sexually mature but still not capable of independently negotiating their own way, adolescents face the predicament of a strong thrust for autonomy tempered by a dependence they often consider vile.

"I love my parents," says fourteen-year-old Johnny, "but sometimes I'd love to blow up the room that they're in."

Johnny has a small, innocent face, with silver bands around his teeth. His white windbreaker is tied around his waist. He wears Levi's jeans and a checkered shirt. "I'm not allowed out on weekdays during school," says this engaging young man. "On weekends, I can go on dates and to parties and to movies. They're strict with me. They're always saying I can't go here or there. Like this one night, I didn't get back here until two o'clock and they were really mad about it. They were all worried. Like if I don't tell them I'll be in at twelve and then I get in at 12:30, that's okay. But if they think I'm supposed to be here at twelve and I'm not, then they get mad."

Of course, most teenagers appreciate some limits. Even when they don't directly acknowledge their appreciation to their parents, they say that they know their parents care about them. The limits give them a sense of security and comfort. Sometimes it's also very helpful to young people to be able to say, 'My mother said I couldn't.'

"My mother always wants to know where I am, who I'm with and what time I'll be home," says Rosinna, a sophomore in high school in Detroit, Michigan. "That doesn't bother me at all. I have to call her and tell her where I am, and I have to be in at ten. At nine-thirty, I have to be on my stoop, because my neighborhood's getting bad."

"Sometimes I'm glad they say no," says Alice, a sixteen-year-old in

Brooklyn. "Like if my friends want to go somewhere and I don't really
want to go, I ask, and if they say no that's better than if I say no. Even if
I want to go, it's better than having parents who don't care. The girl
next door can go out anytime. She's younger, too, but her parents don't
care. Sometimes she's out until early in the morning. She's been having
boyfriends since she was eleven years old.

"There's this other girl on my block, too. She's nine years old. She has
a brush in her pocket and she's always carrying a radio. She was going
out with this boy ten years old. They'd go off by themselves, and her
mother wouldn't say anything. The girl acts older than I do. She doesn't
really look nine years old or act it, but she is. I can imagine her when
she's my age! Forget it!"

Sometimes parents think they're being wise letting their children "do
their own thing." But not establishing perimeters for them is often the
same as denying them limits, which they need in their development.

Since Lillian had a dearth of rules or guidance from her parents, she
had to set up her own rules, which often felt paralyzing. For her, restrictions imposed by an adult would have been a saving grace. Now she says
she's afraid of everything; she has a difficult time establishing boundaries and she rarely relaxes. She always rides with her brakes on.

"I find myself very hung up on spirituality," she says. "I need to feel
giving to someone. I know it's okay to want an emotional commitment
before there's anything physical, but I carry it to an extreme. I ask
myself existential questions to the point where it's almost repulsive.
Like, do I mean this kiss? Is it coming from a genuine emotion?

"It's self-imposed because I've always been let loose all night. Sometimes I wish that didn't exist within myself. I abort relationships before
they have a chance. I ask myself these questions—should I, shouldn't I,
and like, What do I really feel? before I can know what I feel. When
you keep such a tight rein on yourself physically, you can cut yourself
off from healthy experimentation and interaction."

Of course, value systems vary greatly. What is perfectly acceptable in
one family is unheard of in another. At one end of the spectrum was
Jackie's family, in a small Michigan town.

"My brother Eddie, he was about ten years old and he was looking at
Playboy magazine one day on the playground," said Julia, a high school
junior at Columbia Central Senior High in Brooklyn, Michigan. "Anyway, he got caught by the principal. The principal wanted to spank him,
but they called home first. The principal's secretary called my parents
and asked what they should do after they caught him. My dad and mom
were home, and my dad said to spank him. So they spanked him. My
mom said he couldn't look at that magazine. . . ."

At the other extreme are parents who overidentify with their children
and project their own interests and curiosities onto them. Often these
parents encourage teenagers to get involved in situations for which

they're not ready. Or they push them into competing for acceptance and popularity in ways that may have more to do with the parents' needs than the children's. By extension, if the children are accepted, than the parents are accepted. Another aspect of this dynamic is that if the parents treat the teenagers as equals, the parents can keep themselves feeling young.

"There's a tremendous role to be played by the parents," says Dianne Stern, a mother of two teenage sons in Scarsdale, New York. "Some parents are very concerned that their kids are part of the group, and they actively discourage friendships with anyone they consider on the fringes.

"I have spoken to parents who were unhappy because their daughter was not in class with the 'in' group. . . . I couldn't believe my ears with this one mother. She was so upset because her daughter had been put into a class with 'unpopular' kids. I said to her, 'Maybe she'll get something positive out of being with some new children in a different classroom.' That's all I said, but I was horrified. . . ."

Dynamics within families have a much greater impact on individual teenagers than the more superficial rules and regulations, which are a means of working out behavior acceptable to the family unit. The interactions between fathers and their daughters, mothers and daughters, mothers and sons and fathers and sons ultimately have a far greater impact on the teenagers' growth than do restrictions put on a child who comes in late. Oftentimes, issues that can be traced back to the childhood and adolescence of a parent become central to the parent's ability to let a child grow up. In some cases, for instance, a parent can quite easily move from being the interested listener and parental confidant into the role of wanting to be number-one friend and manager—social manager, business manager and sexual manager.

"Last vacation, I had a lot of trouble with my parents," says Julia Todd an eighteen-year-old college freshman from St. Paul, Minnesota. "My sisters and I were in the kitchen doing dishes, and my sister said to me, 'Well, Julia, how's your sex life?' I said, 'Oh, it's really great.' Well, my mother overheard that and flipped out. Later, Mother sits me down and tells me you shouldn't have sex at your age, but if you do, use protection. Then she says, 'Do you really love him enough to spend the rest of your life with him?' I was saying, 'Enough, Mother!' I can remember my mother saying when I barely knew boys were boys and girls were girls, she's saying, 'Your dad would be very disappointed if you ever got involved sexually with a boy before you were married.' "

One problem Julia talked about, and other girls mentioned as well, was the problem of their *mothers* falling for their boyfriends. In this situation, the mother is competing with her daughter, living vicariously through her or using her in a way to fulfill her own fantasies.

"The thing that really bugs me," says Julia, tossing her long brown

hair out of her eyes, "is there was this one guy I was going with in high
school and my mother fell in love with him. She'd always say to me, 'Oh,
how can you do that? Or, 'How will Sam feel about this or that?' Like
she considered his feelings first, over mine. Now it's the same with
Brad. She's always saying, 'How is Brad going to feel about your doing
this or that?' She has all her energy invested in *him!*"

This sort of involvement can be a way of hanging on.

"It's hard when they won't let you grow up," says Julia, who's the
youngest of five in her Catholic family. "At Thanksgiving, for instance,
I was talking to my sister, and I told her that during my first month at
college at the University of Wisconsin, I'd gone with some friends into
Chicago to get pizza one night and then that we'd gone to the Playboy
Club and danced there. I told her we didn't get back to Madison until 4
o'clock in the morning. My mother blew up. 'You didn't tell me before!'
She was screaming about it. She was so hurt and angry. I didn't tell her
when I did it.

"It's almost like she's driving me away on purpose. I want her to have
an interest in my life, but not in telling me what to do and not to do. I
told her I'd been to see *The Rocky Horror Show* and she said it was
trash. Thank God I didn't tell her I saw *Deep Throat*.

"Part of it's because I'm the baby in the family, and she's trying to
hold onto me.

"When I started school, she called me every day. Sometimes she
called me two and three times a day. She wanted to know who I was
meeting, how I liked my classes, everything! I finally told her, 'Don't
call me everyday, please!'

"I told her I appreciated her being interested in me, but it was too
much. Her reaction was, 'Okay, I won't take an interest in you at all. I
won't ask you anything. If you want me not to take an interest in you
like my parents didn't in me, okay, I won't!' "

For James, like Julia, the same air of parental competitiveness and
involvement was a real problem. "Every time I bring a girl over to our
house, or if anybody just stops by, my dad starts talking to her," says
James, a tall seventeen-year-old who plays basketball for his high-
school team in San Francisco. "My dad's real charming, and he doesn't
think I pay enough attention to the girls, so maybe he thinks he's showing me how. But it really bugs me. It's gotten so I don't want anybody to
come over. I never get a chance to talk to them. He's always telling
them about his ideas and showing them pictures of our trips and everything."

Dr. Maj-Britt Rosenbaum at Albert Einstein College of Medicine
talks about the need for a "healthy gap" between parents and teenagers,
enabling teenagers to have some privacy and autonomy and to build
confidence in making and managing their own decisions. It's a balance

of guidance and involvement that maintains a fine line between interest and overinterest. When parents and their teenagers strike this balance, a sense of trust and mutual respect can be built between them.

"I'm really shocked when my parents don't let me do something," says sixteen-year-old Jeannie Fox in Boston. "I'm so used to them trusting my judgment. When they say no, I rarely question it because they save their *no*'s for things they feel strongly about.

"The only thing that bothers me sometimes is if I come in from a party or a date, my mother is ready to sit down and talk about what I did. They're really interested in everything that happens to me, and even though I tell them a lot, sometimes they're offended when I don't want to talk to them. Usually they understand, but when they don't, it drives me up the wall."

"My parents have faith in my moral system and the way they brought me up," says Liz Kelly, a freshman at Northwestern University. "I really appreciate it because they trust me and I know they do, so I feel responsible and good about myself.

"They seem to know what's going on with me. Some parents don't know about their kids—or they project their own fears. I guess my mother knew it wasn't a big thing to go bowling with a boy in the fifth grade."

Liz said that her mother, who has six children altogether, has a good sense of herself, and thus has a warm relationship with her children. Liz said that wasn't the case for some people she knew. She suggested that when I write about parents and their children, I think about parental jealousy and how some mothers get jealous of their daughters, which can be a source of great conflict.

As a result of her advice, I did think about it. In the course of my interviews, I heard several young women talk about their mothers' jealousy, which was usually disguised in competitiveness or in accusations, lack of affection or setups for unpleasant results. "My mother told my father she thought I was a lesbian," Joanie reports. "She got him all riled up, and it was so ridiculous. I wasn't going out with anybody special, and so they get into this whole thing over maybe I had homosexual tendencies. I was having a bad year anyway, and that just made it worse. It was hell. I couldn't figure out why she would say that except for I think she just hates me. She's told me a couple of times that I ruined her figure when she was pregnant with me. She says she wouldn't have flab on her stomach if I hadn't been so late. . . ."

"With my mom, it's just the opposite of jealousy," Julia had said. "She's not jealous. She just lives through me, which might be worse. She got married when she was too young, so she never really established a life of her own. My mother is the kind where if I got the lead in the school play or whatever, she'd go around telling everybody."

One of the most difficult aspects of a daughter's or son's growing up is the seductiveness toward the parent of the opposite sex and the mutual feelings of attraction. Of course, feelings of attraction and interest are quite normal and healthy. In many ways, the parent of the opposite sex and the parent of the same sex each provide a model. But often the feelings frighten both the parents and the adolescents. The incest taboo is strong, but because many family structures are less stable and clear-cut than they used to be, erotic behavior and incestuousness have fewer built-in and ritualized obstacles. Particularly if the parents are divorced or if the parents' sense of themselves is not strong, the tension often mounts. The problems often seem more overt and difficult for fathers and daughters than they do for mothers and sons, whose sexual interplay is more subtle but often just as troublesome.

"My father's very possessive of my relationships and my attitudes," says sixteen-year-old Annie, who lives in Hartford, Connecticut. "There was a period of my life when he was absolutely my best friend—from eleven to fourteen. But that doesn't exist anymore.

"Now we sort of play chess with our eyes about my sexual concerns and his sexual concerns. He'll tell me things to tell my boyfriend as sort of a substitute for him. Like he'll say, 'Tell so and so don't forget to tell you not to worry. . . .' Or he'll say, 'Have you seen that exhibit at the such and such gallery? Why don't you ask him to take you there.' He knows what I like. When I was younger, he would take me places, to see exhibits and shops and all. Now he'll say, 'Do you go to museums with your friends?' like they've taken over for him."

Annie, whose long brown hair drapes over one eye and the shoulder of her jacket, was thrown into the role of surrogate mate to her father when her mother deserted them after a marital separation. It was a situation that intensified their normal feelings of interdependence at a difficult time in Annie's development.

"Just after they were separated, two and a half years ago, my mother rapidly moved out of the country for a year, so my dad and I had the house to ourselves. I did all the cooking, Dad did the cleaning and we'd have dinner together every night. We really played house together, and I had all the responsibility since I was the one left at home." Annie, a lovely girl with a wide, somber face, studies her long, unpolished fingernails. At sixteen, she's yet to discover childhood.

Although the role of surrogate wife and girl friend to her father kept Annie from making friends and being with peers her age, there was no physical contact or overt sexual interactions between her father and her. For Melissa, it was different. Her father carried his own problems and lack of limits to her and gave her an incestuous introduction to the sexual world.

"I always had sexuality," says Melissa, a high-school senior in Baltimore, Maryland, who has frizzy blond hair and a sweet, heart-shaped face. "It only got complicated after puberty.

"That was about the time that my father got a lot of interest in me. He started tucking me in at night, and then he started touching me. This was in the summer, when I didn't wear clothes, and he'd tuck me in. That didn't bother me, but then he started kissing me and I didn't like it. My sexuality didn't include males yet.

"I was confused and I didn't know what was going on. Then he'd say I'm glad you are growing into such a lovely young woman. It felt good to get his praise. He'd tuck me in and then he'd sit and talk to me. We'd sort of cuddle. That was nice. Sometimes he was naked, too. I don't know where my mother was.

"A couple of things really scared me. One time we were touching. We were in the bathroom and he pushed my hand toward his penis. It felt so big and hard it scared me. Another time he was touching me, and he said, 'You know this is your vagina, don't you?' I said yes. He was touching me inside. I know it was when he was starting to feel sexy towards me I got scared."

When Melissa started feeling sexually turned on by her father, she got particularly scared. Since he seemed to have no limits, and she didn't know the rules of the game, she had reason to be frightened. Now Melissa is in college, and she's going steady with one particular boy her mother likes and her father hates. Unfortunately, it may take her many years to unravel an understanding of her own sexuality, her own angers and anxieties and confusions.

Even in households where the parents have been married many years and the rules of family behavior are well defined, and in situations in which the parents are clear about their priorities and values, fathers still have a difficult time relating to the changes in their daughters and mothers to the changes in their sons. It's confusing and disorienting for the child they have known for years to become a developed young woman or man who has a crush on them. "It worries me," said the thoughtful father of a fourteen-year-old. "It's so clear she has such a crush on me, and she's so seductive. I just don't want her thinking that a boy her age will be as mature as I am—or for her to compare him to me. It's flattering, but I don't really know what to do with it." It's a normal, healthy phenomenon. And with time, the crush will transfer to a person her own age. In the meantime, parents have to cope with their own discomfort. Most muddle through quite well. They appreciate the special attention, and they enjoy discussions and exchanges that have moved on to a new level intellectually as well. When their teenagers begin to date, they learn to deal with a new set of discomforts and, again, do a good job of it. Some parents, however, turn off and withdraw or make teasing, mocking comments as a way of coping. Sometimes

they also provoke arguments and situations that create safe distance
through hostility.

In Harold's case, his mother's teasing and inability to give him privacy seems to maintain distances. It has also played a part in his reticence to date. At seventeen, Harold is tall and blond, restless and unsure
of himself. When he tells me his parents had just finalized their divorce
that year, the bottled anger and fury seem ready to burst the fragile
container of his body. "I believe in certain gods," Harold says, picking
at his fingernails and studying them in great detail. "It's a religion I've
figured out for myself. It's matriarchal, run by a matriarch, not a
patriarch. . . ."

Harold attributed the reason for his parents' breakup to his father's
paying too much attention to his job. "He thought my mother was happy, but she wasn't," Harold says. "Finally she got fed up with it all."

And now Harold lives with his mother, who teases him about nonex-
istent girl friends, and sees his father once a month. "My dad's pretty
liberal," says Harold. "He doesn't think sex is all evil or anything. My
mom, though, she tries to act liberal, but she really isn't. I have some
girls who are my friends, not girl friends, who come by sometimes. If I
have one of them, like Pat, up in my room, just talking, she gets all
uptight. She tells me I'm supposed to entertain them downstairs. But if
we're downstairs, she listens to everything we say. She thinks any girl
who's been in my room is a slut. She thinks all the girls who are my
friends are sluts. We go to school together, and she calls them sluts.

"I don't have any girl friends," he says, shaking his head furiously.
"I've never even had my arm around a girl yet! I want to tell her off
when she says things like that. Next time I will!"

I asked Harold what he would tell his mother if he told her off.

"I'd tell her, 'How stupid! She's not my girl friend. She is my friend,
so if you think she's a slut, keep it to yourself. You're old-fashioned and
Victorian and you try to act like you're not Victorian! I'm tired of you
buttin' in like that. Quit buttin' in!' "

Seventeen-year-old Nicki and her father also seem to use hostility as
a way of coping with one another. Nicki, perky, lively and neat, is wearing small gold earrings, an orange blouse and a flowered skirt when we
talk in New Hartford, Connecticut. Nicki's father is a teacher, as is her
mother. Nicki's parents have lived in this town for the twenty-three
years of their marriage.

"If I go bike riding, my dad says, 'I don't want you stopping and
talking to every boy you see,' " says Nicki. "See, sometimes I stop on
my bicycle to talk to a boy, and that's no big deal, but my dad makes a
big deal out of it.

"One morning last fall, I was in a bad mood and I was sitting in the
car. My dad was going to give me a ride to school. He said, 'Why aren't

you smiling? You're always pouting.' I didn't say anything. I was really feeling bad about having broken up with my boyfriend and I just didn't have anything to say. Then my dad got mad and bam, he hit me. I got out and walked to school and bawled all the way. . . ."

Sometimes, because a father feels inadequate and awkward about expressing affection toward his daughter in an appropriate way, he reacts violently when his attempts to soothe are rejected. Misunderstanding, of course, breeds on itself, and the affection and good feeling that are there in both people are lost in the shuffle.

"I've never told my dad I love him," says Nicki. "That's terrible. I had a dream two nights ago that my dad died and I had never said I loved him. Now I want to, but I don't know if I can."

Nicki said her father puts her down at every opportunity. Her theory was that all fathers put their daughters down like that. Once again, the put-down seems to reflect an inability of the father to express directly a healthy affection for his daughter.

"Every girl I talk to, their fathers tell them they're fat," says Nicki. "Mine, too. Every time I dress up to look nice and go out, my dad cuts me down. Like the other night, I put on my dress and you know how you say it, I said, 'Oh, does this make me look fat?' in hopes of a compliment because I wanted to be reassured that I looked nice. I thought I looked pretty nice, but I wanted to hear it. He said 'Everything makes you look fat.' The night of the prom, when I had on a long dress and I felt like I looked really good, he says, 'You have a zit on your face. Cover up the zit on your face.'

"When John and I broke up, and then later when I started going out with someone else and we broke up, my dad said, 'Doesn't anybody like you?' "

Jennifer's father reacted to her development with hostility similar to Nicki's father. Jennifer's father's focus, however, was to mention to his daughter on many occasions that she "better never come home pregnant or you'll be out of the house!"

"He thinks I'm going to be exactly like our neighbor," says seventeen-year-old Jennifer, "just because I'm friends with her. She got pregnant three different times, and now she's got two kids. She had a miscarriage once, but her sons are by different fathers. Anyway he's always telling me, 'If you turn out like her, I don't want to see your face in this place!' "

Jennifer, of course, doesn't understand the source of her father's misunderstanding of her; nor does she understand his conflicts. She just hears the unjustified accusations and feels guilty for withholding affection from him, feels angry and, at the same time, in need of his approval.

She sits, tears in her eyes, talking about him and the interactions in her home. She told about what had happened the night before our interview, when she was going to bed. Her parents had just had a fight, and Jennifer was angry at the way her father had treated her mother.

"Good night, Mom," Jennifer called from her bed.

"Good night, honey," her mother called upstairs in a litany the two repeat each evening. "Have a good sleep. I love you."

"Good night, Mom. Have a good sleep. I love you, too."

Then Jennifer's father called from the bathroom. "Good night, Jenny."

"Good night, Dad."

"I love you."

"Okay."

"I just couldn't bring myself to say I love you to him," Jennifer said. "I'm too mad at him for the way he treats my mother. I despise the way he treats her. I don't like the way he treats me, either. Like the other day he said to my mom, 'She's your daughter, not mine.' That really hurt my feelings."

Tears rolled down Jennifer's eyes. "I used to kiss my father every night, but I haven't. Not since I was thirteen years old."

If parents' reactions to their child's sexual development is a complex network of feelings and concerns, then their reaction to their child's actual sexual behavior is even more complex. Again, parents of daughters seem to react much more negatively to their sexual behavior than to that of their sons. Although sometimes the discovery that a boy is having sex is very traumatic for the family, more often the family takes a boy's sexual behavior in stride. His sexual relationship is considered more normal and healthy, whereas when a girl starts having a sexual relationship, you would think, as one girl put it, "that a hurricane had hit the house!"

When Candace told her parents that she was sleeping with her boyfriend of two years' duration, for instance, their response was hysteria and tears. They set down restrictions to try to prevent it from happening again.

"I'm not allowed to go to my boyfriend's house anymore," says Candy, looking at the pattern her tanned toe was tracing on the floor as we talked. We were in Atlanta, Georgia, sitting in a small park near the high school where Candy is a senior. At seventeen, Candy is long-legged and lean, a country girl in her blue jeans and bare feet. Her large hazel eyes are bright and sincere, and her straight black hair brushes against the shoulders of her orange T-shirt as she talks.

"I've been going through hell the past month," she says. "They found out we were going to bed, and it's been hell ever since I told her. She asked me and I told her. I'm not ashamed. They made us go and talk to our minister. He looked at our reasoning, and listened to us and he didn't make us feel like we were bad or anything. He didn't give us a no or yes.

"My mom was real scared. She cut down Dave a lot. She said she never liked him anyway and a lot of other things that just weren't true. She carried on and on, and once she got started, she'd lose control completely, it seemed. She'd start screaming at me. I'd take it up to a point, but when she got real mad, I would just walk out.

"We talked a lot about it, and I said we'll try to compromise and reason about it so you can understand. She gave me articles on sex, and we read them. We've done what she's asked us to do, but she hasn't really listened to me.

"Dave and I are real close and real open with each other. We can talk about *anything*. There's no subject that's off limits or that's uncomfortable whether it's close to us or far away.

"My dad, being a lawyer, he copes more. My dad looks at me as a little girl. Now he says, 'My little girl's not a little girl anymore.' He said before, 'Just tell your mom you're gonna stop having sex, that will make her feel better.'

"I said, 'No, I'm not going to tell her that because it's not true.' He'd like me to stop, too. That's part of why he said that. The truth is since I've been through all this, we haven't had sex because I've been too nervous.

"They know they can't tell me exactly what to do. They can influence me, but they can't tell me what to do."

Candy got tears in her eyes talking about her mother's reactions. "That's one of the worst things parents can do," she said. "They can cut the things that mean a lot to you. We don't do that to them. That killed me that my mom cut Dave down the way she did, and that she would let herself say such mean things about him. It's one thing to cut me, but to cut the person I love is worse than cutting me.

"I've realized lately that parents are people. I try to consider their viewpoints, but I don't think that they consider mine. I don't think my parents understand what it means that Dave and I care about each other the way we do. Making love means something to us. . . ."

Besides being aware of a child's sexual relationship, parents these days often find themselves in the position of making a decision about whether they'll accept their youngster sleeping with his or her lover in their house. They may have come to terms with their teenager's sexual relationship, but next they have the question of whether or not they will let it into their home. In some situations, the parents' opinion is clear. They don't want their children having sexual interactions in their homes, no matter how old they are, either because they don't think it's right or for the simple fact that it makes them uncomfortable.

Some young people, of course, aren't interested in sleeping with a boyfriend or girl friend in their parents' house. They know they'd be ill at ease or at the least, self-conscious.

"I don't think I'd want to do that," says eighteen-year-old Nellie in Los Angeles. "You have to have some distance. I don't think my parents worry about whether I've slept with anyone or not. They trust me and my judgment. But I don't really know that they'd want me to bring someone home. I think it'd be too close for comfort. Our apartment isn't that big—all the bedrooms are off one hallway. They wouldn't be shocked, but it'd just be tense. It would interrupt everyone's privacy."

In other situations, teenagers feel that it's appropriate. Usually when they discuss it with their parents and decide that they can all be comfortable with it, the arrangement works.

"My parents liked Miriam a lot," says Keith, a high-school senior in Manhattan. "They let us sleep together here. It didn't start easy. We had slept together at her mother's house, but not here. And then I told my mom, 'Listen, Mom, Miriam's going to sleep here for a week. Her mother's in East Hampton, and she doesn't want to stay alone at her house.'

" 'Okay. Should I make up the bed for her in the guest room?'

" 'No. She'll sleep in my room."

Pause. " 'Oh, okay.'

"My father was against it," says Keith. "But then my mother convinced him that there's nothing wrong with the act of love and that Miriam and I loved each other, and that if that was what we were doing, and we were being responsible, that there was no reason we couldn't sleep together in their house. . . ."

Clinton, a nineteen-year-old in Los Angeles, and his eighteen-year-old girl friend, Laura, also worked out an understanding with their parents.

"We'd sleep together here or over at her house," the tall, brown-eyed teenager said. "Laura and I were very open and very positive and very mature. No one ever questioned it because we gave them no room to really object to our behavior. We weren't overt and careless. We appreciated the situation we were in and respected it.

"The first time she stayed at our house, we didn't sleep together. We were studying and stuff and it was hard to get a ride home for her, so I volunteered to sleep on the couch, and that's the way it was the first couple of times.

"Her mother was open. She didn't like secrets or sneaking around, so she put it out on the table. She was hesitant about my parents' reaction, but that was all. I slept there before Laura ever slept here.

"Then I independently explained the situation to my parents. As soon as they knew her mother was aware and consented, that was that. That was all they were worried about. They didn't want her saying she was staying at a friend's house when she was staying here or anything like that. They didn't have to ask us about birth control. We were both mature enough to take care of it."

Many parents surprise themselves with attitudes they didn't realize they had. In theory, for instance, they might think that they will react in a liberal way to their child's sexual life, but when they're confronted with the fact of it, they often feel they've somehow been betrayed.

"One time when my folks went to San Diego, Randy spent the night at my house," says Kathleen, crossing her long legs and brushing back her hair. "Before that, I would never have sex in my parents house— never! But I broke the barrier that time. Well, after a couple of days, when my folks were back, my mother confronts me with a condom wrapper. She says, 'I found this in the wash!' I said, 'Oh really, I wonder how it got there?' I didn't let on that Randy had been in the house. I acted like maybe it had fallen into my clothes or something.

"All my life, my mother's been really cool," Kathleen says. "She's said things like, 'If you want birth control, come to me. Ask me anything.' You know, really laid back and cool. Well, two weeks after she'd told me about finding the condom wrapper in the wash, she went into a flying rage. She started screaming and yelling at me and calling me a little piece of trash, telling me she was going to tell my father.

"I said, 'Hey, wait a minute. Are you the same mother who was telling me to come to you and tell you whatever I wanted?' She was yelling and screaming, 'We don't want a motel here in our house or anything like it!'

"That really blew me away. I thought, 'What does my mother think—that I'm really promiscuous? If I go out with other people, will she think I'm sleeping with them? That kept me with Randy for a long time—more than I think I would have stayed with him otherwise, because I was going through all those head trips over my mother and what she thought of me. But finally we broke off anyway. . . .'"

"I think that trust from the parents to the child and the child to the parents is most difficult in adolescence," says Toni Donnelly, a mother of two teenage sons. "The child needs to be confident that his parents trust him. But the parents are remembering what they did at that age and you *don't* trust them half the time. . . ."

Certainly trust is difficult to achieve. But it comes from both directions, from allowing one another space and not flaunting disregard or disrespect. It's possible for teenagers and their parents to disagree and still live together harmoniously, as long as they can learn to appreciate the concern involved in a different vantage point.

"Looking back," says eighteen-year-old Lauren, "I learned a lot [during that rough period of time with my parents]. But I realize now that they were telling me their position. They were learning just as much as I was. One thing I learned is that I don't want to go out with a boy who can't get along with my parents. It's a sign of maturity to get along with them. A relationship is not something that has to be out of the home to be good. It makes it so much easier with my parents because they know me better if they see me with my friends. It also keeps me from being different with grown-ups than I am at school. Some kids are afraid of their parents, but I'm not afraid of mine. I like them, and I like to be with them and their friends, too."

It seems to me that the best relationships between parents and their teenagers grow out of mutual regard and a trust that parents will be parents—will set limits and guidelines, but will listen with respect to how their teenagers feel. From what I heard, teenagers want their parents to have authority but not be authoritarian. They also very much want and need their parents' trust and esteem. When adolescents behave in mature and responsible ways, their efforts should be recognized. Certainly, they are sexual creatures and have sexual feelings, sensations, desires and emotions. How they learn to deal with what they feel reflects in large measure how they feel about themselves, which in turn reflects how their parents feel about them. If parents support and respect their teenagers and treat them as individuals in their own right, they'll most likely be happy about their future relationships.

"You think you'll like your kids when they're grown up because you expect them to grow up just like you and your husband, don't you?" demanded eighteen-year-old Chris.

"No, I don't think that's the reason," I said.

He studied my face. Then he nodded his head.

"You're liberal because there wasn't that much you didn't do," he said knowingly. "You were probably a wild kid. But what if your kids grew up to be Nazis? What then? You wouldn't like that now, would you?"

Ah, he'd gotten me. "No, I wouldn't like it one bit. I'd hate it."

"Well, they could," he said victoriously. "Anything is possible. You've got no control ultimately. You can't force what you believe down your children's throats. No matter what it is!"

Yes, I admitted, with or without me, my kids would grow up. They would become who they are. But didn't I have a responsibility, as a parent, to guide them?

Chris was silent for a moment. Then he spoke. "If I were a parent, I would let my child know what I thought but I wouldn't try to make them believe the same way," he said. "There's a point at which you realize you're an individual, and you want other people to recognize that. And when they don't recognize it, that's when you begin to rebel."

Dave nodded his head in agreement as Chris continued. "Parents are so sure their kids are going to grow up the same as them, and when they don't, they get so annoyed. The basic trouble is that parents won't accept their kids for who they are." Chris sipped his beer and looked at me. A truce had been established.

PART III

10.

Spin the Bottle

Although there are some eleven and twelve and thirteen-year-olds who find themselves in bed with a person of the opposite sex, most do not. The vast majority of our preteens and young adolescents are still quite deeply entrenched in discovering themselves, their same-sex peers and the phenomenon of the opposite sex. Rituals, hocus-pocus and group mythology most often guide them in the realm of boy-girl land and their first experiments in the ways to behave. The folk wisdom of the young has its own distinct logic that addresses the quite indistinct vision they have of themselves and The Other.

"If you're dating *before* Easter holiday, it's a fact that you'll break up after the holiday," said thirteen-year-old Zach, explaining to me why he was no longer "going steady" with his girl friend. "We agreed to break up beforehand, since we would have afterwards anyway."

"Why would you have broken up anyway?" I asked.

"It's that period of three weeks you don't see 'em," he said. "You always break up afterwards. It's easier, too, because of the holiday, you don't want to risk two-timing your girl friend."

Parents who dread the onset of their child's puberty rites in the 1980s only have to remember what it felt like the summer before they grew three inches in two months, when they had a crush on the boy down the street and gave him an elbow in the stomach whenever they had a chance. If they remember themselves and listen closely—as well as watch—their fears will be allayed.

"My first crush was on this boy, Bobby," says Lana, a brown-haired fifteen-year-old from Brooklyn, New York. "He and Danny were my best friends. We were a trio, and we used to go to Danny's house. His parents would take us swimming and to the movies. One time Danny whispered in my ear, 'Bobby loves you.' Oh, I loved him, too. I was madly in love with him. We used to write notes in class. I remember his notes. He'd say things like, 'You're my best girl friend. I love you so much. How do you love me:

A little
A lot
Very, Very Much
TONS

"I'd have to circle one. And of course I'd circle TONS."

Young adolescents, who in fact should be defined by emotional age rather than chronological age, are in a state that is more thought and talk than action. It's a time when they're beginning to try on the bodies, the emotions, the roles and the thinking of the adults they are *in the process* of becoming. They are still at a great distance from being firmly established inside their own bodies and responses. Although people can find themselves in this stage of development when they're in their twenties, the most common time people experience it is when they're near the end of middle childhood—between the ages of ten and fourteen. This is a time when great safety is found in hiding behind a role instead of being exposed in a one-on-one setting. It's a stage of game playing and talking to people of the opposite sex through the media of roles, groups and rituals. In this way, they can experiment with very scary things in a safe environment.

"I'm really attracted to this boy in my class," thirteen-year-old Judy tells me. "And I think he's pretty attracted to me, too."

"What do you talk about?"

"*Talk?*" she said, her face turning bright red. "We don't talk!"

"What do you do?"

"I don't even look at him, let alone talk to him! I wouldn't know what to say! He says things to this friend about me—I can tell he's talking about me sometimes, but talk . . . !"

Usually this time of life coincides with the beginning of early adolescence and its subtle bodily changes. As secondary sexual characteristics begin to develop, a quiet courtship dance begins. It happens in all species. The male of the lion attracts the lioness. The smell of the female dog attracts the male. Salamanders literally dance, and so do adolescents. Breasts begin to grow, hips begin to spread, shoulders begin to broaden and the dance begins. Before boys have their first wet dream, before girls begin to menstruate, their bodies begin to change and they begin to get an inkling of unpredictability about themselves. They understand that they will become adult someday, but they still have not grown into their bodies. They work hard trying to get a clear picture of what happens sexually.

"I remember being aware of sex and being intrigued and excited by it in the fourth grade," says Clinton, who is now six feet, two inches tall. "It opened up my imagination and fantasy and all that stuff. I used to do a lot of wondering what it was all about and trying to get a clear picture of exactly what happened. I grew up in the middle of a city, and when you grow up in the middle of the city, you hear everything on the streets. You're made aware very early on. I never even pictured my parents doing any such thing. I never *imagined* that they would have anything to do with what I was hearing about or thinking about. What you heard on the streets was dirty and exciting, not what could take place on the old homestead."

Sex is funny, unreal, mysterious and at the same time, an exciting, almost unbelievable prospect.

"When we were younger," Ingrid told me, "they started tearing down houses around our house, and us kids in the neighborhood were always scavenging things out of the rubble. Well, one time I found this torn-up book. It was all covered with dirt and had ripped pages and all—but it was a book with pictures of a man and a oman and it showed all these different positions and all these graphic scenes. Well, when I found it, we ran to this empty house and I was the narrator and this girl and boy got into all the positions as I described them. It was really funny. We just about died laughing."

The difference between gender identification and sexual contact is wondrously thin, almost an invisible line.

"In the fifth grade, we had this really good teacher," says Ingrid, whose large brown eyes and olive skin create a vision of Greece in the summertime. "One time he said something in class about the sex of a woman and we giggled and said 'Ooohh . . .' And he said, 'Not *that* kind of sex. I mean the *gender* of a person.' And he got out the dictionary for all of us to look it up together.

"Then Charles Simpson says, 'So what about the coatroom kind of sex and the other kind of sex?' He explained that sexual intercourse was when a man and a woman got together and merged into this union. Sometimes babies came from this union and sometimes not, he said."

Many times, when discussing sex with one another, when thinking about it themselves, it seems so fantastic and farfetched that it is quite difficult to imagine "it" actually happening to *them*. It must be something they dreamed up—and most certainly, like Columbus finding America, they often feel that they are the first explorers in this new territory.

"Here's a good question for you to ask teenagers," thirteen-year-old

Tom said, picking up the pleat of his pressed jeans. " 'How do you feel that you differ from the children of the fifties and the forties?' All the kids think they're more advanced, but in talking to my parents, I find they went through the same stages.

"I remember coming home when I was ten and asking her [my mother] if she knew what sixty-nine was. I was sure it was invented three days ago in my generation. When she got it right, I said, 'How did you know that?' She said, 'It was our favorite number when I was young.' "

Many young adolescents are light-years older intellectually than they are socially and emotionally. Tom, for instance, is about five foot two and quite thin. At thirteen, he hasn't started his growth spurt. He has thick brown hair and he tosses his head every time I look down at my notes. Actually, he shakes his head violently and then brushes his hand over it and pats his hair into place. He does it over and over again as we talk. He stretches out on the couch in the guest room of his parents' lovely home in Grosse Pointe, Michigan. He is very serious, thoughtful and reserved. He thinks hard about what he says and measures his words.

"I live in a neighborhood that I'd call too fast," he says. "Some kids around here start at age nine or ten what some people don't start until they're much older. Possibly because of extreme boredom or rebellion against Republican parents. There's an extreme amount of boy-girl parties, a lot of feeling out and heavy petting in the fifth and sixth grades."

Later, Tom said, "I expect that I'll have intercourse for the first time anywhere from sixteen at the earliest to twenty at the latest. Whenever it happens, it will depend on a) how long we've been together, b) how old she is and how old I am, c) how much we like each other, d) circumstance presenting itself—and e) contraception. I don't want to get in trouble. Basically it depends on mutual feelings."

Tom estimated that "About one percent of my age group have participated in sexual intercourse. The people who brag about it are the ones who haven't. The ones who have are usually unknowns."

Often, because young people articulate sophisticated thoughts, parents have the impression that they are operating on an emotional level that is equally mature. Just how far off base we get sometimes in bringing our adult expectations and concerns to our children's reality is often demonstrated during candid exchanges with them. One father told me about a discussion he had had about sexuality with his son, Mickey. Mickey had talked about his views on girls, dating, schoolwork and sports when he said, "Puberty's a problem. In my school, we take showers and some kids put a towel on because they're embarrassed because they have pubic hair.

The father reports that he then asked his son: Is there competition about penis size?

Mickey answered: No. But there's a lot of water fights.

When I interviewed fourteen-year-old Louis in Hartford, Connecticut, I made the same mistake.

"One of the problems with girls and taking them out," Louis had said to me, "is that you have to try to entertain them. It would be much better if you just saw it as being friends so nobody would have to entertain anybody else. Some people say being friends spoils things, though."

"Why?" I asked.

"Because you can't do the same things with a friend as with someone else because you respect a friend and don't want to hurt a friend."

"Like what?"

"Like things on their mind."

"Like what?"

"Doing things."

"Like having sex?"

"Oh, that's too much! Not that much!" he exclaimed, reddening, hitting his head with his hand. "Not *that* much!"

"Then what, exactly?"

"Oh, like sticking your hand under her shirt," he said, blushing again, "or under her pants. That other is on their mind, but they wouldn't go that far at this age because they're too scared themselves!"

The fact is that the actual interactions of young adolescents are quite exploratory and, more often than not, ritualistic. They use magic formulas to explain how things really work between the sexes. The quality of charms and the baffling aspects of many of their transactions are quite striking. During one interview, for instance, eighth grader Nathan explained to me what he had meant when he said he was "starting to get a girl friend."

"Like, one time we were talking on the phone, and she says, 'I'm going to the movies with a bunch of my friends and if you want to come along, that's okay.' So I went. Eventually, I'll ask her to go out with me. . . ."

"See, the thing is these days," Nathan's friend Stan explains, "you ask them to go with you—and that way, the girl belongs to you. You ask her to go steady and then she won't go out with any of the other guys and the other guys know she's off limits."

"Do you give her a ring or anything like that to show that you're going steady?" I asked.

"Well, you can give 'em a ring if you want to," said Stan, "or you can give 'em something, but you don't have to give them anything. It's just that you say they're going with you and you're going with them. Usually it gets around school by the next morning so you don't need a ring or anything like that."

"How do you do it?"

"You just say, 'Do you want to go with me?'" Stan said, his face lighting up in a fabulous smile. "And they say, 'Sure,' or, 'I'll think about it,' or 'Get lost.'"

"Of course, they don't really say get lost. You wouldn't ask 'em if they were going to say that."

"You make *sure* they'll say yes before you ask them," says Nathan, "so you won't be a fool if they say no. You don't ask them otherwise."

I asked Stan about what it meant, going steady, and how long he and his girl friend had been together.

"Her name's Penny," he started. "She's in the same grade as me . . ."

"She's taller than him," interrupted Ricky, one of Stan's friends.

"Only by an inch," said Stan. "We're at the place where we have gone walking around holding hands, and we've kissed a few times. We go to dances and get pizza afterwards. That's about all. We've been going steady since September. In the sixth grade, I had another girl friend, Janet. I talked to her on the phone. In the seventh grade, I had one girl friend at the beginning of the school year and one at the end of the year. The first girl, I saw her at school and talked to her on the phone at night. The one at the end of the year came to my baseball games."

Group activities and parties often serve as the medium for social interactions. There's protection in numbers. Social know-how does not spring full grown out of these boy-girl parties, but it gets a start. What more often occurs at these pre- and early-adolescent social events is that the kids have practice in how to behave. ("It was a good party, but I kept getting hit in the head with a basketball," a sixth grader told me. "The boys weren't supposed to throw it around, but they did!") These are practice sessions with the opposite sex in what to do ("We'd see how long we could kiss," Chad said, "which basically meant how long you could hold your breath with your mouth on hers.") Sometimes schools sponsor dances: sometimes the parties are at private homes. Wherever they are, they are the places young people often learn to kiss and to dance before it's *serious*. They facilitate touching without taking risks the kids can't handle. In a group, they can observe each other and feel support for what they're doing. Being all together somehow makes it okay, for instance, to kiss or to dance more than once with the same person and still be somewhat anonymous.

And when you're playing a game, nobody asks for commitment.

When you're 'it,' you're not really responsible. You don't have to choose. You just have to kiss.

"We used to keep track of how many times we had kissed at a party," said Sarah. "Like I remember the night I kissed Roger Strauss twenty-two times and Jimmy Larsen sixteen times. It helps you get used to the idea."

At some dances, boys and girls do choose, but the risks are still quite low, since everyone else is doing the same thing and there are clearly identified sets of values to follow. Here everyone has permission to flirt and make advances. Even with permission, it's still nervous making.

"For boys, it's sort of rough because the girls expect you to dance and you have to go up and ask them but you don't know if they want to dance with you or not," says brown-haired Bradley. "You want to dance, and you want to dance with this girl 'cause you know she's cute, but you don't know if she accepts just because you ask her or because she also wants to dance with you. And with the girl, it's probably hard because even if you ask her to dance, she doesn't know if you really like her or not. I think it would be better if it was just more open and girls asked boys to dance and boys asked girls to dance because then people would know more how they feel."

At fourteen, Bradley has been going to parties with his classmates in New York City since the sixth grade. In the sixth grade, they often played spin the bottle. That's the game where everyone sits in a circle, the person who is "it" spins the bottle in the middle of the floor and kisses whichever person of the opposite sex the bottle points to when it stops spinning. It's a game I remember playing when I was in the sixth grade in Kansas.

In seventh grade at his junior high school in New York, Brad said the main activity at parties was seven in heaven, a game in which "you go with a girl into a closet or a dark room for seven minutes or longer and you both do what you want to do."

"It's usually a half-hour," says Bradley, his fingers tapping his desk. "Really, if you don't get in during the first shift, you don't get in at all. I mean nobody's about to say, 'Seven minutes, that's it! Time's up!'"

"With seven in heaven you find the same problem as with dancing," Bradley said. "You never know if she wants to. And rejection is tough to deal with, too. Also, it doesn't really make sense unless you really like the girl. I like the idea of it, though, because I'm excellent in the dark because of my experience in the darkroom. I can do anything in our darkroom by feel. Once there were three girls in there with me. Of course I didn't do anything with them because they were friends, but I thought about it." Bradley smiles, and then laughs.

These preliminaries, of course, serve as a laboratory from which our young social scientists can observe and then dissect behavior, analyze it, compare notes and come up with new conclusions about themselves and the ways the world works. Many times they sit with their second-best friend, analyzing the motivations and behavior of their first best friend, or, after a party, sit with both best friends comparing notes on their boyfriends, who looked at whom when, and why who said what to her, or why he was really mean! or *gross!* or *fabulous!*

Fourteen-year-old David Jensen, an eighth grader at King Junior High School in Berkeley, California, meets me in the comfortable living room of his parents' home. He is a younger, curly-haired version of Robert Redford. In jeans and a red T-shirt, his feet bare, his manner is friendly, unassuming and seemingly unaffected. He invites me to this room to talk; we leave his attractive, well-dressed mother speaking with a friend in the living room. He's offered me the chair and he sits on a large, green bean bag. "Last week I went to a Berkeley High School dance with a friend of mine and his girl friend and a bunch of other girls. During the dance, we were sitting outside and talking about what we did," he said. "I said I play the saxophone, and this girl says, 'You do? I hate the saxaphone.' So we kept talking, and then I said something about how I loved gymnastics. 'I love gymnastics, too,' she says. 'I studied it for five years.' Then she goes on to say how good she is. She thinks everybody loves her. All the girls who were with me thought it was pretty gross.

"The main group I run with has two times as many girls as it has boys," says David. "There are about ten girls and about three boys. We're mostly at school, or we go down to Center and Shattuck and we hang around the bus stop and talk. Mostly at break and lunchtime, that's who I talk to. . . ."

Often, when boys or girls do have a favorite person of the opposite sex, it turns out that the person is "shared" with a best friend. "John's my number-one boyfriend," twelve-year-old Melanna told me, showing me a picture of a brown-haired boy who looked like he was ten years old instead of twelve. "He likes Sherry better than he likes me, though. He says he likes me next best to Sherry, and then Lisa." Sherry, of course, is Melanna's best friend, and Lisa is her second-best friend. There's an innocent, casual nature to all of this sharing, which comes from the distance and lack of intimacy that is comfortable at this stage of development.

Often, these kids have arrived at their current state directly from a time when they wouldn't be caught dead alone with a person of the opposite sex and when they would hit rather than speak to one another. They're still borderline children. Their understanding of individuals of the opposite sex is still remote, and they are one step removed from really understanding what's going on with themselves, let alone anyone else. The feelings they have about their girl friends and boyfriends are intense but still painted in broad strokes, exaggerated and without detail.

"I had my first steady girl friend from the sixth to the seventh grades," says David. "She was in my class. Me and my friend liked her a lot. She went with my friend for two weeks, then I went with her for three weeks before I went on vacation and then again in September and October. During the last month we were going together, she started ignoring me. That bothered me a lot. She wouldn't talk to me. She just talked to her friends. Then one night she called me up and said, 'I don't think things are going that well . . . we ought to break up.' I wasn't about to protest because I thought she must like someone else. Things weren't really going that bad except on her side."

The ebb and flow of affection and the shifting objects of affection also seem to be a norm in social interactions during this time.

"There was this girl I liked named Hillary Green," said thirteen-year-old Gary, an eighth grader in Denver, Colorado. "I didn't know she was real conceited, but she was. At school, I'd walk up and say hi and she'd walk away. One time I was out for two days sick, and when I went back, this guy came up and said, 'Did you hear, Gary, did you hear?'

" 'What?' I asked. 'Well, if you didn't hear,' he said, 'I'm not telling you.' Then a friend of Hillary's came up and said, 'Hillary doesn't like you. You turn her off.'

"She wouldn't even talk to me," he said. "She acted like we couldn't even be friends. Then she started acting nice to me again and I started liking her again. Then one night we went ice-skating at Iceland, and she acted nice to me and I acted nice to her. I thought she had decided she liked me okay. Then Monday at school, this girl came up and said that Hillary said, 'Gary Fulton is so in love with me, but I don't like him. I like Johnny Gale.'

"Well, I know Johnny Gale," Gary says, shaking his head and rubbing at the knee of his jeans. "He's a real nice guy. He's a friend, and I know he doesn't like her at all. In the end, I didn't feel so bad because if I'd gone with her, I wouldn't have ended up with her."

Outside the Ice Capades in Santa Monica, California, dozens of eleven-, twelve-, thirteen- and fourteen-year-olds lined up, ice skates over their shoulders, waiting for the doors to open. Mostly they stood in clusters. A few couples were scattered through the line and two or three were holding onto one another, kissing, rocking back and forth.

Outside six glass doors that opened from the inside out, Patrolman Jim Martz stood attentively, dressed in a blue security force uniform, which he wears when he moonlights from his regular job on the Santa Monica police force.

"These kids are too young to hit any big parties on the weekends, but they're too old to be home in bed," he says. "They're too young for dope and drinking and too young for beach parties, but they're too old to stay at home. . . .

"In Santa Monica," Martz says, "the Ice Capades Chalet is 'the place' for the early adolescents. Their parents drop them off, then pick them up afterward. It's a lot better to have them here than having them in the streets or at a party."

Inside the Ice Capades, the lights had gone on and piped disco music filled the large expanse. The line outside had filtered past the pay booth and now, skates on, youngsters poured onto the icy surface of the rink and seemed literally to fly from one boundary to the other and around the perimeter, touching each other as they passed, spinning, bumping, sailing, falling.

Often, when kids this age do something on their own, the force of their comrades is with them. They are behaving as if they are still in the middle of the group with the support of the group. Approval from their friends gives them the courage to move. Their dial of personal vulnerability is still set on remote control when it comes to the opposite sex.

"My first real boyfriend was in the eighth grade," says brown-haired, brown-eyed Vanessa. "He was really cute. He was in my homeroom. We'd chase each other around the hall. Finally he asked me out. He took me to his friend's house and we turned on the television. He sat in the chair looking at the television, and I sat on the couch. That's all we did—just sitting there watching TV. As soon as his friends came in—he heard them coming in the front door and down the hallway—he came over and sat beside me on the couch and put his arm around me—like, 'Look what I've been doing.' I laughed, and he said 'What's funny?' I said, 'Nothing.'

These kids are the norm. Life for some of their classmates, usually but not always classmates with problems, sometimes gets much more intense, and the games turn into experiences they aren't always ready for. There's no doubt that many of our young adolescents *hear* about somebody in their class or in the class ahead of them who is sleeping around, who is into drugs or sex in a serious way. They know about homosexual activity and oral sex and other things that would have shocked our grandmothers, but they're basically just kids groping for their identity. They may have seen many pictures of nudes, they may have seen people in bed together at the movies, but that doesn't mean they will personalize the information at this point in their lives. Having information does not mean acting on it.

"I'm always worrying about how all this flesh and gore on cable television and in the movies is going to affect my sons," says the mother of a thirteen-year-old and an eleven-year-old in Boston. "I hear about kids in their class acting up in different ways and I get all worried—and then something happens to bring me back to reality.

"The other night, for instance, Wilson announced to me that he was taking a date to the sixth-grade social night. I was totally caught off guard. I was expecting it from the older one, but not from him!

"Anyway, as it turns out, I was a chaperone for the social that night, and I found out that what a date entailed for him was the same thing as when I was in the sixth grade . . .

"Each of them came separately, and then the idea was to stay away from each other. They don't go to the social together and they don't stay together, they both go off with their friends, but everybody knows that Wilson and Karen are together.

"They did play one game of Ping-Pong together. It's apparently important within his peer group that you have a date. It reminded me so much of when I was in the seventh grade and Larry Dalton gave me his ID bracelet to wear so that we were going steady. He actually got his friend to hand it to me. Then everybody knew we were going together, but we avoided being seen together at any cost.

"Everything changes, but it really does stay just the same."

II.

A Kiss Is Still a Kiss

When two human beings connect themselves to one another despite their underlying belief that the person they face possesses alien, if not supernatural powers, they have made magic.

Talking with teenagers about the first time they *really* kissed, touched or communicated intimately, I remembered the grand canyon we all had to fly across to make that connection. What was on the other side was unknown. Yet we made that leap on the basis of faith or courage or some inner challenge that compelled us into space, not knowing where we would land. Perhaps a biological imperative, magic in itself, drove us, lifted us off the ground.

It's easy to forget, if we've bridged that chasm, how very alien the opposite sex was when we were young and exploring the new territory of our emotions, sensations and sexually mature bodies. What do *they* think? How do *they* feel? Or, more specifically, how does *he* feel about me? What is *she* thinking?

A sense of awe and wonder arises when one crosses the bridge to another person. Could this be happening to me? The excitement, the magic of actually doing it, whatever *it* is, is awesome. You become at once spectator and participant, reporter and reportee, transformed. As I heard these stories, I thought of the lyrical songs birds sing when they begin to court one another. The tones of the songs are clear and high.

"I've had four girl friends," thirteen-year-old F.G. tells me. "The first girl friend was when I was eleven. I liked her a lot.

"I didn't really know what to do at first. It all started when we met at a track meet at this school. We got to be good friends and all that. . . . I didn't know what to say to her when I saw her. I had some feelings I'd never had before. Before that, I didn't like girls. But then when I'd see her, it was different."

F.G. smiles and looks at his hands. He's a small, very handsome boy, neatly dressed in beige dungarees and a red plaid shirt. He looks up, his dark brown eyes looking directly at me, and speaks clearly, a soft Spanish accent barely grazing his words.

"Being close to her was like having something different happen to me," he says. "My hands got wet and shaking. My head felt pretty good, but my mouth would get dry, and it was hard to think of things to say. Once I got to know her, I felt better. I could talk to her more freely about stuff.

"We held hands, but we never kissed. Sometimes I wanted to kiss her, but it never came to that certain spot where it happened."

When F.G. was twelve, in the seventh grade, he had his second and most serious girl friend. It was with her he took a giant step.

"I kissed her about five or six times," he said. "The first time we kissed, it felt good, but then after that, I was a little shaky.

"It was at the park. We were there by ourselves, and we went back of the building where the amphitheater is, and that's when it happened. I had that feeling ahead of time that I was going to kiss her, and then when we were there, it happened. It was the first time she'd kissed somebody, too.

"My mouth got dry again. Then we did it a couple of more times and I started getting used to it. My body felt better after that and my hands stopped shaking. Before, I used to feel nervous around her. After that, I wanted to be around her. It felt good to be around her.

"When it first happened, I felt like this couldn't be happening to me. Now I feel comfortable about kissing. I like it."

As F.G. talked, I relived the feelings of my first kiss, the first real kiss, which I had waited for expectantly through the entire summer of my thirteenth year. When it actually happened, I just sat there and didn't move a muscle. My lips didn't even twitch. Turner kept his mouth on mine, waiting for a response, and then drew away and sighed. I remember the mortification: I'd missed my chance! How could I just sit there! Fortunately, after a few minutes of silence hanging in the air between us, he said, 'Maybe we should try that again?' We did, and as far as I was concerned, it was the most wonderful moment of my life. And certainly life was never the same. Really connecting, really touching, removes you from the category of spin the bottle into the real world where people of the opposite sex talk to each other.

Leonore Tiefer, associate professor of psychiatry at the Downstate Medical Center in Brooklyn, New York, writes of her first kiss:

> He was, at 16, an older man. He was tall. He was dark. He was handsome. I was, at 14, hopelessly in crush. . . . We drove to the top of a hill overlooking Los Angeles, where millions of dancing

lights reflected the midnight moon. We stood regarding the view in silence. He put his arm around my waist. Soon he drew me to him. He held my face between his hands and kissed me leisurely, provocatively, on the mouth. He knew what he was doing. He inhaled my awkwardness and exhaled grace.

My memory has made of this first kiss a thing of beauty and joy forever, although I seem to have no recollection at all of the physical details. I have no idea where our tongues were, for instance, or whether our eyes were open or closed. . . .[1]

Women's liberation, sexual liberation, erotic atmosphere or no, nothing seems to change the significance of that first real conversation or that first real contact and response with someone wonderful. The teenagers I talked to remember those firsts with just as much pleasure as we do. They're just as scared, excited and awkward as we were.

"At camp, it was my first time with a girl where you weren't just at a party or with a group or playing spin the bottle or whatever," said fourteen-year-old Louis, from Hartford. Connecticut. "It was something where you had to talk to her, and you know, *make conversation.*

"I was really lucky, because she was really understanding. We mainly talked about how I didn't know what to say and how hard it was to do this sort of thing.

"At our camp, see, you have to ask a girl to the banquet the last night, and I lucked out with this real cute girl. I was dancing with her a lot before that, and then I asked her and she accepted. But then it turned out that this other guy, who was going to ask her, asked her that night. So I went with my second choice, who turned out to be better anyway.

"Anyway, it was one of those things where we were dancing, and I said, 'Do you want to take a walk? It's stuffy in here.' [Lou pulls his shirt out and waves it back and forth to indicate heat and embarrassment. He flushes.]

"Well, then we walk out and walk through the woods and all these people are off necking here and there. This is not like spin the bottle. This is like nothing I've ever done before. I was so nervous. We were walking around for an hour before I got my nerve up and asked her if she wanted to sit down. We sat down on this bench and then after a couple of minutes, I said, 'Well, do you want to walk again?' and got up.

"We kept walking, and finally I said, 'I'm real nervous about this. This is the first time I've been with a girl like this.' She said, 'Me, too. This is the first time I've been with a boy like this.'

"Of course, neither one of us said what it was that we were nervous about or what 'like this' meant—but we both knew what we meant. Finally we got around to it. An hour and a half later! We sat down on a park bench and I put my arm around her and then . . ." [He puts his arm out into the air and then closes his other arm around her and nestles his head into the space.] I kissed her.

"It's really tough. You don't even have to be particularly shy for it to be tough. It's so funny, because I've practiced it so many times. In my mind, I've gone through all the motions, but in real life, it's just not the same. In my mind, it's so smooth and easy, but in real life, all these other things happen. Like once, she was sitting close to me, and I couldn't get my arm back and then move up next to her again to put my arm around her." [He puts his arm out and shows how his elbow got stuck.]

"I felt like I had to lead, but I didn't have any experience. After we kissed a few times, though, when we got comfortable, she could lead me a little more. It's one thing if the boy knows what he's doing and the girl doesn't, he can lead her. Or if the girl knows what she's doing and the boy doesn't, she can lead him. But when you get two that don't know what they're doing, then it's really tough.

"I was so embarrassed. I was smiling the whole time. I couldn't think of anything to say. When all you're thinking about is how you're going to get around to kissing her, you can't think of anything else to say. Finally I just said what was on my mind. . . .

"It's different than you think it will be. Also, in your mind, you do a little bit more, and of course in real life, you're not doing nearly that much.

"But it was so much more than just kissing a girl, because you really had to confront her and talk to her. It took me an hour and a half to kiss her! When you spin a bottle, it takes two seconds!

"Spinning the bottle is like practice.

"I kissed her a lot afterwards. Once you get used to it, it's a breeze. It's just getting there that's hard.

"It's so much easier in your mind. You go through the whole thing with a magazine and it's just one two three. But it took me hours just for kissing. Imagine doing something more!"

How alien *they* are is emphasized when you have no sisters (if you're a boy) or brothers (if you're a girl) close to you in age. The opposite sex is truly an enigma. Nothing so clearly demonstrates how strange they are as being locked into a "date" with one of them and not knowing what to say. I remember standing around a lot with one of "them," kicking the dirt. We couldn't think of anything to say, and yet we wanted to talk, be together, so we would stand, facing one another, kicking the dirt, saying nothing. Then the bell for the next class would ring and we would say, "See you later." We didn't know what to do with our attraction, our helplessness in one other's presence.

"I guess when you're in high school, it's the hardest situation between a boy and a girl," says Lanie, who's sixteen and a junior at a small private school in Brooklyn, New York. "There was this boy in the tenth grade who asked me to a movie. We went into the movie and sat down and I felt really strange. We sat down in the movie and he put his arm around me. The whole time I felt so strange. His arm felt strange. I couldn't think of anything to say. Before that, he'd call me and we'd talk for hours. I thought I liked him for a long time, and I did like him, but then when he finally asked me out, I didn't like him. I'd envisioned something fantastic, so that was a letdown. He kept calling me afterwards, and I finally told him I just wanted to be friends."

"Last year, I had just turned sixteen, and I liked this girl Valerie," says Jud, a football player in Minnesota with wide shoulders and thick, long legs . "I always wanted to be around her. I was too shy to go up and talk to her, so I'd plan a route and work out little things so I could see her when I'd walk down the hall. Finally I called her up and asked her to go to a movie, and we ended up going out for six months."

"You're always worried about what to say and how you're going to come across," says seventeen-year-old Curtis, talking about how, when he finally liked a girl, he called her up and asked her to a movie. "I felt nervous the whole time, from when I picked her up, through the movie, until afterwards, when we really started talking. Then I couldn't believe how much more relaxed I felt."

Besides the fact that you speak opposite sex language, fantasies interfere, emotions interfere and lack of familiarity interferes. Even when the impetus to get there is strong, forays out into the wild jungles of excitement and unknown emotion are fraught with dangers and murky unknowns.

Worry about what the girl is thinking, or vice versa if you're a girl, is crowded by your basic need to know you're okay, and that you are attractive and acceptable. Just as much as you want to know what she thinks, you want to know that your desires are valid and that she feels you are special. In fact, it seems you want to know that she finds you absolutely devastating. What she actually thinks or feels is baffling.

"I wonder what girls are saying about us," says Graham, a tall and good-looking sixteen-year-old. Graham and his friends are sitting around Ian's chilly living room, where we are drinking hot tea and shivering with cold and with laughter. "You know, when you see this girl at a dance and you go off in the dark with her, you wonder what she's thinking and why she's gone with you. . . ."

"If you want to dance, you think, 'She doesn't want to dance with me,' " says Phillip, also sixteen. "They *must* think some of the same things. . . ."

Ian looked thoughtful. "In a real close relationship," he said, "with the same things happening, you'd know what she's thinking."

"Do you think so?" Phillip asks, his forehead wrinkling.

"The first time I touched a girl's breasts, I felt real guilty," says

Graham. "I was twelve and she was sixteen. I sort of apologized the next day, but she didn't seem to feel a bit guilty about it and so that made me feel better. I didn't tell anyone about it until I told these guys, and that was three years later.

"We were in the grass on top of the cliffs one summer vacation, and we were kissing, and it just happened. I'd been reading my dad's naughty books—he didn't know I had—and anyway, it just happened. I put my hand in her jumper and touched her breast. I couldn't believe it was happening, but I thought, it really *does* happen!"

"I wonder what the girls talk about when they get together," Les said. "After a party when we all go back to someone's house, we're all saying these things, like, 'I got a bra strap stuck!' Or, 'shit! she had no nipples!' What do the girls think and talk about?"

"They talk about the emotional side," said Phillip.

"It's so embarrassing when you get a hard-on," says Graham. "When you're at a disco, dancing, for instance, and you get a hard-on. You think, what must she think? It happened the other night when I was dancing a slow dance with this girl and she tickled my back and got me closer to her. I was surprised, but I liked it."

"I don't find it embarrassing at all," said Les. "I just enjoy myself. I don't know what they think about it, but I don't think they mind."

When you break through the rituals, ceremonies, embarrassments, one of the most exhilarating aspects of that first real contact is the flow of communication, learning what he or she thinks and feels. The sense of sharing, and of finding someone who wants to know how *you* feel, too, is like being given a lantern when the lights are out.

Lanie, who had such an unhappy time on her date in tenth grade, couldn't believe her good fortune in finding Charles the next year. "It was *different* with Charles," she says. "I looked forward to seeing him each time. Usually when you're with a boy my age, you have to think of *topics* to talk about. But when I was with Charles, we'd just talk about anything. We'd talk for hours, and I wouldn't get bored."

George, who's now seventeen and a high-school senior in Detroit, Michigan, talks about the excitement and relief of his first emotional connection.

"My mother has a younger sister just three years older than I am," says George, "who was coach for a girls' basketball team. Well, she asked me to help her coach the team, so I went over there to help, and I met this girl, Cheryl. It was really puppy love. The biggest problem was that she lived twenty-five miles away and I was only a freshman, so we only saw each other at practices. She was the seventh child of ten children in her family. We saw each other once a week and, rarely, on weekends. We must have been on the telephone together about an hour every night.

"The biggest thing was at the time that my parents had just come off a separation, and they were kinda quiet. It was tense at my house; you could just hear it. What was good for me was I could talk to her, and since she was a middle child, she didn't get that much attention. I guess I gave her that attention she needed, so it was good for both of us. I used to feel so good after we talked; she said she felt the same way.

"The distance caused the breakup. It finally kinda burned out because basketball season ended and we didn't see each other for almost a month and then we kinda called it off. It was good, though—it was the first time I ever felt so close to anybody. I still think about her."

Moving into a real interaction with a person of the opposite sex shifts the teenager into a new gear. He's experiencing private feelings for someone else and beginning to see himself through the eyes and responses of that other person. In a brand-new way, he's considered special for himself, and life inside his own body takes on new meaning.

Because having a private boy-girl relationship is so unlike anything else previously experienced, and because it has so much to do with defining one's individuality separate from one's parents, it's an arduous task to integrate the experience into the family world. Many teenagers experience so much trauma about letting their parents in on their feelings that they wind up having their first dates in secret. Some nurture their feelings in private for a long time and then drop the news of having a boyfriend to their parents casually. In the middle of a discussion on the Sino-Soviet situation, for instance, Mark will say, "That's what my girl friend, Debbie, thinks," by way of introducing Debbie.

Like Mark and many other adolescents, Jerome went to great lengths not to let his family know he was asking a girl out. It made him feel safer and less worried that he would be knocked off his balance before he had gained it.

"I had a girl friend in the first grade when the guys and girls didn't even play together," says Jerome, a football player in San Diego. "I never had a real girl friend, though, until the seventh grade. The first time I asked her to go to a movie, we were both living on a navy base. I was embarrassed to tell anyone, so we met outside the gates of the base and walked down to the movie. I told my family I was going to the movies with friends, and I even told them the names of my friends. I told them when I got home more lies—like what Joe said at the movie and that kind of thing. Later, like a few months later, I told them the truth. They thought it was funny. My sister teased me for a long time, but by then it didn't bother me anymore."

Even after the initial breakthrough, teenagers still can have enormous difficulty trying to integrate their new involvement with normal family life. The intensity of their feelings, the insecure nature of the role and the transfer of affections sometimes tip the balance totally out of whack while the teenager learns to manage. In some ways, it seems a psychological equivalent to the biological processes going on inside the adolescent body.

"The summer between seventh and eighth grade at music camp, I met Shelley," says fourteen-year-old David, in Berkeley. "We started going together then, and we went together August, September, October and November. That was going real good. She played the flute and I played the sax. We had the sectionals for instruments and we'd see each other between them and say hi in the canoe, and after dinner, we'd go talk and stuff. We'd have about an hour. We'd kiss a lot, and french, but nothing more than that.

"During the time I was at camp, I wouldn't even talk to my mother or sister. Then when school started, every day after school, I'd go to Shelley's house from three to six. I'd sometimes be late and Mom'd say, 'You're late,' and I'd say, 'I know! I know!' I wasn't very nice to my mom or to my sister. I was kind of grouchy. I just didn't think of much else besides Shelley. I didn't know how I was acting to my friends, but they started getting mad at me and disliking me.

"With my best friend, he started going out and having a close relationship with his girl friend. He was doing things the exact same way for a while, cutting everybody out and being real grouchy. I told him about it, and he told me I'd acted the same way. I looked back and realized I'd done the same thing. I told him and I told my mom 'The next girl friend I get, you've gotta tell me if I start acting that way, 'cause I don't want to start acting that way again.'

"I felt really guilty after I broke up with Shelley, and I tried to regain my friends and my family friendships. I hadn't realized how mean I'd been to everybody."

Because hormones have opened up a whole new world of sensations for teenagers, and because their drives are so strong and their excitement so new and tremendous, love at this early age and stage of development has incredible impact. The whole chemistry of being sexually excited is transforming and sometimes stunning. It is as if the nervous system of teenagers has been turned on. Lips, tongues, the interior of the mouth come alive. Even for teenagers who may have gone through the motions of kissing or petting or whatever before, the level of excitement after puberty makes previous experience pale.

"In the eighth grade," says Miles, "it was fumble in the dark. You'd get stoned and go out in the bushes and get some petting and that was the thing everybody did.

"At the beginning of the ninth grade, I felt more inhibited with girls. But then later in the ninth grade, I started more to experience sensual things. This one time I got bombed and went to a dance and picked up a girl there. Like the eighth grade, it was somebody I knew, but it was much more exhilarating. Petting her and kissing her was something

different from eighth grade. There was a *rush!* It was more exciting.
There was something more than just going out to pet and kiss. It was
like the first time ever!"

"I had a real sexual awakening last summer," says fifteen-year-old
Jacquie, in Boston. "It was the first guy I went out with who wasn't
from my school. He was so totally different than anyone I saw from my
school. He was from New Jersey, and he was just natural. He wasn't so
oh, I respect your feelings and all cerebral. He did respect my feelings,
but he didn't talk about being in touch with his feelings and that sort of
thing. Yuk!" [She makes a face.]

"I hadn't done anything with any guy before him. I hadn't even
french-kissed before that. I didn't have sex with him, but we held each
other and kissed a lot—and somehow it was as if I'd never done *anything* before. It changed the way I thought about everything. I didn't
really notice that I had a body before that. He touched my breasts, and
it was like he made me see my breasts in a whole new way—like, when
he touched them, I discovered them. It was nice. But then he went away
and I didn't even like him when he came back. . . ."

The intensity of those early emotions and sensations is extraordinary.
All parts of the body come alive. It's a special time that can never be
duplicated. It stands on its own as a beginning, a time of discovery that
initiates a person into intimacy.

"I had a girl friend in the eighth and ninth grade who was my first
real love," says Dennis, smiling as he remembers. "We slept together,
and it was wonderful. She was the same age I was, and she was a beautiful girl. She was a little Jewish-American princess. I totally lost my
heart and soul to her. We didn't ever have intercourse, but we did sleep
together a lot. Our mothers were friends, too, so I stayed at her house
and she stayed at mine. We'd be in different bedrooms, but we'd sneak
into the same bed after everyone was asleep and kiss and hold each
other. It was so intense and so beautiful. . . ."

"A guy came along in the tenth grade," said Courtney, "and he was
the first one I'd loved. He was totally mystical to me. He played the
guitar. It was real moon, stars and candlelight. All of a sudden, one
night he kissed me and it was like magic. It was like a fairy tale to me.
We got really close."

The feelings of being in love are extraordinary, but often it is the
physical and sexual aspect of that first relationship that looms in the
mind. In addition to the excitement and the pleasure, that focus often
seems to create a great deal of anxiety after the fact.

"Me and Carrie went out for about eight months," says fourteen-
year-old Ben. "I went with her twice, really—from March until the end
of the summer, and then because we were in different schools, we
stopped going out because we didn't see each other very much. Then we

got together again for about a month and a half and then it just didn't work out. But we're still very good friends.

"We still see each other and talk on the phone. I was real close with her whole family. At first, her father didn't like me, but then he started liking me because we'd do things together and he'd talk to me about things. He even took me hunting a couple of times.

"During the summer, I'd go to her house every day. Her mom would come get me, and then I'd be over there from morning until the late afternoon. Carrie and I got real close. We talked a lot. If one of us had a problem, we'd talk about it with each other. I'd never done that with a girl before.

"With Carrie, I held her hand and stuff and I kissed her, and well, we did more than that. I'm embarrassed to say what." At this point, Ben, who has bright red hair and who is tall and well developed for his age, wriggled around in his chair and looked at the bottoms of his sneakers and said, "I don't know how to say it—well, what we did." I said, "Well, you can just say it, what it was you did. It's okay."

Then he said, "It was like my hand went up under her shirt and down the other way, too. Like inside." He turned deeper shades of red as he spoke. "I feel like a bad guy now." "Well, I really don't know why it's bad, either," he said. "People say if you've had intercourse in the eighth grade, that's really bad. But you aren't going to go through your life without it. You're going to have it sometime, so I don't know why it's so bad if you have it before if you feel you're ready for it."

Parents often worry that their young adolescents are getting too involved too intensely and quickly. They worry that if their child gets "carried away," he'll regret it. For the most part, I think that our worries come from our own experiences and ideas, not theirs. Most children know their own limits and, if they feel good about themselves, will make decisions that work for them.

Sometimes, however, teenagers do get very serious sexually as well as emotionally at a very young age. It may or may not be too soon for them, but it's important for adults to know it is possible for the very young to be quite responsible in their relationships and in their feelings for one another. Certainly the beginning may in retrospect have been too early, but if the setting is loving, the experience can be positive.

Nicholas and Mia, for instance, first had intercourse when he was twelve years old and she was thirteen. Now he's sixteen and she's seventeen. Since they broke up, Nicholas hasn't had sex with any other girl. Does he think they made that leap into intimacy too soon?

"I sort of regret it," he says. "I think it was too early. In the relationship I had with Erica, when I was fifteen, that would have been a better time in terms of knowing what we were doing and being more mature and ready for it.

"But at the same time, it was beautiful with Mia. We really cared for each other, and we were learning. I wish I'd known Mia two years later. Thinking back, I don't know what to say to people because they're surprised that at twelve years old, you could be making love. Not everyone would believe that I cared so much for her.

"We used to write each other letters. It was a letter I'd written her that caused our breakup. Her mother searched through her drawers and found the letter. We were forced to cool down our relationship and not see each other again.

"My mother took it fairly well. We just discussed it. My father was a little bit upset. He was distressed, though not angry. Mia's mother went crazy. She wouldn't let Mia go out or do anything; she was screaming and hysterical. Mia and I had gotten hints that something had happened to her mother when she was young. I don't know whether she was molested or hurt, but whatever it was, that made her react even more.

"Mia told me, and then I went straight home to tell my mother, but she already knew. Mia's mother had already called. I called my father and told him.

"We were in school together, but I wasn't supposed to go to her house anymore and she couldn't come to my house for dinner. We finally broke up, essentially because she was older than me and she was going to high school and I was still in my last year of elementary school."

Later, when we were talking about college and goals and dreams, Nicholas said, "I'm sure I'll be married and we'll have a family. I can see this just in terms of dealing with my little sister and brother. They're so great, and I love them so much. It makes me know I want a family. Also, I think about Mia and what we had. I know that I can love somebody and that we can be happy together. What we had was very special. We really grew up together, and I really cherish her. . . ."

I suppose in some special place in each of us, we have tucked away memories of that first one-on-one, boy-girl connection. The moments we spent together during that time of our lives—moments fraught with tension, electricity, surrender, absolute joy and terror—are small monuments to our courage and fortitude and faith. They carried us into the world of contact and touch and miracles to come. Although we may have moved into deeper and more substantial relationships, and although nothing can match the comforts of experience, nothing can ever erase those first moments of making magic.

12.

Sexual Drives and Decisions: To Bed or Not to Bed

One day as I drove away from interviews at Lowell High School in Whittier, California, I passed two Adults Only peep shows on the Imperial Highway not far from the school. Beyond the peep shows, more buildings marked Adults Only advertised everything from Live Nudes to Pervert T-Shirts. On my car radio, Donna Summer sang "I need your hot stuff baby, tonight . . . Gimme little hot stuff, baby, this evenin' . . ." I was singing along with the lyrics when it occurred to me that no matter what age they are, today's teenagers are so inundated with sexually explicit information that they must learn to make decisions about what they do or don't want to do in their own relationships. Unlike yesterday's teenagers, they are exposed to information about sex before they are aware of their own sexual drives or have established their own social limits.

In addition, they are exposed to stimuli and suggestions about sex that may be unrelated or inapplicable to their own lives. Our popular mythology, for instance, depicts the sexual act as mature, casual and glamorous. It's Bo Derek in a hot tub; Paul Newman whispering into your ear. It's J.R. going home to his secretary's bed (while her husband's out of town) and his wife starting a hot affair with an old high-school sweetheart. It's sex for recreation, rarely procreation. The couple falls into satin sheets after the sun sets, and in the morning, love songs and full orchestration accompany the orange juice and champagne.

In strong contrast to the advertised promises of perfection are warnings that invest sexual intercourse with a frightening, death-defying life of its own. "My mother said God would punish me if I ever did it before I was married," seventeen-year-old Elsa told me in Detroit. The threat of venereal disease and moral reprisals can be even worse. "If I ever did it, he'd kill me, or kill the guy," Amy said about her father. By what is said and what is not said, the issue of premarital sex is often blown into a larger-than-life matter.

Some church literature and some parents suggest the false notion that once a person gives into the "the sex urge," they will no longer be able to control it. So, many emotion-laden, real and unreal issues are wrapped into the powerful decision of whether "to do it" or "not to do it." The decision looms large.

In fact, for each person, whether to have premarital sexual intercourse—and when to have it—depends on a complexity of factors. For the teenager who has strong moral or religious beliefs against it, the decision is clear and other outlets must be decided on. For the teenagers who are not devoutly religious and who believe that it is all right to have premarital intercourse, then the challenge is to determine the conditions and circumstances appropriate to their personal beliefs and expectations. The right time for one person might be when she is fifteen years old, for another when she is twenty-one. It might be right for one who is merely "comfortable" with his partner, but for another, only when he is engaged to be married.

Most teenagers begin to make sexual decisions on a more limited scale before they get to the decision of whether to have intercourse. In fact, although it's not talked about very much, many make decisions about a great deal of sex that stops short of genital union but is very exciting, passionate and satisfying. In our culture, people for many generations have remained "virgins' and still found sexual satisfaction in hours of erotic play that involves everything from kissing to exploring each other's mouths with their tongues, to petting and massaging one another, to "dry humping"—simulating intercourse but with clothes on—to oral sex and mutual masturbation. All of this sexually exciting play can lead to orgasm that involves no threat of pregnancy. The explorations can also be quite helpful to the teenager in becoming aware of himself or herself as a sexual person. Because it stops short of intercourse, most petting can be experienced free from anxiety and serve as a wonderful outlet for sexual energy.

"I figure that for me, I want to be a virgin until I get engaged," said Marina, a high-school junior in Atlanta. "That's what's right for me. I'd be pretty upset if I had sex at this point in time. But messing around doesn't bother me at all. I feel really good about it. It doesn't worry me."

"Last year, I went out with a girl who was more liberated than I was," says eighteen-year-old Peter. "She had had more sexual experiences than I had, and she'd had intercourse. My idea of virginity until marriage was a conflict, because she couldn't understand me. She got very frustrated, and then she broke up with me. She said she didn't want to see me anymore at all because it was just too painful. We'd spent so much time together—nearly all the time—so it was a total severing, which really hurt.

"From the experiences I had with her, though, I felt a lot of loving emotions I'd never had before. I also experienced myself sexually like I hadn't before. I became aware of my body and my responses. I felt that having intercourse just to show that I cared, though, wouldn't be right for me, even though there was a lot of love there, and a lot of wonderful feeling. . . ."

In fact, many of the teenagers who are counted among the "sexually active" may have had only one experience of sexual intercourse, while a "non sexually-active" teenager may be regularly having orgasms through petting and, overall, be having a much more satisfying sex life.

Nevertheless, parents are justifiably concerned about their children's decisions about premarital sex, about the quality of their early experiences and the social consequences of their behavior. Timing, partners, education, options for the future, values, life patterns—all are a matter of concern. Another natural factor for parents is that the sexual act itself does take their children from them. It literally and symbolically replaces them.

Thus for teenagers and for their parents, the dilemma is decision making. Just what should teenagers do with their sexual energy, their responses to another person, their desire to be close and loving? How do teenagers decide what is right for them—and how should parents help guide them into behavior that is suited to their own temperaments, beliefs, goals and needs?

"One of the things I'd like to communicate to children and to young people is that what they want might be a lot of touching, what they want might be a lot of loving. Sex may or may not be the thing they want right now," says Marsha Lawrence, senior communications consultant for Planned Parenthood in New York. "Part of the cultural mythology is the informal message reaching kids that after puberty, if you want comfort, cuddling or just warm, sensitive reassurance from someone— you have sex. This is so turned around. Here we are inventing sex therapy to teach grown-ups that they can lie down in bed together, that they can pat, stroke each other, make each other feel good and not have any pressure to have sex right then. That's something teenagers know naturally if we don't push them into sex before they're ready.

"We do very little to teach kids decision making, whether it has to do with sex or anything else. The teaching of decision making should rank with reading and writing. We should tell children that when it comes to sex, we can make clear, rational decisions about it. We should convey a wonderful, joyous, proud feeling about this marvelous capacity we have. We can control it completely if we know we can."

Because of the mixed messages they receive, because of guilt over their sexual excitement that seems to come with the energy, most teenagers move toward the decision to have intercourse with great expectation and apprehension. Popular adult notions often don't give them credit for having emotions connected to their behavior. Although a wide range of behavior is normal, research has shown that the majority of teenagers who have had premarital intercourse have done so only with one partner and have not done it very frequently. Girls aged fifteen to nineteen reported to Drs. Melvin Zelnik and John Kantner in their 1979 survey, for instance, that in the month before the survey, nine out of ten who had had relations had done so with only one partner. Only 16 percent of whites and 11 percent of blacks had had four or more partners since they first started having intercourse. Fully 38 percent of the nonvirgin girls in the study had had no intercourse at all during the month before they were questioned; 30 percent had had intercourse once or twice; and 18 percent had it three to five times. Only 14 percent had had intercourse six or more times in the month before the survey.[1] Despite the evidence, however, some adults continue to characterize today's youth as sexually promiscuous. Even people who work with teenagers often have fantasies about their behavior that are not reflected in the statistics from dozens of reliable studies.

"It used to be they'd do it for love," a high-school principal from Queens, New York, told me. "Now they don't mention love. They do it as an experiment, because it feels good. With movies and everything so open, and because they hear so much—and what with their mothers not getting home from work until five and school out at one, they have all that free time. It's a time for experimenting. They have free time, and they want to satisfy their curiosity. Our whole society sets it up for them."

I think he was right that many teenagers have intercourse "because it feels good" and because it satisfies their drives and curiosity. The same is true for adults. It's also true that teenagers have more convenient places to have privacy when their parents aren't home and feel less pressure generally to marry the first person with whom they sleep. But none of these factors is evidence of a lack of caring or seriousness when it comes to sexual decisions and interactions.

More often than not, teenagers have had earlier, clumsier manifestations of sex before they first have intercourse. These experiences—petting, touching one another's bodies and learning how to be comfortable in the close physical and electrical proximity of another person's body—

are very important in helping adolescents or anyone else move into an acceptance of their own sexual feelings and responses. They become part of a process and a prelude to intercourse—whether that intercourse comes before or after marriage. They become a way of identifying the perimeters of one's own body, an important part of a process in becoming a sexually mature adult.

"I love it when no one's in the house," says Josie. "I love walking around with no clothes on, turning the music up loud. It's nice not to have your parents around. They went away this last weekend, and they were saying, 'Hey, Josie, come with us,' and I just kept saying no. I didn't have anything to do, and I wasn't going out. I just loved being there alone."

Sexual experiences of kissing, petting and holding have a similar flavor to Josie's sense of freedom at being in the house alone. As well as being a way of learning about another person and connecting to that person, they're vehicles for discovering yourself. Quite literally, discovering your own body, your own skin, your own sensuality is, in fact, also identifying yourself as a unique entity.

"When Tom touched my breasts, I was so shocked that I couldn't move," said seventeen-year-old Betty. "He was the first guy who had ever touched my breasts. I don't know why it hadn't ever happened before, but I felt like my body was going to go crazy, it was so exciting. The next morning when I was in the shower, I just kept running my hands over my breasts. I couldn't get over the fact that they were there, even though I had had them for a long time already. I had a whole different feeling about my body after that."

One of the most positive results of teenagers exploring their feelings and responses and not rushing into intercourse is that they have time to get used to owning and managing their own bodies. Several teenagers told me that the first time they felt skin against skin—when he took off his shirt and she took off her shirt—was wonderful and unlike anything else. For Clair, the first time of being naked with a boy was a giant step in her easy and slow-moving progression into her life as a sensual woman.

"It was summertime, the first time I was totally nude," she says. "It was last summer, ans we were lying up on the roof nude. I think a lot of people think if you take off your clothes, you have to make love. But we were just lying there, feeling skin, touching each other with our fingers. The skin was not hot and not cold, but just warm. It was a very specific feeling. That was the first time I really turned on to the art of sex.

"I was going with this guy Johnny. I was really open with him and frank. It was no big deal. I knew his body quite well by then, and he knew my body quite well. But this was the first time he'd seen my body in full sunlight. I wanted to get tan, and that's why we took off our clothes. In most ways, it was extremely unsexual, which was kind of curious and nice.

"Afterwards, we went down and laid on my big double bed and just kissed. That's all. It was very passive. I'd only been partially naked before that. I was still very cautious about sex.

"This experience gave me a fresh outlook on sex. It helped me arrive at a new perspective sexually. It was a nice starting place."

Most teenagers I met said they felt that learning to have fun together physically was important. "I feel sorry for anybody who just jumps into bed when she's thirteen years old," said Grace Anne, an eighteen-year-old who went with her boyfriend for three years before having intercourse. "It's so much fun having all that buildup. We learned about how to make each other feel good without having to worry about all the other junk. I didn't feel guilty at all about our messing around, and that was a big help. What I was worried about was having sex, so we just did everything else until finally I got comfortable with the idea and figured I was ready to make the move."

"I wouldn't have wanted to miss all the buildup," said Jeannie. "It was so great just holding off !"

Also, without having intercourse, many teenagers find it easier to learn how to say no as well as to identify what they want and don't want for themselves. No expectations for performance are pushed quite as mindlessly, and putting a penis into a vagina for five minutes of pumping is not substituted for more quality interaction.

Sometimes when a couple has many months of exploring one another's bodies and have prolonged foreplay that basically includes the techniques of foreplay sophisticated adults use, the act of sexual intercourse in and of itself can even seem anticlimactic.

"Jack and I had fooled around a lot, but I really wanted to wait until I was eighteen," said Brenda, a freshman at the University of Maryland. "I felt like I was growing up too fast. I felt like there were years and years to be involved in that sexual sense. He understood, but in the heat of passion, he would tell me how much he wanted me and how we should start making love.

"One thing about not having intercourse is that we had oral sex a lot. I think if we'd had intercourse, we wouldn't have gone in that direction, and I think we would have missed a lot that was really satisfying and pleasurable to both of us.

"It started because Jack encouraged me to do that to him. I did and he enjoyed it, and finally I felt very comfortable about it. Then he went on vacation, and we missed each other very much. When he got back, we went into my room and got in bed together, and were nude and he did it to me. I thought it was really touching, and it was a really pleasurable way of expressing our love for each other. I had never thought about it before, but I enjoyed it.

"My birthday was in August, and that was when we were going to do it officially. That was when I was going to be eighteen. But anyway, in May, we were driving along, not talking much, and I said, 'Jack, what would you think if I told you I just got the Pill?' He started to swerve off the road and then he pulled off and stopped the car and hugged me. He was saying, 'Oh, I'm so excited! I love you so much.' He was so sweet and so thrilled. I explained how I had to wait seven days after I started taking the Pill. I was sort of sick the first day, and he called every day after that to see how I was feeling.

"When we finally made love, we both said, '*this is it*?' The actual sex act was nothing. In our heads, we knew it was going to grow, but initially, it was nothing. The first few times were awkward, but after that it grew into a nice thing. . . ."

Once teenagers decided to have sexual intercourse, the reality of it was almost always different from what they expected. The first time is almost inevitably clumsy. It's never as good as it has the potential to be, and the pleasure is limited. Besides the anxiety that each person brings to the first encounter, besides the emotional conflicts, the sheer mechanics of it get in the way. It's rarely if ever a smooth slide into home base or silk sheets.

Kathy and Wyatt, for instance, decided to have intercourse during Easter vacation, when her parents would be gone on a weeklong trip to Europe. Kathy says she was thrilled at the prospect of finally making love. She put fresh flowers in vases in her room, and they made a dinner of baked chicken, potatoes and peas and ate it by candlelight ahead of time.

"We put music on in my room and slow-danced and it was just so exciting I thought I'd die," says the laughing eighteen-year-old. "And then when we got in bed and he got on top of me, I couldn't believe it. I thought I was made wrong. There he was and I thought, oh, my God, I'm too little. His penis felt like it was twenty times bigger than my vagina; it was horrible. I couldn't believe the pain. Here was this big moment I'd been waiting for, and it was a nightmare. I didn't think we'd ever be able to do it. I started crying and he got all worried. Finally we gave up. But he tried it again the next night and it worked."

Whether it's in the backseat of a car or behind the bandstand or in the girl's bedroom when her parents aren't home, the actuality of intercourse stands in stark contrast to the romantic notions people have about it ahead of time. "I remember the blood" says eighteen-year-old Anita. "There was so much blood. I got hysterical. I thought it was disgusting and that we were terrible. I started screaming at him,

'You've got to marry me now!' I was only fourteen, and I went berserk."

"It wasn't anything like what you read in *Playboy*-type books," said seventeen-year-old Allen. "It was *physical*. In those books, they use all those neat little adjectives that make it sound like silver—all polished. And, of course, they use their beauty queens and the men are real macho and you get it all blown out of proportion. After it happened, I didn't think it was such a big deal. It was a letdown. I realized it's the love that must make it unique and nice, not the physical thing itself."

And no matter how "prepared" they are, the experience comes as a surprise.

"My mother had explained everything to me," said Leslie, "but I didn't understand it until I was involved in it! I had orgasms before that, fooling around, and I had an orgasm the first time. Then it was a long time before we had sex again and before I had another orgasm.

"In high school, I never fantasized while I was having sex. Not *while* I was having sex. I was very involved in it. It was too total to have room for any fantasies. But at home by myself, I would fantasize. It's still that way for me."

"Even the first time was a good experience," Leslie says. "But we didn't know if it was the right thing for us to do, so we didn't do it again for months. We didn't really plan it, we just did it. It was right after my period, so we were pretty confident I wouldn't get pregnant. I felt good about it. I really loved Worth, and I knew he loved me. In fact, I think he was more worried about it than I was. He thought I might eventually regret it if we broke up. He was also worried that I was so young that maybe it would damage me psychologically. I was fifteen and he was seventeen."

Most of the teenagers I met who had had or were having premarital intercourse seemed to me to bring a great deal of caring to the experience. Although many didn't feel they would marry the person, more often than not, they had real affection and concern for the person they chose as a sexual partner. The teenagers who acted as if their partners were interchangeable and unimportant vehicles for their own satisfaction were few and far between. Those few I met who were scornful about their partners—angry or contemptuous—seemed to me to be quite lonely little boys or girls, disappointed in their dreams, who used sex as an unsuccessful solution to intimacy. They usually had low opinions of themselves and behaved sexually in self-punitive ways while often fooling themselves into believing they were sexually liberated.

Sometimes the casualness with which teenagers first had sex reflected their immaturity, and intercourse was akin to playing spin the bottle or, depending on your perspective, Russian roulette. Because they weren't fully conscious of living in their own bodies, had no individual boundaries or firm sense of their own wants and desires, their experiences were quite impersonal.

"The way it worked was everybody in the neighborhood had a partner," Angela explained of her initiation into sex in the city of Philadelphia. "It wasn't even puppy love. You'd just hang out with the gang and this person was the one you'd mess around with and sit on his lap. Or when he was horny, you'd have sex. There was no commitment, and I didn't care that much one way or another about him.

"I was forewarned about the kids and the experimenting, but I didn't listen. I started hanging out at Arnold Thompson's—and there was Paul and Allen, Lynne, Mimi, me, James, Sammy and Melissa. . . . Arnold introduced all of us to joints and sex. They were all one-night stands, and there weren't that many during that time. They weren't that good, either. I can count them on one hand that were any good. There were some people got so off they can't remember them all. . . .

"I was never that way. It was good to learn early those things about myself. You have to learn somehow. The way I learned wasn't the greatest, but I'm past it. Now I know. . . ."

Most of the teenagers I met seemed to have made decisions that reflected how they felt about themselves and their partners. They usually had thought about how premarital sex would fit into the overall pattern of their lives. I met some teenagers who cared for and loved one another deeply and had decided, as a result, to have intercourse. No doubt some of them will part, and some will stay together. But it seemed evident that they had a constructive relationship and were learning with one another how to be intimate, how to share pleasure and how to build their own adult lives, separate from their parents.

"After Jimmy and I had sex the first time, I asked Jimmy's dad, who knew about it, if he thought I should tell my mother," remembers Ellie, whose mother had been quite adamant that her daughter not have premarital sex. "He thought for a little while, and then he said, 'No. This is something that belongs to your adult life.' I've always appreciated that. It confirmed that it was my own decision, my own life that I was dealing with."

Elaine, who was planning to begin college in the fall, said she had been going steady with a fellow senior for nearly a year before they first made love. "Neither of us talks about it to anyone else," she said. "I'd be very upset if he talked about it. I don't think he would, but if he did, he would be less one girlfriend. I don't talk about it to the girls, either. . . .

"Making love is what we call it," she said. "There's a difference between making love and screwing. Sometimes we call it sleeping together, but usually we call it making love because that's what it is. That's what it means to us."

I think most parents would be surprised, and pleased, if they knew how their children made their decisions and how they had incorporated their sexual relationships into their larger sense of themselves and their lives.

For instance, Suzanne Taheshi and Glenn Anderson, high-school seniors when I met them in Seattle, Washington, told me they had evolved quite slowly into their relationship and their decision to have intercourse. Both of them were virgins when they met.

At sixteen, Glenn had assumed he would be a virgin until he got to college. Suzanne had assumed she would have sex before she graduated from high school.

Suzanne is Japanese-American, with long black hair and a thin, elegant figure. Glenn's father, a banker, and mother, a pediatrician, are wealthy WASPs from an old Seattle family. Suzanne's father is a surgeon; her mother is a housewife. Glenn's hair is several shades between blond and red, and his fair skin is scattered with freckles. He's wearing white pants and a short-sleeved shirt with a floral Hawaiian pattern on it. Suzanne is wearing white jeans with a turquoise-blue Indian shirt of soft cotton. The two touch their heads together occasionally while they talk, shifting positions, smiling at me and each other. They're comfortable together physically; they have said they would feel free to talk about their separate histories in front of each other because they've already told each other all the things they would tell me.

"The first time I ever went out on a date was my sophomore year," says Suzi. "I went out with this guy I'd had a lot of fun with, and it was an innocent relationship for a long time. At the same time, I had this heavy relationship with a friend of my brother. He had a pretty bad reputation. Everyone came up and was warning me to stay away from this creep, including all three of my brothers. Anyway, I saw him for three months off and on. His parents were divorced and his mother was always in California for some reason.

"Up until then, I was really innocent. Part of it's because of my Japanese background. It's very conservative and traditional. My mother never talked about sex, and my father doesn't mention it at all.

"They're really against sex. They believe it's not before marriage. My mother thinks people my age who are having sex are insecure or want revenge against their mothers. She can't consider or think that kids can make grown-up decisions of their own.

"My mother didn't know I was going out with this guy, who was my brother's friend. But he had moved out and gotten an apartment of his own. He had eight hundred dollars a month from his job, and a water bed and a sauna in his apartment, and he'd call me up and say, 'Why don't you come over here and stay with me?' I'm glad I didn't. The last thing I heard was that he was going to get married.

"The other person I was seeing was more like a big brother. He cared about me a lot, but I couldn't handle any other relationship after that one with Doug, so I dropped out of everything. I didn't talk to anyone except for my best friend, Angie.

"I was scared. Everything was happening too fast for me. I wasn't used to feeling so much and I wanted to slow down the pace. I couldn't handle everything that was going on inside me or outside me.

"Up to that year, I was very shy. I had a lot of problems about being accepted. When I started the ninth grade, though, I said to myself that I'm not going to be shy anymore. I'm going to be extroverted and see what happens.

"I volunteered for everything, and people got the impression that I was open and carefree. That reinforced me.

"I also started being aggressive in that I started to initiate group activities and started having lots of fun. Then I met this one person, Skeet. If you saw him, you'd call him a hunk. Anybody would call him a hunk. And then I instantly fell in love with an image. Well, he fell head over heels in love with me. He was in love with an image, too.

"I'd been in a play, and by looking at me, he decided he wanted to know me. After the play, I backed up into him and he was hugging me. We went out a lot after that, and he put on a good front, but when I got to know him, I got sick of him.

"I stopped dating over the summer, and then this year, I started to date Glenn."

Suzanne looked at Glenn, and he looked at his white duck pants and grinned. "Well, my story's pretty innocent," he said.

"I really had absolutely no contact with the opposite sex up to the age of sixteen. At that point, we were in Vancouver, and I was with my brother and sister-in-law. My brother and I were in the pool, and my brother asked me if I was a virgin and whether I wanted to be with someone who had had a lot of experience. So we went into the house, and I went into the bedroom. The room was dark, and my sister-in-law was lying on this nice big water bed. I was sort of fumbling around with her, trying it, but I was too drunk to do anything.

"Then I went back to being an innocent. I had no girl friends as girl friends. I went back to school and started going out with this girl—Suzanne. We'd go out to the movies. A couple of times we snuggled on the couch at my house. Then we went up to this mountain cabin on a school retreat. We were up there and it was real snowy outside and real warm inside and we spent a lot of time inside talking. It was this big dormitory room sort of thing—a big room with a bunch of cots in it—

and I ended up on her bed, sitting there and talking with other
people.

"I didn't expect it, but I ended up sleeping there. It was a lot of fun.
We were kissing and petting. We didn't have intercourse, but it was
warm and comfortable and exciting. The weather wasn't so hot the
whole time we were there, so we stayed inside a lot. We talked about sex
a couple of times and whether we'd have sex, but it was abstract. . . ."

After that school retreat, they started spending all their free time
together and eventually started going steady. Deciding to have intercourse was, for them, as for most of the kids I talked to, a major
step.

"I was really scared about it," said Suzanne. "I had to come to grips
with myself. I sat down with myself and tried to think about it. My fears
were connected with the act of having sex and with pregnancy."

"I was afraid of feeling guilty afterwards," said Glenn. "For me, it
was a lot about what my parents think versus what I think. I couldn't
figure out any solid reasons why I was scared.

"One thing I knew was that I didn't want to do anything and afterwards have her say, 'I wish I hadn't done it with you,' he said, studying
his sandal. "Certain girls want to be virgins. I didn't want to push her
and have her regret it afterwards or say she wasn't ready for it."

"Before the retreat, we talked about our beliefs and whether it was
right to have sex and that sort of thing," said Suzanne. "After the
retreat, it was, 'Are we going to . . . ?' instead of, 'Am I going
to . . . ?' "

"When it happened, it was a surprise to me," Glenn said, blushing. "I
felt like all of a sudden, she did that to me!"

"With Glenn, I decided I'm going to be more aggressive, because he's
so shy," Suzanne explained. "I really went after him, in a way. I talked
to him whenever I could, and then I started to suggest going out to
lunch, going to the movies and all. If a bunch of us were going out, I'd
say 'We're going, why don't you come along?' Later, I was pretty agres-
sive sexually, too."

"When we did it, it came as such a surprise," said Glenn, laughing
again. "I have a very little car. We were in the front, which is a little
shorter than this table, and it was really cold outside. I didn't even
expect to do anything that night. I just wanted to see her and talk to her.
I hadn't seen her for a while, and I just really wanted to see her. I didn't
expect to see that much!

"Afterwards, I felt it was no big thing in itself. But the next morning,
I felt sort of guilty. I wondered if she regrets it now. I was also going,
hm, I lost my virginity. I was sort of sad about that, too. There were
times in the past when I have felt embarrassed about being a virgin.

There's this whole big macho image on campus; everybody acting like a stud. But it was sort of okay with me if they looked on me as slow. Nobody really paid much attention to it, and I didn't go around advertising it. Suddenly I wasn't a virgin anymore.

"I wasn't really surprised that we made love," said Suzanne. "I knew it was going to happen sometime this year. I was only surprised that it happened that night. Afterwards I felt really rushed because I was supposed to be home an hour and a half before I was. I wanted to talk, but I really didn't have any time. I didn't even think about feeling guilty or regretting it. The only thing I worried about was getting pregnant.

"Glenn and I had discussed it and vaguely decided we would use birth control, but then it happened and we didn't have any. A friend and I went down to this clinic and got the Pill afterwards.

"My mother told me that if I ever decided to live with anybody, she wouldn't throw me a wedding. She said she wouldn't look favorably on me and wouldn't be supportive if I had any problems or if I had a child. One of my beliefs is that I should live with someone before I get married, so I know it's going to be a horror house when that time comes. I believe in being spontaneous in things I do day-to-day—but life decisions shouldn't be spontaneous."

As we talked, I realized that most likely Suzanne and Glenn wouldn't be seeing each other after another five or six months. She was going to the University of California at Berkeley; he had no definite future plans. She was a real academic with career goals; he couldn't stand school and thought he might become a pilot. They both said, "Whatever happens is going to happen," about the future of their relationship, but they admitted the future looked dim. Nevertheless, each of them has given the other something special of herself and himself. They know each other in a special way that's a common denominator to all humankind, no matter what customs or attitudes or values they have brought to the experience.

Suzanne and Glenn made their decision together and grew together. In many relationships, however, one partner coaxes or pressures the other into sexual behavior before he or she is ready. Andrea was one of several girls I had talked to who would fall into the statistical category of being "sexually active"—but, in fact, she's only had intercourse once.

"Carey and I did it when I was sixteen," says Andrea. "We had been going out for about six months. We had talked about it before and I had said no, there was no way. I was really firm about it. He always said, 'But I love you!' He said sometime we should do it, whenever I was ready.

"Then this one time, my parents were gone for a week. They went to London on a business trip. I'd thought about it beforehand and thought that if I was going to do it, this was the time. Then when he was there one time, we'd been making out for a while and he was asking me if I wanted to do it and I said oh, why not. I was scared to death, though.

"We were in my room, and we took off all our clothes and did it. During and afterwards, I cried and cried. I had wanted to save it until I was married—until The One came along. He thought I was stupid for crying. He kept saying, 'Why are you crying? Didn't you enjoy it? Didn't you want to?' But I didn't.

"My problem is that I'm a very insecure person, and I felt that I had to have him because he liked me. I felt sorry for him. I also figured, he wants it, so I might as well do it.

"One night about two A.M., we got into a fight. He followed me home after a party. My parents told him to leave me alone. It wasn't a relationship like we had before.

"Also, I didn't like him after we had our big fight. Finally I told him I didn't want to go out with him. He bugged me and called me and gave me presents. But finally he gave up.

"I haven't gotten involved with anyone since then. I've dated, but I haven't had a steady boyfriend.

"The next time I get really involved with somebody and really care about somebody, I'll probably have sex again," Andrea confided. "The pressure I had has a lot to do with my bad feelings about sex. I realize it could be a lot better."

Often, the decision to have sexual intercourse happens quite spontaneously when "one thing leads to another." This approach seems to remove responsibility for having thought it out ahead of time, but also increases the chances of pregnancy if birth control is not being used. Some teenagers, however, take the gamble.

"I lost my virginity when I was sixteen," says Freddy, a tall, eighteen-year-old basketball player from Brooklyn, New York. "She was a friend of my cousin, and she'd just graduated from high school. Anyway, we were kidding around, and I asked her to give me a real nice kiss. That's where it started, with a real nice kiss. That was about five thirty in the afternoon. We were out in the hallway behind her grandmother's door, this little foyer kind of place. I said, hey! I'd never been kissed like that or felt that way before. We didn't leave that hallway until two thirty in the morning. This girl, she'd been raped once, so sex was a pretty heavy thing for her. We got into some very heavy petting, and I promised her and myself that I wouldn't have intercourse with her. I didn't keep the promise, though, because she wouldn't let me keep it until we were through.

"It was so weird. We were right next to her grandmother's room. Right out in this little cramped hallway. I'd had to go to the bathroom for hours, and I almost broke my neck from the weird position we were in. I'd never been so uncomfortable in my whole life for such a long time, but it was worth it."

Some couples survive what seems an exploitative or nonmutual initiation into sex, but they make the process much more difficult for themselves. Barbara, like Andrea, reacted violently to the first experience and bitterly resented Jason's pushing her and lying to her.

"We started going together in January, and he was interested in having sex right away," says Barbara, a seventeen-year-old who speaks in a clear, mature voice. "I didn't really want to. I was embarrassed. But for some reason, he was different from anyone else I'd ever dated.

"The first time we had intercourse was that spring, when I was fifteen. I didn't love him then, but I do now. How it happened was he weasled me into it. He kept telling me he loved me and I kept saying no, you don't. You don't know me that well to love me.

"That first time, we were in his room. He'd kept on telling me he loved me, and you start to believe what they say. His parents were at a wedding, and his brother was home. Well, he got really drunk and his brother and I carried him into his room, and then I was going to go out into the living room with his brother to watch TV. He grabbed my hand and said, 'Hey, come here and lay down with me for a little while. I won't do anything, honest. . . .' So I laid down, and he started going to sleep. I said whew! to myself. Then he woke up and started kissing me, and then things just kept happening.

"I cried *extremely hard* during and afterwards. We talked about it afterwards. I told him, 'You don't love me,' and he said, 'I know.' Then I thought, what if I'm pregnant? I regretted it then. I don't know. The main thing I was afraid of was rumors and that he would dump me, but he never said anything to anybody."

Barbara and Jason have gone together now for more than two years, and survived that sexual initiation together. She said that after that first time, he also thought she was just using him. "He used to say, 'You're popular and I'm ugly. You don't really like me.' I liked him, but I don't know why. I chased him. I was the one who started it. I'd call him up, and he'd say, 'Why are you calling me?' I'd say, 'Cause I like you!'

"He said recently that it didn't mean a whole lot to him that first time, but it does now. It was the same for me, really. And when he stayed with me afterwards, even without sex, then I knew he wouldn't have stayed with me so long if he didn't really love me.

"It bothers me still sometimes, and it bothers me that he did it with other girls, too, but he never stayed with them that long and that makes me feel better."

Barbara told me that she and Jason make love about once or twice a month at her house or his house, or sometimes in his car. He uses rubbers for their protection. As for the future? They think that they're likely to get married within two or three years if they stay together during that time.

"We can't break up," she says. "We've tried. Sometimes we need more space, but now I'm getting better at giving him the space he needs. I used to get mad at him when he went out with his friends. Now I don't anymore, because I know he needs that and I do, too."

Once a couple had begun to have intercourse and continued to have it, even infrequently, they said that their pleasure usually progressed with their experience and confidence. Many of the girls said that they started having orgasms only after they had become familiar with what they wanted and liked. Some had their first orgasm only after they had ended one relationship and begun a more serious and "mature" relationship. Part of this enhanced enjoyment had to do with learning what they enjoyed and being more relaxed with the experience. Sometimes enjoyment came when a teenager had a mature and thoughtful partner who was sensitive to his or her feelings.

"There was this one guy last summer, Brian, who worked at the same restaurant where I was working," says Annette. "He was eighteen, and he'd just gotten accepted to Yale and Princeton. He was going to go to Yale. He gave me this line about why don't you come up to my room and I'll read you some poetry. Eventually we became friends, and finally I did go to his room with him and I had sex with him, and it was such a good experience for me. He was so nice about it. He gave me some very good feelings about myself. He asked me, 'How are you feeling?' He asked me, 'What do you like?' I felt very well taken care of, and I didn't feel self-conscious at all. He's so much more experienced than me that he was able to teach me quite a bit.

"I come across as a self-confident person. But I'm so nervous about people. I'm so paranoid."

The pleasure of discovering and developing an intimate understanding of one's own body as well as another's most often depends on being able to communicate and to relax. For teenagers, like anyone else, the newness of body fluids and smells and orgasms of another person take getting used to. Touching and being touched, giving and receiving, take getting used to. Learning your own and another person's responses also takes time. So if the experience is overlaid by fears or feelings of being rushed, used or disconnnected, it cannot be very full or emotionally satisfying. Almost always, teenagers said, the extent of their sexual pleasure was dependent on their feelings of mutuality and comfort with their partner and security about themselves. Being respected and confident enough to assert what they wanted and didn't want was their key to feeling real satisfaction and confidence in their sexual relationship.

When teenagers are not worried about getting pregnant or getting caught, when they have come to terms with their personal conflicts about having sex and reach a comfort zone about their own bodies, their sexual interactions can be quite wonderful. The interactions can set a standard and even establish patterns for a person's life.

"Katherine was really romantic," said sixteen-year-old Mitchell. "She wanted everything perfect for my birthday, so she planned it out. Her dad was a conductor, and he was at a concert the evening she had planned, so we had the whole evening and no pressure.

"She made it so that we had our clothes off and we had a bed. We did it all slow, with candlelight and everything. It was really perfect. It couldn't have been better. I'd never done it before with all my clothes off and all the girl's clothes off. That was a great feeling. She was something else. If she could have made a bed of roses, she would have made a bed of roses.

"Our relationship ended when I moved here, to Colorado, from Arizona. But it was really the best relationship I ever had. I've had several girl friends since then. I care about the girls I go out with. Not enough to marry them, but I care when I go out with them. I think I'll marry somebody who is the kind of person Katherine is, though. That's the closest to my ideal so far."

According to Kinsey's studies, there was considerable evidence that premarital petting and even premarital sex contributed definitely to the effectiveness of sexual relations after marriage if one partner didn't have moral beliefs that made him hold the other in contempt for specific premarital sexual behavior. Kinsey found that the sexual factors that most often caused adults difficulty in their marital relationships were the failure of the male to show skill in sexual approach and technique and the failure of the female to participate with the abandon necessary for the successful consummation of sexual relations. Both these difficulties, according to Kinsey, stemmed from the restraints people developed during premarital years and the "impossibility" of freely releasing those restraints after marriage.

Certainly it seemed to me that many of the teenagers I talked to would have fuller and richer marital lives because of healthy patterns they established in premarital experiences. Many said that even without intercourse, what they had learned about their sexual responsiveness and about foreplay would eventually contribute to a more complete experience. Others, who had begun to have premarital intercourse, also seemed to have learned and grown through the experience.

"I can't say I loved him the first time I made love to him," said Candy, in Atlanta. "But I wanted to be close to him. I wanted to touch him and have him touch me. I knew I wanted that closeness and that touching, and I knew it was right.

"The first time, it wasn't that bad for me. But I've grown so much in my mind since then. We've talked about it more, and we've both grown more. Now it's good for me. It's like he gives so much to me, and I give so much to him, and it makes us feel so good and so right showing our love that way."

Once they feel free to express themselves in sexual ways, teenagers also begin to explore a range of sexual feelings. When they give themselves play room, like Jeana and Brian, they often find that much more than sexual intercourse itself enriches their union.

"This one afternoon it was raining and we went up to my room" she says. "We were talking about sex, and we took off our clothes and were kissing and stuff, and then he'd say something like, 'Would you like me to give you some head?' This wasn't a smooth thing where you went from one thing into the next. We talked about it all and were kind of trying it out. This was really my breakthrough into the sexual world. I trusted him, and it was really nice.

"We talked a lot about regions where we liked to be touched, and how we liked to be touched. We had oral sex and made out and stuff. We didn't have intercourse at that time.

"There's different kinds of sex, like fun sex, jab, jab, jab, and just touching. Another time this summer, Brian and I just stroked each other all over. One time we took off all our clothes and just stroked each other's bodies for the longest time. I think we fell asleep arm in arm. It was so wonderful. I'd never felt anything that felt so good. . . ."

Just as learning what feels good is important, so is learning to communicate what you don't like.

"I hate it when something is being done for a long time," says Terri, a sixteen-year-old from New Haven, Connecticut. "If it's too long, it starts to get boring. A little is fine, but if he goes on for too long, I take his hand away or move his head up or move my head up or something.

"Usually I do it in actions rather than in words. That's with a hand job or oral sex. Sometimes, even with sex, though, they go on forever. Like, you want it so bad, and then when you get it, you're saying, 'com'on already!' It seems like guys never get tired of it. They can just keep pumping away! How can they be so different?"

With the freedom to explore comes the possibility of experimenting with fantasies and what one likes sexually. Sometimes teenagers told me about grown-up-sounding adventures that at first glance were rather risqué, but really, beneath the surface, were quite innocent and reflected, more than anything else, a lack of sexual experience or maturity.

"The best sexual experience I ever had, well, it sounds odd, but it was with this guy I met at the beach," says Claudia, a seventeen-year-old from Long Beach, New Jersey. "That day we were together all day, so I felt like I knew him. We went to this party, and the whole atmosphere was nice. It was a wedding party, and about seven people were there and laughing and having an excellent time. Then we went back to his house and to his room. It was the best experience I ever had. It was the only time I remember having had an orgasm. I remember saying, 'I can't stop! I can't stop!' It was great. The next day when I woke up at my house again, it was like, where are you? I felt like I could hold him and squeeze him forever. It was really wonderful. The first time I'd had sex, I was so nervous. I wasn't relaxed, so the only thing I felt was that I was relieved to know what it was. I'd wondered so much about it. But now I really like it. I guess it's just like anything else—practice makes perfect."

Raymond, an eighteen-year-old in New York City, also had his sexual fantasies fulfilled with someone he met and "slept with" the same night. For him, the experience sets a standard.

"I met a real nutty girl over this weekend," he told me. "It was the most intense sexual experience of my life. I normally don't go to discos, but the people from work were going, so I agreed to go along. I went, and there was this woman who was absolutely gorgeous. She was throwing a kick when I met her. Anyway, we danced, and then we went to breakfast and then back to her room at the YWCA.

"At breakfast, I was telling her about my great abilities of cunnilingus, and she said she'd have to see. I'd had a lot of oral sex before I had intercourse, starting with a friend of my mother's who baby-sat for me when I was little. But I'm glad it worked out that way. It made me a very patient lover . . . Anyway, we went back to her room and started at it. During her first stages of orgasm, I pulled her up and took me inside her. I've never had such an intense initial sexual experience before. Something that intense usually comes after several sexual encounters.

"Usually I'm a very gentle lover, but she was so lubricated and wound up, there wasn't any need to be. I'm not overly large, I'm just average, but I've found that if I'm not careful, I can cause a girl discomfort. She didn't have any discomfort. We got back to her place at 3 A.M., and when the sun was coming up at six, she fell right to sleep in my arms. I was up a couple of hours just looking at her.

"My greatest sexual fantasy is to come at the same time as a woman, and that's what happened. We had simultaneous orgasm. It was *great*. She's great, too. When she smiles at you, she looks like she's fourteen years old, but she's really twenty-one."

Experimenting with sexual fantasies can teach people—young or old—what they do or don't want or introduce them to areas of their psyche that surprise them. Again, several teenagers I talked to handled these experiments in a very mature and responsible way.

"You're not going to believe this," Sharon tells me, pulling the brightly colored suspenders that hold up her dungarees. "But the other day, I tied him up to my four-poster bed. I'm still freaked about that. I can't believe I tied him up and that we were that gamesy. But see, we had this bet. The bet was that he'd scream for mercy after a half-hour because he'd be so sexually aroused. The bet was for dinner at The Clam Bar. So I tied him up and I did everything and anything I could think of to turn him on. I was outrageous. But he didn't get aroused. It was terrible. After fifteen minutes, I untied him. I felt then like I didn't do a damn thing to him. I got this whole attitude. I felt so rejected and hurt. It's crazy. If he'd begged for mercy, I would have felt great, but he won and I felt rejected.

"I still can't get over it. Once I had him tied up, I had the devious idea of leaving him there. I had these weird feelings in my body, seeing him laying there helpless. It felt really powerful."

"The kinkiest thing I ever made come true was when Ron and I were into whipped cream," she said. "We put it all over ourselves and ate it off each other. Another time when we were together and we were all hot and bothered, we took a shower and then filled the bathtub with Mr. Bubble and watched TV from the bathtub.

"Sometimes I get into fantasies related to some kind of public sex. The idea of maybe getting caught turns me on—of course, that depends on getting caught by whom. If I got caught by my mother and father, I think I'd die."

Some people might be mortified at the idea of an eighteen-year-old who is becoming so sexually knowledgeable. They might use Sharon as an example of depravity and moral casualness. But she has a value system of her own that does not allow "casual" sex.

"When I was seventeen, I did something I think is really embarrassing," she says, swinging her legs back and forth under the table on which she's sitting. "There was this guy—he was my neighbor's gardener, and we decided we were supersexually attractive to one another. I was seventeen and he was thirty-seven, yeah? Well, we had coffee and talked about it. We talked about where we could go and everything, but then I backed out when it came right down to it. I said, 'Hey, I'm all talk; I can't handle it.' It was like *talking* about having an affair is one thing, but doing it is another. So he said, 'Okay, that's cool.'

"Then one morning I saw him and he says, 'What are you doing this morning?' 'Nothing,' I said, so he says, 'Well, let's go have some coffee.' So we go to this coffee shop and then he pulls these keys out of his pocket and jingles them. And I say, 'Hey, what's that?' He says, 'Keys to a room at a motel down the block.' I said 'Hey, oh, hey, no!' And he says, 'Oh, let's just go over there and talk.' I said, 'You know we won't just talk!' And anyway, I went. Well, that was a trip. That was the first time I'd ever been to a motel. I felt like such a sneaky little criminal.

When I went to work, I felt like it was written all over my face and anybody could read it just by looking. 'Sharon Altman just went to a motel for casual sex.'

"After we had our little encounter at the motel, I decided I didn't want to see him. I felt I was an evil person for having a casual affair without the 'I love you' first. I didn't think I could have casual sex without feeling rotten afterwards. I don't know—maybe I had to do it just to prove to myself I couldn't do it."

Making explorations into their sexual feelings and into sexual interactions with another person at the age of sixteen or eighteen does not mean that today's teenagers will be any better or worse off than we were when we did the same things at the ages of twenty or twenty-five. Some of them will make right choices for themselves, and some will make wrong choices. They will have relationships that affect them in a variety of ways. But when they behave sexually, when they respond to another person, they are doing something that human beings have done for as far back as the history of humans extends itself. Even though each sexual experience is individual and intimate and unique, in it, we become part of the human race, linked to humankind, past and future, regardless of what language we speak, what customs, beliefs, cultures, attitudes or perspectives we bring to the experience.

Today's teenagers may be aware earlier, they may be exposed to more, they may make decisions sooner than they would otherwise, but they'll most likely find their way through the hazards and the squalls and the ways of the world as well as we did. And in their own way.

13.

Sexual Encounters of the Third Kind

Being part of a couple in love means seeing through the loved one's eyes as well as your own. It's a matter of gaining sight and sharing the view.

Certainly the quantum leap from standing single to identifying and committing oneself to another is propelled by faith, courage and suspension of disbelief. For many teenagers, it's a process for practicing marriage, testing values and ideals and working out what it means to care and be cared for. From eighteen-year-old Chip's perspective, "One and one makes one" and moves you into a new dimension where love takes over and "goes the distance."

Sometimes, particularly with teenagers, the distance a relationship goes is not measured by time as much as by intensity. And that intensity sets a standard. It serves as a foundation from which teenagers will build relationships. Some will stay with that first real love and build from the commitment for the rest of their lives. Most learn from it and move on through other stages of development to new life partners.

Since being part of a couple requires intimacy, loyalty and any number of possibilities for rejection, the terrain around each unit is mined with explosives. The reshuffling of childhood loyalties and the transfer of attention create anxieties that reverberate internally. Nevertheless, most teenagers, like most adults, venture into couple commitments bravely, with their eyes closed.

"The year I turned sixteen from fifteen, I didn't see anybody," says Takey, an eighteen-year-old in jeans and a blue sweatshirt who still has the playful child in her face and a dimple in her cheek. "I was just tired. I did so many things I regret, back when I was dumb and wild and stupid. I hate thinking about it. But by the time I hit sixteen, I didn't see anybody at all, and I wasn't interested. I knew I'd meet somebody when the time was right for me.

"Then I met Vince. He came with Thomas to a party at Marty's house. His looks weren't that great. He *had* looks, but they weren't that noticeable to me. The way he danced was the first thing I noticed about him. Later I went into the kitchen to get something, and he wouldn't let me out. He stood in the doorway blocking me. I said, 'Excuse me,' but he just stared at me. I said, 'What can I get you?' He said, 'Give me your phone number.' I don't know why I gave it to him, but I gave it to him."

That magic click happened, once again, without conscious understanding. Now Takey says she wouldn't trade her life with anybody's. She and Vince, who's Jamaican and nineteen years old, spend the majority of their time together. The two are monogomous, and loyal, but they don't see legal marriage as something they want at this point in their lives.

"We didn't get really close until this past summer," she says, poking her comb into an Afro already combed to perfection. "I wasn't going to get serious about it. I wasn't going to climb the mountain to get pushed off. To get to know someone—to really know them and let them know you—it takes so much energy to know all the sides. I didn't want to go through all that and just break up. But it turns out that I came along at a good time for him and he came along at a good time for me. He used to be a real Casanova, and he just got tired of all that. He wanted something deep with someone, and so did I."

The depth and energy of teenage love is often startling to adults who may have momentarily forgotten how they lost twenty pounds after the breakup of their first affair or how they sat, crying night after night, longing for the telephone to ring, and then laughing with joy when it did. The agonies, obsessions and ecstasies of being in love when you are sixteen or eighteen or fifteen are just as real and just as important and critical to the people involved as they are to someone twenty, sixty or thirty. Sometimes, in fact, they are even *more* critical and more important than what follows because they are so formative.

Chip, talking about his relationship with Kay Ellen, nearly flies with the memory. "She was the first girl I ever felt in love with," says Chip, an eighteen-year-old who has ushered me into his parents' elegant apartment overlooking Central Park. "The first time I ever made love with a girl was with her the summer right after I turned fourteen. We had a relationship for nine months. It was beautiful.

"I went on this ski tour in Switzerland, and we met each other there. We were both from New York City. She moved into my room and so we lived together for eight weeks. Then when we came back to New York, it lasted eight months.

"With Kay Ellen, I tripped LSD a couple of times and we smoked a lot. We did everything together. I came out of the relationship definitely changed. My emotions were so much different than they were when we started. She was very sensitive. She used to cry all the time. We got very, very close. In many respects, we became one person. You know that song, 'One and one don't make two, one and one make one'? That was true of us. Really . . . We were hippies in love. The beautiful thing was we communicated so openly.

"My parents liked her a lot. They let us sleep together here."

When Chip and Kay broke up after nine months, it wasn't a ruptured or fractured ending. It was, somehow, a natural conclusion to what they each considered a very good part of their lives.

"We were just growing apart," says Chip. "It all happened in a week. I was getting very involved with my music, and she was very much involved with her acting. We were only seeing each other two or three times a week, so we stopped seeing each other. She told me she'd never loved anybody as much as she'd loved me. It was a wonderful first love. We never once had a violent argument, because if something was on our minds, I'd tell her and she'd tell me."

Chip, who was planning to go to college, wants to "be very well off" and wants "to settle down with one girl."

"I think I'm going to marry a very deep girl—who's open and who really understands me, like my best friend understands me, like Kay Ellen understood me."

In a long-term, ongoing affair, girls often feel secure enough to enjoy sexual intercourse, if they chose to have it, whereas their previous experience might have been too anxiety ridden to be pleasurable. Shyrell, for instance, had hated sex with Andrew, her first boyfriend. He came over to her house almost every night and snuck into her bed and she did it "only because he wanted it." She was constantly worried about getting caught or getting pregnant, and each time just "counted off the minutes until he'd come and it'd be over with."

When she started going out with Peter, however, she was older—eighteen instead of sixteen—more confident and more relaxed. Peter was older, and he had his own apartment. On account of the privacy and the feeling that she was loved and that she could assert her wants, she felt quite differently about sex with Peter than she had with Andrew.

"With him, I feel wonderful," she says. "Like when he kissed me the first time, I had chills. I never had that before. He's older than I am, too, and I feel more comfortable with him. We're having sex pretty regularly. Before, I always felt guilty and cheap. I don't feel guilty at all having sex with Peter. I feel it's what we're supposed to be doing."

Girls and boys alike say that when they really are in love, sex is better than it ever was before.

"I'd never had an orgasm until one night Danny and I were at his dad's house for overnight, and he said, 'You know I love you. Now I just want you to lay back and relax,' and he went down and started licking my clit," says Margaret. "At first I felt really nervous, but then I relaxed and I started feeling it, and then after a while, this incredible feeling came over me and it just took me up inside the feeling. Like waves washing up to my brain and blacking everything out. It was so wonderful. I felt so total. After that, I started coming more often, even when we were having sex."

"The first time I ever felt totally loved with anybody was with Shelley," said Joe. "We were making love and when I came inside her, I really felt like my whole body was exploding. I kept coming—it lasted so long I couldn't believe how it kept coming. I never felt so happy in all my life."

For Angela, sex was never satisfying or joyful until she and Mark began their long-term affair. At nineteen, Angela is very attractive, lively, lithe, warm and funny. Her father was black, her mother white, and she herself has tawny, smooth skin and soft, curly brown hair. Wire-rimmed glasses slide down her nose as she talks about herself and Mark, the love of her life for the past three years.

"The way I look at it, there's two levels of sex," she says. "One is purely the act of pleasure, and the second level is when two people really care about each other. Then it's a lot more real, and *a lot* better! It's like real whipped cream as opposed to Redi-Made whipped cream. If you can have the real thing, why take a substitute?"

"One person gets boring," Angela's younger sister called out from the other side of the kitchen.

"It doesn't get boring," she said back. "It just gets better and better."

"I want to do something meaningful with my life," says Angela, who has worked for the past two years in a bank. "The one thing that would complete me is a college degree. My chances of making money would be better and I could do some kind of work I'd enjoy. Maybe we all want to do one step better than our parents did. There are a lot of things I'd like to do. I would like to hang-glide. I'd like to sail around the world with Jacques Cousteau once I get over my fear of fish. I'd like to play the flute and make stained-glass windows. These are some of my fantasies.

"I'm a poor person with ultraclass tastes," she says, spinning her spoon in her coffee cup and chuckling. "I have this fantasy where once in my life, I'd like to do the cancan in Paris with a red ruffled skirt on and have men throw money at me."

Angela's humor, her gentle warmth and perspective on herself didn't arrive suddenly in a night's dream. She's had many difficult times and a rocky beginning as an adolescent, doing her share of screwing around, smoking joints, getting drunk to try it all out. When she was younger, her parents worried a lot about her.

Angela remembers why. One time, for instance, when she was fourteen years old, she got up one morning and went to school, where she drank three shots of tequila, smoked two joints, went to a friend's house near the school and passed out. During the same period of time, she had intercourse for the first time, and it was an impersonal, unsatisfying experience.

"I consider myself settled in life as far as that's concerned," she says. "I'm not interested in going to bed with a lot of men. There's more to a relationship than sex, and you get more out of sex when there's more to the relationship.

"When Mark's gone, I don't want to go out with other men. I don't want to sleep with anybody else. I want to do something like skydive. I'd like that: that'd make me happy.

"Mark is *so* gorgeous. I didn't like him when we were kids. He was a big jock at Friend's Select School, and I thought he was stuck up. . . .

"Now we're going into the end of our third year. It's not that long when I look at it. But as long as it lasts, you enjoy it. . . . As far as I'm concerned, it could last a lifetime. . . ."

It may be that as Angela and Mark each grow and evolve, their needs and interests will shift or change focus. New goals or new concerns may come between them. But no matter whether they stay together or part, they've given each other great nourishment and comfort and care that has contributed to making them the people they are.

Sometimes couples who start together very young do stay together and choose to marry. Evelyn, a thin, attractive girl with very pale skin, adjusts her shorts, crosses her bare legs and pushes her glasses to the top of her head. It's summertime in Chicago, and she has been married to her childhood sweetheart, James, for three months. The two have known each other since they were in second grade and have gone together since they were fifteen years old. They broke up once in high school and once during Evelyn's freshman year in college.

We are sitting in a small, cozy apartment, sipping iced tea. James is at work downtown; Evelyn doesn't go to work until two in the afternoon.

"I started college three months before I turned seventeen," says Evelyn. "At the end of the first semester, I broke up with James and got involved with other people. But all the other guys were jerks. I did it with them more because it was expected of me than because I wanted to. At that point, I felt badly about our breakup and I didn't care. I didn't care about myself or anything. I tried drugs, acid and grass and that sort of thing. It was a pretty crazy time.

"I wouldn't characterize any of these relationships as good. There wasn't any communication. There wasn't any love. They were only interested in self-gratification.

"Finally James and I wrote letters that crossed in the mail saying we wanted to see each other again. We got the letters the same day. We got back together again, and I transferred to his college."

One of the main attractions of Evelyn and James' relationship was that they cared deeply for one another—enough to let the other have enough privacy to evolve into the separate and distinct individual he or she is. From the beginning, their sexual relationship reflected other good aspects of their interaction. They always thought of sex as very private and very important. "We didn't take it casually at all," she says. "The love that was involved was the most important thing," she says. "Sex without love, without caring, is nothing. The way we feel, our marriage is an extension of that same caring. . . ."

Both Evelyn and James were products of very happy two-parent homes, and they felt they had realistically appraised their own relationship and would be able to make a good marriage. "We have good models," Evelyn said. "We know there will be rough times, but we also know that we each have the love and flexibility to grow through bad times as well as good times. We've done it before."

Although Census Bureau figures show the chances of wives who marry in their early teens getting divorced are twice as high as for women married between the ages of eighteen and nineteen, and four times as high for wives married when they are twenty-five or older, some teenagers do manage to "grow up" together and to change together whether they marry at fifteen or at eighteen. The couples who aren't able to maintain their marriages often are unable to manage their developing identities and their conflicting roles as teenagers and "adult" marital partners. Sometimes they've chosen a socially acceptable means of escaping home but haven't escaped the problems that plagued them there.

In some cases, however, it seems that very young couples are quite innovative in trying out new roles and learning together how to make their marriage work. In Beverly and Bill's marriage in Los Angeles, the two were molding what worked for them, which was quite unlike either of their parents' relationships.

"Bill's such a good cook that I'd feel dumb cooking," says Beverly, an eighteen-year-old high-school senior who has been married for nearly a year. "Not that he'd say you did this wrong and that wrong . . . just that he's so good and he does it so well that it'd be dumb for me to do it.

"He hates doing dishes, so I do the dishes. I do most of the housework, but I hate vacuuming, so he vacuums for me. He's Mr. Neatness. He'd have me iron his T-shirts if I would, but I wouldn't.

"Sometimes we fight. You're not going to agree all the time. You're two different people. You're going to fight. You've got to be secure within the relationship to fight in the first place. . . .

"We got married because we wanted to and because we're ready. I wasn't pregnant or anything. He's twenty, and it just seemed right. We didn't want to sneak around. We wanted to live together like a woman and a man, and that's what we're doing."

For most teenagers, relationships are practice sessions for future marriages. They also serve as vehicles into adulthood and as opportunities for the intimate release of primitive feelings and urges, from the warmth of infantile cuddling to the intensity of sexual release, from jealousy and possessiveness to oedipal fantasy and anger. The pool of feelings from young years are stirred in close relationships, and sometimes ghosts appear out of the brew. In day-to-day interactions, they often find themselves reacting to each other as they would react to their own parents or in a way their parents would react. They see their fantasies blown to bits as well as fulfilled. Sometimes they cope well; sometimes they don't. Michael and Jennifer, for instance, seem to be behaving toward one another almost exactly as they have seen each of their same-sex parents behave—a complication not unusual in any relationship.

"Remember when I told you we were going to go on that picnic on Saturday and have so much fun?" Jennifer asked, tossing her hair back over her shoulders and picking at the butterfly sewn on the pocket of her denim shirt. "Well, Michael picked me up and he was tired from work, so he asked me to drive his car. I was driving down the road and I swerved to miss this dead cat, and there was this car coming, so we just missed it and he said, 'Goddamnit, can't you drive a car?'

"When we got to the park, I pulled up too far and he yelled, 'Don't you know how to drive?' Each time, I just hung onto the wheel and didn't say anything.

"Before we went to the park, we'd gone to get some fried chicken to take with us. When I stopped the car, he said, 'I suppose now you're not hungry.' And I said, 'No, I'm not. I don't want to eat your food anyway.'

"So I walked away from the truck, and then when I came back, he threw the Frisbee at me, and he said, 'Think you can throw a Frisbee?' and I said, 'I can't throw it good enough for you!'

" 'Okay, then, you might as well go back home.'

"So we got into the car and we were driving back to town and I felt terrible and I said 'Was it all my fault again this time, Michael?' And he said, 'No, it wasn't.' He said, 'I shouldn't have yelled at you.' Then he apologized, and we made up and everything was fine after that."

Michael works at the electric company in Tulsa, Oklahoma. He already "graduated" from his first year of college, as Jennifer puts it, and plans to go back to finish four more years for an engineering degree while she's working. Jennifer plans to go to college, too, and hopes to get a degree before she gets married. At seventeen years old, Jennifer has been going with Michael, who's nineteen, for a year and a half.

"One time we broke up and I cried for three days straight," she says. "I didn't eat anything. I lost six pounds within those three days. Well, after those three days, Nicki and Kate made me call him at lunch one day. I dialed his number and he answered the phone. When I heard his voice, I said 'Oh My God!' and hung up. Well, then they said I had to call him back, so I dialed his number and I heard his voice and then I said, 'Michael, can you pick me up?' He said, 'What for?' and I said, 'Well, I'd like to talk.'

" 'Well, what for?'

" 'Well, I don't understand everything.'

" 'Well, I don't either,' he said.

" 'Well, can you pick me up anyway? So we can talk.'

"He said, 'Well, I'll have to see what my work schedule is, but I guess I could pick you up for a few minutes.'

"Well, then he picked me up and we went to the park and we were standing by this willow tree and he just kept looking at me. Inside I was hoping and praying. I was saying oh, ask me to go back together with you, and I said to him, 'Why are you looking at me?' He said, 'I'm just thinking.'

"Then I said, 'Michael, I'm not asking you to go back with me or anything. I want you to know that. I just want to know why you broke up with me.'

"He said, 'I don't know why.' Inside, I was saying, oh goody, goody. Well, then we walked down towards the river without saying anything and then back up to the swings. Then he sat on one of the swings and I was standing there and he wrapped his legs around me and said, 'Won't you go back with me?' I said, 'Oh yes, Michael, I'll go back with you.' And he said, 'Don't say it so quick—think about it for a while. I'll call you on Saturday.' Then I said, 'I guess I should be able to make up my mind by Saturday.'

"I was so happy then.

"When we got back, he wouldn't say I love you. He said he'd made too many commitments before, and he didn't want to do that again at this point. See, before when we broke up, I really threw it back at him. I said, 'You promised you'd love me and you promised me you'd never leave me, and now you're leaving me.' So now he won't say I love you to me because he's afraid that I'll throw it back at him again if we ever break up."

Even when a relationship is complicated by role playing and fantasies and other dynamics that interfere, the ardor of that love between two high-energy people meeting in one common space is extraordinary. The emotions can literally go sky-high.

Just as teenagers learn through relationships that love isn't always perfect, just as they learn to cope with another person's interests and habits, they also learn to live with disappointments in relationships and, often, to cope with losses. The breaking up of a love affair is always painful, but when one partner doesn't let go, and feels tormented and frustrated by something that's clearly no longer mutual and no longer operable, the pain is extraordinary. This may be all the more true for young people who still are forming a sense of themselves, who may have been depending on the other person for much of their identity or self-worth.

Even when the affair has been one-sided all along, giving up the dream and the security of it is very traumatic. With Ned and Laura Anne's breakup, Ned had to deal with many emotions he found in himself that he didn't like.

"One of the problems always was, she flirts," says Ned, a tall, chocolate-skinned eighteen-year-old in pressed denim pants and a trim, blue plaid shirt. "She can't help herself. The problem with that was, I was jealous. I hate jealousy. My father was an extremely jealous person, and that was something I never wanted to be. But she kept going off, and I kept telling myself, that's okay, I don't own her. She'd flirt with this one and that one, and I'd say, that's all right, but then it got to me.

"My first omen was when her mother asked me to their country house (outside Boston) for the weekend and Laura Anne didn't say anything. I could tell she didn't want me to go because she wasn't in love with me anymore. After they left for the summer, I wasn't able to have her magic reach out and grab me.

"I just worked that summer and I flowed in and out and tried to keep my sanity.

"In the fall, when she came back, we'd start getting close again, and then she'd disappear on me. When she was upset and confused about all these guys surrounding her, she'd turn to me. And I was always there, waiting.

"Finally, though, I couldn't take it anymore. I decided I was going to make my last and final plea to her. I couldn't stand being second guy anymore, so I asked her to make the decision about how she felt about me. I told her to think about it and let me know. I was waiting for her that afternoon, but she didn't come down to gym class, so I went up to her locker. She was standing there with Matt. I saw them. They didn't see me. But they were standing there with their arms around each other, looking so good and so comfortable with each other. I felt this empty, nauseous feeling in my chest. It just hit me, so I walked away.

"When I saw her later, I said, 'It doesn't look too good, does it?' She said, 'No.' And then we took a walk and we both started crying.

"Then I began my week of agony. It got worse as it went. I couldn't sleep, I couldn't eat and I started drinking. That first evening, I needed someone to talk to, but I didn't have anybody. I felt alone. I felt cold. I felt bitter and angry. I loved her too much to be angry with her, but I was angry at what she did.

"I'm a musician. I play the piano—and I couldn't do it. I'm in a group, and I just couldn't do it. At work, I kept dropping things—and breaking dishes and forgetting orders. I started smoking. That helped a bit."

Even though the agony of their breakup seemed unending, Ned did find out some positive things about himself from the experience. "One thing I found out," he says, "was that I had a lot of friends. They'd say, 'You'll meet someone else,' and I'd say, 'Yeah.' That didn't help, but it was sort of good to hear. My mother even realized what Laura Anne had meant to me. She came up and said, 'I never realized it, but you are really in love with that girl.' I said, 'Yeah, I guess so.'

"Our main problem was that Laura Anne didn't know me. She couldn't accept me and who I am. Whenever I tried to give her something of myself, she ran away. I needed someone to share myself with, and I wanted to share myself with her, but it became a one-sided kind of thing. I was doing all the sharing. . . ."

Sometimes, because ending that first affair is so excruciating, because the sense of failure and loss and desperation is so overwhelming, teenagers can be very cruel to one another. They don't have a monopoly on cruelty, of course. Adults do the same things even though theoretically they're wiser because they're older. In the meantime, the cruelty does its damage, as it did to Nicki's ability to trust.

I first met Nicki at her high school in St. Paul, Minnesota. I was talking to a friend of hers when I saw Craig, wide-shouldered, with a bounce in his walk, striding down the corridor toward Nicki.

About the same time, a boy behind him said, "Hey Nicki, where's Bill?"

"Probably at home in bed with VD," Craig shouted. "Where else would he be?"

Nicki turned and glared at Craig. "Shut your dirty mouth! I hate you, I really hate you!"

"You know if you could get me back, you would."

"I'd sooner get a rusty combine." In tears, Nicki turned and walked down the corridor, then broke into a run and went sobbing into the girls' rest room.

Craig and Nicki had gone together for two years and broken up the summer before this exchange. After a year and a half of going out with one another, they had decided they would make love.

"I was his first girl friend, and we weren't too smart about it," she tells me later. "I thought it would be dirty, but it wasn't at all like that.

I'd been going with him, and I knew he loved me and I loved him. I didn't feel embarrassed or ashamed. It was romantic, too. Afterwards we had a bottle of wine. His best friend gave him the key to the house, and when we went there, we knew we were going to make love.

"After that first time, though, it got worse between us. Our relationship didn't grow any closer. After a while, sex was all he wanted. When we broke up in May, then when we'd go out, he'd still want to do things. Then I felt really used. Like when my folks went away on vacation, he was really nice to me because he wanted to have sex.

"I thought if I did things with him, he'd love me more. But it didn't work that way. He was the first person I ever told I loved. Now he's so mean to me. He practically spits on me in the hallway.

"Now I'm afraid to get close to anybody, and that's really bad. The other bad thing is that Craig's got a runoff mouth. About a month after we first made love, he started wanting to do this and that, like oral sex. He told his friends, and this one guy said to me, 'Everybody knows you're screwing Craig.' Someone said I gave him blow-jobs all the time, and that he ate me out, but that wasn't true. Now when I go out with someone, Craig always says to them, 'Oh, did you screw her yet?' "

As Nicki talks, she keeps wiping away tears that continue to fall from her eyes. Her face is red and splotchy. "At the beginning of school, I cried every day because I felt so lost I couldn't stop crying. He was the only person I ever cared about and trusted, even more than my mom and dad."

Unless you make the same bad choices over and over again, you're learning about being intimate with people, and it can be instructive for all the relationships that follow. You learn what to look out for in the other person as well as yourself. You learn, by experience, what values are most important to you. You also learn that sometimes you say things through your behavior that you had not articulated to yourself in words.

"I went with Ted half my junior year and all of my senior year," said Karen Schmidt, a nineteen-year-old from Detroit. "We were quite serious, and now we're not even hardly talking.

"I like him a lot and I loved his family—and I had mixed feelings about him. We talked about getting married, not real serious like setting a date, but we'd say things like, 'When we get married. . . .'

"I've realized that one of the reasons I stayed with him was because people talked against him. My dad didn't like him. He thought he was lazy and selfish and self-centered. Everybody was always saying, 'You can do better than him.' That made me mad. I wanted to prove we could make it. . . .

"Now I'm going with Weston, and it's so different. Everybody thinks that we're such a perfect couple; I'm not used to it. But I decided I'd never make my own personal decisions in reaction to other people's reactions again. I know I want to get a guy who has the same type of desires I have; that's really important to me. I don't want to waste my life. We have to have the same kind of desires and commitments.

"Weston, he likes to have fun and do fun things. He's really crazy sometimes. We toilet-paper-decorated someone's yard and put tin cans on cars. . . . It was so much fun and so crazy. Weston is also very understanding. Like the other night my dad lost his temper at my sister and hit her. He was yelling at her and it was pretty awful. I felt really bad that Weston had to be there and hear it all. He said, 'Every household has its problems.' He's really intelligent, and he feels like everything he does, he likes to do it the best he can. I'm that way, too, but not as much as him. . . . I'm a poor reader and a poorer speller. . . .'"

Trisha learned a great deal from her relationship with Turner that she values; but from their breakup, perhaps, she learned even more. The two went together her junior and senior years of high school and her freshman year of college.

"The breakup was initiated by him," Trisha says, folding her long, slender fingers around her thin arms, almost hugging herself at the memory. "The whole time we went out, he'd go out with other women and make inferences to me that he'd had sex with them. I knew about it and accepted it. He was honest from the beginning. He'd gone with this other woman and felt really trapped by her and didn't want that to happen again. He'd always tell me how much he loved me, and how seeing other women made him know how much he loved me.

"At one point, he started going out with a friend of mine, though, and I said, 'If you go out with someone else on a regular basis, I'm going to have to go out with someone else, too.' So I did. That made him lose interest in her real fast. Eventually it became very rare that he'd go out with anyone else, but in the meantime, I started college.

"At college, I met this guy Stan, who I became friends with. We decided that one night we'd sleep together to see what it would be like to have an 'affair.' It was real fun, like a pajama party. I brought a candle and an album. It was an experiment, and it wasn't great. It was like the first time with Turner, really nothing. But we both learned a good thing from this. We had loving feelings for each other, but we learned there has to be more. There has to be sexual excitement. And electricity. If you want to have an affair, you have to ask, 'Do you feel a real attraction for each other?' If the answer is no, then it won't be any good.

"A few weekends later, Turner and I got together and he told me that he wanted me to know he'd gotten drunk and lonely the night before, and picked up this woman and slept with her. 'It wasn't any good,' he said. 'It just made me know how much I loved you.'

"Then I told him I'd slept with Stan and it wasn't any good and how it made me realize how much we had going for us, and how much I loved and cared about him.

"He flipped out. He said, 'You slept with someone else! How could you do such a thing?' Even to this day I've remained the eternal virgin to him. Even though we slept together, he always treated me that way. The whole night, Turner kept saying, 'Why did you do it?' I kept telling him, 'I love you; don't be threatened by it!'

"Anyway, we'd spoken about it for twelve hours straight, and I said, 'I can't talk about it anymore. I have to get some sleep.' The next day he called me and said, 'I can't live with the idea of you going out with anyone else.' He said he wanted to break up. I said, 'You're being ridiculous!'

"After that, even though he had said he was breaking off with me, he'd call me up and hassle me and see who I was with.

"He said he was coming to see me that weekend, and I said, 'Don't come.' I told him, 'I don't want to see you. It won't serve any purpose.' He came anyway, and all weekend, he said everytime we passed someone or he thought of someone, 'Would you sleep with him, or him, or him . . . ?' He came Friday night and I wouldn't sleep with him. He left Saturday morning, and for the first time, when he left, I felt really relieved. That morning when he left, his heart was really broken, but I felt he did it to himself.

"He called me about once a week for a long time after that and started each time by being nice, and ten minutes later, he'd end up being nasty. In the end, I started seeing someone else, and that helped him step back. Now we're friends—but I'd never get involved with him again."

In a good relationship, even if it doesn't last forever, both people can learn a great deal about their own beliefs and values. They can define themselves as individuals and learn about their own limits, responses and psychological investments. Because they each have an extra set of eyes, they learn to see themselves from another's perspective. The experience can be extremely expansive.

Jerry stretches his long legs out onto the coffee table in front of him. He's a tall young man who will only be a teenager for another month. Currently he's on a work break, and we're sitting in his parents' home in San Francisco. The neighborhood where they live is an old neighborhood where the architecture is an interesting blend of Spanish and modern, Mexican and Oriental. There seems to be a comfort here, an atmosphere of bohemia that pleases the senses.

"In the beginning of high school, I was always falling in love with beauty," he was saying. "I had beauty as my high criteria. The ones who fit all the pictures. Then I'd get disillusioned with them because I'd discover the dissatisfaction of experiencing sex with ladies I didn't care about. I knew there were more important things and there were more valuable things.

"It was partially because I was still influenced by my peers. I found out quickly that you exploit yourself when you exploit others. That was a big step for me. Also, finding out that beauty and sex were no big deal was quite significant.

"My biggest fear of getting involved with someone was the one of rejection—that very primal thing of not being loved. So I put up defenses like the male macho image of being cool and strong, to keep women at bay or whatever. Well, I learned that was a fallacy and all you have to do is truly care about someone to get through that."

Jerry chooses his words carefully. He somehow sounds like the son of college professors, which he is. He wears new, tight jeans and a light red plaid shirt, a light brown leather belt and loafers. His fingers are long, and he fans them as he speaks.

In eleventh grade, he says, he started having a relationship that "officially" lasted three years. "I'm still very close to her," he says. "We have an ongoing relationship. We've had a lot of learning, a lot of sharing, a lot of pain and a lot of insight through the pain—through compromise and being willing to change and not being stuck in self-righteousness."

I said that sounded a lot like a modern marriage, California-language and -style.

"We always considered it a spiritual marriage," he said with a serious expression, displeased with my levity. "In a way, we're still together now. We've never formally broken up. Our relationship is based on honesty and being supportive of each other.

"The biggest low in our relationship was my breaking through the facade of being cold and strong," he says. "She always seemed more openly dependent, but she was strong enough that she could handle breaking up or whatever happened to our relationship. I *seemed* less dependent—but I was doing a real egocentric number, acting and feeling confident that I could do without the love and the support. It was really the fear of not being lovable or okay the way I am.

"She'd always confront me on everything, so to be with her was to face my problems. People always really loved her. She's a very special person. She's not hard to appreciate. She always likes to see what she can do to support people and to help and assist them in any way she can.

"We don't have any agreement not to see other people. It just so happens not much else is going on. Now we're living totally independent lives, but we're spiritually and intellectually just as close as ever, and we're in constant correspondence.

"Because of our relationship, I know some of the things I have to offer, and I know some of the things I appreciate. I also know I won't compromise now, and that narrows things down quite a bit.

"I know we're always going to be best friends. I know I'm going to know her all my life. Maybe we'll continue to be lovers and maybe we won't. Sometimes when we get together, we do have sex and sometimes we don't. It depends only on whether it's emotionally healthy for both of us at the time.

"Sometimes I think we may stay together. Sometimes I think no.

"I'm coming to grips more and more about things I'm here to do and learn. I consider myself very fortunate."

Being part of a couple is an act of stretching. It is a maturing process, an unveiling of one's very self. When we talk about growing up, it's part of the process that includes learning how to communicate, how to be intimate, how to share, how to love and give, how to understand and assert one's self at the same time. Certainly, that process is one of the things that makes life on this planet most interesting.

14.

Homosexual Relationships

"Yesterday my grandchildren asked me what homosexuals *do*," a seventy-four-year-old friend of mine told me recently. "They're eleven and twelve years old, and the eleven-year-old was the one who asked me.

"Well, that got me. I thought for a moment, and then I told them I suspected that homosexuals shopped for groceries like other people, and that they did all the same things as everybody else except that they loved their same sex more than the opposite sex. I couldn't bring myself to say any more and they didn't ask any more.

"I was sixty years old before I figured out how homosexuals do it. I just never thought about it before then. Isn't that amazing?"

Since sex is so openly talked about today, different sexual orientations are a matter of common knowledge. One night recently I turned on the television to find that homosexuality was the theme of shows on three different channels. What once was a matter of personal humiliation, a sexual preference unacceptable on the job or in the schoolyard, is now widely acknowledged and accepted. Through demonstrations, legislation, lawsuits, open forums and articles, homosexual activists have made the public aware of discrimination against them. They have made people realize that homosexuality is not one thing but actually represents a huge variety of separate relationships, a gradation of experiences and responses that are not exclusively homosexual or heteorsexual, and an assortment of separate reasons for moving into predominantly homosexual adaptations.

Most of the teenagers with whom I talked felt that sexual preference was every person's right. They were accepting of individual choice.

"I think homosexuality is fine as long as that's what they want," said

235

seventeen-year-old Dean. "Like those two guys who wanted to go to
their high-school prom together in Nebraska. I think that's their right.
They should be able to choose who they want to be with just like anybody else."

"As long as they love each other," said Michelle, "and it's good for
them, it doesn't bother me. It's when people use each other it's no good,
but that's true for anybody."

Other adolescents expressed far less tolerant views, some quite hostile
and vociferous. For the most part, these views were expressed by boys—
and only a few at that.

"I detest homosexuality," said Stanley, a high-school senior from
Seattle. "I hate it. I couldn't relate to that. I think they're screwed up. I
think it's a disease. There's no way that's normal."

"I'm against homosexuality," said Douglas, a high-school senior in
Santa Ana who had strong religious views. "There's a few places in the
Bible that say it's evil. Most of the time in the Bible, when it talks about
marriage, it refers to a man and a woman. If God had intended two
women or two men to be together, he would have said so. It's just another form of lust. Even if they cared about each other, I still think it's evil.
Men doing evil things with each other is unnatural. The reference to
sodomy is taken from the evil cities of Sodom and Gomorrah in the
Bible."

Much more common was a toleration for the homosexual behavior of
others. When adolescents had family or friends involved in homosexual
life, they had particularly sympathetic perspectives and insights on the
subject.

"My godfather's gay," says Janice, a fifteen-year-old from Boston.
"He's always telling these stories. He travels a lot, and the last time I
saw him, he was saying that when his flight was delayed a couple of
hours in New Orleans, he picked up this guy and went to bed with him.
He's always saying things like that."

"One of our teachers is gay," said Leon, a private-school student in
New York. "When he came out of the closet, he allowed himself to take
on whole new expressions. He started acting differently—more loose
and gay-looking and effeminate at the same time. A lot of the guys
made jokes. They'd back up as if they thought he was going to touch
them and that kind of thing. Some people were pretty mean. But I
thought it took a lot of courage for him to come out. Things have settled
down about it now, but there was a lot of flak at first."

When close friends or peers get involved in homosexual experiences,
teenagers often feel shocked because they identify strongly with their
friends. They find that in such circumstances, they examine their own
attractions and emotions more closely.

"I had a friend who got it on with another close friend of mine, who's also a guy," said Austin," and I said *what?* It made me ask myself a lot of questions I'd never even considered before. It made me start to wonder about myself."

"A couple of weeks ago, I went into San Francisco with a couple of good friends of mine—guys," says Clark, a college freshman at Berkeley. "We all got sort of drunk and we came home really late. I'd been behaving like I was really out of it, which I was, partially. Anyway, I was staying over at their place, on cushions on the floor in this big studio apartment. Anyway, at four or five in the morning, I woke up and they were talking about whether I was asleep. I knew for about five minutes I was being studied to see if I was awake, so I purposely made a noise and pulled the sheets up over me.

"After that, I was 98 percent sure they were going at it with each other. I couldn't believe it at all. I was trying desperately not to make a sound. My heart was beating so loud, I was sure I was going to have a seizure.

"The next morning it was 'Oh, I had a really good sleep' and 'How did you sleep, Clark?' All normal and like nothing had happened.

"They probably look at it in a very logical way. I don't know! They're both very sensitive people, and they're very good friends. One of them lost his virginity at thirteen, and the other one at fourteen. That might have something to do with it. They might have very bad feelings about women because of it. Or they might be saying since there's a momentary lull, we might as well get it on with each other. One of them vehemently denies having a homosexual relationship; the other one jokes about it.

"It made me very uncomfortable, being witness to it all. I don't really know how to react."

Some adolescents told of experimenting with homosexuality themselves on one or more occasions. Although only a small percentage of the population is exclusively homosexual throughout their lives, many people as teenagers or preteens have sexual or sensual experiences with a person of the same sex—a best friend or an acquaintance. (Kinsey found, in fact, that two out of every five males in the total population had at least some overt homosexual experience to the point of orgasm between adolescence and old age.)[1] Most of these experiences are explorations, confirmations of their own bodies and responses—and have little or nothing to do with distinguishing sexual preferences. Certainly they do not affect a person's lifelong sexual identification or serve as cause for categorization as homosexual.

Because we have a tendency in our society to consider an individual homosexual if he or she is known to have had a single experience with another individual of the same sex, many teenagers worry that they are homosexual on the basis of feelings of attraction or isolated experiences.

According to Kinsey, "all such misjudgments are the product of the tendency to categorize sexual activities under only two heads, and of a failure to recognize the endless gradations that actually exist."[2]

"When I was thirteen and fourteen, I was president of this club of boys," said eighteen-year-old Arnold from Columbus, Maryland. "In that neighborhood, everyone would get together and we'd go around the neighborhood and get old rugs and old floodlights. Then we'd go out in the woods and build a house between the trees. We'd build the house up off the ground so if it rained, we wouldn't get wet. Once we got the first floor, we'd try to build the second floor. That was the private room.

"We got into situations where we'd spend the night out there, just boys. . . . We'd do all kinds of things. . . . We'd play swordsmen with old antennas and have wars. Everybody had their own houses, but theirs got burned, mainly from smoking cigarettes in them, and so most of them joined ours [club].

"One night when we were staying overnight, a boy approached me that was younger. He was twelve and I was fourteen. We were up in the private room. We dry humped—that was the only thing I knew. It was new, but I understood it was sexual. I was scared of that.

"I think homosexuality's a normal part of experimenting," says eighteen-year-old Linda. "A lot of people have had bisexual relationships and have heterosexual relationships afterwards. One of my best friends experimented with bisexuality when she was a senior in high school, and now she's very seriously involved with a man. I don't feel it's something I'd personally want to do, but for her, it was an important experience. She needed to do it to find out who she was and what she wanted out of life."

While some adolescents told of their experimentations with homosexuality, others acknowledged strong curiosity about it and said they flirted with the possibility of experimenting with a "bisexual" or homosexual relationship at some point.

"I've been around homosexuality a lot in my life," says fifteen-year-old Sue Ellen. "I've been opened to it through my family and other people I know. Lesbianism is a possibility I entertain. I've always had a very strong relationship with women, but never physical. It's never gotten to that."

"I wonder about my mom sometimes," says Jacqui, in New Haven. "She has a lot of gay friends—lesbian women who are also artists. I don't think she is, but sometimes I wonder. I know she's very comfortable with them as friends."

"I think it's a period everybody goes through," she says. "Some people just go farther with it than others."

As Kinsey pointed out, the histories of thousands of people make it apparent that heterosexuality or homosexuality of many individuals is not an all-or-none proposition. Although there are many people whose histories are exclusively heterosexual or exclusively homosexual, both in experience and psychic reaction, the record also shows that there is a considerable portion of the population whose members have combined, within their individual histories, both homosexual and heterosexual experience and/or psychic responses. There are some whose heterosexual experiences predominate, some whose homosexual experiences predominate, and some who have had quite equal amounts of both types of experiences.[3]

Because many people still believe that homosexuality is immoral or abnormal, and because being homosexual or "gay" in our society is often looked upon as a definition and category separate and apart from the heterosexual or "straight" community, the discovery of distinct homosexual preference is often discomforting.

"The gay situation, well, I was always shy about it because I didn't want no one to ever know because there'd be a lot of heartache in my family," said Randall, an eighteen-year-old who now defines himself as gay. "I also didn't understand it. It scared me to think about it for a long time."

Another young man I talked to was quite distressed to discover his erotic attraction to men and sexual preference for them. "Being gay is not being literally gay and happy," he said, sitting on the front steps of a friend's apartment. "I resent that word. I don't feel *gay* about being homosexual. It's not better than being heterosexual, and in some real, definite ways for me, like with my family and like with getting some kind of stable relationship, it's *worse*."

For some young people, the evolution of a clear homosexual preference is gradual. For others, the focus of their sexual interests is quite clear. Sean Zeigler, a nineteen-year-old college sophomore who grew up in a large family in Indianapolis, Indiana, for instance, had homosexual dreams from the time he was young.

"Between the ages of three and five, I'm told I was always prancing around in my sister's clothes," he says. "That's not so unusual, I suppose, but it was sort of a stigma on me growing up. People would sort of joke about it, but I didn't want to think it was another kind of sexuality.

"Then in junior high, I had a few infatuations with girls, but mainly I loved their faces and their beauty. By the time I was in high school, I knew I was truly gay. My fantasies centered around stereotypical masculine beauty. Then one time during the summer, there was a television documentary called 'An American Family,' and in it, the oldest son, Lance Loud, came out gay, right there on television. It excited me. He did things to his hair and dressed up in different clothes and tried things out. Seeing him gave me courage. When I went back to school that fall,

I had my hair cut short and I started wearing bright-colored shirts and trying out different appearances. I felt a lot looser about myself.

"I had a feeling things were going to be a lot different.They were in my head, but outside, nothing much really changed. I didn't go out with anybody or anything like that. The next summer, though, a friend of my brother's came to visit, and while he was there, he tried to seduce me. He was staying in my room, and he kept trying to convince me there was nothing wrong about two men making it together.

"One night when we were in my room, he kissed me. It blew my mind. I remember kissing girls, but it was all spit to me. I couldn't imagine why anyone liked it. I didn't like it. In fact, I couldn't stand it, and it wasn't any different with him. I just wasn't turned on. I thought I should have been if I was gay, but I had this superman image in my head, and he wasn't it.

"I still had largely a fantasy life. That was like a double life in itself. You have your fantasy life with masturbation, and everybody feels guilty about that to start with, and then I had all these homosexual fantasies to feel guilty about on top of masturbation!

"I was pretty popular in high school by being funny and getting into all the groups. I never got involved with anyone in high school, though. I was friends with this one guy who thought he was homosexual and used to talk to me about it. One night we left this party and went walking in the woods, and he pulled down his pants and started jerking off. I told him that if he thought he was gay, there were places he could go. I never let on to him that I thought I was gay, too. Partly, I suppose, he just wasn't my type."

The summer after his senior year of high school, Sean started going to gay bars in Chicago, and he felt good about getting attention and being an "object of desire." Finally he had his first sexual contact.

"One night this guy asked me to dance," says Sean. "He was real macho in a T-shirt, with big biceps, and it was an immediate turn-on for me. He had a 1930s car with upholstered seats, and we drove out to his place in the country. I had my pastels on, and I rode with it. I felt like I was a character in *The Great Gatsby*. He didn't live in a mansion, as it turned out, but it was nice, and he was a gentle teacher with me. He was twenty-two and I was eighteen. Physically, he was quite nice. I didn't know how nice since I didn't have anyone to compare him to."

Shortly after that, Sean fell in love and had his first affair. Even then, he never particularly liked the actual sexual act of sodomy. "I could never conceive of getting fucked," he said. "To actually have someone stick something up my ass. . . . I thought I *should* like it, but I didn't. It was very conditional with me. I used to hold back on that like it was a treasure I'd give. I was initially the person who got it, not the person who did it.

"I think in that relationship, I was putting myself into a role," he says. "I wanted a prototype of a straight relationship with him, and I wanted to be the feminine half. Later, when I found out he was having sex with other people, I was crushed. I was into a monogamous thing with him, but he was getting bored by me. Basically he was a jerk, but I was in love with him anyway."

Ed's introduction to homosexuality came as more of a surprise.

"When I was sixteen years old, I was thumbing and someone picked me up," says Ed, now nineteen years old, from Baltimore, Maryland. "I was always thumbing. He says, 'Where are you going?' He was a really nice guy. I told him I was going to work. I told him what time I was getting off, too. I don't know why I told him that, but I did. He told me he was gay, and I said, 'That's your thing.' I was working at a taco place. He came in one time after that and asked me if I wanted to go have a few beers. I said, 'Hey, why not?'

"So he waited, and when I got off work, we went riding around and drinking beer. I guess he was waiting for me to get pretty loaded so I'd be loose. Anyway, we drank a lot of beer, and then we'd driven out to this place in the country and we're sitting there talking and he says, 'You ever get a blow-job before?'

" 'No, not really, what do you do?'

"He says, 'I suck you off. If you'd like it, I'll do it.'

"So I did. It was unbelievable. I go for the feeling of it. It made me feel better than it ever could being inside a girl. I just sat back. The feeling was sensitive. It wasn't masculine at all. It was comfortable and relaxed, like hey, kick back and enjoy. I couldn't believe a feeling like that other than rubbing up against a girl or doing it with my hand.

"After I started coming, it lasted longer, that feeling I enjoyed. I couldn't believe it. When you're masturbating, it's quick, like two seconds. This was five to ten minutes. After that, he said, 'Did you like it? Did you enjoy it?' I said, 'Yeah, I did, did I! He said, 'If you enjoyed it, I enjoyed it.'

"It was friendly, and it was personal.

"Before that, it never occurred to me that it would make someone feel good or that it would feel good in my mouth. You can eat a piece of pie and that tastes good. I couldn't imagine that something you piss out of could taste good unless you could get into it emotionally."

Although Ed says he is more comfortable in gay places and with gay people, he still expresses ambivalence about exclusive preferences. "I think every man has a fantasy of finding the right man," he says. "I think if there was a right man for each man, there wouldn't be too many more babies made. . . ." At the same time, he says, "I wouldn't want my kid to be gay, but I'd understand it if he fell into it."

"When you go into being gay, you want to find that special person,"

Ed says, "and then other things happen, and you find various people and think, I like this but I don't like that. . . ."

Like many of his compatriates, Ed thinks the physical aspects of sex with a man are far superior to sex with a woman. His graphic reasons, however, may not have been analyzed in the same extraordinary way by many other people.

"I've had sex with a lot of girls, so I'm comparing," he says. "When I have sex with a guy, there's more control of movement. If that person gets into it, there's perfect control of movement. Also, with a girl, it doesn't come together tight. That would make it better for me. I love to have good sex, and with a man, that does it. It doesn't get loose, so the feeling is better.

"The only thing that's gross about it is that's where you go to the bathroom. But it's cleaner than with a girl. A girl puts these things in her vagina once a month and they're air exposed. They're made in a factory, and you don't know what's in 'em. That's not clean. With a guy, he goes to the bathroom every day and wipes himself. There's nothing foreign going in.

"If a girl gets down and sucks me, I get the same feeling as from a guy, but sticking it in a girl is kind of gross to me. Like that's a hole, and it's cloudy in there. I don't know what's in there or what's been in there. It made me shy from it. The difference is, what goes up inside her has been exposed to germs. With a man, it's coming from inside him, so it's clean.

"I've had it done to me, and the results are pretty satisfying. I was pretty surprised. When you're having it done to you, it hits something on the inside of you that holds the sperm sac, so it gives you this sensation inside. I got off having someone fuck me without anybody touching me. It was unbelievable.

"I want to find someone who will understand having sex with me as well as me having sex with him."

Despite open discussion about homosexuality, despite wider societal acceptance and the fact that the American Psychiatric Association now states that homosexuality is not an illness or psycho-sexual disorder, it's still difficult for heterosexual parents to acknowledge and accept that their child is involved in a homosexual relationship. Most parents want very much for their children to be happy but don't imagine they will be truly happy or fulfilled in a relationship with a person of the same sex. Social pressures and their own expectations add to their distress.

It seems particularly difficult for the teenager who falls in love with a person of the same sex when he or she is still living at home. How does a young woman handle her parents' response to her feelings? What does she do if they won't allow her to see her lover? When a teenager has graduated from high school and is away at college or living on her own, it's much easier.

In Susan's case, she's living at her parents' home and feels enormous strain. She hasn't talked to them about her relationship with Carolee, but she suspects they suspect. At the time we talked, Susan and Carolee hadn't seen each other in any private situation for more than two months. Susan's parents had forbidden her to see Carolee at all, so the two girls had to arrange furtive meetings over lunch or sneak telephone calls to one another. When I met Susan, she was a very lonesome girl. We met at West Philadelphia High, where she was a junior and an honor student. It was through her friendship with Carolee, she said, that she discovered she was gay.

"Our relationship evolved very slowly because I couldn't accept it," says Susan. "In a way, I still can't. I do, but I don't, too. It's just the fact that I'm scared of what my friends are going to think. I'm also scared of what my parents would think. A couple of months ago, they said I couldn't see Carolee at all. I think they know, underneath, but what they said is that she's a bad influence and it was her fault that I tried to run away, which wasn't true. . . ."

Susan was one of the most serious, articulate teenagers I met. She's a slim, attractive girl, but her expression was somber as she talked about Carolee. She says that "for Greeks," her parents are "very liberal," and that her mother, especially, has an open mind. Until our interview, Susan had never told anyone she thought she was gay. She told me when I asked her if she'd had any turning points or discoverings about her own sexuality. "Well, last year was a very important time for me," she said, looking at her hands. "That's when I found out I was gay. It was a feeling I had inside of me for a long time, and then a friend of mine started talking to me about it, and then we became more than friends."

When Carolee was a little girl, Susan said, she had one lesbian encounter. "She was going home one night, and an older girl asked to walk home with her," she said. "On the way, they stopped at this building. The girl said she just had to go in there for a few minutes to get something and told Carolee to come along. They climbed these steps and then the girl started raping Carolee. She doesn't remember exactly what happened, but she remembers she kept hitting at this girl the whole time because she knew it was wrong.

"The same thing happened to me by a baby-sitter when I was nine or ten," says Susan. "One night my parents were going to a dinner or something and so they went out and we had the baby-sitter there. I was allowed to stay up because I was the oldest, so I was downstairs in the living room. I don't know why but I asked her, 'How do you kiss a boy?' Instead of telling me, she showed me. Then she took all her clothes off and took off mine, and tried to make love to me. She was fifteen or sixteen or maybe older. In the time it was happening, though, my parents just happened to call up to say they were coming home then, so that ended it.

"At the time, I was scared. I really didn't know what had happened. Afterwards when I thought about it, I knew I had liked it. I never told my mother or my father nor any one person anywhere about it. I didn't speak to her after that. She got pregnant and didn't baby-sit for us anymore.

"It was like I blanked it out. I never thought about it until I became close with Carolee. So then I told her about it and she told me about what had happened to her. I'm the only one who knows what happened to her, and she's the only one who knows what happened to me."

At the point we talked, Susan had been going with Carolee for a year and a half. I asked her if Carolee, who was eighteen, had gone with other girls before they started going together.

"She had gone to bed with another girl before me," says Susan. "She was so mad because I wouldn't accept it, that one night she went to a party of these people she worked with and went to bed afterwards with the woman who gave the party. She didn't do it to get even with me, she was just frustrated with my refusals. She didn't tell me about it until a long time afterwards.

"I always did want to, but I was just scared. I didn't know what would happen. It was six months before I'd do anything at all. Then this one time, we were at my house and everybody else had gone out to a movie. Since Carolee was there, I didn't go with them.

"As soon as everybody left, I said, 'This is what you wanted, right?' We were in the living room, and she was sitting on this chair and I was sitting across the room on the couch. She sat there a minute and stared at me. Then she said 'Come over here.' I said, 'No, you come over here.' Then she came over and sat beside me and put her arm around me and kissed me. She got mad when she kissed me because I wouldn't kiss her back. I just sort of sat there. Then I did kiss her back, and we stayed in the living room kissing each other, and then I said, 'Well, let's not stay in the living room because all the windows are open, and if someone walks by, they're going to see something they don't want to see. . . .'

"So we went to my room and we sat there on my bed and made out for a while, and then we talked, and then we made out some more. Then her mother called and she went home. That was all that happened that night, but that was a lot. It took six months before we'd even kissed.

"Then on her birthday, we got into a fight. We had been arguing all day. She was saying 'I don't feel like you love me. I don't feel like you care about me. You just take me for granted; you don't treat me right.' We always took the bus home from school together, and when it came to my stop, I got off. I hadn't gotten her a birthday present, so I went down to the florist and got her some flowers and then I went to her house.

"I rang the bell and she opened the door and stood there. I gave her the flowers, but she was still mad, so she just said thanks.

" 'Can I come in?'

" 'Okay, I guess so,'

"Then we went up to her room. I sat down on the chair and she laid down on the bed. She looked at me a long time, and then she goes to me, 'Susan, I don't think I'm going to see you anymore. I don't think you love me because you just don't show it. And I don't want to keep being hurt. I think we just have to call it off. I can't keep seeing you.'

"I was stunned. I started to stutter and then I just got up and ran out the door. She grabbed me before I could get all the way out the door, and I burst out crying. Then her brother came into the room to see why I was crying, and she told him to get out. Then she closed the door and put the lock on and she started hugging me, and it just went from there. That was when we had oral sex for the first time. I felt good about it.

"Afterwards, I did feel freer. I was really scared to even *try* to make love before that, and doing it made me feel better. It made me feel like I *could* make love.

"The first time I had an orgasm, it was a surprise. My feelings were really happy, like bliss. After I had it, all I felt like doing was holding her in my arms. I never wanted to let go of her."

Talking about her first orgasm, Susan got a glazed expression in her eyes and stared for a long time at one spot on the table. When I asked her what she was feeling, she said she was lonesome, and that they hadn't been able to hold one another or sleep together in more than two months.

"We used to be together all the time," she said, fighting back tears. "We did everything together and went everyplace together. Nobody could separate us. When you saw Carolee, you saw Susan, and when you saw Susan, you saw Carolee. Even now I'm not supposed to speak to her. Since I'm not allowed, we have to meet on corners or sneak lunch together. I can't go to her house because I have a lot of relatives around where she lives who would tell my parents if they saw me there. And if I went there they'd see me."

"Why aren't you supposed to speak to her?" I asked.

"I tried to run away from home last month, and she convinced me to go home," Susan said, "so now they blame it on her. They think she caused me to run away. My father says she's ruining me."

I asked Susan if she thought her parents knew about the nature of her relationship with Carolee.

"Well, we got caught one time," she says, tapping her fingers on the red bandanna around her curly hair. "I was in the living room with her one time, and my little sister, who's eight, pushed the door open and came running in when we were kissing. She was freaked out. She says, 'Were you kissing her? like she was stunned. I said 'No! Why did you think that?' It was stupid, but it was all I could think to say. She just stood there, and then she went running into the kitchen and said to my mother that I was kissing Carolee.

"I was stunned. I said to Carolee right then, 'I can't stay here. I can't live here anymore.' Then my mother asked me if it was true and I denied it, but I was all flushed. Inside her, she knew, but outside, she acted like she believed me. She asked me if I'd been kissing Carolee like Sonya said and I said 'No, Mom! Of course not!' She said, 'I knew it wasn't true.' My other sister [who's fifteen] was sitting there and she gave me the dirtiest look possible. She knows. I know she knows, just from the vibes. We share a room, and you just know things like that.

"I went out with a guy once," she said, smiling. "We went to a school dance. I knew he liked me, and I went, really to be polite. Anyway, we danced several dances and then we danced this slow dance. When it finished, afterwards, he kissed me. We were just standing there and he kissed me. It happened so fast that I had to ask somebody who was sitting there afterwards if it had really happened or whether I just thought it had. She said it had happened; she saw it. They had all the lights out, so I couldn't see in the first place, and it stunned me so much I wasn't sure it happened at all.

"I went out with him again. One night my sister and I wanted to go to a movie and my father wouldn't take us. This guy called up right then and asked me what I was doing and I said nothing. I told him that my sister was mad because she wanted to go to this movie and my father wouldn't take us. He said he'd take her if I'd go, too. I knew my sister would be really mad if I said no, so I said okay. I didn't mind. I think he's a really nice guy. He's a gentleman. But we're just friends, that's all.

"He called me quite a bit, but I told him afterwards, 'I don't want you coming to my house anymore. But I'll call you from time to time and we can talk.' That was an ultimatum from Carolee. She said if he kept calling me, that was the end of our relationship. She had reason. One time he had stopped by just to see if I wanted to go out with him, and she happened to be there. She wanted to hit me so bad.

"Now I'm always wondering if my mother's going to show up someplace when I'm seeing her—or my father. My father threatened me that if he ever found out I was seeing her again, he'd kick my ass so bad he'd put me in the hospital and he wouldn't care if I came back home or not."

"Do you think your father would *really* hurt you if he found out you were seeing Carolee again?" I asked.

"He was going to hurt me when I ran away. I'd probably be dead if my mother hadn't stepped in between us and stopped him," she said. "When I was small, he hit me once or twice. But he never really beat me or hurt me bad.

"I'm afraid of how they'll react, though," Susan said. "Especially my mother. She may be a liberal, but that's one thing she won't deal with. I'm just waiting until I go to college, and then if they ask me, I'll tell 'em. Otherwise I won't.'"

When we spoke, Susan had another year and a half of high school left before she would start college. She wasn't sure what would happen to her relationship with Carolee. Her goal, outside of getting her college degree, however, was to get her own apartment so that she and Carolee would be able to spend time together and have privacy without hostile relatives or invasions from other people.

Before our interview, Susan said she had "talked around" the subject of homosexuality with a counselor at school, saying she had a friend who was worried about being gay.

"The counselor kept saying, 'Either she's one way or she's the other,' " Susan said. "She kept saying, 'She'll have to make up her mind; either she's lesbian or she's not.'

"I'd be open to having a relationship with a guy," said Susan. "Believe me, I have a lot I don't know. I want my relationship with Carolee to be long-term, but if anything happens, I guess eventually I could care for someone else. I know I have a lot to learn, and a lot to explore."

I had the feeling that if Susan stayed open and didn't feel too constricted by her definition of herself as gay, she well might have relationships with men as well as women as she grew older. I felt the counselor was wrong; she didn't have to decide one way or another. It was hard to know, but because Susan is so young, she might in time look at her relationship with Carolee only as the important first love and the first commitment of her life. With time and experience, she might discover other layers and feelings in herself that also involved men.

Unlike Susan, who did not identify herself as homosexual from the time she was young, other adolescents said they had been clear about being exclusively homosexual very early. They had no doubts about their sexual preferences or their lifelong orientations. Their self-categorizations were unequivocal.

Alec, for instance, has no question about his sexual identity. He has no sexual interest in girls. He likes them "okay," he says, but he can't imagine ever going out on a date with one of them, let alone being attracted or erotically excited by one.

Alec comes from a small town outside San Francisco, where his father is a sanitation man and his mother works in a factory. "She works hard," he says of his mother. "She's also like a household freak.

Everything has to be perfect. The house and the floor always have to be clean and shiny. . . ."

When I met Alec, he was manning the telephone office of the Gay Alliance at San Francisco State University. He had moved out of his parents' home eight weeks before we had met because he didn't feel he could maintain his love affair with his friend, David, any other way. At sixteen, Alec is slight in build. Because he was so thin, I asked him about his eating habits. He admitted he hadn't eaten much since leaving home. Recently, however, he'd gotten a job at a bakery, which covered rent on his room and literally supplied him with some bread. As far as he was concerned, he had no complaints about his life on the loose.

"I love the freedom," he says. "I have posters all over my walls. At home, I couldn't put posters on the walls. They were afraid to have holes in the walls. They'd say they worked hard for that house, and they weren't going to have it all torn up because of me. . . .

"Now it's so great. For once I can do what I want. They [my parents] wouldn't let me come to San Francisco—it seemed so big and bad to them. They think it's so rough and tough, but it's not. For once, I'm free, and I'm beginning to see a few things. I'm going to movies. David likes the X-rated ones with women and men—not the gay ones. I think they're disgusting. I fell asleep at the last one we went to. I'd rather go to a really good show. . . ."

Tom answers the phone: "Gay Alliance," and tells the caller that a business meeting and social are scheduled for Tuesday night at 8 P.M.

"I couldn't take living at home," he says, hanging up the phone and pushing the hair back from his eyes. "I really didn't know why. Then I met David, and I didn't want seeing him only on weekends. The last week of school, I was really depressed. My mom was yelling at me all the time. I'd just look at her with no expression on my face. I went to my counselor at school, and I said I wanted to leave home, but I wanted to do it right, so she helped me get an apartment two blocks from Glenn here in San Francisco. The rent is fifty dollars a month, and I can do that.

"I had some money saved up, plus a Christmas savings. After I got here, I got a job at a hot-dog stand, but they wanted me to work Saturdays, and Saturday is our special day to go out. We go out every day, but Saturday is our special day. I explained that to my boss but they still wanted me to work Saturdays, so I quit. Now I got a job at the bakery down the street, at the same place David works. Everybody there knows about us."

Alec beams his smile and pride at his and David's relationship. He tells me that David is also sixteen, and that he goes to high school and takes some classes at San Francisco State under a special arrangement for bright high school students. "He's really smart up here," says Alec, tapping the side of his forehead.

"I was never really attracted to women," he says. "When I watched a program or read a book, I always focused on the male. I could never do much about it. Then I read in the paper about some of the gay groups here in San Francisco. I called up and asked what the Gay Alliance was, and they told me some about it, so I came down on two or three Sundays.

"I decided in the seventh or eighth grade that I was gay. I knew this one neighbor who was fourteen, and I told him. I felt okay about it. As soon as something came out in the newspaper or magazine, I'd read about it and try to find out more about it. Nobody I knew knew anything about it, and I couldn't talk to anybody about it.

"Then in high school, I had a relationship with this kid Jim. I took it more serious than he did. We went together about a year—to the beginning of my sophomore year. We used to go to each other's house and go bowling and we'd ride on the bus together. Then one time he was taking a shower, and I was in his room and then he came out and he started coming on to me. I was surprised. I never knew he was and he never admitted he was. We never used to talk about it at all. We never kissed. I really wanted to, but I couldn't do it and he didn't. Also, I didn't like him in that way. We were such good friends—he was just there.

"We didn't have sex. I didn't really want to with him. I always thought it was something special. Jim and I, we'd hug each other and we'd masturbate each other—but not like *inside*. David was the first person I had intercourse with. He was the first person I ever fell in love with. He felt the same way.

"The first time I came down here [the Gay Alliance] on a Sunday, I took off from work to come down. I got my neighbor (the one I'd told I was gay) to come with me. I didn't know what to expect—except that they were having this picnic that I'd read about. Leo dropped me off and went to a movie."

At the picnic, Alec met David and they both had an immediate "click" about the other. When Alec got home that night, they talked on the phone for nearly two hours. A week later, Alec took his neighbor, Leo, along with him to pick up David after work.

"He got out a little early, and we three went in the car together for a ride. He drove and I sat in the middle. I felt nervous about what to say or do, and then he goes, 'Let's do something tomorrow night.' I didn't have to say nothing but okay. I was so happy. So Saturday night, I came in and we met here at the Gay Alliance, and he goes, 'Well, this is our first date'—so I knew it was more than just friends to him, too. I was so relieved. We went to this little gay café and then he said, 'Well, do you want to go dance?' I said, 'Would you care if we just went to the movies? Don't get mad, but would that be okay instead?' He said sure, so we went to the movies, and then we went to this gay bar afterwards.

"I was scared to make the first move, but I wanted to hold his hand or something before the night was over. I didn't know what to do, so I said, 'Let's do something really special tomorrow. . . .' So he knew. The next day I quit work early and went to pick him up. Then we went to my house and he took me to this little park and we started walking around. He said, 'I want to go to my house,' so he called and nobody was home, so we went to his house and into the living room. We were just listening to a radio and he was sitting right next to me. Then we went up to his room and just started talking.

"He sat next to me on the bed. He kept touching my sweater. It was for about a half-hour, he was playing with my sweater and talking. I was really scared. I'm not the kind to pray, but I was praying to have a real relationship with him. Then he said, 'Come here,' and he kissed me. And then that really got us going. One time I'd kissed Jim good-bye, but it wasn't like that. . . . Then we just got into bed. We were holding each other and kissing and then we had oral sex.

"I remember when I was younger, I read about oral sex in the paper. I didn't know what it was, so I looked it up in the sex encyclopedia. My parents had bought this sex encyclopedia for us to answer any questions we might have. It was pretty nice. It was the only thing we had like it in our house. Anyway, they said in the sex encyclopedia there's nothing basically wrong with it or with homosexuals, so I believed that. I had always wanted to try it, but there was no one there. I could never ask my parents or anybody else what it was. . . ."

When Alec arrived home at midnight that night he first made love with David, his parents grounded him. They had told him to be home by six, and punishment for his violation was that he couldn't go anywhere but school and work for two weeks. Alec's response was to take the car to school, leave school after his first class and drive into San Francisco to meet David.

"We were riding in the car one day and he told me he loved me and I just about cried," said Alec. "I got home and he called and he started crying, 'Alec, Alec. . . .' I couldn't get over it. It made me feel so good. No one ever really cared for me that way before." Eventually Alec decided he'd have to move out. He dropped out of school and told his parents he was leaving home.

"My parents cared about me and bought me things—not much because they don't have much—but I could never really talk to them. Now I'm happy. I save my pennies and buy little presents for David. He thinks I'm extravagant, but I have fun."

Although David has told his parents that he's gay and is having a relationship with Alec, Alec hasn't told his parents.

"My father always told me, 'Don't do nothing wrong. Don't do nothing to hurt us,' Alec says. "They both say it all the time. 'Don't do nothing to shame our name. You'll kill your mother.' She's kind of sickly, so he's always saying, 'If you do anything wrong, you'll kill her.' My father says, 'Why do you hang out with this kid? He's going to change you.' They know he's gay. It's so obvious that he is, and I'm with him seven days a week.

"I don't want to tell 'em. I could have the counselor there when I told them, but then they have to bring me back to San Francisco and I don't want to sit in the car and hear them all the way back here. That's right before I go to work, too.

"In a way, I want to tell 'em, though. I want to get it all out in the open and have the relief of having it over with.

"I don't like planning it all out because then I get all nervous. I'll tell them eventually.

"My sister, the older one, she knows. She assumes it. She saw this sign David gave me and on the back, he wrote 'I love you.' She told my parents, so they suspect. One time I went over there with a hickey on my neck and she said, 'Where'd you get that?' I said, 'A girl,' 'cause I didn't want to tell her. She says, 'Yeah, I know who gave it to you.' I said 'Shut up.' She's just worried about herself, though. My sister basically thinks of herself only. The two younger ones, they're too young to know anything or if they do, I don't know it.

"I like going to bars sometimes, especially bars downtown. I love it there! People go around holding hands. We do, too. I feel so much freedom there. Some people do hold hands all over the city, wherever they are.

"Sometimes when we're driving, I try sitting close to him in the car. One time he sat close to me when we were driving in my town, though, and I felt nervous. I made him move over.

"It's so obvious when we're together. When you look at somebody the way we look at each other, you can tell. Sometimes in the library, he'll be doing homework, and I just sit looking at him. He reads all the time, all these hard books. I read about ten books in high school. Maybe I'll take it up again since I have so much free time now."

I asked Alec how long he thought his relationship with David would last.

"I look at it lasting forever," he said. "When I say that to David, he goes, 'You shouldn't say things like that'—but that's the way I am. To me, it should last forever. I can't look at it any other way."

PART IV

15.

Contraception: It's Magic

From the time we are small children, the idea that we will be able to reproduce another human being from our own bodies is incredible and intriguing. It's a fantasy—a mysterious and awesome proposition that never seems quite possible.

"When I was five or six, I'd play doctor with the girls down at the end of the road," sixteen-year-old Donald recalls. "Oh, God, it was so exciting. I'd pull the baby out of them. I was always getting to be the doctor. Then, when I was six years old, I got married. We went out in the woods and walked up the aisle. Then we pulled our pants down and kissed and hugged. I don't think anything happened, but it felt good."

Even when we have grown out of our children's bodies, even if we've learned about human reproduction, we still hold onto some of our magical ideas about the process. Though as children, we may equate making love with making babies, when we are teenagers, we sometimes use the same kind of logic to separate one act from another.

"The two different guys I went with before Alan always carried little silver condom packages in their pockets, but I didn't want to have sex," says a woman friend of mine recalling her teens. "I didn't love them and I wasn't ready for it. Then when I fell in love with Alan and decided to stay overnight with him, it never occurred to me that he wouldn't come equipped with one of those little silver foil packets like all the other guys. I think that I was so shocked and excited and passionate about what we were doing that I kind of forgot about it after I found out he didn't have anything with him. I also think I felt safe *because* I loved him. The next day I thought, 'Now I'm a woman. I have to get a diaphragm.' I was so lucky!"

My friend's gap between doing and thinking isn't unusual. Like her, the majority of teenage girls who have intercourse do not use contraceptives the first time. In fact, there's a delay of approximately one year between the time they initiate sexual activity and obtain contraceptives. The effect of this delay is that one-half of all initial premarital teenage pregnancies occur in the first six months of sexual activity.[1]

"I was worried about it but I didn't think a lot about it," said seventeen-year-old Steven. "When it started happening, I think we both just threw our minds out the car window. We had even talked about it ahead of time and decided that when we made love we would definitely use birth control, but then when it happened, we didn't."

Although some teenagers never use contraceptives and others use them "sometimes" or "often," recent studies show that teenagers are thinking more about contraception and are using it consistently more often. Although contraceptives are less easily accessible to teenagers than to married adults (some doctors and clinics still refuse to give teenagers contraceptives without their parents' consent),[2] evidence shows that their access to contraceptives has improved, and so has their use. In a survey by Drs. John F. Kantner and Melvin Zelnik, of Johns Hopkins University, 49 percent of "sexually active" teenagers said they always used contraception. This was a dramatic increase from parallel surveys in 1971, when only 18 percent of sexually active teenagers "always" used contraception, and 30 percent in 1976.[3] These figures clearly demonstrate that a growing number of teenagers are taking responsibility for the consequences of their behavior and are trying harder than ever to avoid pregnancy and childbirth outside of marriage.

"It's pushed in your head, don't cross on the red light," said Aaron, an eighteen-year-old senior from Pomona. "Well, this is the same thing. But you haven't come into contact with it before. Look, it's there. This is what happens if you have sex and you don't use your head and you don't use birth control. Being promiscuous, if that's your preference, is your choice, but you should know that you don't do things before you take precautions. Like they say, you don't go out and play basketball without a basketball. And it's the same thing here. You don't go out and have sex without using contraceptives."

Despite their efforts, however, the number of teenagers having unintended premarital pregnancies is on the increase. According to Drs. Kantner and Zelnik, it is more difficult for teenagers to achieve their goal of avoiding pregnancy and childbirth outside of marriage for two basic reasons. The first is the growing disinclination of teenagers to marry earlier, even when faced with pregnancy. The second is that even though more teenagers are using contraceptives and more of them are using birth-control methods more consistently, they have become more disinclined to use the Pill or the IUD, which are the most effective methods of contraception, and are substituting one of the least effective methods—withdrawal.[4]

"I wouldn't put those pills in my body," one sixteen-year-old girl named Sandra told me. "My boyfriend wouldn't let me take them, either. He says he doesn't want me getting cancer or a blood clot from them. . . . Basically we use withdrawal. I have a diaphragm but neither one of us like it very much. . . ."

Some teenagers cite reports of the Pill's side effects as the reason they're afraid of using it; others say that Pills are too expensive. One girl said, "Why should I pay $21 a month to take Pills when he can pay $1.19 for a packet of rubbers?" Although condoms usually cost $1.50 for a packet of three and the side effects of the Pill for the average teenager with no medical history of varicose veins or heart difficulties seem quite minor compared to the side effects of pregnancy, I heard other, similar remarks. "It's no good to put drugs into your body," Sarah said. "Besides that, even if I was willing to use them, I couldn't afford them."

According to Zelnik and Kantner, use of the Pill and the IUD declined by 41 percent over the three-year period between 1976 and 1979, and use of withdrawal and the rhythm method rose by 86 percent. In 1976, they report, the three most popular methods were the condom, the Pill and withdrawal, in that order. In 1979, they were withdrawal, the condom and the Pill.[5]

Certainly withdrawal is not a foolproof method. And although the condom is quite effective both against venereal disease and pregnancy, particularly when it's used in conjunction with foam, many teenagers say they don't like the way condoms feel. They're uncomfortable or "smothering," and so they're often not used until right before ejaculation (which is sometimes too late) or they're used inconsistently. Maybe these teenagers haven't been told by their doctors, as one young woman was told by hers: "Use it. Use it every time. Don't ever not use it."

"I don't like 'em 'cause they don't feel natural," said Ethel, a vehement and colorful seventeen-year-old from Harlem. "I don't like using no rubber scum bags. He don't, neither. He comes inside me and then it goes all down my leg."

Milton, an eighteen-year-old at Pomona High School, explained why he thought many teenage boys don't like using condoms.

"Most adolescents are into the feel of things," he said. "They want to feel it. I mean, like the rubber, it'll stop the feeling. To take off the rubber and have the feeling, well, it's two different things. Most adolescents would take off the rubber to have the feeling."

Milton, a tall young man who was wearing a suit and tie when I met him at a conference in Los Angeles, said he personally felt the feeling should take a backseat to being careful.

A variety of studies show that of the 55 percent of teenagers who have sex by the time they are eighteen years old, most say they do not want to have a pregnancy as a result of their behavior. Even without using the Pill or an IUD, however, teenagers adamant about not getting pregnant, who have the proper information about what they're doing and the resolve not to have sex unless it's safe, usually don't get pregnant.

"Even after I was *on* the Pill," said Marion, who had been having intercourse with her boyfriend since she was fourteen, "he would use condoms and we'd only do it right after my period or right before my period."

Thirty-four percent of the teenagers between the ages of fifteen and nineteen surveyed by Zelnik and Kantner said they always used birth control, yet 14 percent of them became pregnant.[6] Some of the reasons for their pregnancies may have had to do with faulty birth control, like the use of withdrawal or the rhythm method. Sometimes it's because they have misunderstandings about the biological facts of conception. They have heard and believed popular myths that are "guarantees" of safety:

You are most likely to get pregnant during your period, just after your period, or just before your period; the rest of the time is safe. (Of course, just the opposite is true, and no time is absolutely foolproof.)

If you take the Pill every time you have intercourse, you won't get pregnant.

An IUD is no good because it will get lost in your body and it works only if the man is on top of the woman, not if the woman is on top of the man.

If you have sex less than once a week or have it infrequently, you can't get pregnant.

There's a shot that will bring down your period even if you're pregnant, so don't worry about it.

Sometimes teenagers have a very good understanding of the facts, maintain real discipline about using birth control and get pregnant anyway. It may be that some sperm slipped past the diaphragm somehow, that there's a tiny hole in the condom or that the diaphragm was not properly fitted or inserted. ("I hate my diaphragm," one eighteen-year-old told me. "It's always slipping out of my fingers when I try to get it in. It falls on the floor and then I have to wash it and put the jelly in it and start all over and it never feels like it's in right!") Some begin to have intercourse while they are still on a waiting list for their doctor's appointment at the clinic.

The odds for teenagers who use contraceptives getting pregnant are far lower than they are for teenagers who don't use them. Some 50 percent of all premarital first pregnancies occur among teenage girls who have never used a contraceptive.[7] In 1979, 27 percent of the young women fifteen to nineteen with sexual experience had never used a contraceptive at all. Forty-nine percent used it sometimes, but not always.[8]

Lack of information is often cited as the reason teenagers don't use contraceptives and also as the reason they have unintended pregnancies. It's true, I'm sure, that some teenagers don't know anything about contraception. On the other hand, studies don't show that having information about contraception correlates with contraceptive behavior. Other factors are involved. It also seems that even if teenagers have not had sex education about contraception in their schools, even if their parents haven't talked to them, it's quite unlikely that they won't hear about birth control, the availability of Planned Parenthood or other family-planning clinics from school friends or even from spot announcements on the radio. Recently, for instance, when I was driving my car in Philadelphia, I heard a public service announcement from country singer Loretta Lynn. "Kids today, they need to know about the Pill because they don't need to be having a baby and not know what's going on," she said. "They need to be taking the Pill. I think . . . I know people my age probably think I'm crazy, but this is how I feel because I grew up with my kids. I had . . . my oldest kid is fourteen years younger than I am, so I know what it's like. If I had had the Pill back then, I'd have popped them like popcorn." At the end of her statement, a voice came over the air saying: "The Center for Population Options asks you to think about having a child before you make a baby."

Later I found out that the Center for Population Options located in Washington, D.C., broadcasts tapes like these all over the country, featuring stars popular among teenagers, including Linda Ronstadt, Bonnie Raitt, Jerry Garcia, Fee Waybill of the Tubes from San Francisco, Boz Scaggs, the Bay City Rollers, War and Neil Diamond, among others. The spots get your attention and hold it: "Charlie Daniels says, 'Having a child isn't like a damn automobile or something you can take home and try out and if you don't like it you can take it back.' The Center for Population Options asks you to think about having a child before you make a baby."

Despite such public information, there are still youngsters who don't make the connection between what they're doing sexually and having a child.

Not having the ability—for whatever the reasons—to anticipate the consequences of their actions seems to be a major factor that influences birth-control usage. In a study conducted among 730 teenagers in family-life classes at three high schools and a Teen Clinic Group in Philadelphia, 22 percent of the teenagers indicated that having a child now would make life "no different" or "better." Thirty-five percent indicated pregnancy now would make life "worse" or "ruined." I found it amazing that 43 percent of the total sample said they *"did not know"* how a child would affect their lives.[9] While in one sense, being unable to judge experience that has not occurred is a rational response, the inability to understand or to link cause and effect is no doubt associated with many unwanted pregnancies.

Another factor Dr. Freeman and her colleagues in Philadelphia found in their study was that although male and female students agreed that responsibility for contraception belonged to both sexes, males were less likely to recognize the risk of pregnancy and had less information about contraceptives and fewer attitudes that supported contraceptive use.

Some boys with whom I spoke said quite clearly that they felt birth control was the girl's responsibility, not theirs. None of these boys was involved in a steady relationship.

"It's up to the girl, the way I see it," said eighteen-year-old Morris. "If she doesn't want to get pregnant, she should be on the Pill or make sure she takes care of herself."

The assumption in these cases was either that the girl had more information than they did about contraception or was the person in charge of this outcome of the transaction. A few boys were quite contemptuous about not using contraceptives, expressing the view that because a girl "slept around," there was no reason to show caution.

"I couldn't care less with April," said Rick, a seventeen-year-old in Minneapolis. "She had it too many times. You could tell she was a whore by the way she acted. Like how she came on to me and the little games she'd play. We had sex about three times more after the first time and we never used anything."

I asked this same boy if he was having intercourse with his steady girl friend. "I don't want to talk about it," he said, stiffening, seeming both offended and proud about their privacy. "But let's say I would use birth control if I had sex with Shelly. I would definitely use birth control."

I met some boys who were extremely conscientious about using birth control and expressed real concern and involvement in the decision to use it.

"I think that the decision to have sex is mutual, and the responsibility not to have a baby is mutual," said seventeen-year-old Roger, who had been having sexual relations with his girl friend for nearly a year. "I think that if guys are going to have sex, they should make sure the girl's protected. My dad always said it's better to be responsible before the act than eight or nine months later."

"I think the complete brunt of contraception should be borne by the male," said Nick, a college freshman majoring in political science. "Sometimes I can't believe what I hear guys say. You ask some of them if they use contraception and they say no. I say, 'How can you equate five minutes of pleasure with ruining someone's life and ruining the child's life?'

"I think part of the reason that some guys are so cavalier is because they're jealous they can't have a child. It comes from an inherent jealousy. I know I'm jealous. I'd love to be able to bear a child. . . .'"

James pointed out that even when you're mature about planning against pregnancy, it's often difficult or embarrassing to buy the contraceptives. "If a guy walks into a store to buy a condom, he's embarrassed," seventeen-year-old James said, obviously talking about himself. "There may be a woman at the counter, or the druggist may look at him funny. It's not as easy as it seems. Also, with a girl, how is she going to explain a juicy oversize bill from the gynecologist at the end of the month? If she can't talk to her parents, and she doesn't have a job, it's pretty expensive."

Most boys, like Curtis, a broad-shouldered high-school senior who intends to play professional football, feel that birth control involves the boy as well as the girl, and that it's not fair for the girl to depend totally on whether the boy has birth control. "I was with a seventeen-year-old girl a few weeks ago, and she said she wasn't on the Pill," he said. "She goes, 'Are you going to use a rubber?' I said, 'Sure, I'll use a rubber.' But with her, if a male doesn't use a rubber, she's going to get pregnant right off." He shakes out his long, large hands by his sides. "She just has this attitude, you know, it's up to you, whether she's safe or she should get pregnant."

Although a boy's attitude about contraceptives and his commitment to using them can make all the difference, girls are the ones who bear the brunt if neither of the partners uses birth control and she conceives as a result. She is the one who will end up pregnant.

Over 1,100,000 girls got pregnant last year. Twenty-seven percent of sexually active girls who had never used birth control accounted for two-thirds of the pregnancies.[10] Of course, some of these girls wanted to have a baby. Some were married before they conceived the child. But what about the ones who didn't want to get pregnant but still didn't use birth control? Didn't they understand cause and effect? Why didn't they use contraception?

It seems that conflicted feelings about their sexual excitement and their sexual behavior, confusion about their emotions, relationships and roles, play a dominant part in unwanted pregnancies.

Much of the risk taking for teenagers who don't use contraceptives or use them sporadically seems to stem from a feeling of invulnerability and the notion that if sex is premeditated, it's not romantic. Girls, particularly, and boys to a lesser degree, seem to feel that sex should be spontaneous, which is one of the reasons the Pill is so effective. Stopping the romance to put in a diaphragm, put on a condom or insert foam seems to lessen the pleasure of the lovemaking. They feel that the mood is broken by mechanics when they have to stop the action to "get prepared." This is particularly true, of course, if teenagers feel conflict or are confused about their behavior and would rather be carried away by the candlelight and love songs and the passion of the moment.

"I know it's crazy," said eighteen-year-old Kathleen, "and I should know better, but it's worth the risk to me sometimes not to use anything. Sometimes, it's just too wonderful to stop. . . ."

Although many people who are against sex education in the schools think otherwise, studies show that teenagers who have information about contraception are more likely to delay first intercourse and be more cautious when they do begin to have sexual intercourse. It's also not surprising that all the studies of the subject indicate that teenagers who talk to their parents about contraceptives are more likely to use them than teenagers who don't talk to their parents about them. Ironically, girls who have a support system in their family that's in favor of using contraception are more likely to delay their first intercourse and less likely to have a premarital pregnancy.

"It's a big thing and an important thing to have someone they can talk to without getting mixed messages," says Marsha Lawrence, senior communications consultant for Planned Parenthood. "As far as birth control goes, too many people say to their kids, 'Don't have sex, but if you're going to have sex—which is the wrong thing to do—use birth control.'

"This puts kids into a real bind. The only way kids feel that it is okay to have sex and still be a good person is to not *intend* to have sex. By making it out of my control, and making myself a victim, then I am still a good person and I can have sex."

Marsha Lawrence says that it is very clear in all of the surveys Planned Parenthood has done that youngsters use birth control *if* they feel good about themselves and about their decision to have sex.

"Somehow people think it is a very difficult and complicated thing to teach young women how to use birth control," she says, "or how to use a diaphragm. Yet women can attach false eyelashes, they can dye their hair, they can give themselves permanents, they can do incredibly complicated things to themselves, but we put birth control in a separate category. The diaphragm is always off limits because somehow it is offensive for a girl to explore her own vagina or touch herself to put it in."

Behind this myth of young women's inability to manage birth control, says Lawrence, is a very clear conflict about sexual behavior. She points out that even though premarital sex, pregnancy and motherhood are much more tolerated than they ever were before, single teenage mothers participating in Planned Parenthood programs often hold that it is wrong to have sex before marriage. They may have felt that it was okay because everyone else was having sex or that it was socially necessary to keep their boyfriends, but at the same time, they maintained the belief that it was wrong to have sex before marriage. Many of these girls say they will teach their daughters that premarital sex is wrong.

Everywhere I went throughout the country, I heard the same thing from teenagers and people who work with teenagers. The reason many girls don't use birth control is because they feel they would be "bad" or "cheap" if they planned to have sex. In other words, they feel that "good girls" should wait until they're married to have intercourse. If they don't wait to have it, it's an accident—and if it's an accident rather than something planned for, they're not bad. They just couldn't help it. One mother of an eighteen-year-old in San Diego actually said to me, "She's a good girl. I know that if anything ever happened with her, it wouldn't be planned. It would be an accident."

So girls who are trying to stay "good" in their mother's eyes don't go behind their mothers' backs to a doctor or a clinic to get birth control, because doing so would prove that they're bad. Ironically, as pointed out before, two-thirds of these "good" girls do have "accidents."

Girls often attribute this lack of planning on their part to not wanting their boyfriends to think they're "bad," either. In Barbie's case, she was trying to use protection, but she was frightened of acknowledging her own desires.

"I bought a package of Trojans," she said, "and I am so nervous about it. I got them because I want to have them if Ronnie and I ever decide to have sex, but I think like, if we're, you know, starting to get into it and I pull a rubber out of my purse, what will he think of me? He'll probably think that I wanted to have sex with him! That would be so embarrassing!"

Even when the girl is the one who is really quite aware of what she wants, she often feels she should lead the boy into thinking he planned it and she never thought about it until it happened to her—like a good girl should.

"The main thing is with kids who get pregnant, when you ask them why, they say, I didn't want him to think I was planning on having sex with him," says Monica Johnson, a counselor at Scottsdale High School in Scottsdale, Arizona. "They knew where to get the Pill. They say they didn't want to plan because then he'd think badly of me. Or else they really weren't consciously planning and they got swept up in their emotion. In their head, they're still being told it's wrong and that you shouldn't have sex before you're married.

"They don't talk with their parents," she says. "If they could talk more to their parents, I believe, they wouldn't have some of the relationships they have and they wouldn't go so far. They're running around with all these ambiguous feelings and feeling in love, and they don't know what to do with it all. They want to talk about it, but they still have the stumbling blocks at home."

I found myself terribly frustrated when I spoke with immature teenage girls who were having intercourse regularly and were not using birth control. If they had made a positive decision to have a baby, I wasn't upset when I listened to them. Even if they seemed young, I could listen to their plans and their dreams with a measure of equanimity and respect. But girls not adept at taking care of themselves, who refused to make any active decision, who were passive about themselves and their lives, aroused my crazed maternal instincts as I listened to them. Norma's a case in point. At seventeen, her self-esteem is rock bottom. She says she has no idea what she wants to do after high school. She's afraid of making decisions, and she's quite ambivalent about having a baby. One evening when I was talking with Norma and her friends Rita, Bert and Bill, I asked Norma if she and Robert, her new boyfriend, were using contraception. I felt sure that since she characterized this relationship as "more mature" than her last, the answer would be positive.

"We haven't been using anything, but I might," said Norma, putting her arm up over her eyes and laughing. "I'll use it if I start my period again."

"If?"

"It's late," she said, blushing.

"You're not using *anything*?" I asked, having trouble keeping the pen in my hand.

"He doesn't believe in any birth control," Norma said. "He says 'I'm not worried about it.' He says he'll take care of me. We've talked about the future and all, and he says if I get pregnant, it wouldn't matter. We'd get married. He's with the Catholic religion like I am, so we don't really believe in birth control."

"We?"

"Yes."

"You and him, or just him?" asked Bill.

"Both of us."

"I'm not really worried about it," Norma said in a different tone of voice, a different cadence from her own, in what seemed a direct imitation of the way she had quoted Robert saying "I'm not worried about it."

"But you *are* a little worried about it, aren't you?" I probed.

"Well, yes," she said. "I'm kind of scared. Especially when I think of my parents and how they'll take it. See, my parents are pushing me into college. I don't really want to go, though."

At this point, the cadence of Norma's speech changed once again and she said, imitating Robert's voice: "It doesn't interest me to have a career or anything. And I really don't want to go to college if I have a baby. I wouldn't want to leave my baby with a baby-sitter.

"It'd be okay if I had a baby. It wouldn't matter. Robert graduates from junior college in February and he has parents . . . his parents are really understanding. So are the people he hangs around with. . . ."

"Do you know how much it *costs* to have a baby?" Bert yelled at Norma. "Robert's just a hamburger man! You can't support a baby working at a hamburger stand!"

"You expect his parents to support you and him and the baby?" Bill yelled. "How do you know he feels the same way about you that you feel about him? What makes you think he'll stay around if you get pregnant?"

"He would," Norma said. "I know how he feels. I see him about twice a week. And I stayed with him for the last two weekends. I told my folks I was staying with Rita. If they found out, it'd be move-out time."

Norma pulled a blanket around her shoulders and seemed to curl into herself, away from her friends. She looked at me from the folds of the blanket, and her face was like that of a vulnerable little girl, a scared child.

"Do you know where to go for birth control if you do get your period again?" I asked, tossing any shred of objectivity I might have possessed out the window.

"I could get them free from the air-force base if my mother didn't go with me," she said. "But my mother always goes in with me. My dad's retired from the Air Force, so we have benefits there, and that's where we go for our medical checkups. Last year the doctor asked me if I was on birth control, and my mom blew up at him. She goes, 'What do you mean, is she on the Pill?' Do you know how old she is?' my mother yells at him. 'She's only seventeen years old!' "

Before we left, Rita promised that she would take Norma for a physical exam and birth-control pills once Norma got her period again. Norma said that she would go, but then, her eyes glazing, she said, "I think when it's not planned, it's the best. When it's planned, it's not as good. It ought to come naturally, when you're in the mood."

I imagined Norma a year from then, having a daughter and beginning to raise her in the same way she was raised, telling her the same things she was told, unexamined. I was surprised at the intensity of my reaction, and I realized that it was the child I was imagining, the child who would be cheated by being born to an ambivalent mother who would, like her mother before her, blame her child for her problems.

"I don't know," said Norma, her dark eyes seeming to shadow. "If I had a problem, I wouldn't go to my parents. Never. It would tear my parents apart. They would feel like it was their fault somehow."

My own feeling is that most young women who don't use birth control or use it only sometimes may be quite ambivalent about the idea of having a baby or dealing with the real decisions that will face them once they are pregnant. When they take the risk of having sex without contraception, I believe that it's usually because they want to tempt fate for a variety of complex reasons that have as much to do with magical thinking about their own bodies as it does with anything else. I think that they often want the relief and reassurance of knowing that their bodies work properly and they *can* get pregnant. Of course, sometimes they would like this knowledge without suffering the logical consequences of pregnancy.

"Women really want to know if their bodies work well," says social worker Sue Cohen in New York. "You hear kids say, 'Whew, it works,' after they get pregnant. It's the same thing I've heard with older women friends, only in more sophisticated language.

"Then there's the kid who has *not* gotten pregnant, and all her friends have gotten pregnant. Nobody can look inside her body and say, 'Of course you'll be able to have children.' But she wants to know what's the matter with her. She wants to be sure she can have children. It's not a scientific question to her; it's part magic and part science. . . ."

"I had one girl come back seven times for a pregnancy test," said a registered nurse who works in a Planned Parenthood clinic in New Jersey. "The seventh time, it came out positive. Then she said, 'Oh, no, what am I going to do now?' Some kids want to get pregnant just to know they can. But they don't want to have a baby right then, and so they're faced with a very serious decision."

Jenny was one teenager I talked to who told me she didn't want a child at this particular point in her life, but that since she hadn't used birth control and hadn't gotten pregnant, she was worried about why she hadn't gotten pregnant. Before our interview in Jenny's suburban Chicago home, she had been thinking about going to a doctor to find out what was the matter with her. She was sixteen and hadn't finished high school and wasn't sure at all that she could handle a baby—but she felt that she wanted a baby eventually and wanted to know she would be able to have one. I told her it seemed to me she had a lot of time left to find out—that at this point in her life, she ought to get on with her education so that she'd be able to afford all her future children. A year later I called to see how she was doing, and her mother answered the phone. I asked after Jenny and asked how everything was going.

"She's still going with Stephen," her mother told me. "She practically lives over there. She's over there now. I think she really wants to get married and have a baby. Stephen doesn't want to get married, and she knows that, but last week, she went to see the doctor to find out why she hasn't gotten pregnant.

"I no longer worry about it. I don't because there's nothing I can do about it. Three of Jenny's friends have babies, and I look at their children and they're beautiful, but it still makes me sad.

"Jenny's friend Miriam is different. She's far more mature than Jenny or the others. She has far-reaching goals. Even with the baby, she's planning to go to college. She went back to get her high-school degree, but the baby's in day care from eight to six every day because of that. If these girls want to do anything to better themselves, they have to leave their babies in someone else's care all day long.

"I can't encourage Jenny to do anything. She doesn't have enough confidence in me at this point in time to sit down at the kitchen table with me, let alone listen to me. She doesn't trust anything I say. Thank God Stephen is encouraging her. He's encouraging her to go to college or to get into some kind of training. The other day she brought home a brochure from the University of Chicago. I don't know who told her about it, but I was glad to see it. I'm just hoping, but that's about all I can do at this point. She won't let me do anything more."

Jovina Hankins, supervisor of school nurses in the Oakland, California, public schools, came to her present post after ten years of work with pregnant teenagers in a program called CYESIS (the Greek word for pregnancy).

"The reasons for pregnancies are far more complex than we'd like to accept," said Mrs. Hankins, a tall, attractive woman who is mother herself to a teenage son and daughter. "Before I started working with pregnant teenagers, I thought that if we had all this information and education and the Pill was available, then girls wouldn't have these unwanted pregnancies. But I was in for some new insights.

"With most of these girls, it's not a lack of education. They *wanted* a baby. They didn't *want* to take the Pill. They want to have something of their own. It's unfortunate that people think that if you shower love on this thing, it automatically loves you back. But the fact is that these cute little things are little individuals who may or may not love you back."

Mrs. Hankins feels that the lack of clear-cut goals plays a major part in a girl's not using birth control. "In all the years I was doing CYESIS, I found maybe two girls who didn't know what was happening. The others knew, but they haven't bothered with it. Either they think they won't get pregnant or they don't care, and the result is their lack of motivation to take this information and personalize it. But then we're dealing with teenagers, and with them tomorrow is not part of the picture. It's only today."

Some teenagers, like some grown women, may want to get pregnant for a variety of reasons. A girl may be going with a young man who wants a baby; she may want a child to love and someone to love her; she may be wanting her own child as a way of getting out from under her mother's wing; or she may be having a baby because her mother unwittingly has given her a cue to have one. "When am I going to be a grandmother?" She may want a baby as a way to hang onto her boyfriend. Teenagers have other issues going, like competing with a sibling who has had a child, giving their parents a baby the parents want; or doing it to spite the parents or to resolve Oedipal issues that don't seem resolvable any other way.

Wanting to be pregnant is a very private and a very intimate desire, however. It often involves the magical thinking that you can be pregnant without having to deal with the *actuality* of being pregnant. Being pregnant, in and of itself, is an extraordinary experience. Until the point that a young woman—or any woman—has to acknowledge that she's pregnant, it's a very personal, spiritual, illusive miracle. It doesn't seem real. It is a fantasy: a dream come true.

"Instead of parents freaking out at their child using birth control," says Norris, "it would be much better if they said, 'Hey, my daughter's responsible for herself, isn't that terrific. It shows she's mature enough to make her own decisions.' To have that kind of support would make it so much easier. If you had support from parents, you wouldn't have venereal disease or all these unwanted pregnancies among teenagers."

16.

Conception:
Beyond Wishful Thinking

"I'm pregnant. Now what do I do?"

In 1881, a teenager who found she was pregnant would have begun knitting booties. In 1981, her response is not so automatic. She has choices to make. Should she have the baby and keep it? Have the baby and give it up for adoption? Have an abortion? Unless she's already married, should she marry the father of the child? Should she stay single or marry someone else?

Most of the teenage girls who find themselves with an unexpected pregnancy don't want *any* of their options. As one woman who has worked many years with pregnant teenagers put it: "Their preference is divine intervention."

Barring that intervention, however, or some equally potent magic, the pregnant teenager must make decisions about whom to tell and whom to ask for help. One out of every ten girls in the United States, at some time during her teenage years, finds herself in this dilemma.

Some people, of course, have all the answers spelled out for the pregnant teenager. My father's was: If you get pregnant, you get married. That was the rule. In other households, the choice seems clear and obvious: A teenager is ill-equipped to deal with a complex society and has no business bringing an innocent child into the world when she can't take care of it. She should have an abortion.

Equally clear is the view that abortion is absolutely wrong. The answer is to have the child and keep it or give it up for adoption. Formulas often boil down to: If you play, you pay; no if's, and's or but's.

Absolutes, however, rarely apply to the multiple layers of an individual's experience and to the effect that a child would have on that person's life and vice versa. Even when the choice for marriage or an abortion is obvious to the young people and the families involved, it is never an easy decision. It's almost always a painful one. An enormous sacrifice of one's fantasy and often one's sense of integrity is involved in an abortion. On the other hand, an enormous sacrifice of one's future plans and fantasies is involved in the birth of a child. No matter what the individual chooses, there is no absolute wrong or right when it comes to the health and the life of the individual teenager. What's wrong for one might be ideal for another.

"When I found out I was pregnant, all I could do was cry," said Lucy, an eighteen-year-old who got pregnant the second time she had intercourse. "I kept thinking, how can I tell my mother? She didn't even know I'd made love with Steven. It was so awful. I wanted to go to college, and my dad was dead, and I just couldn't believe it. Finally I told her and she was really calm. She said, 'Well, you have a lot of fast thinking to do.' She got me to go talk to a counselor about what to do. I didn't want to do anything. I thought my life was ruined no matter what I did. . . ."

Ultimately Lucy opted for an abortion. According to the Alan Guttmacher Institute's report, nearly four out of every ten pregnant teenagers chose abortions last year as a way of dealing with an unwanted pregnancy. One out of every ten teenage pregnancies ended in a miscarriage, and the other five carried their babies full term and gave birth to them.[1]

Of the 48.5 percent of pregnant teenagers who have their babies, 21.9 percent gave birth to their babies out of wedlock, 9.8 percent "legitimated" the births of their babies by marrying and 16.8 percent were married before conception. Although the pregnancies of the married teenagers may have been unplanned, these girls are for the most part in their late teens; they've finished high school, chosen a mate and, in effect, set out upon an adult life. They have a family structure into which their child will be born.

For the girls who've decided to have their babies but aren't married— or don't marry—the question remains: Will they raise it, or will they give it up for adoption? For many girls, this is not a question. Nine out of every ten teenage girls who give birth keep their babies. One gives hers up for adoption—an extremely painful decision.

Nothing about teenage pregnancy is as easy as the conception itself. The consequences are enormous—for the girl, for the life inside her, for the girl's family, for the boy and, often, for his family as well.

The ways families react to a child's unwanted pregnancy vary enormously. Mothers and fathers just getting used to their children's growing up, are oftentimes almost as shocked by their children's having sex as they are by the potential grandchild. Some parents disown their children or react with fury and don't retreat from that position, but they are in the minority. Fortunately, most families seem to absorb and to understand without making the teenagers pay any more of a price than they're already paying.

Changes in societal attitudes toward sexuality and sexual behavior apparently have made a difference in the way families handle the news of their teenagers' pregnancies.

"There are fewer pressures from parents for shotgun marriages than there were fifteen years ago," says Carol Toney, director of the CYESIS program in Oakland, California. "And there's more acceptance of abortion than there used to be as well."

"I've seen a lot of mothers who are incredibly supportive of their daughters," says social worker Sue Cohen. "The mothers all feel terribly alone. They ask themselves, 'What did I do wrong that this happened?' They go through a lot of self-searching. It's the rare parent who turns around and says 'It's all your fault.' With some parents, the whole experience means that they've gotten much closer to their child than they were before. They're talking to each other.

"Some parents feel that this life crisis has opened up communication and made them much closer. The parents always know what's going on with their kids, but this kind of event forces them to acknowledge it and talk about what's going on."

One of the least considered parties in the process of decision making is the boyfriend. To him, the news of pregnancy is often staggering. Some boys see the threat to their own future as so overwhelming that they deny responsibility and walk away. They don't come to terms with the news or the problems and decisions involved. Some literally can't imagine that they had anything to do with the pregnancy; magically, it does not seem possible. Most boys, however, feel quite invested in their girl friend's decision and equally responsible for the outcome of the pregnancy. For boys as well as girls, feelings of pride that their bodies work properly, that their sexual identity is confirmed, blend in with the shock. At stake, however, is their future relationship with their girl friend, potential fatherhood, changed status, financial considerations and responsibilities beyond their wildest expectations. For boys, it's often as emotionally wrenching as it is for girls.

"One time, after we'd been going together for about five months, Christy went out to Vancouver to visit her father," eighteen-year-old Kent told me. "Before she left, she told me she might be pregnant. I was so much in love with her, and I was nervous because this friend of mine had lost his girl friend because he got her pregnant and she never forgave him for it. I was scared the same thing would happen to us. When she was gone, I was lost. I felt as if part of me was missing. The torment of waiting for her to come back and to know what was what with her being pregnant nearly drove me insane. I woke up crying several mornings, and my parents were really worried about me."

When Christy got back, they decided upon an abortion. "It was the most painful experience of my life," Kent said. "She was wonderful about it, but neither of us could bear the idea that we had our baby aborted. I couldn't help myself, I thought of it that way. At the same time, I couldn't live with the idea of not going to college or having a real baby, but it was awful. Even though we really loved each other, things were never quite the same after that."

"One of the things people don't think about is how males feel when females get pregnant," says eighteen-year-old Darrell. "Everybody acts like the male doesn't feel nothing; well, he does. Maybe the majority don't care, but personally, I care. Emotionally and financially, I care. It's my child, too."

Although the consequences of conception are simplified by having an abortion, the experience of terminating a pregnancy is usually very upsetting and disturbing. Even when the rationale for having the abortion is crystal clear, it's an emotionally complex experience. A teenager may have no alternative; she knows she is too young to be a good mother, she has no way to support the child, her family could not take over for her. She may believe that the fetus is just that—a fetus—and technically, it is. But no amount of legalistic explanations let her forget, deep within herself, that the fetus she conceived had a *potential* for life. Even if she knows that potential life would not have had a *good* life had she let it develop into a baby, that conception—that lost possibility—is something most women never forget.

"The girls who have abortions have a lot of guilt afterwards," says Mary Garfield, a social worker in New York City. "It's a very difficult thing. There are a lot of thoughts about what might have been. We try to get them to come back and talk about it, but a lot of them won't because even coming into a clinic reminds them of having had the abortion, and they want to put it out of their minds. Those girls probably have the most problems with abortions."

"The girls who do have abortions instead of babies are usually more goal-oriented, have plans for college and career, and it's very clear it would not be accepted by their families to have a baby," says Ms. Garfield. "Knowing that a baby doesn't fit into their life plan at this point doesn't dull their consciences."

"Not much credence is given to what a major decision it is to get an abortion," says Sue Cohen, "no matter whether you're twelve or thirty years old. There's a mourning process kids as well as older people go through.

"After a woman has had an abortion, there are two mourning periods. The first reaction, right after it's over, is *whew* . . . But then on the birthdate of the child, there's a reaction. I can pinpoint it," says Cohen, who follows through after the girls' abortions. "They know when the baby would have been born. And I can predict I'll hear from them about the time the baby would have been born. I get a call and they come in. It's very difficult. They also have another reaction on the anniversary of having had the abortion. It's very hard on a person even if they're ambivalent."

Sometimes girls who are so young that they don't even seem to own the bodies they live in find themselves pregnant. They're little girls, barely past the stage of playing with dolls, and they have grown-up women's tears. These girls haven't learned algebra and often couldn't get themselves across the city without a map drawn by their mothers, but they end up, probably in the best interests of everyone involved, getting an abortion.

I visited one little girl at a hospital where she was having a therapeutic abortion. She was small and blond, and silver braces glittered from her teeth as she smiled up out of a sea of white sheets.

"How are you doing?" I asked her.

"Pretty good," she said. "I just want to get it over with, oh, I just want it to be over with."

Helene was her name, and she was fourteen years old. She stroked her belly through her white hospital gown and waited for labor that had been induced. She was five months pregnant. She looked as if she should be playing jacks in the hallway or marbles in the dirt. It was hard to imagine someone as young as she looked even having a boyfriend.

"I'll tell you one thing," she said. "I'm never having sex again. It's just not worth it."

"Well, if you ever do have sex again, you could use birth control and you wouldn't have to go through this kind of thing," I said, feeling like I was going to start crying momentarily.

"I'd rather just not have sex," she said, biting her bottom lip, her eyes glazing. "I didn't like it anyway. I don't care if I never do it again."

I looked at her thin white hands gripping her stomach.

"It hurts," she said, looking plaintively at me. "It hurts! Why does it hurt so much?"

"It's labor pains," I told her. "They're like sharp cramps, and they'll push the baby out." This is why it's better to have an abortion the first trimester, I thought, when suction can be used and the procedure is simple. This is why it's so painful emotionally and physically to have an abortion so late.

"I just want to get it over with," she cried. "Oh, oh, oh, it hurts, it hurts!"

Last year, out of the 1,142,000 teenagers who got pregnant, some 434,000 had abortions.[2] Some people assume that any girl who could have an abortion takes it lightly. They don't. I talked to many who had chosen abortion, and not one of them felt easy or casual about it. For each girl, the magnitude of ending a potential life was a grief they learned to live with, even if they felt it was the right decision and one they would make again if they had to. Many say they would have made the same decision if abortion had been illegal, except then it would have been more difficult and dangerous, and their own lives would have been at stake.

Marleen Dougherty, who is "more Baptist" than any other religion, got pregnant when she was fourteen years old. At the time, she was going with Carlos, who was four years older than she. He was her first "real love."

"We really had a good time together," she says. "Even though he was eighteen when I started going with him, he was really young. I always felt I was older than him. I felt I could handle things better than him, and that I was more logical then him. But we went together a year and half. He made me feel loved, and I felt secure around him. We both needed somebody. We both were lonely. We met at a school dance. He wasn't very good-looking, but he was a nice guy.

"In May of 1977, I got pregnant. Before that, I'd been pestering my foster mother to help me get pills. She kept on saying 'Okay, I'll make the doctor's appointment.' Finally we went and I got a pap smear. The doctor called up later and said a little malignancy had showed up inside my uterus.

"Then I was waiting to get my period so I could start my pills, but I never got my period. As it turned out, it wasn't a malignancy. It was a pregnancy. I had no appetite and I was throwing up in the mornings. We went to the doctor and I found out for sure I was pregnant.

"My foster parents were telling me to keep it, and that Carlos and I should get married. I didn't want to get married, but I would have. Then Carlos said he didn't believe it was his kid. That hurt me because I really loved him. See, he had gotten another girl pregnant while we were going together, but I was faithful anyway because I loved him.

"Anyway, I talked to an attendance counselor here at the school who I felt really close to. He took me to a birth-control clinic and I had some counseling. They just told me my options. Well, I thought about it and I decided to have an abortion. I didn't tell anyone except Carlos and my sister.

"After I had the abortion, it just tore me up. I was crushed. I realized I could not have handled a baby in my life right then, but I still was crushed. I just went home afterwards and cried and cried. I didn't want anyone to know. But they found out. My foster mother accused my boyfriend of being a murderer and me of being a murderer. They wouldn't let Carlos come over anymore. Our relationship lasted a few months after that, but then it was over.

"I kept thinking about what he'd said when I was pregnant. 'It couldn't be my baby.' He didn't want to get married—that's why he was saying it. I'm glad now we didn't. It would have messed up my life, and it wouldn't have been any way for a child to grow up."

As we sat at the table, Marleen leaned forward, watching me write my notes. She propped her arms under her chin and the soft cotton sleeves of her Indian blouse absorbed the tears that fell from her eyes as she talked.

Other girls I talked to felt much of the same distress that Marleen felt at having had her abortion. People who take an absolute view that abortion should not be legal often don't take into account compelling personal reasons that make a woman decide to have one. Nor do they seem to consider that woman intent on having an abortion will do so whether or not abortions are legal. Illegal abortions are a horror not forgotten by women over twenty-five today. They know that illegal abortions put the lives of women in jeopardy.

Ten years ago, when abortions weren't legal, a sixteen-year-old girl showed up on my doorstep one evening. She had just been given a D & C by a doctor in the suburbs of Philadelphia. The girl was seven months pregnant and had come from a small country town to Philadelphia because she had heard about a "doctor" who would perform abortions. She had gone to him and he had cut inside her uterus and told her that after a day or two she would dilate and "abort naturally." No legitimate doctor would see her because she was under age. And by the time we got her to the hospital for emergency treatment, she'd almost bled to death. She had come to me because a friend of her boyfriend's had met me and said he thought I would try to help if she'd had any trouble. It turned out that the doctor who performed the abortion had charged her $500 cash. He did not have a license to practice medicine, yet regularly performed these surgical procedures in his office. The story may seem horrific, but it is representative of what life was like without legal abortions. Some girls, unlike my young friend, weren't as lucky as she was. They died at the hands of people who have performed sloppy, medically unsound, unsanitary abortions when there were no legal options for woman intent on not having the baby.

Today, when they live in metropolitan areas, teenagers do not have to risk their lives at the hands of butchers if they have an abortion.

Claire is small and blond. At seventeen, she has a sweet, almost cherubic face, and a soft, sometimes inaudible, voice. She smiles a lot as she speaks, her blue eyes looking worried and the skin on her forehead wrinkling in concern.

"The first time I had intercourse, I was fifteen years old. I was a freshman, and it was with the boy I was going with. I used to live in Ohio, and then we moved out here [to Denver, Colorado] at the end of my freshman year. It was sad. It took me awhile to get over it. I really cared about him.

"Then my sophomore year I was seeing this guy Duke. I didn't even like the guy. I was still interested in my guy back home. I feel really guilty about it. We weren't that close at all. But then we had intercourse. I only had intercourse once with him and that's when I got pregnant. It was rotten luck.

"I had a feeling I was pregnant. I was a week or two late, and I'd never been late before. I got bummed out. I went with a girl friend to a clinic and found out I was pregnant. I thought about it for one night and decided it would be too scary to have a baby and I wasn't ready for it. Oh, it was terrible. I just cried and cried. Then I made an appointment to have an abortion.

"Duke wasn't some kind of mean guy. He was willing to marry me. He took me down there and paid for it. He wasn't leaving me out in the cold.

"I felt really bad about it. It makes me feel I'm not a part of God anymore. It was against my Catholic religion to have an abortion, and it was against my own feelings. Oh, it was terrible. It still is," she says, tears rolling down her face.

"I was writing a letter to a girl friend back in Ohio about it, and dummy me, I left it out on my bed. My mother found it. Then she came to me and told me she knew about it. I guess she expected me never to have sex again after that.

"She told me she wanted me to go to confession. My dad didn't talk to me at all. Whenever he gets angry, though, he brings up the abortion. If he ever found out I was having sex again, I couldn't live in the house anymore.

"After the abortion, I didn't have sex again until I met Jeremy, and then we started getting closer and one thing led to another, and then it just happened. I'm on the Pill now, but my folks don't know it. I know they don't want to know it, either. I get tired of lying to my parents, but whenever I try to tell them who I am, they put me on restriction, so if this is the way they want it. . . ."

Some young women, when faced with the option of having and raising a child, decide to have the baby and give it up for adoption. These girls face the same medical risks to their life and health as do the teenage girls who will take their babies home. The death rate from complications of pregnancy, birth and delivery is 60 percent higher for girls under fifteen than it is for women aged twenty to twenty-four and 13 percent greater for girls fifteen to nineteen than it is for mothers in their early twenties. The chance of having toxemia is a "special hazard" they face because of the lack of development of the endocrine system, emotional stress of such early pregnancy, poor diet and poor prenatal care.

They are 91 percent more likely to have anemia and 23 percent more likely to suffer complications from premature births than mothers aged twenty to twenty-four.[3]

It seems to me that carrying a baby for nine months, going through all the physical and emotional changes of pregnancy and childbirth— feeling the baby kick, watching him emerge, having your breasts fill with milk—and then giving the baby away must be one of the most heartbreaking experiences possible. Yet many young women make that humane and courageous decision. Apart from the pain of it, they have the satisfaction of knowing they gave life to a child who is being raised by parents who are capable of loving and guiding and nurturing that child's growth in a way the natural mother was not.

For Lauren McPherson, like other girls who decided to give their babies up for adoption, it was the best possible choice in a situation where no alternative was a happy one.

Lauren, at seventeen, had just graduated from high school when we met. The fourth of six children, she lives at home with her brothers and sisters, her architect father and her mother, who had recently gotten her Master's degree in philosophy.

"I was four months pregnant before I found out," she says. "My periods were so irregular, I didn't know. I was really nervous about telling my parents, but then I went to Planned Parenthood and they told me that if I had an abortion at that stage that I'd have to be in the hospital for about three days and that it was risky. They didn't recommend anything. They just told me my options. So then I had to talk to my folks.

"I didn't want my mom to tell my dad. But she and I went to a doctor together, and he recommended that I tell my father. When we told him, he didn't say anything, but he let me decide what I was going to do about it.

"The first person I talked to about it was my boyfriend. We had broken up then, and he said, 'Are you sure?' I said, 'Yes, I'm sure.' I only talked to him over the phone, and then he said, 'What are you supposed to do now?' and I said I was going to have the baby and give it up for adoption, but that he'd have to sign some papers. So he said he'd sign the papers. I mailed them to him. I didn't want to talk to him and I didn't want to see him, not at all. We'd broken up already.

"After a while, I didn't go out. I didn't feel very good about myself. I mainly stayed inside. I had one friend, but she was pretty giddy, so I mainly hung around with my sisters and brothers. I went on the school's Home Bound program after spring vacation, so a lot of kids didn't know, but word got around. Nobody said anything to me when I came back. I'm not friends with enough kids that they'd have any reaction. I guess also in my school, it's a usual happening. I had two other girls in my class who were pregnant. I talked to one a little bit, but I didn't talk to the other one.

"I didn't have any problems physically from being pregnant. I didn't have morning sickness, and I didn't gain a lot of weight. I gained about fourteen pounds in all, and I lost that after I had the baby.

"I really felt like it was a big letdown for my parents. My mother was hurt, but understanding. She was hurt that I actually did go to bed with someone before I was married. They didn't expect me to do that. But there's a lot of other pressures with that, mainly from boyfriends. Like if you're not going to do it, well, then forget it. It was six months after we'd gone together that we first did it. We didn't use any birth control. I had this idea, well, it won't happen to me. But it did. You think it won't happen to you, but it does.

"I decided more between abortion or adoption than between adoption and keeping the baby. I knew I didn't want a baby right now. I felt it would cut into my life a lot and there are still a lot of things I want to do that I couldn't do if I had a baby.

"So I knew I couldn't keep it.

"And at the stage where I was, though, it was life. It even had a heartbeat. It was life. If I'd had an abortion then, I would have felt bad about it.

"I went in about seven o'clock one morning to the hospital, and they induced labor. They induced it because I was overdue and I was going to be starting school soon, so they induced it. It came out about eight o'clock that night. My mom and my grandmother were both with me. It didn't seem like that long. I watched television and stuff, and we talked, and my grandmother told me about her births, and they gave me pain-killers along the way. I was awake when the baby was born. It was a boy—and I only saw it out of the corner of my eye—like a flash.

"I didn't look at the baby, and I didn't see it, because I knew if I saw it, later I'd want it back and then I couldn't get it back. I knew if I saw it, I'd always think about it afterwards, so I didn't see it. It was hard knowing the baby was down the hallway and not going down there to look at him. But I thought about it a long time ahead and I knew if I saw it I'd always think about it afterwards.

"Now that I didn't see it, I don't really know . . . so I don't have a picture of him in my mind.

"I did a lot of thinking about it ahead of time.

"An attorney was the one who took the baby. He came down from the adoption agency and I signed papers that I was giving it up for adoption. They said it went to a pretty well-off couple, and that they were really nice. They said the couple had waited five years to adopt a baby. I'm not sure exactly how it happened, but I think the attorney took them the baby. I wasn't sure exactly what did happen with them taking the baby from the hospital.

"I was hoping that it was a good family who would love the baby and want it. I think if I would have kept it, it would have changed my life a lot . . . to a way of life I'm not sure I would have liked. I didn't want to change my life that way. I didn't want to have to grow up that fast!

"Right now I'm happy with my decision. I'm glad I made that decision. I couldn't make that decision for anybody else between getting an abortion or giving it up for adoption. I wouldn't advise either way. I don't advise getting pregnant—not until you're married. There's no easy way out. My parents said, 'Don't take the easy way out,' meaning abortion, but I don't think there is an easy way out. An abortion wouldn't have been easy. Whatever you choose, it's tough."

I asked Lauren if she thought she would have felt differently if she had had an abortion than she did having the child and giving it up for adoption. "I wouldn't say that I'd feel any less guilty," she said. "I think it's equal. I don't know about how I'd feel if I'd had an abortion. I think when you think about abortion, you don't think of it as a child, you think of it as a fetus. So it might not be so bad. I don't think of the baby now. If I do, I figure it just makes more problems for me.

"Every once in a while, the fact that I have had a baby gets to me. I have had a baby, but I don't have it. Sometimes I wonder what he looks like, and things like that. Every once in a while, people come in the restaurant where I work and ask, 'How's the baby?' and I don't have a baby. They saw me when I was pregnant, that's why they ask. When they ask me that, I tell them I didn't keep the baby, and go on being busy doing what I'm doing. The people who I care what they know, they know already I didn't keep the baby.

"I try not to think about it.

"It is a comfort knowing it went to a family who wanted it instead of just going to some people who didn't care about it."

Giving up a baby for adoption can be enormously difficult for the young father as well as for the young mother. Just as the girl feels the loss of her child, so does the boy. Even though the father of Lauren's baby was not involved in her pregnancy, he had feelings about the adoption. "It makes you feel kind of weird knowing you have a son out there somewhere," said James, Lauren's ex-boyfriend. "Sometimes when I see a baby who looks a little like me, I wonder if that could be my kid. It makes me feel kind of sad and kind of funny inside."

"We think of all the weight as being on the girls, but it works the other way with a lot of guys," a high-school counselor in Denver told me. "One young guy came in to see me last year and he was all upset. His girl friend had gotten pregnant and he wanted to support her and do whatever was right, no matter what it was. But her parents spirited her away from him. They wouldn't let him talk to her. He'd circle their house, but they kept their curtains closed so he couldn't see a thing. Whenever he called, they hung up the phone on him. He was frantic. He used to come in and see me every day. I'll never forget the day he brought the social worker in to me to witness his signing away his rights and giving up the baby for adoption. I've never seen so much pain.

"He went through hell that nine months. He worked three jobs and went to school. I helped him get word to her that he really cared and that he was there for her. His folks were supportive of him, thank God.

"If boys are worth their salt, they go through just as much emotionally in their own way as the girl. Of course, they don't carry the baby, but they go through hell. You don't hear about that side of it."

When teenagers decide not to have the baby or not to raise it, they often think about what might have been. Usually, they say, the choice they made was right when they think about what kind of life the baby would have had if they had had it or raised it.

"If I had kept my baby, I don't think it would have had a very good life," said Roslyn, a nineteen-year-old who gave her baby up for adoption when she was seventeen. "You've heard of people blaming their kids for their problems. I think that would have happened with me, because I didn't really want it at that time in my life. I'm not a violent person, but subconsciously, I don't like the father at all, and that might have showed through, and I might have resented the baby for making my life different."

Roslyn, now a college freshman majoring in civil engineering, plans to work in Paris next summer and to travel extensively. Eventually, she says, she wants to marry and raise a family of her own. Because she made the decision she did about her pregnancy, the path of her life has not been drastically altered.

But for the half-million teenage girls who have and keep their babies, life is changed enormously. For keeps. No longer will they merely be kids growing up. They'll be mothers or fathers, waking up to feed the baby or change a diaper or stop the crying. Just how different life will be for them is something they can't imagine until after they've given birth, come home from the hospital and run out of diapers or milk in the middle of the night.

17

Taking the Baby Home

"The first month was fine, but then from the time she was one and a half to three and a half months old, she was crying all the time and she was awake every night," says nineteen-year-old Gina, slipping a diaper onto the moving bottom of her lively two-year-old daughter. "I lost weight and I looked terrible. I got sick and I was running a high fever. It was the middle of July and it was very hot. I remember her little body breaking out in a heat rash. It was awful.

"Right off the bat, I started resenting Donald. He'd come over and pick her up and say something like, 'She's going to boil in those clothes, Gina!' I didn't know what I was doing, so for me, it'd be like, 'Don't tell me what to do, I know what I'm doing!' I wanted to do everything right, and I was so insecure about what I did that if he criticized me at all, I'd jump all over him!"

Life changes dramatically for every woman when she has a child, but it often changes even more profoundly for a teenager than it does for an older woman. Many girls are still growing themselves when they have their babies. ("I changed shape after Michelle's birth," says Jessica, running water for her daughter's bath. "When I got pregnant, I was five foot two and weighed 125 pounds. At the time of the birth, I was up to 145 pounds, and afterwards, I went down to 115 and was two inches taller, so I really stretched out.") Most have never worked or been responsible for anyone other than themselves, and have never taken care of anything but their own room. Suddenly they emerge from the hospital with a real live baby that cries when it's wet, hungry or tired, never looks at a clock or says thank you. There's an unyielding need on the part of this infant for attention, and often young mothers find themselves feeling exhausted, isolated, helpless and frightened. Besides the physical aftereffects of childbirth, the day-in and day-out, hour-to-hour details of caring for a baby leave little room for any other activity.

"Can you imagine what it would be like to bring a baby home by yourself, even at the age of twenty-five, with no notion of what's going on with yourself, let alone with what it means to be a parent?" asks Elizabeth Graham, executive director of the Northside Center for Child Development in New York. "In the hospital, you've held the baby for twenty minutes or so at a time, and then the nurse takes it away and that's been your exposure to the child. All of a sudden, you go home and you're totally alone with it. For a new mother who's older and married and totally prepared for the experience, the whole reality of taking care of a baby totally changes her life. A teenager doesn't know anything about life changes—and she still needs to be taken care of herself."

Elizabeth Graham points out that most young parents are in need of nurturance themselves, so the drain of always giving out takes an extra toll on them. Many girls had the fantasy when they had the baby that the baby would love them and become a person "all their own" who would care about them.

"Boys' needs are just as acute for caring and loving and support as the girls," she says. "Boys just ask for it in a more aggressive way.

"A boy doesn't know what being a father is, either. His image of what it means to be a parent is total fantasy, much like the girl's. He may hold and burp the baby every now and then and think he's making his contribution. Both boys and girls have a sense of pride of having produced something, but the notion that this little doll is a real life—it takes a long time to hit them.

"They often have expectations that the baby will love them, but all the baby wants is to be taken care of. It can't give back yet and won't be able to for a long time . . ."

"At first it was really overwhelming," says Robyn, the nineteen-year-old mother of a six-month-old daughter. "I think it would have been a lot more overwhelming if I'd been younger. But you go from being really a very carefree person, almost a child yourself, to having all that responsibility. Having a young baby is harder maybe because they're demanding of you all the time. They always need to eat and be changed. . . . I think it's a good responsibility, and I'm glad I feel that way, but it's still hard sometimes. . . ."

"I didn't know what it was to be a father," says Phillip, who was a father at the age of eighteen. "The only thing I could go on was to flash back to what my parents did with me. That was the only thing I had to go on. I was from a family of nine and we always did things together, and he [my father] kept us all close."

While it's difficult for teenage parents, babies of teenagers also face some tough odds. A baby born to a mother fifteen or under is three times more likely to die in the first year of life than a baby born to a woman twenty to twenty-four years of age. Babies born to teenagers are also much more likely to be born prematurely and to have low birth weights. Teenage mothers—who give birth to 19 percent of all the infants in this country—have 26 percent of all the low birth-weight babies. Low birth weight is not only a major cause of infant mortality, but it also hosts a number of other childhood illnesses and birth injuries.[1] Through ignorance, teenage parents sometimes neglect their children, and some experts say that because of the teenager's frustrations at being held back by the child, the odds that a baby will become a victim of child abuse are increased.

The life prospectus for the teenage mothers of these babies is also rather bleak. Last year some 600,000 teenage girls gave birth to babies. Although a sizable proportion of them were married before they conceived their children or were married shortly after conception, the nature of their marriages will be affected drastically by the arrival of a baby. Brides seventeen and younger are three times more likely to split up with their husbands than brides twenty or over when they marry. Bridegrooms who marry at seventeen or younger are twice as likely as men of any other age to end their marriages in divorce. More than one-quarter of first marriages in which the bride is fourteen to seventeen years old end in divorce or separation, compared to 10 percent in which the bride is twenty to twenty-four years old.[2] The rates are even higher for young mothers who were pregnant before they were married. One-fifth of their marriages are dissolved within twelve months—two and a half times the proportion of broken marriages among classmates of the adolescent mothers who were not pregnant before they were married.[3]

For the 250,755 single girls who gave birth "out of wedlock," prospects are said to be even more dismal. Families headed by young mothers are seven times as likely as others to be poor.[4] One social worker to whom I talked called young unwed mothers the walking wounded. "They're wounded because they're essentially alone when it comes to caring for and raising their babies," she said. "The boy may have pressured her to have the baby—and he wants to have his baby born. But then the realization hits him that this is more than he bargained for, and she loses the boy before she even goes to the hospital. These girls feel particularly alone emotionally."

"I'd been going with the baby's father for three months when I got pregnant with her," says sixteen-year-old Cookie in San Francisco. "It was right around my birthday I got pregnant with her. I was fifteen. He was against birth control for some reason. He wouldn't use nothing, period. He was against abortion, too, and I was for it, but we just talked about that. He didn't want either of us to use any birth control period."

"If I didn't want to have, I wouldn't have kept her, though," says Cookie, picking up her daughter and rocking her. "I couldn't believe it when I was pregnant, but I believe it now. Now, the baby's father? He's moved to Los Angeles. He calls to see how the baby is, but lately, I wish he wouldn't. I don't like him anymore. I did at first, but I don't now. . . ."

The vast majority of unwed mothers come to a standstill educationally, don't complete high school and don't develop a skill or vocation. In Baltimore, sociologist Frank F. Furstenburg of the University of Pennsylvania found that two-thirds of the unmarried teenage mothers he studied were on welfare five years after the birth of their first child and 50 percent were unemployed.[5]

Just as career advancements are limited, so are social situations. "It's been my experience that girls who keep their babies never have a normal adolescent life," says Georgia Anderson, director of Family Services of Pomona Valley. "The experience affects the girl's sexuality and her concept of herself. Boys put the press on her because there's the scarlet letter, her child, that says she's an easy make. A certain element of men take advantage of this kind of girl. Certain patterns get established and they're hard to change. . . ."

In many school districts, various individuals and groups have moved to incorporate the realities of teenage births into the regular high-school curriculum. One of the oldest public-school programs for pregnant teenagers, begun by the Oakland School District in California in 1954, has a full academic program for teenagers as well as psychology classes on the growth and development of the one- to five-year-old child. It also offers health-education classes in childbirth, delivery, prenatal care and child care. Girls who graduate from this program are usually several steps ahead of their peers in being prepared for the arrival of their children.

In most areas of the country, however, young teenage mothers do not get much instruction on motherhood, nor do they get much support in their mothering. Despite the fact that they give birth to one-fifth of the babies in this country every year, they have few services available to them that facilitate their school attendance.

At Coronado High School in Scottsdale, Arizona, Alta Lands, chairman of the home economics department, proposes that regular high-school programs should address themselves to the issues of teenage parenting and child care. Mrs. Lands has proposed that the nursery school currently run for the Child Development program at the high school should accommodate the children of high-school students while their mothers and fathers attend classes. She also proposed that the school provide parent-effectiveness training for teenagers. Mrs. Lands, like others, wants to make sure that young mothers have continuing education, early and consistent prenatal care and counseling, as well as day care and vocational training. The program before birth, and after birth, would aim to help young mothers have positive attitudes toward their child-rearing responsibilities, teach effective parenting and homemaking skills and provide opportunities for these young people to develop marketable skills.

People working for these changes say, however, that they encounter a greal deal of hostility. Some of that hostility is the same sort that confronts the proponents of sex education in the schools despite the fact that the majority of parents favor it. Of course, some of the hostility simply reflects the resentment people seem to feel toward pregnant teenagers.

"You'd be surprised at people's attitudes towards pregnant minors," says Jovina Hankins. "A lot of older people and a lot of taxpayers feel that pregnant girls should be kept at home and hidden away. They think that they shouldn't enjoy the benefits of education because they've 'done wrong' and they should pay for what they've done."

Despite the official lack of support services for young mothers, and despite the hostilities or complexities they may face, more and more teenage girls are choosing to keep their babies and raise them without being married. These girls come from every socioeconomic group. The most drastic increase is among younger white girls.

"I've been here for seven years, and it's clear to me that getting pregnant and having the baby is on the increase," says Olive Cameron, Chief Midwife at Mt. Sinai Hospital, who has delivered the babies of hundreds of young women aged eleven to seventeen over the past eight years in New York City. "The big fad is for intelligent, educated people to have babies. It's spreading through all strata of our society. Our society is an *environment* for having sex and babies."

"In the first six months of pregnancy, the girls sit back and fantasize," she says. "Oh, it's beautiful. They think the baby's father will be there and that it's all going to be wonderful. Then he splits, and in the last three months it hits them that something real is coming out of them, and they get fearful. Some of them withdraw. They get scared, and some of them get nasty. They're depressed around labor and delivery, and very frightened about delivery. When the baby comes, they're happy again, but the big depression comes later when they want to go out and find out that it's a real live baby that has to be taken care of."

Ms. Cameron shakes her head. She's a large woman with deep brown skin who comes from Jamaica, West Indies, and her accent is soft. Her jet black hair is piled on her head, and she wears small gold hoop earrings that sparkle over her white jacket.

"It's terrible for kids to have kids," she says. "They don't go back to school; it cuts off their job advancements; it cuts off their chances for advancement. It cuts off chances for jobs at all! How do you go out looking for a job with a baby on your hip? It's terrible for the children of children, too. They suffer!"

Family attitudes are particularly critical to the young woman who has her baby by herself. It used to be that many families, particularly middle-class families, spirited off a young, unmarried and pregnant daughter to a maternity home where she would have the baby quietly, away from community attention. Over the past ten years, however, maternity homes for unwed mothers have virtually closed down. Up until 1970, these homes were full and had lists of girls waiting to get in. After 1970, however, with increased information about contraception, legal access to abortions and a significant shift in acceptance of sexual-behavior attitudes and mores about sexual behavior, maternity homes across the country began closing down or changing their orientation.

After their initial shock, parents seem to take the news in stride. "My mother was really upset at first because she didn't want to be responsible for raising a baby," says seventeen-year-old Lois, whose father is a doctor and mother a librarian. Lois mixes yogurt and peaches in a bowl for her daughter as she talks. "But once she got that straightened out and realized I planned to take full responsibility, she was fine. She loves her. My whole family is crazy about her."

"When I told my mom I was pregnant she asked me what I was going to do," says Cookie, leaning over to check her baby girl, who is now asleep in the baby carriage with a hand-knitted pink cap on her head and a soft white blanket wrapped around her body. "I said I was going to keep it. Then she gave me a lecture and asked me a lot of questions about school and the baby's father. She only finished eighth grade herself, and she didn't want me dropping out. I told her I was going to finish school.

"At first, she didn't like the idea of me having one, but she's gotten used to it. Everybody was telling me she'd take over my baby when I had one, but she didn't. It's all my responsibility. I'm glad she didn't. I wouldn't like that. My neighbor was fourteen when she had her baby, and her mother took over the baby. She's like the baby's mother instead of her grandmother. But there it was better, because the girl runs the streets. She's never home, and she's never with her baby."

Often, because the teenager's mother is concerned about her, the daughter gets nurturing from her that she has needed, and the two form a bond they didn't have before. The mother feels she can talk to her daughter about things she never before told her, and the two establish a new, positive relationship. Often, the mother is with her daughter when her daughter gives birth, providing companionship during the baby's first lesson to its mother that the mother is no longer in charge of her own life. The baby will be born when it's good and ready, not before.

"I was in labor fourteen hours and I hadn't dilated at all," says sixteen-year-old Lorna, stroking the forehead of her eight-month-old son. "After that, I only dilated to about three and a half centimeters. My mother was with me, and I was really grateful. It would have been so much worse on my own. As it was, I was miserable. Finally they gave me an epidural to help with the pain. All in all, it was thirty-two hours from the time I started labor to the time he was born. I can't remember being happy or sad or anything at all when I saw him come out of me. All I remember feeling is relief. I didn't think he'd ever get born. I was so tired, all I could think of was, it's finally over!"

Some unwed mothers, like eighteen-year-old Dee, have the active involvement of the baby's father and have experience in baby care. As the second of seven children, Dee is used to taking care of babies, and her nineteen-year-old boyfriend, Herbert, took lessons to boost his ability.

"He always wanted children," says Dee. "He went to the Lamaze class with me to learn about natural childbirth, and he went to the How to Raise a Baby class and the How to Bathe the Baby class and How to Feed It Right. Most of them classes he went to by himself because I couldn't go because I was in school or I just didn't have time." Dee was in labor only six hours before having her son, Rachid, who has Herbert's last name.

Dee's hair is deep black, tied up on top of her head with a red ribbon, and her skin is smooth, rich brown. She's tall, probably five foot ten, and very slender. She wears a green checkered shirt over her tall, lanky frame, blue jeans and sandals.

She's wonderful to look at: She radiates an elegance and playfulness unusual at any age. Her laugh is uproarious, and despite the fact that she's seventeen years old, unwed and living part-time in her mother's home and part-time in Herbert's two-room apartment, she's relaxed and optimistic about her life.

Right now she's sitting at her mother's kitchen table in Los Angeles, intently studying pictures out of *Modern Bride* magazine. She isn't looking for a wedding dress, she explains, she's looking for a formal for the senior prom three months hence. Her mother has already promised to baby-sit.

"I can hardly wait. I'm going to rent a limousine for the evening," she says. "We got to do it up right. Herbert's paying for the dinner and the flowers—my corsage and his flower—and I'm paying for my dress and the car. It's going to cost us a couple hundred dollars, but it'll be worth it."

Although many young women never plan to get pregnant, Dee was one who consciously wanted a baby. It wasn't by accident that she and Herbert didn't use birth control.

"All my kids will be by the same man," she says, smiling, her arms folded on her belly. "It was planned, this baby. I like kids, and I don't want to be too old when I have 'em. I want to have four or three of 'em. And I don't want to be fifty when I have the fourth baby. I plan to stay with Herbert. I'm not leaving him. We'll get married in 1983, when I'm twenty-one."

Unlike many girls her age, who find themselves with a baby and no concrete plans or life goals, Dee is full of ambitions. She's in the process of finishing high school and she plans to start college in the fall. "They have a nursery school at the college so you can leave your baby there while you're in class. I'll be majoring in accounting. I mean to get rich, too—and I will."

At this time, Herbert and Dee are in an unusual position for teenage parents. They are not worrying about finances. Herbert has a job as a chef's assistant and makes about fourteen thousand dollars a year. Additionally, Dee's father owns a children's clothing store, her mother works as a teacher's aide and both shower their grandson, their daughter and Herbert with gifts.

For most teenage parents, the logistics and the finances of having a baby are staggering. Particularly when a young mother truly makes her own way, she must work and manage her time and money as well as arrange for her child's care. I interviewed one young woman, Jessica, on her day off from her job as a telephone answering service operator. As we talked, Jessica played comfortably and warmly with her diaper-clad daughter, Michelle, an alert, happy two-year-old.

"I make $90 a week working six days a week, nine to five," Jessica says. "In addition, I get $76 worth of food stamps a month." Jessica pays $210 a month rent on her one-bedroom apartment in West Philadelphia, plus electricity and gas. The month before, her food stamps hadn't arrived.

"It's so unreliable," she says. "A person could starve. If I didn't have anybody, how would we eat this month? Really, if I didn't have my mother and my friends in town, we'd be hungry."

Every day Jessica drops Michelle off at a federally funded day-care center at 7:30 in the morning and picks her up at 5 P.M. "I'm looking for a good nursery school for her now," she says, smiling a smile that lights her hazel eyes and strawberry blond coloring. "I've got my eye on a Montessori school and I'm trying to get a scholarship there. If we get it, she'll start there in the fall."

The financial realities of Jessie's life are startling. Even though she blames herself ("I'm really bad at managing money," she says. "I save, but you always find something you need at the last minute"), she doesn't have much latitude. What's even more alarming, is that her finances are in better order than those of some young mothers because she has some help from the baby's father.

"He gives me a money order every week for her day care, which is nine dollars, and five dollars for her Pampers every week," says Jessica. "So it works out to about fifteen dollars a week, which is a big help. He said when we broke up that he wanted whatever he gave to go directly to Michelle, so we both feel comfortable about it this way."

Although the amount may seem small, it shows concern and commitment on the part of Michelle's father, who is under no legal obligation to pay anything for his daughter's support.

"I'm trying to find a better job so I can start school at Temple by next Christmas," says Jessie, running water for Michelle's bath. "I figure right now I'll concentrate on secretarial skills and start from there. A good secretary is as good as a lot of professions. At the telephone-answering service, I've heard a lot of people say, 'You know anybody who types?' I figure if I can type, I can do better than I'm doing now, anyway!"

Although teenage fathers get a lot of bad press, many teenage fathers, like Michelle's, stay closely involved with their children, despite difficulties between themselves and the mothers. They may decide that they can't maintain a relationship living together, but they can both be good parents to their child.

"I see my daughter almost every other day, sometimes every day," says Phillip. "She calls me over, and I always go with her to doctor's appointments when I can. I take her out a lot. Usually, too, I take her shopping for her clothes and I give her mother money. We don't have any formal agreement, but I give her money for food, and I buy all my daughter's shoes and clothes.

"I back my daughter all the way. I guess I'll back her all the way until she's grown up and even afterwards. . . ."

"Sometimes I get this guilt feeling, like I think I should be there with her no matter what the sacrifice is, even if I'd be miserable, but then I think all the tension and hostility and all that could build up and wouldn't do her any good, so it's better this way. Usually it's when I'm out partying or whatever, that's when I get that guilt feeling. . . ."

Certainly it's easier for teenage fathers to party than it is for mothers. Even when teenagers have liberal views of gender roles, most child care falls to the mother. When the mother and father live apart, when the mother is in her own apartment or living with her parents, it's difficult to make time for friends, let alone for parties or romance. The choices about where to go and when to go must be planned. A girl can't go to a spur-of-the-moment party unless she takes her baby along. When she gets involved with a boy, he has to accept the fact that she has a child, and then the mother has to consider the child's attachments and feelings as well as her own.

For instance, Lorna has been seeing her current boyfriend, Jim, for four months, but it's not an average eighteen-year-old's carefree relationship. When I arrived at Lorna's apartment in Minneapolis, Jim was just leaving for his job at a gas station. We sat on a mattress on the floor while Lorna's baby, Ronnie, took his nap in the crib in the same room. Lorna rents the room from the couple that owns the house, and she and Ronnie live, play, sleep and eat in that room.

"Jim likes Ronnie a lot," Lorna says, "but I try to do most everything for him myself, because if we break up, I don't want it to be hard on Ronnie. I know he's young, but those things make a difference. Jim is here about three or four days a week overnight and he used to do more to help me, but recently I told him I was feeling funny about it, and so now he's trying to relate more to Ronnie as one of Mommy's friends rather than as *the* friend."

Lorna hasn't gone out with the baby's father since about five months after Ronnie was born. "When I went back to high school, I realized there was life after pregnancy," she said. "I started seeing other people secretively, but I felt like I should be seeing only him. You feel like you have a child by this man, so you should stay with him. But after a while, I lost my attraction for him. I would get annoyed just being around him, and I couldn't stand sex with him.

"Also, I think I'd grown up a lot after Ronnie was born. Not when I was pregnant, because people were still doing everything for me, but after he was born, I had to do the decision making and I was responsible for myself and for him.

"We grew more and more apart, until finally it was to the point where I was desperate not to see him. I'd say quite bluntly, 'I don't want to see you anymore. Leave me alone.' Finally he agreed.

"He's very dependable now if I need anything, and his family is more than willing to help. I don't ask for help, but when his mother says, 'Does Ronnie need anything?' I whip out my list!"

One of the biggest changes for Jessica has been the lack of free time she has to spend with friends. "By the time I pick up Michelle and get home and do everything I have to do, I'm ready to go to bed again, so I don't see a whole lot of my friends. I have three main girl friends, but I don't see them much, either. It's not like you can just go out whenever you want," she says, running water for Michelle's bath and putting her in the tub.

"Having sex is also in slightly different perspective. "At first, I was afraid. I didn't start to enjoy it again for a few months. I'd go through the motions, but I didn't really enjoy it. Now I feel real pleasure again. . . ."

Although she's very careful and does use birth control, Jessie says if she got pregnant again, there's a strong possibility she'd have the baby. "But I'd set up a formal agreement with the other party about financial arrangements, because I'm not into being a welfare mother for years. I'm not against marriage or anything. I just want to be sure when I do get married.

"I suppose if I could do anything right now, I'd have a lot of money. It sounds very intriguing to live comfortably. I'd like to do that."

Jessica squeezes water through a yellow duck onto Michelle's hand. "I never could have realized exactly how much of a change it could have been to have a baby," she says. "I couldn't have believed it. Nobody telling you, no book, nothing in reading could prepare you.

"I remember my mother telling me, 'You won't be able to go out as much'—but it's something you have to learn for yourself."

Married teenagers face many of the same problems as unmarried parents. They have day-to-day responsibilities that make them grow up so fast they're almost dizzy. They have financial debts and pressures, limits on their social time. They often feel quite isolated from friends, because with a baby, their lives are different. They don't have much in common anymore with their single friends.

"Most everybody our age *isn't* married," says Scott, a twenty-year-old father in California. "We don't have any friends who are married— well, one couple we met who live quite a ways from us. But we're pretty solitary."

Scott and his wife Robyn got married after they learned Robyn was expecting. "It was kind of a moral thing with me," says Scott. "We wanted to be with each other. What we had was like a very new blossom of love just started. We had known each other for a while, but we had just begun to really know each other. . . .

"When we decided to get married, I was thinking more about Robyn and me than I was about the baby. The pregnancy was almost an imaginary thing to me. I'm a very visual person, so if I couldn't see the baby, it was like she didn't exist. I just felt this getting married was the thing I had to do, so I did it."

According to the 1980 census, approximately 10 percent of all teenagers are married. Historically, teenage brides become mothers quickly. Although most teenage brides are not pregnant when they marry, approximately 70 percent of married first-time mothers aged fifteen to nineteen have a child in the first year of their marriage. In 1979, according to figures from the Alan Guttmacher Institute, over 192,000 teenagers who were married before they got pregnant gave birth. One hundred and twelve thousand gave birth within eight months after their marriage. These married teenagers accounted for nearly three-fifths of all teenage births.

Even before the baby arrives, it begins to change the relationship between a young husband and wife.

"We started arguing more," says nineteen-year-old Wayne, who works at an automobile factory outside Detroit. "At times she'd go into a lot of moody ways she didn't have when she wasn't pregnant. There was a lot I had to put up with that wasn't normal. Like, in the middle of the night, she'd want ice cream. At 3 A.M., a ham hoagie or pizza.

"When she first got pregnant, I was shocked. We'd only been married about three months, and I didn't want to have kids for at least a couple of years. At that time, we discussed alternatives she didn't want to hear about. She had made up her mind she wanted the baby, and finally I just accepted it. I didn't realize how much I would like it until right before she went into the hospital. Then I had really warm feelings. And I was so happy when our daughter was born. I'd wanted a son, but I really liked our daughter."

When the baby comes home, it nearly always disrupts normal life and routine between the father and mother. Their sponteneity and fun and romance are overshadowed by the needs of the baby.

"I went through a period feeling like our relationship would never be the same," said Robyn, who is nursing six-month-old Rebecca. "It was for three weeks or a month after she came home from the hospital. We had such a loss of privacy. I was afraid we'd never regain that one-on-one contact we'd had with each other. It sure changes everything.

"You have a little nostalgia sometimes. You wish you could go back and go out when you want and where you want to go, and you wish you could be spontaneous again. You miss your freedom.

"Being a girl, you also worry cause it makes your appearance less appealing. Like your figure is not quite as nice and trim as it was before you had a child. . . ."

Often the arrival of a baby and the new scheduling of events and priorities reshuffle a couple's relationship. The new mother is fully occupied with baby care and often feels quite unattractive and unappealing.

When she's feeling unattractive and preoccupied, she may also feel quite uninterested in sex. Particularly after the birth of the child, she may not be interested in having intercourse for weeks. In fact, doctors recommend waiting six weeks. The father who is feeling insecure—and who may be used to confirming his masculinity and good sense of himself sexually—feels all the more shut out and displaced by the baby.

"What happened after she'd been home from the hospital for about a week and a half was I started getting pretty upset," said Roger, Jeannie's eighteen-year-old husband. "She wasn't interested in sex at all, and that's all I could think about. I started looking at other girls on the street, and feeling rotten about it, and then I'd come home and all she did was fuss over the baby all the time. Nothing was ever right anymore. After about two months, we started getting things straightened out again, and now we're pretty together about sex and everything else."

One advantage young mothers have is that because they are young, they seem to regain their good shape fairly quickly after childbirth. "I was really happy I didn't get any stretch marks or anything," says seventeen-year-old Edie. "It went back very fast. After Tony was born, when I went in for my first checkup, the doctors were oohing and aahing that my stomach wasn't hanging out me. They attribute it going flat again to being young and having your muscles be pretty elastic."

Besides taking on new roles by themselves and with each other, losing contact with friends and feeling isolated seem to be common denominators for all young parents. "I was scared and nervous about having a baby—very nervous about what the future held," says twenty-year-old Scott, holding Rebecca as he talks. "I wasn't sure about myself at all. Sometimes I'm still not. The biggest thing you lose with a baby is freedom. I was rather flighty before. I did a lot of partying. And I kept my own hours. I had my own place or I lived with other guys.

"Now I'm getting used to it, though. I'm enjoying it, and it gets more fun with time. I look forward to coming home more lately. I was more skeptical before about what would happen. But as Robyn and I get to know each other, things start running a lot smoother and we have our timing more together. We've gotten so much into our own timing that when my little sister came up to visit us last week we almost couldn't function because we're so used to being solitary. We couldn't keep our timing together. . . ."

During the days, Scott is being trained for a job in electronics. It's a technical job, he says, "one of the human machine" jobs, but he hopes to find more challenging work later. While he's working, Robyn is at home with their six-month-old daughter, Rebecca.

"I had to learn a lot of things awfully quick," she says. "Like doing housework and cooking; it has to be done. At first, it was overwhelming to me, all the things that needed to be done, as well as spending valuable time with Rebecca. But now I've learned that sometimes I have to let some housework go and just spend time with her. It's getting a lot easier to adjust to things now. I'm feeling stronger, and Scott is very helpful. He's always there when I need him—I'm lucky like that. He's changed almost as many diapers as I have since Rebecca was born."

When Scott's away from the house, however, Robyn is basically isolated. "I have one friend who has a child, but she's too far away and neither of us has transportation during the day," she says. "The other women around here are either younger than I am and don't have babies, or they're older—they're twenty-five or twenty-seven, and I feel that they think I'm too young to associate with them. It's hard for me. I think a lot of women go through a time when they're having children when they feel pretty unattached and isolated. I've pretty much lost contact with my old friends.

"I'd love to spend some time with other mothers. I think I could learn from them and the way they interact with their children. But it seems like they're all inside their houses."

The strains on young married couples with children are often enormous, and probably have to do with the low odds on their marriages surviving. One of the big problems besides the isolation is that teenagers are still developing their interests and their definitions of themselves, and sometimes, as with older couples, they grow in different directions.

"We were living together when she went into a religious type thing," says Phillip, who now shares an apartment with a male friend. "She got saved and sanctified in the Pentecostal church. I tried to follow the same route as her, but I had mixed emotions about it. I'd grown up Baptist, and it was just too different for me. It caused a lot of problems and tensions.

"We had always had fun partying together, too, and then she didn't want to go out. Then I was working six days a week, and on Sundays, I'd get up and try to go to church with her. If I stayed home to watch TV, she'd get mad, and if I went to church and missed it, I'd get mad.

"We became two different people. And finally we decided to have a temporary separation, but it's never gotten back together, and it probably won't. I don't want to get into a permanent relationship with anybody else 'cause I keep thinking someday we can get on with it, but I don't know.

"I wanted to keep my family together in the same way my folks did," said Phillip. "My mother and father have been together since they were sixteen, and now they're sixty-three. I wanted to have the same kind of thing for my family. I felt it was my responsibility as a man. But times were different then than they are now. I guess a lot has changed. . . .

"The thing I care about is making a blend between both of us where it won't affect my daughter in any bad way. I go over there a lot, and she seems to bounce along. They can always call me, and I'm always there for them. Some people stay in bad relationships, though, and get to the point of no return. Instead of breaking up, they call names and fight and get to the point of vengeance things with each other. The kids know what's going on. They can feel all the hurt and pain. I couldn't live that way, and I don't think it'd be any good for our daughter."

Although the realities, hardships and logistics of being teenage parents are often discouraging, there are also joys. None of the teenagers to whom I talked said she or he would be willing to give up the joys of having a child. Many said that there are advantages and disadvantages in starting their families young, but they don't regret their decision.

"You turn on the television and you hear them talking about teenage pregnancies," says seventeen-year-old Charity, a small-boned, blond seventeen-year-old whose roly-poly daughter is nudging her mouth against her mother's neck. "They act like it is such a terrible thing—like, 'Your daughter could be next!' Instead of acting like it's so terrible, they ought to provide support services for people who do have kids when they're young so they can do more for themselves.

"It's not so terrible to have a child when you're still a teenager."

Charity put her daughter Mikeeda down on the floor and filled a baby bottle with milk. She offered me potato salad and apple juice. I kept doing a double-take at seeing her with her daughter because I knew Charity when she was eight years old, and it was hard now, nine years later, to think of her as a young woman with a child. Though technically an unwed mother, Charity lives the life of a married woman, supported by Mikeeda's father, James. Since she has had Mikeeda, Charity has finished high school and begun a program in commercial art. A good day-care program in her neighborhood makes it possible. Mikeeda's father, James, works construction and maintenance jobs during the day and has begun driving a car at night to supplement their income. He wants to become a pediatric nurse.

"We're glad we started our family early," says Charity. "We didn't really think about getting married. We said we'll get married when we're in our forties and the kids are raised and the real pressures are over. Then we can sit back and enjoy ourselves."

"A lot of people tend to categorize teenage mothers," says nineteen-year-old Jessica. "I tend to think of teenage mothers as thirteen, fourteen and fifteen. I'd rather be called a young mother. I like that better. My mother was married at eighteen and had her first child when she was nineteen, and I don't think anybody would have called her a teenage mother."

"When we had the baby, it was a motivating thing for me," says Phillip. "It gave me a motive as to how I was going to take care of my child. It gave me a need to provide for my daughter and to be somebody other than just being one of the fellows. I started listening to positive ideas and opportunities, and started to heed what I wanted to do with my life.

"At the time, I was working, but it made me think about where I wanted to go and what I wanted to do with my life. It made me feel more responsible as an individual. I wanted to have something and be somebody for my daughter to identify with. . . .

"She's given me something special in my life. She's just so happy and bubbly. She just bounces along. There isn't anything like the feelings of love I have for her. . . ."

"Every day now it's better with her," says Robyn, smiling at her baby and tickling the baby's toes. "It seems like each day she's doing something new. She responds more and she smiles more. . . .

"Sometimes I think, looking back on my teenage years, that looking back makes it more glamorous. When I look back, I know there are times I was just bored out of my mind.

"Now sometimes if it's raining and I'm inside with Rebecca and I feel nostalgic about old times, I remind myself that there were times I couldn't think of what to do then, too. . . . Even with my freedom, it wasn't all that great. . . ."

PART V

18.

Moving On

Nothing quite prepares parents for their child's move away from home. Although everything from a baby's first steps to a teenager's written declaration of independence is part of the process leading to future separation, the actual leave-taking is traumatic, if not shocking. Parents say that letting go is one thing. Acting grown-up about it is another.

When Cindi and her mother went out to celebrate Cindi's eighteenth birthday, for instance, Cindi asked if she could have a gin and tonic. "I said sure, she could have two if she wanted," said her mother, Meta, an attractive woman of forty-one. "It nearly killed me. But she's eighteen now, and she's out of the home and I have to stop thinking of her as my baby. At this age, she's got to be responsible for her own decisions.

"Things will never be the same at home. I'm very emotional about it, but it's true. It's just not the same as it was. It never will be. She'll be home for a week after this summer job, and then she'll be off to college and just come home for weekends here or there.

"I can't say don't do this or that anymore. I can give advice and I can tell her what I think, but she's on her own. She'll have to make decisions and some of them won't be good, but she'll learn by experience.

"Yesterday we were walking on the beach, and I wanted to say don't slump. Stand up straight. But I didn't. I tried so hard not to criticize. We were walking, and I kept noticing things, but I managed to keep my mouth shut."

Fred's mother, Linda, labels her feelings about her son's life away from home as "primitive."

"It just kills me to think about his living with a girl at his age," she said, running her hands through her curly gray hair. "He's so young!

He's nineteen. I mean, the idea of her being there at all hours of day and night—it's like they're married, but they're not. I just hope she doesn't get pregnant or anything like that. I just don't want him to cut off his options so young."

Linda, who gave birth to Fred when she was twenty-one, admits she's doing some projecting when she thinks about Fred's future. "I didn't get to start my career until I was almost thirty years old," she says. "And I know they just aren't thinking realistically about what's ahead of them. They're just too thrilled with the freedom of making love whenever they want to and doing their own thing. I remember what it was like, feeling so free. I should trust him, but I'm so afraid he'll make foolish decisions or get hurt or do things he'll regret. Really, I'm most afraid of her hurting him or talking him into marriage or something crazy like that. I might feel differently if I liked her, but I can't stand her. I don't think she's up to him at all!"

"Mark can't wait to get away from the family," says Toni, shaking her curly black hair and inhaling, then blowing smoke out past the mother-of-pearl cigarette holder she's balancing between the fingers of her right hand. "He can't wait to go to college and be independent and a man on his own. It's not a problem for us. We're anxious for him to go.

"But I don't know . . . I get very emotional at times. It's like a part of myself is leaving. He's leaving, and that separation is final. It hurts your heart a lot, but you know it's right, and it's time. Yet part of me is going away.

"I'll have a close rapport with Mark always. I know we'll always be in touch, but there will be a void for sure. There's always holidays and vacations, but he'll be gone, and even if he came back to live with us for a while, it wouldn't be the same. He'll look at being here with different eyes, even, because it will no longer be the same for him. He'll be visiting us."

Toni takes another drag from her cigarette. She wears three golden rings set with diamonds on her right hand. I follow her eyes to the Chinese vase filled with giant white mums and across the carpeted floors to the large, spotless windows. Light casts afternoon shadows across the cushioned, elegantly furnished living room.

"It's so strange. Here's this person you've loved and cared for since birth. You've gone through every stage, from his first step to his first love, and then he goes out of your life and your care, and it's so *final*.

"I worry. Is he going to be all right? Is he going to care for himself as well as we did? He will. But he'll make mistakes . . . It wouldn't be natural if he didn't.

"I can't help but think about the first time he comes home from college. How will he present himself when he comes in? Will he try and crawl back into that little capsule we built for him for a short while, or will he come home as a man and try to show us how grown-up and independent he is?" Toni sighed and smashed out the embers of her cigarette in a porcelain ashtray.

"You look back and remember when your mom said to you, 'When I was your age . . .' and you said 'But Mom! Those were the olden days!' Everything changes so *fast*."

Teenagers as well as their parents often see their eighteenth or nineteenth birthday, moving into an apartment they will support with what they earn themselves, or going away to college, as the definitive step into adulthood.

When I first met eighteen-year-old Victoria Kramer at Duke University in Raleigh, North Carolina, for instance, I asked her her permanent address. She gave me the address of the dorm where she lived. "I'm independent," she insisted when I pressed her for a *home* address. "*This* is my permanent address.

"When I decided to leave home," she explained, "I wanted to leave home permanently. I was living with my mother and stepfather, and they have their own life. They have their own daughter and son, who are younger. I figured I need time to get my life organized on my own. I wanted to move out last summer and get my own apartment, but I realized that was just my way of saying, I want to hurt you. The problem was basically a clashing of style. That was the basic difference. Without constant contact, it's not a problem. Now I can visit them and we can just enjoy each other without rubbing the wounds."

From now on, as she puts it, "Wherever I am is where I live."

Even when a young person doesn't view the break away from home in as distinct a way as Victoria, even when home base is still "home," most young people say that once they've experienced a world of their own, home can never be quite the same again.

"When we go home after having been away, it's different from when we're living here," says Annette, a freshman at Northwestern University who comes from Silver Springs, Maryland. "Now we have our own life-style, and we're going to visit them in their life-style. It'd be great, even for vacations, to live in the house next door to theirs. It's living *with* them that's so difficult. Our relationship may be strong—and ours is—but it's still like trying to mend broken fences. . . ."

Something else that happens when young people leave home or move away emotionally is that they measure their parents' lives against the life they want for themselves. When they're home, they're often reminded of ways in which they are like their parents and comfortable in their patterns, and they find distance in identifying how different they will be, ways in which they will change the status quo for themselves.

"I could never live a life like my parents live," says eighteen-year-old Christine, a college freshman at UCLA, who plans to become a stockbroker in New York and marry when she's twenty-eight or thirty years old. "They live in a residential neighborhood, my dad has a nine-to-five job and they go to church on Sundays. That's about it. My mother is so dormant. I couldn't stand it. It seems to me that neither one of them is aware of the life around them. They don't even know what's going on in the rest of the world, and what's more, they aren't even aware that they're missing anything! I don't want to be like that!"

Certainly the world teenagers enter upon departure from home is quite different from the one most of us stepped into when we left our parents' homes. The world they move into for the most part makes no severe judgments based on their sexual behavior. At most colleges, what once would have caused scandal and perhaps suspension from college causes not a ripple of surprise. It's socially acceptable for a young woman and a young man to have intercourse with one another with no intention of marriage or future plans. Theirs is a world of no accountability when it comes to where they are or how they spend their free time. It's quite acceptable for unmarried college students to live together in intimate heterosexual or homosexual relationships that twenty years ago would have meant automatic cessation of academic studies.

"We don't have any rules here," says Adele, a sophomore at Northwestern University in Evanston, Illinois. "Boys can be here all night if they want to be.

"When I came here from Texas, I thought I'd act just like I did in high school when I went to a party. There was no way. I hated it; I couldn't believe it. When you went to frat parties, you'd walk in and it was like a lineup with the guys standing there looking you over like you were livestock: 'Let's give her a number seven.' "

Six of us had gathered around a small wooden table in the living room of a girls' dormitory on Northwestern's large, snow-covered campus. Five of the students were freshmen; Adele was the only sophomore. While the girls collected cigarettes and gum from their various rooms, I thought about my freshman dorm and how, within the first week, I had gotten into trouble for (1) going barefoot in the lobby, (2) chatting with a male guest in the living room of our dorm when it was, unbeknownst to me, off limits to boys, (3) taking a dog and a bird, at different times, into my room and (4) making hot chocolate in my room. The list of known and unknown violations was endless.

When all the girls were settled, with Tabs, Pepsis, ashtrays, gum and candy, I told them about the concept of colleges being *in loco parentis*—taking the role of parents—that had been the norm when I was in college. It was difficult for me to imagine the freedom they had. When I was in college, we had to sign out and write down where we were going (including phone numbers) and be back in our dorms at 10:30 on week-nights and by 12:30 A.M. on Friday and Saturday nights. Girls were not allowed in boys' dorms or apartments, nor were they allowed to live off campus themselves until senior year. This was a normal, average, run-of-the-mill state university. I described the scene on the porches and steps outside the girls' dormitories five minutes before the doors were locked at curfew: couples stood body to body, kissing, snuggling, whis-pering, giggling, "going to bed standing up," as one counselor put it, until the dorm mother stood with the door held wide, ready to pull it shut and lock it. Girls kissed their last good-bye before charging up the gangplank; it was akin to soldiers getting on the boat to go to war. (The boys, of course, were free to roam under an institutionalized double standard; they had no curfews.) If girls were late five, ten minutes, fifteen minutes, the demerits accumulated. After three tabulated "lates," you were grounded for a weekend. If you were late too often or if you failed to sign in at all, you could be suspended from the university. Clearly all guards were up against casual sex.

"Who gave them the *right* to tell you when to come in!" eighteen-year-old Theda Lloyd demanded, incredulous. "Who gave them the right to tell you what to do or where to go?"

I felt as if I had told a story from ancient history; I had.

"I think it's *terrible*," said Adele. "It just makes people more de-vious."

The girls had heard a few "horror stories" from Baylor and Nebraska and a few other schools that still have locked dorms (after certain hours) or restrictions on being in the girls' or boys' part of a dorm with-out an escort—all of which they thought ludicrous. I was as amazed by their sense of outrage as they were by my lack of it when I was their age.

Of course, they acknowledged, with no authorities making the rules for them, they had to make rules for themselves, which was definitely hard on some students, particularly if they had been restricted at home and felt they had to go wild at school to prove themselves "normal."

"That doesn't happen with many kids," said Karen, an eighteen-year-old freshman. "But the ones who feel pushed and pressured to perform are usually insecure in the first place. Most people conduct themselves pretty well, and with respect."

Of course, when eighteen- or nineteen- or twenty-year-olds leave home, they do have new freedoms. They have an oportunity to complete the tasks of adolescence—learning to deal with stress, to feel autono-mous, to transfer their loyalties to new friends, to understand their own controls and to be able to integrate themselves into a larger society, outside the family.

Many people wait until they leave home to explore freedoms they will have as adults. In fact, for most, the majority of their sexual experiences come after they are eighteen years old. Away from their parents and their family setting, they say they feel less restricted in exploring their own sexuality and establishing intimate relationships.

"I felt I had to be an adult before I undertook a sexual relationship," said Wally, a twenty-year-old who works for a telephone company in Wisconsin. "I didn't have any really intimate sexual relationship with a girl until I was nineteen, last year. It was right after I got my job and my own apartment. I think for me I had to be away from home and of age to do what I pleased. I always felt it was all right to explore and to have sex once you were more grown up. I think also, for me, I had a lot of anxiety about the technical details and I didn't have the idea that it could be as natural as it is. Maureen was the first girl I slept with, and afterwards, I felt like I should marry her, but she wasn't interested in getting married. She taught me a lot about myself. I still have a lot to learn."

Although people often equate being adult with being sexual and having intercourse, the equation is erroneous. Just moving away from home or getting an apartment doesn't throw most teenagers into wild, frenzied sexual behavior. Although college students and older teenagers sometimes accord status to their sexually experienced peers and put down sexually inexperienced teenagers, those who have a clear sense of their own priorities are not intimidated.

"People get so hung up about relationships and sex," says Elizabeth, a college freshman from Baltimore, Maryland, whose straight brown hair is topped by a baseball cap sitting at a jaunty slant over one eye. "It's ridiculous. It's like the opposite of junior high . . . like this big gap between the seventh to the ninth grades, where you can't be seen talking to a guy. They'd say all kinds of things like, oh, you love him, if you ever talked to a boy. Now it's like if you talk to him, you must be sleeping with him. It's really ridiculous.

"To have a normal sex life isn't meaning necessarily making love," she says. "For some people, it might mean making love. For other people, a normal sex life would be hugging and kissing and not doing anything else. That would be normal for them at that particular time in their lives. It might mean doing nothing at all that would be normal too. It depends on what's normal for that person."

Virginia Landwehr, dean of students at Northwestern University, says, "It's overwhelming to some freshman women to have no limits when they're making all their personal decisions and career decisions on their own. Making all these decisions can be overwhelming," she said, "but career choice tends to be the most difficult and cause the most stress. In my generation, it was: If you find the right mate, then happiness will follow. Now it seems that if you find the right job, then happiness will follow. It's the old work ethic. Find your job and you'll find satisfaction.

As for sexual decisions, Ms. Landwehr said, "The question now is not about finding the right mate. The question is shall I have an intimate relationship with this person? Why am I not having an intimate relationship like everyone else is?"

"I think in some ways I enjoyed high-school sexuality more because there were so many rules," said Eric, who had just passed his nineteenth birthday. "We spent most of our time avoiding rules. In college, with no restrictions, I have a lot of leftover guilt and anxiety with the message from my parents that sex is wonderful with love, but without love, it's bad. My father said it would be pleasant, but bad."

Sometimes, particularly in a college community, individual freedoms reign supreme—at the expense of consideration for others. Since it is now popular to be sexually liberated, at least in attitude, and since college students are often still reveling in finally being free of the parental eye, sometimes students directly violate a roommate's privacy or show a lack of thoughtfulness for another's feelings. It's a tyranny of liberation.

One young woman at UCLA told me, for instance, about an incident that year that had caused a stir of protest in her all-female dorm. It happened when one of the freshman women had her boyfriend stay with her in the dorm's common lounge for ten days. What people objected to, besides being barred from a common room, was that the couple didn't pick up after themselves, left liquor bottles scattered around, played the radio quite loudly and were overly loud in their lovemaking at all hours of the day and night.

"One night I was sound asleep when I heard this funny sound coming out of the bottom bunk," said Candace, a freshman at UCLA. "My roommate wasn't back and I was paralyzed for a few minutes, wondering what it was. Then I realized that my roommate was back—and her boyfriend was with her. I could have died. I was still a virgin, and she knew it, but it didn't bother her. It bothered me plenty, and I told her the next day. After that, we made arrangements about when she wanted the room, but she bad-mouthed me to everybody because de facto, to be so mad at my privacy being invaded, I had to be out of it."

In high school and in the homes of their parents, teenagers are living in an environment where they usually understand the rules, the value systems and the moral interpretations of different behavior. Home is a familiar place with familiar people, and it often serves as a refuge and comfort from the differentness they encounter in the outside world. Most college freshmen, no matter what experience they've had before, look forward with real longing to Thanksgiving vacation and their first trip back home to their families and high-school friends. After Christmas vacation, however, they're no longer homesick and for the most part have adopted their new world as their own—even though it's a world occupied by people with outlooks, values and backgrounds that don't parallel their own experience.

Often in the crush of new encounters and conflicting expectations and assumptions, feelings get trampled and eyes opened to attitudes that are shockingly new and different.

The pressures are just as difficult for boys as they are for girls, sometimes even more so because of "macho" expectations.

"The first day I was at the university [of Michigan], I walked into my room and this kid Steve was in the room with his parents," says eighteen-year-old Roger, who is tall and has a sandy complexion. "They were in their forties, and they were very young-looking. The father was very dominantly masculine. He hadn't gone to college, but I didn't know that. I asked him what school he had gone to, and he said, the school of hard knocks. I didn't know what that meant, and I didn't really understand him, so I said, 'Where's that?' He just repeated that it was the school of hard knocks. The kid, Steve, isn't on work-study, so they had some money, and they were dressed really nice, too.

"When they left, his father kissed him good-bye, which I thought was uncommon for someone so macho acting. . . .

"Anyway, the following night, Steve was having sexual intercourse with this girl and it was *in* our room. They had a very tactile relationship—they were always touching and kissing, and they were very exclusive about it. They spent all their free time together, and it was in our room because she didn't want her roommates to know. When they didn't want people to come in, the memo pad outside the door would say 'Busy: Come back later!' No one's going to keep me out of my own room! I tried pushing the door open, but they had it all barricaded with chairs and furniture so no one could get in.

"Several times they made love in the room after I was in there and theoretically sleeping. For the most part, with them, sex wasn't a very private or heightened act. If it was really that important, they would have needed privacy, but they didn't.

"I was uncomfortable because of the sounds they were making. And when they were doing fellatio, all the sucking sounds were so loud. I couldn't see it because I wear contact lenses and can't see anything even five feet away, particularly in the dark. But I could hear it all.

"The way Steve dealt with it was he said, 'Hey, you bring a girl in here and I'll leave.' That was his way of rationalizing his screwing in my presence. . . ."

Roger said he couldn't imagine having sex in front of another person even if it didn't matter to that person. It seemed too private and too important a matter to him.

"With them it was like, let's make love, and if anyone comes in, who gives a damn," he said. "She cared about fucking in front of *her* roommates, though, and that's why they always fucked in our room. She had the gall to tell her roommate in front of me one time that someone had started a rumor about her sleeping with Steve! Can you imagine? She was acting all serious. I couldn't believe the gall—in front of me!

"Another time they did it on my roommate's bed in the back room and got stuff on the sheets and my roommate demanded that Steve wash the sheets, but he never did. Steve's response was, 'Use my sheets—they're the same size.' "

Cicely's values were assaulted even more dramatically than Roger's when she moved to Boston to take a job in computer programming. That was when she got involved with Larry, a senior at Boston University. She considered her involvement a love affair. He considered it at most a casual fling. The two had very little in common and, in fact, didn't communicate with one another on any significant level outside their sexual interactions.

"I started going with him spring term," says Cicely, a brown-eyed nineteen-year-old who eventually wants to work in banking. "That's the way I thought of it—going with him. He wasn't thinking of it that way at all, which I realized one night when he and his roommate got really drunk and they were going to trade me back and forth. I didn't realize it until the roommate started dragging me out of the room. Larry didn't do anything at all until I started crying. I got really scared and was screaming and crying. Then he started talking to me and calmed me down, but that was the end of that.

"Later, I found out that he was married *three weeks* after he graduated. I was his last fling, apparently. He knew he was getting married, but of course I didn't.

"My problem is that I have this morality thing where sleeping with people is a big thing for me. First of all, I make it too big, and so then I have to fall in love with the person. I tend to ignore their bad parts and only focus on what's good about them.

"I didn't have any rules put on me when I was younger, but I had *hurt* in a way. Part of my problem was because my dad was having affairs. I think I shut myself off because of it. Like I feel I can't flirt and I can't play games with my female self or my femininity.

"That's tied in with my confused attitude about men and relationships. I have a way of anticipating sad endings and hurt as part of the relationship."

Once a person gains confidence in her own value system, no matter what it is, she can look on different ethics and assumptions with a comfortable sense of perspective and not be threatened by them. Several young people told me that when they knew what they wanted, even when it didn't fit peer-pressure expectations, other people found them even more appealing.

Adele, for instance, after the initial shock of being "treated like a piece of livestock" at college, decided that she needn't accept the criteria or play the game according to rules she didn't like. A very pretty young woman with long brown hair, brown eyes and olive skin, she comes from a Southern Baptist background in Texas. Her father is a bank manager and her mother is a university secretary.

"In the spring," Adele, who is now a college sophomore, says, "I had a period that was unique. I felt very good about myself, and I decided that I was going to be myself and ignore that evaluation process because it was stupid and I wouldn't subject myself to it. If someone started giving me a line, I'd just say, 'Hey, I'm not interested in that line. I've heard it too many times,' or flip things like that.

"Anyway, in the spring, guys would just ask me out, wherever I was. I had twelve straight weeks of dates. Everyone was asking me out. It was really a lot of fun. I couldn't get over it. I couldn't do anything wrong. . . ."

June's experience working in a Los Angeles bank was similar to Adele's in college. Her confidence and freshness draws people to her.

"There aren't that many guys I'm interested in," she says. "There are a lot of guys thirty-five years old and just divorced who ask me out, though. I wouldn't think of going out with them. I tell them, 'You're almost old enough to be my father!' or I say something like, 'You're not even tall, blond or tan!'

"Some people draw conclusions real fast. It's easy to like someone just because they like you. But that's not the way to be."

When I talked with young people about how their dating habits, sexual views and experiences changed when they moved away from home and took total charge of their own time, I was struck over and again with what a personal exploration sexual behavior is. So many components of one's sexual feelings are wrapped up in the matrix of one's childhood and stirred by old feelings of love and warmth. In the same way, when we care deeply for someone, our infantile fears of separation and abandonment are also stirred. How young people respond to their new freedom and the new pressures they face are also intimately connected to their personal history and the perspective they've gained on themselves from their family.

"I never felt that much pressure here," says Bill, a sophomore at Yale. "For me, it's easier to relate to women as friends. I figure there's that half of humanity and now there's a much greater opportunity to learn how they think about things than there was in high school. I live in a coed dorm and share a bathroom with women, and I like that. We all observe decorum. We don't bang open the shower curtains when someone's taking a shower, but you wouldn't do that to anybody. There's nothing intrinsically gross about seeing a girl brush her teeth. It's possible to say good morning without wondering, oh, wow, are you a sex object?

"Sexual pressure depends on the way you relate to people, and to some extent, to where you are.

"I think that not having limits is good because you learn to accept responsibility for your own actions and decisions," says Bill. "I had one 'talk' with my father. It was when my parents first learned I had a girl friend after I was in college. He came to me all nervous, pacing around and cracking his knuckles. 'There are some things you should know,' he said. 'There are some things you should know about women and men . . .' He asked me if I had any questions, and I just kept quiet. I didn't ask him anything.

"I think it's really tough on parents to accept that their children are acting sexually."

One essential ingredient that young people seem to look for from their parents when they leave home is trust. Being able to have that confidence is an important part of a young person's feeling of security in leaving and making independent decisions. Despite their efforts, though, parents still worry.

"My parents and I can communicate on every level," says Delia, "but I don't think they can see I can be totally independent fifteen hundred miles away from home and be free and not be promiscuous or totally off the wall. I'd say, 'Mom, you know how I was raised. You know my values.' But she still worries."

"My parents have faith in my moral system and the way they brought me up," says Liz. "I really appreciate it because they trust me and I know they do, so I feel responsible and good about myself."

Long before I ever thought of doing a book on teenage sexuality, I'd interviewed and written about adolescents who acted out their frustrations about separation in dramatic ways: the boys stole or struck out or committed delinquent acts, and the girls, for the most part, ran away from home or were self-destructive. Many of these youngsters were legally classified as juvenile delinquents; others were called status offenders—in other words, the laws they broke were only offenses because they were underage. The offenses range from breaking curfew, drinking or smoking in public, using obscene language in public and running away from home, to having sexual intercourse or being sexually promiscuous. Three-fourths of the girls who are in juvenile institutions are status offenders—and most of them were put there by their parents because they were "uncontrollable."

What I heard from these teenagers, over and over again, with many different manifestations of behavior, was that their parents could not bear for them to grow up. Their parents could not allow them a successful separation. Often, by rejecting their children or pushing them out into a premature separation, knowing the children would break down and have to come back, parents have kept them dependent, kept them at home and emotionally connected. It also seemed clear, in many cases, that the girls who were punished for their presumed sexual behavior were victims of a mother's jealousy or a father's attraction or both. These families did not handle separation well; in fact, they were very destructive of one another.

Many parents who are more mature emotionally and who are more self-aware often find themselves having very similar, very difficult problems about the time their children are pushing for independence. Parents, often without understanding why, resist being forced out of parental roles. They don't want to face their middle age without their maternal or paternal roles. Often, they don't want to make the difficult adjustments required in getting used to themselves or free time or one another without children as a buffer or a point of focus. Teenagers, too, can force renewed dependency out of fear of autonomy

Separating isn't particularly easy for anyone, although I suspect that more often than not, it takes the biggest toll on parents. When parents have trouble, it compounds an already difficult task for the teenager.

"My mother would call me up and cry about my dad on the phone to me," said nineteen-year-old Randy, speaking of his first year in his own apartment. "He'd go out drinking and then he'd be mean and nasty when he came home. They split up more times that year than they'd ever split up before. I spent most of last year racing over there to patch things up. It was crazy. I felt like I might as well move back sometimes, because I felt like I had to take care of them. Now things have cooled down a lot. I can eat dinner without worrying about the phone ringing with another crisis."

Sometimes, when a parent can't handle the separation, a teenager obliges by quitting college and going home or having a nervous breakdown or just never getting around to leaving.

"For an adolescent to be successful at separation and individuation, a parent has to allow it," says Carol Silbergeld, who holds a master's degree in social work and is a therapist in Santa Monica, California. "If the parent is holding on it's much harder for the adolescent.

"When one doesn't feel loved, it's very hard to separate. If a parent wants to keep the kid forever, and keep him from successfully separating, the best way to do that is to reject him a little bit all the time.

"No matter his age, the child is always trying to get from the parent what he's not getting, and the child feels responsible for that lack within himself. He feels it's his own shortcomings that are causing the rejection, and this interferes with his own development, with separating and developing a good self-esteem. Without good self-esteem and good separation, it's hard to move on to new relationships. . . ."

Just as teenagers move on to new relationships and into adulthood, so parents move on to new ways of defining themselves as adults separate from their children and their children's decisions. They learn to think about themselves in new ways, whether they're living on Park Avenue or on Main Street in Cleveland or on 136th Street in Harlem.

When Matina's only child, Eva, got married secretly at the age of seventeen, for instance, Matina felt her heart was permanently broken. She had worked hard all her life so that Eva would have an opportunity to go to college and better herself. Matina had dreamed for Eva to be well-educated, independent and settled in a career. When Eva married an eighteen-year-old boy in her class who was unemployed and rather aimless, Matina gained weight and walked heavily, as if bags of sand were balanced on her shoulders.

"I don't know why she do this to me," Matina cried. "I don't know what I do wrong! I do everything so she can go *up*, so she can do better things and get an education. I say to her, you don't want to be like me and have to work with your hands! You can get an education! You can make good money and lead a professional life!

"But no. She throws it all away to marry a bum!"

Four months later, I saw Matina again. She's lost weight, and her face looked bright again. "I am better," she admitted, smiling. "I'm learning to let go and to think about *me* every now and then. All my life I have centered my thinking around her. Now I have to think for myself and let her go. It's better for both of us.

"She's in training for a nurse's job. Who knows. Maybe she'll do okay—we'll see. But I tell myself, remember to think about me and what I want. It's not easy, but I learn!"

"One time when my mom and dad were going out," says Cindi, "I walked around my mom, the way she always walks around me to check out if I've forgotten anything before I go out. I said, 'Not bad! You look really pretty, Mom. Now go out and have a good time, but be careful and don't stay out late. Don't be back any later than 12:30—you need a good sleep tonight. Do you have a dime in case you need to call? And, oh, Mom. Did you remember to brush your teeth?' She just about died laughing. She kept saying, 'I never sounded that bad, did I?' I told her not quite, at least not most of the time. And I told her I appreciated it anyway—everything but the line about brushing my teeth—which she still asks me every time!"

19.

Sex and Love for Tomorrow's Child

There's more to teenage sexuality than problems. There's joy to consider. There's also the foundation of self-understanding and intimacy upon which teenagers build experiences and confidence for the rest of their lives.

When their bodies become reproductively capable, it's normal and natural that they take an interest in sex. In addition to having active mental and spiritual lives, in addition to our many senses and our abilities to observe and communicate, we all have sexuality. We have a natural capacity for euphoria, for the bonding of bodies as pure enjoyment, entertainment, warmth and well-being, in addition to creating future generations.

Adolescents today are in the very special position of being able to integrate their sexuality into an awareness of themselves as whole, mental, spiritual and emotional people. They have the potential to witness an evolution of their senses and to understand their physical bodies, their sexual excitement and their own responses from the time they are young.

They have the advantage of living in a day and age in which sexual feelings and desires are openly acknowledged—and no longer considered sick or sinful. And although many people still repress their feelings, although many are secretive about the source of their eroticism because of personal feelings of shame rather than a healthy need for privacy, teenagers have a vast amount of available information to draw upon and learn from if they wish to do so. They have the vocabulary and the cultural sanction to talk about sex and to learn about it.

If they take the time and the care, they can also become comfortable and intimate with other human beings to whom they're attracted. They

312

can learn how to touch and be touched. If they give themselves permission, they can discover how they like to be held and handled, what feels exciting and gratifying to their skin and their senses, what thrills them and in turn, what makes that other person feel whole and good, and sometimes enchanted.

If adolescents allow themselves a gradual move into intimacy and into sexual experience, they can savor the delicious satisfactions of getting to know themselves sexually and can build a foundation upon which their adult sexual experiences will thrive.

In his scholarly and unparalleled research, Alfred Kinsey found beyond doubt that life patterns of sexual behavior are greatly affected by the experiences of adolescence—not only because they are initial experiences, but because they occur during the age of such great sexual and physical capability, activity and drive. People are extremely impressionable during adolescent years and are in the process of developing their individual life patterns. Kinsey found that adults who had had sexual experiences as teenagers made much happier marital adjustments than adults who had not.

From what we know of sexual excitement, the source of much of our personal eroticism is fixed during infancy and early childhood. The sexual scripts, or playlets, to which we consciously and unconsciously respond are woven into the intricate tapestry of our psychic lives.

The extent to which we allow ourselves freedom in our private sexual feelings and fantasies, the extent to which we allow ourselves sexual expression, has to do with habits, beliefs and behavior patterns which we develop through the years, but which begin to take real shape during adolescence.

With information and encouragement, teenagers today have an opportunity to integrate their sexual feelings and behavior into their lives with a lot less pain than their parents did.

Erring in the opposite direction is also possible, however. A danger today's young adolescents face is jumping into intercourse at the first opportunity because of the status involved in being "cool," "adult" and nonvirgin. Many are not emotionally or intellectually capable of understanding what they're doing and such an experience can give them a setback emotionally or merely give them a less than satisfactory introduction to what otherwise can be a very fulfilling evolutionary experience.

It seems to me that adolescents of all ages should be encouraged to have foreplay and to defer intercourse until they are extremely comfortable in their own bodies and very much at ease about themselves and their sexual partners. Teenagers should think about their own requirements for sexual intimacy and have great respect for their own feelings and values. They should decide what conditions they want in their relationships. For some, that will mean being in love and being secure about the love of the other person. For others, it might mean literally sleeping with and knowing the other person for a period of time before being relaxed about intercourse. For others, it will mean marriage or a commitment to a long-term relationship, and for others, it will mean having their own apartment or merely knowing what the experience means to their sexual partners.

Young people who do not want to have children need to be told that if they do not want children, but they want to have sex, it's okay to have sex as long as they use birth control. Girls should be encouraged to plan and to be prepared. They should be told that it's good and proper for them to take care of themselves, to be interested in sex, and to prepare for it. They should also be told that it's perfectly normal for them not to have sex if they don't want to, and that it's good and proper to wait until they feel sure they're ready for the experience. When they are ready is time enough.

Parents are often unduly frightened by the whole phenomenon of teenagers deciding to have sex at younger and younger ages. Sometimes it may well be that age does make a difference, but I believe that it is the teenagers' ability to make decisions based on their personal wants, needs, realities and values that matters most. Some younger adolescents often do need guidance because they don't have the cognitive ability to understand cause and effect. Later on, however, they have the ability to be responsible, and don't need the same kind of intervention.

We should remember, however, that sexuality is not something that begins at age fourteen—or arrives with the onset of puberty. It begins at birth and is rooted in our feelings about ourselves and our parents. I believe that it's essential we teach our young children, as well as our teenagers, how to make decisions. We should help them see that they have the power to make decisions in all different areas of their lives. They need to know that when it comes to sex, they can also make clear and rational decisions. It does *not* connote promiscuity to know about birth control and to use it, for instance, if you're going to have sex and you don't want a baby. It connotes being responsible for your own life and being responsible for another very important life, the life of a child.

A goal for teenagers moving into their adult lives is that they form intimate relationships, that they fulfill a sense of themselves as independent individuals in a larger community. Today's teenagers are no better or worse than those of twenty and fifty years ago.

In today's environment, we have the freedom to talk to other people about sexual matters and to find out that our responses are "normal," that sex isn't perfect and that it's something that can be an enriching part of the totality of our lives.

"In many ways, kids in this generation are healthier than in our generation," says Dr. John O'Brian, psychoanalyst and director of Child and Adolescent services at St. Vincent's Hospital in New York. "Today there's a more conducive attitude toward good discussion about sexuality and about our own experiences.

"Sexuality is a part of the person's being—not all of the person. We have to have that perspective. And with sexual experience, you have the giving of one person to another. At first, you're so caught up in your own experience that you're not giving very much. But as time goes on, you're giving and getting more. We have to put sexual experience in its place as part and only part of an intimate relationship."

It may be that in addition to being psychologically healthier, today's young people are biologically healthier, as well. Although there has been alarm that girls are having sex at earlier ages, it seems to me that overall, it's a biologically natural and thus a psychologically healthy development. In every other species, when females come into maturity, males are waiting at the gate. It's almost unheard of in nature for a female not to copulate when she is ready for reproduction.

Dr. Winnifred Cutler, a reproductive biologist who conducted research at the University of Pennsylvania, has found direct correlations between the age of first intercourse and infertility later in life. The degree of the inability to conceive a child intensified in direct correlation with how advanced the age at first coitus was. The critical period for the first intercource appeared to be seven years after the first menstruation.[1]

"It may be that the price we pay for delayed copulation when a woman is ready for reproduction is infertility," says Dr. Cutler. "It's been my premise as a biologist that everything animals do is normal and natural. As human beings, we are animals, too. But unlike animals, who have no mores, no theories and no ethical values, we do have mores, theories and ethics, and we do things differently. My question is, to the extent that we do things differently from other mammals, there might be a price to pay in reproductive capacity."

In her research, Dr. Cutler has also found correlations between sporadic sexual behavior and infertility, and a disrupted, feast-or-famine type of sex life associated with patterns of infertility. The woman who has regular, stable and continual sexual activity seems to be the more fertile and the most fit.

Likewise, Dr. Cutler's research also supports how natural female aggressiveness is. In the course of studying the length of menstrual cycles of three hundred women students at the University of Pennsylvania, Dr. Cutler asked them to record their menstrual cycles and eating and sleeping habits when they had intercourse and when they masturbated. She found that women who had regular weekly sexual activity tended to have stable, fertile-type menstrual cycles and had an increase of sexual activity at the time of ovulation. Even women with sporadic activity almost never missed having sex around the time of ovulation.[2] This leads to a simple, remarkable and biologically obvious truth: Nature tells us somehow (is it genetic programming?) what we ought to do to reproduce the species. And we do what comes naturally.

Even though what many of our children are doing may be biologically natural, it doesn't always work to talk with them about it. I'm reminded of a story I heard about a real 1980s relationship between father and daughter. The father, a Wall Street lawyer in his fifties, got together for dinner with his twenty-year-old daughter, who was home for vacation from Harvard College. The two had always been very close and had always had free-wheeling discussions about many aspects of their lives. At dinner, the father asked his daughter how she was, how she'd been and what had been going on in her life.

"I'm really okay," she said. "The only trouble is that I've been having trouble having orgasms."

The father was silent for a few moments. Then he said, "I think we need more of a gap in our relationship."

Obviously it isn't necessary for parents and their children to talk about everything. Details of their sexual relationships are just as private for parents as they are for their teenagers.

Parents *should* talk to their children about what they value, what they care about. They should talk about love and loyalty and commitment and what taking care of another person, what giving and receiving, mean. Parents often feel reticent when talking to their children about values and about love. Perhaps they think they're old-fashioned or feel unsure whether it's appropriate. Whether children agree or not, they should be exposed to what their parents feel and what their parents care about. Teenagers need a measure; they need a starting place in order to know where they're going.

" As a culture, we're almost ashamed to talk about love or ethics, not about sex," says Joyce Banzhof, a teacher and counselor at Beverly Hills High School in California. "We depersonalize our talk about love."

Mrs. Banzhoff, who teaches sex education as part of her health-education course at the high school, says, "I don't tend to talk about my marriage because I'm afraid to come across smug. I find myself leaving out of my discussions my feelings about the importance of marriage and family.

"You tend to slight morals and ethics—loyalty, faithfulness and commitment—because it sounds old-fashioned to people," she says. "The omissions are acceptable in a very loving environment because the kids *see* it for themselves, but for kids who don't happen to have that in their experience, one tends to wonder what happens to them and where they get their values."

Many of the people I talked to repeated how important values are;

how vital it is for young people to learn how to be responsible to themselves and other people in their lives. Teenagers also seemed to want and need support for the ethics and values they formulate.

"*Everybody's* shaking up the importance of sex," says Olive Cameron, Chief Midwife at Mt. Sinai Hospital in New York City. "The television, the media, the movies, they make it all sound exciting, like it's the thing to do, so the kids go out and do it and they get pregnant.

"The answer to the situation is that we've got to go back and teach values. We have to give kids a value system, a sense of self-worth and self-aspiration. It's the family's responsibility. And we have to get back to these things, back to the basics."

As a culture, we are probably approaching eighth or ninth grade. Certainly we're in our sexual adolescence. Sometimes, when I see grown men on the street intensely focusing on every pair of breasts that passes by, I'm reminded of the seventh-grade boys who told me that they really can't concentrate on their studies because they're so busy looking at the girls' breasts. Certainly many of our true adolescents are watching as we try out the sexual roles we missed when we were teenagers, when we experiment with new attitudes and behavior or go into therapy to learn how to hug and hold one another.

The extent of the difficulty we adults have had coming to terms with our own sexuality and integrating it into our lives is reflected in the growing numbers of books and therapies that address themselves to sexual disfunctions. We have fears and inhibitions in our thirties and forties that we might have been able to rid ourselves of in our late teens or early twenties had we had the information available to us.

Rather than worry about teenage sexuality as a "problem" that leads to pregnancy, adults should focus on how to give their children the information they need to grow into their new bodies, ideas and feelings with a sense of equanimity. We should help them learn how to deal with their new attributes and capabilities, so that as they mature and form relationships, they can do so with as much pleasure and ease as possible.

As for concern about teenage hostility or depersonalization of one another in sexual matters owing to overexposure to television and the movies, I seriously doubt that teenagers are any different from adults in this regard. Certainly there's no evidence that they have a monopoly on neurosis, on sadistic or masochistic inclinations. If anything, they have the advantage of minimizing disturbances by airing them, expressing them and working them through at an early age rather than operating on them for years in secrecy.

Certainly, if they start younger, many of today's teenagers may have more sexual relationships in the long run than did their parents. This won't necessarily hurt them. Life is different for them, and if they are so disposed, they do have more options than we did to experiment sexually, to try on roles and relationships with society's sanction.

"It seems things have changed rapidly with teenagers," says Evelyn Caskey, the principal of Scottsdale High School. "Yet they've got to be capable of changing faster. Life is changing faster because things around them are changing faster.

"Recently I visited an old cemetery in San Francisco. If you look at some of those old cemeteries, you see how young people were when they died. There are so many grave stones where people had died at the age of twenty or the age of thirty. And so people had a second wife if the first one died, and a third wife if the second wife died. They didn't stay with the same spouse all those years. Yet we say there's so much promiscuity today. Maybe things are just more honest. I'm not ready to put a value judgment on it."

Many of today's teenagers are involved in "serial monogamy"—one relationship after another that's exclusive, the route of their great-grandparents. It's also true that today's teenagers have more freedom to get into trouble and more freedom to err.

As Evelyn Caskey said, "When you think about the growth of freedom that's been provided in this country, it's amazing. What's happened and is happening for blacks, what's happened and is happening for women, for the handicapped, for the young . . . with this comes the freedom to have children out of wedlock and the opportunity to make even more mistakes. It's all part of the growth of freedom.

"It's fantastic," she says, sitting back in her large leather chair. "All men are equal. What a wonderful, radical idea. It's an idea we have to be willing to follow. We have to recognize that allowing freedom also means making mistakes and going in directions we didn't always expect."

There's much we don't know about where we are or where we're going, much we don't know about adolescence and the chemistry of our own bodies, much we don't know about sexual fantasy, sexual excitement, eroticism and sex itself—whether it's gender identity, the act of intercourse or other aspects of sexual interaction. By the time today's teenagers are their parents' age, much more information will be available. From what we've heard from teenagers so far, I imagine that in addition to new information, today's teenagers will be telling their children that love is integral to the most satisfying sex. That commitment makes a difference. That sex is important, but that other issues are just as important. In their children's lives, most likely, the notions of love and loyalty and mutual care will take center stage again as the matrix from which the most satisfying, fulfilling lovemaking emerges. Sex without love won't be condemned, but sex with love will be the aim.

Notes

Chapter 1

1. Lloyd D. Johnston, PhD, Jerald G. Bachman, PhD, and Patrick M. O'Malley, PhD, of The University of Michigan Institute for Social Research. *Highlights From Student Drug Use in America, 1975–1980*, pp. 7–9.

2. Johnston, p. 19.

3. Melvin Zelnik and John F. Kantner, "Sexual Activity, Contraceptive Use and Pregnancy Among Metropolitan Area Teenagers: 1971–1979." *Family Planning Perspectives* 12: No. 5 (Sept./Oct. 1980), pp. 230–37.

4. Ellen Freeman, PhD, and Karl Rickels, MD, "Adolescent Contraceptive Use: Current Status of Practice and Research." *Obstetrics and Gynecology* 53, No. 3 (March 1979), p. 388.

5. Freeman, p. 389.

6. National Center for Health Statistics, "Final Natality Statistics, 1978," *Monthly Vital Statistics Report*, Vol. 29, No. 1, 1980.

Chapter 5

1. Roger Revelle and Rose Frisch at Harvard make this speculation. Their research shows that the adolescent growth spurt begins at relatively constant weights for girls and boys, and that menstruation begins at a relatively constant weight-to-height ratio for girls.

2. Dr. Anne C. Peterson, director of the Laboratory for the Study of Adolescence at Chicago's Michael Reese Hospital and Medical Center

and research associate and assistant professor in the department of psychiatry at the University of Chicago, says that available data show that the age of menarche began to get earlier around the time of the Industrial Revolution, a period associated with an increased standard of living and advances in medical science. Cross-cultural data, she says, show that better nutrition, higher social class, fewer children in the family and living in urban rather than rural areas are also related to earlier maturation. She speculates that if improved nutrition and corresponding decreases in disease and illness are responsible for the trend toward earlier puberty, then the trend should level off when people are nourished at an optimal level. In fact, there is evidence that this is occurring in industrialized countries. Where major variations exist, she says, there also appear to be large differences in nutrition and health care. Recent research by Alan E. Treloar has shown that a trend back toward older menarche has begun, which may support this theory.

3. James Leslie McCary, *McCary's Human Sexuality.*

4. James M. Tanner, *Growth at Adolescence.*

5. Herant A. Katchadourian, MD, and Donald T. Lunde, MD. *Biological Aspects of Human Sexuality.*

6. Alfred Kinsey, Wardell B. Pomeroy, and Clyde E. Martin, *Sexual Behavior in the Human Male.*

7. Tanner.

8. Tanner.

9. Tanner.

Chapter 6

1. Peter Blos, *The Adolescent Passage.*

2. Blos, *pp. 125–26.*

3. Blos, *pp. 125–26.*

Chapter 7

1. Robert C. Sorenson, *Adolescent Sexuality in Contemporary America.*

2. Sorenson.

3. Robert J. Stoller, MD, *Sexual Excitement: The Dynamics of Erotic Life*, p. 13.

4. Stoller, p. 14.

5. Alfred Kinsey, Wardell B. Pomeroy, and Clyde E. Martin, *Sexual Behavior in the Human Male.*

6. Kinsey, p. 506.

7. Aaron Hass, PhD, *Teenage Sexuality.*

8. James W. Maddock, "Sex in Adolescence: Its Meaning and Its Future." *Adolescence Magazine* 8: No. 31 (Fall, 1973), pp. 325-42.

9. Hass, p. 86.

10. John Money, "Pornography in the Home: A Topic in Medical Education." In *Contemporary Sex and Behavior: Critical Issues in the 1970s, p. 415.*

11. Money.

12. Kinsey, *Sexual Behavior in the Human Male*, p. 503.

Chapter 9

1. Elizabeth J. Roberts, David Kline, and John Gagnon, "Family Life and Sexual Learning: A Study of the Role of Parents in the Sexual Learning of Children."

Chapter 11

1. Carol Tavris and Leonore Tiefer, "The Origin of the Kiss." *Redbook* (May 1979), p. 41.

Chapter 12

1. Melvin Zelnik and John F. Kantner, "Sexual Activity, Contraceptive Use and Pregnancy Among Metropolitan Area Teenagers: 1971–1979." *Family Planning Perspectives* 12: No. 5 (Sept./Oct. 1980).

Chapter 14

1. Alfred Kinsey, Wardell B. Pomeroy, and Clyde E. Martin, *Sexual Behavior in the Human Male*, p. 650.

2. Kinsey, p. 650.

3. Kinsey, p. 639.

Chapter 15

1. Laurie Schwab Zabin, John F. Kantner, and Melvin Zelnik, "The Risk of Adolescent Pregnancy in the First Months of Intercourse."

Family Planning Perspectives (Nov. 1979), pp. 215–22.

2. Frank F. Furstenberg, Jr., Richard Lincoln, and Jane Menken, eds., *Teenage Sexuality, Pregnancy and Childbearing,* p. 11.

3. Melvin Zelnik and John F. Kantner, "Sexual Activity, Contraceptive Use and Pregnancy Among Metropolitan Area Teenagers, 1971–1979." *Family Planning Perspectives* 12: No. 5 (Sept./Oct. 1980), pp. 230–31.

4. Zelnik, p. 231.

5. Zelnik, p. 236.

6. Zelnik, p. 236.

7. Laurie Schwab Zabin, John F. Kantner, and Melvin Zelnik, The Risk of Adolescent Pregnancy in the First Months of Intercourse." *Family Planning Perspectives.* 11: (Nov. 1979), pp. 215–22.

8. Zelnik and Kantner, "Sexual Activity . . . and Pregnancy," pp. 236–37.

9. Ellen W. Freeman et al, "Adolescent Contraceptive Use: Comparisons of Male and Female Attitudes and Information."*American Journal of Public Health* 70: No. 8 (Aug. 1980), p. 195.

10. *Teenage Pregnancy: The Problem That Hasn't Gone Away.*

Chapter 16

1. *Teenage Pregnancy: The Problem That Hasn't Gone Away*, p. 29.

2. *Teenage Pregnancy*, p. 17.

3. *Teenage Pregnancy,* p. 29.

Chapter 17

1. *11 Million Teenagers: What Can Be Done about the Epidemic of Adolescent Pregnancies in the United States.*

2. John R. Weeks, *Teenage Marriages: A Demographic Analysis.*

3. *11 Million Teenagers . . .*

4. *Teenage Pregnancy: The Problem That Hasn't Gone Away.*

5. Frank F. Furstenberg, Jr., *Unplanned Parenthood: The Social Consequences of Teenage Childbearing:*

Chapter 19

1. Winnifred Berg Cutler, Celso-Ramon Garcia, and Abba M. Krieger, "Infertility and Age at First Coitus: A Possible Association." *Journal of Biosocial Science* 11 (1979), pp. 425–32.

2. Cutler, "Lunar and Menstrual Phase Locking," *American Journal of Obstetrics and Gynecology.* 137: No. 7 (Aug. 1980), pp. 834–36.

Bibliography

Adelson, Joseph. *Handbook of Adolescent Psychology*. New York: Wiley, 1980.

Akpom, C. Amechi and Kathy L., and Marianne Davis. "Prior Sexual Behavior of Teenagers Attending Rap Sessions for the First Time." *Family Planning Perspectives* 8:203–6.

Barbach, Lonnie Garfield. *For Yourself: The Fulfillment of Female Sexuality*. Garden City: Doubleday, 1975.

Becker, Ernest. *The Denial of Death*. New York: Free Press, 1973.

Bell, Robert. *Premarital Sex in a Changing Society*. Englewood Cliffs: Prentice-Hall, 1966.

Best, Winfield. "Teensex: How Far Do They Really Go?" *Ladies' Home Journal*, February 1973.

Bettelheim, Bruno. *The Uses of Enchantment*. New York: Alfred A. Knopf, 1976.

Blos, Peter. *On Adolescence: A Psychoanalytical Interpretation*. New York: Free Press, 1962.

———. *The Adolescent Passage*. New York: International Universities Press, 1979.

———. *The Adolescent Personality*. New York: Appleton-Century-Crofts, 1941.

Burr, Hanford M. *Studies in Adolescent Boyhood*. Springfield: Seminar Publishing, 1913.

Butterfield, Fox. "Love and Sex in China." *The New York Times Magazine*, January 13, 1980.

Byler, Ruth, Gertrude Lewis, and Ruth Totman. *Teach Us What We Want to Know*. New York: Published for Connecticut State Board of Education by Mental Health Materials Center, New York, 1969.

Calderone, Mary S., and Eric W. Johnson. *The Family Book About Sexuality.* New York: Harper & Row, 1981.

Caplan, Gerald, and Serge Lebovici, eds. *Adolescence: Psychological Perspectives.* New York: Basic Books, 1969.

Cates, Willard Jr., and Christopher Tietze. "Standardized Mortality Rates Associated With Legal Abortion: United States, 1971–75." *Family Planning Perspectives* 10: No. 3, May–June 1975.

Chess, Stella, et al. "Sexual Attitudes and Behavior Patterns in a Middle-Class Adolescent Population." *American Journal of Psychiatry* 46: October 1975.

Comfort, Alex. *Sex in Society.* Secaucus: Citadel Press, 1963.

Cottle, Thomas J. *Children's Secrets.* Garden City: Doubleday, 1980.

Crawley, Lawrence. *Reproduction, Sex and Preparation for Marriage.* Englewood Cliffs: Prentice-Hall, 1964.

Cutler, Winnifred Berg. "Lunar and Menstrual Phase Locking." *American Journal of Obstetrics and Gynecology* 137:384.

—— and Celso-Ramon Garcia. "The Psychoneuroendocrinology of the Ovulatory Cycle of Woman: A Review." *Psychoneuroendocrinology* 5:89.

—— and Abba M. Krieger. "Infertility and Age at First Coitus: A Possible Association." *Journal of Biosocial Sci.* 11:1979.

——. "Lunar Phase Defects: A Possible Relationship Between Short Hyperthermic Phase and Sporadic Sexual Behavior in Women." *Hormones and Behavior* 13: 214–18.

——, Celso Ramon Garcia and Abba M. Krieger. "Sexual Behavior Frequency and Menstrual Cycle Length in Mature Premenopausal Women." *Psychoneuroendocrinology* 164: January, 1980.

Cutright, Phillips. "The Teenage Sexual Revolution and the Myth of an Abstinent Past." *Family Planning Perspectives* 4: No. 1, January 1972.

Dodson, Fitzhugh. Cutright, Philip. "The Teenage Sexual Revolution and the Myth of an Abstinent Past." *Family Planning Perspectives* 4: No. 1, January 1972.

Dodson, Fitzhugh. *How to Father.* New York: Signet Books, New America Library, 1974.

Douvan, Elizabeth, and Joseph Adelson. *The Adolescent Experience.* New York: John Wiley and Sons, 1966.

Duvall, Evelyn Millis. *Facts of Life and Love for Teenagers.* New York: Association Press, 1956.

11 Million Teenagers: What Can Be Done About the Epidemic of Adolescent Pregnancies in the United States. New York: Alan Guttmacher Foundation; Parenthood Federation of America, 1976.

Erikson, Erik. *Identity, Youth and Crisis.* New York: W. W. Norton, 1968.

————. *Insight and Responsibility.* New York: W. W. Norton, 1964.

Esman, Aaron, ed. *The Psychology of Adolescence.* New York: International Universities Press, 1975.

Evans, Richard I. *Dialogue with Erik Erikson.* New York: E. P. Dutton, 1967.

Forrest, Jacqueline Darroch, Ellen Sullivan and Christopher Tietze. "Abortion in the United States, 1977–78." *Family Planning Perspectives* 11: No. 6, November–December 1979.

Fort, J. "Youth: Drugs, Sex and Life." *Current Problems in Pediatrics* 6: January 1976.

Fox, Greer Litton. "The Family's Influence on Adolescent Sexual Behavior." *Children Today.* May–June 1979.

Fraiberg, Selma H. *The Magic Years.* New York: Charles Scribner's Sons, 1959.

Freeman, Ellen W., PhD, and Karl Rickels, MD. "Adolescent Contraceptive Use: Current Status of Practice and Research." *Obstetrics and Gynecology* 53: No. 3.

Freeman, Ellen W., et al. "Adolescent Contraceptive Use: Comparisons of Male and Female Attitudes and Information." *American Journal of Public Health* 70: No. 8, August 1980.

————, et al. "Self Reports of Emotional Distress in Urban Black Adolescents." Research Report, Departments of Obstetrics and Gynecology, University of Pennsylvania, July 1980.

Freidenberg, Edgar Z. *Coming of Age in America.* New York: Random House, 1963.

————. *The Vanishing Adolescent.* New York: Dell, 1959.

Freud, Sigmund. *Sexuality and the Psychology of Love.* New York: Collier Books, 1963.

Friday, Nancy. *Men in Love.* New York: Delacorte, 1980.

Furstenberg, Frank F., Jr. "The Social Consequences of Teenage Parenthood." *Family Planning Perspectives* 8: 1976.

————. *Unplanned Parenthood: The Social Consequences of Teenage Childbearing.* New York: Free Press, Macmillan, 1976.

————, Richard Lincoln, and Jane Menken. *Teenage Sexuality, Pregnancy, and Childbearing.* Philadelphia: University of Pennsylvania Press, 1981.

Gadpaille, Warren J., MD. *The Cycles of Sex.* New York: Charles Scribner's Sons, 1975.

————. "A Psychiatrist Discusses Myths About Childhood Homosexuality." *Today's Health,* January 1971.

Glass, Esther Eby. *When You Date.* Scottsdale: Herald Press, 1952.

Glazer-Malbin, Nona, and Helen Youngelson Waehrer, eds. *Woman in a Man-Made World*. New York: Rand McNally Sociology Series, 1972.

Goldstein, Bernard. *Introduction to Human Sexuality*. New York: McGraw-Hill, 1976.

Gordon, Sol. *The Sexual Adolescent*. New York: Duxbury Press, 1979.

―――. *You Would if You Loved Me*. New York: Bantam Books, 1978.

Grinder, Robert E., ed. *Studies in Adolescence: A Book of Reading in Adolescent Development*. London: Macmillan, 1969.

Hanckel, Frances, and John Cunningham. *A Way of Love, A Way of Life*. New York: Lothrop, Lee & Shepard, 1979.

Hass, Aaron, PhD. *Teenage Sexuality: A Survey of Teenage Behavior*. New York: Macmillan, 1979.

Hatcher, Sherry L., PhD. "Understanding Adolescent Pregnancy and Abortion." Primary Care 3: No. 3, September 1976.

Hauser, Stuart T. *Black and White Identity Formation*. New York: John Wiley and Sons, 1971.

Hendin, Herbert. *The Age of Sensation*. New York: W. W. Norton, 1975.

Henshaw, Jacqueline Darrock Forress, Ellen Sullivan, and Christopher Tietze. "Abortion in the United States, 1978–1979." *Family Planning Perspectives* 13: No. 1, January–February 1981.

Hettlinger, Richard F. *Growing Up with Sex*. New York: Seabury Press, 1970.

Hite, Shere. *The Hite Report*. New York: Dell, 1976.

Hurlock, Elizabeth B. *Adolescent Development*. New York: McGraw-Hill, 1955.

Jensen, G. D., and M. Robbins. "Ten Reasons Why Sex Talks with Adolescents Go Wrong." *Medical Aspects of Human Sexuality*, July 1975.

Johnston, Lloyd D., PhD, et al. The University of Michigan Institute for Social Research. *Highlights From Drug Use Among American High School Students*. Rockville, Maryland: National Institute on Drug Abuse, 1975–1977.

―――. The University of Michigan Institute for Social Research. *Highlights from Student Drug Use in America 1975–1980*. Rockville, Maryland: National Institute on Drug Abuse. 1981. (U.S. Government Printing Office: 1981–341–166:6170.)

Journal of Clinical Child Psychology, "Adolescent Sexuality" 3: No. 3, Fall–Winter, 1974.

Kagan, Jerome, and Robert Coles, eds. *12 to 16: Early Adolescence*. New York: W. W. Norton, 1972.

Kaplan, Helen Singer, MD, PhD. *Making Sense of Sex*. New York: Simon and Schuster, 1979.

Katchadourian, Herant A., MD, and Donald T. Lunder, MD. *Biological Aspects of Human Sexuality*, 2nd ed. New York: Holt Rinehart & Winston, 1980.

Kinsey, Alfred Charles, *Sexual Behavior in the Human Female*. Philadelphia: W. B. Saunders, 1953.

———, Wardell B. Pomeroy, and Clyde E. Martin. *Sexual Behavior in the Human Male*. Philadelphia: W. B. Saunders, 1948.

Kirby, Douglas, Judith Alter, and Peter Scales. Mathtech, Inc.: "An Analysis of U.S. Sex Education Programs and Evaluation Methods." Written for the Department of Health, Education and Welfare, Public Health Service, Center for Disease Control. Atlanta, Georgia: July, 1979.

Kirkendall, Lester. *Premarital Intercourse and Interpersonal Relationships. New York: Julian Press, 1961*.

Konopka, Gisela. *The Adolescent Girl in Conflict*. Englewood Cliffs: Prentice-Hall, 1976.

———. *Young Girls: A Portrait of Adolescence*. Englewood Cliffs: Prentice-Hall, 1976.

Landis, Ludson T. and Mary G. *Personal Adjustment, Marriage and Family Living*. Englewood Cliffs: Prentice-Hall, 1975.

Lester, Julius. "Being a Boy." *Ms. Magazine*, July 1973.

Levinson, Daniel J. *The Seasons of a Man's Life*. New York: Ballantine Books, 1978.

Levinsohn, Florence. *What Teenagers Want to Know*. Chicago: Budlong Press, 1967.

Lewis, Howard R., and Martha E. *The Parents' Guide to Teenage Sex and Pregnancy*. New York: St. Martin's Press, 1980.

Lipsitz, Joan, ed. *Barriers*. New York: Ford Foundation, 1979.

———. *Growing Up Forgotten*. Lexington, Massachusetts: D. C. Heath, 1977.

MacDonald, Charlotte. "The Stunted World of Teen Parents." *Human Behavior* 8:53–55.

McCary, James Leslie. *McCary's Human Sexuality*. New York: Van Nostrand Reinhold, 1978.

Maddock, James W., PhD. "Sex in Adolescence: Its Meaning and Its Future." *Adolescence Magazine*, Vol. 8, No. 31, Fall, 1973.

Masters, William H., and Virginia E. Johnson. *Human Sexual Inadequacy*. Boston: Little Brown, 1970.

Masterson, James F., Jr., MD. *The Psychiatric Dilemma of Adolescence*. Boston: Little Brown, 1967.

May, Rollo. *Love and Will*. New York: W. W. Norton, 1969.

Maynard, Joyce. *Looking Back, a Chronicle of Growing Up Old in the Sixties.* Garden City: Doubleday, 1972.

Mead, Margaret. *Coming of Age in Samoa.* New York: Morrow Quill Paperbacks, 1928.

_____. *Culture and Commitment: A Study of the Generation Gap.* Garden City: Doubleday, 1970.

_____. *From the South Seas: Studies of Adolescence and Sex in Primitive Societies.* New York: William Morris, 1939.

Miller, Derek, MD. *Adolescence, Psychology, Psychopathology and Psychotherapy.* Jason Aronson, 1974.

Money, John. "Pornography in the Home: A Topic in Medical Education." In *Contemporary Sexual Behavior: Critical Issues in the 1970s.* Baltimore: Johns Hopkins University Press, 1973.

_____ and Anke Ehrhardt. *Man and Woman, Boy and Girl.* New York: New American Library, 1972.

_____ and Robert Athanasion. "Pornography: Review and Bibliographic Annotations." American Journal of Obstetrics and Gynecology 115: 130-46, January, 1973.

Morgenthau, Joan E., MD, et al. "Adolescent Contraceptives." Followup study, *New York State Journal of Medicine* 77: No. 6, May 1977.

_____ and P. S. S. Rao, MD. "Contraceptive Practices in an Adolescent Health Center." *New York State Journal of Medicine* 76: No. 8, August 1976.

Morrison, Eleanor S., and Vera Borosage, eds. *Human Sexuality: Contemporary Perspectives,* Palo Alto: Mayfield Publishing, 1973.

Muus, Rolf E., ed. *Adolescent Behavior and Society: A Book of Readings.* New York: Random House, 1971.

"Normal Adolescence," By the Committee on Adolescence Group for Advancement of Psychiatry. New York: Charles Scribner's Sons, 1968.

Offer, Daniel. *The Psychological World of the Teenager,* New York: Basic Books, 1969.

Petersen, Anne C. "Can Puberty Come Any Earlier?" *Psychology Today* 12: No. 9.

_____. "Coping with Puberty." Presented at Conference for Medical Research Week, Michael Reese Hospital and Medical Center, Chicago: September, 1979.

Rank, Otto. *Will, Therapy and Truth and Reality.* New York: Alfred A. Knopf, 1936.

Reiss, Ira L. *Premarital Sexual Statements in America.* New York: Free Press, 1960.

Roberts, Elizabeth J., David Kline and John Gagnon. "Family Life and Sexual Learning, a Study of the Role of Parents in the Sexual Learning of Children." Prepared by Project on Human Sexual Development, Population Education, Inc., Cambridge, Massachusetts, 1978.

Rogers, Carl R. *On Becoming a Person.* Boston: Houghton Mifflin, 1961.

Sarrel, Lorna, MSW, and Philip M., MD. *Sexual Unfolding.* Boston: Little Brown, 1979.

Semmens, James P., and Kermit E. Krantz. *The Adolescent Experience.* New York: Macmillan, 1970.

Shiloh, Ailon, ed. *Studies in Human Sexual Behavior: The American Scene.* Springfield: Charles C. Thomas Publishing, 1970.

Sorenson, Robert, C. *Adolescent Sexuality in Contemporary America.* New York: World Press, 1976.

Spacks, Patricia Mayer. *The Female Imagination.* New York: Avon Books, 1976.

Stoller, Robert. *Sexual Excitement: The Dynamics of Erotic Life.* New York: Pantheon, 1979.

Stone, L. Joseph, and Joseph Church. *Childhood and Adolescence.* New York: Random House, 1957.

Storer, Robert V. *Sex in Modern Life.* Melbourne: James Little and Son, 1933.

Sugar, Max, MD, ed. *Female Adolescent Development.* Chapter 2, "Female Pubertal Development" by Anne C. Peterson. New York: Bruner Mazel, 1979.

Sullivan, Harry Stack. *The Interpersonal Theory of Psychiatry.* New York: W. W. Norton, 1953.

Talese, Gay. *Thy Neighbor's Wife.* New York: Doubleday, 1980.

Tanner, James M. *Growth at Adolescence* 2nd ed. Oxford: Blackwell Scientific Publications, 1962.

———. "Sequence, Tempo, and Individual Variation in the Growth and Development of Boys and Girls Aged Twelve to Sixteen." *Daedalus,* Vol. 100, No. 4, Fall 1971, pp. 907–30.

"Teenage Pregnancy and Family Impact, New Perspectives on Policy." Family Impact Seminar, George Washington University's Institute for Educational Leadership, Washington, D. C., 1979.

Teenage Pregnancy: The Problem That Hasn't Gone Away. New York: The Alan Guttmacher Institute, 1981.

Thornburg, Hershel D. *The Bubblegum Years.* Tucson: H.E.L.P. Books, 1978.

Tiefer, Leonore. *Human Sexuality: Feelings and Functions.* New York: Harper and Row, 1979.

Tietze, Christopher. "The Effect of Legalization of Abortion on Population Growth and Public Health." *Family Planning Perspectives* 7: No. 3, May–June 1975.

Treloar, Alan E., Ruth E. Boynton, and Donald W. Cowan. "Secular Trend in Age at Menarche, U.S.A.: 1893–1974." Reprinted from *Excerpta Medica International Congress*, Series No. 394, "Biological and Clinical Aspects of Reproduction." Amsterdam: 1974.

Tripp, C. A. *The Homosexual Matrix*. New York: McGraw-Hill, 1975.

Vander, Arthur J., James H. Sherman, and Dorothy S. Luciano. *Human Physiology: The Mechanisms of Body Function*. New York: McGraw-Hill, 1970.

Van Houten, Therese, and Gary Golembiewski. "Adolescent Life Stress as a Predictor of Alcohol Abuse and/or Runaway Behavior." National Youth Alternatives Project. Washington, D.C., 1978.

Vincent, Clarke E. *Sexual and Marital Health*. New York: McGraw-Hill, 1973.

Weeks, John R. *Teenage Marriages: A Demographic Analysis*. Westport, Connecticut: Greenwood Press, 1976.

Weinstock, Edward, et al. "Legal Abortions in the United States Since the 1973 Supreme Court Decisions." *Family Planning Perspectives* 7: No. 1, January–February 1975.

Zabin, Laurie Schwab, John F. Kantner, and Melvin Zelnik. "The Risk of Adolescent Pregnancy in the First Months of Intercourse." *Family Planning Perspectives* 11: 1979.

Zelnik, Melvin, and John F. Kantner, "Sexual Activity, Contraceptive Use and Pregnancy Among Metropolitan Area Teenagers, 1971–1979" *Family Planning Perspectives* 12: No. 5, September–October 1980.

Zilbergeld, Bernie, and John Ullman. *Male Sexuality: A Guide to Sexual Fulfillment*. Boston: Little Brown, 1978.

Zubin, Joseph, and John Money, eds. *Contemporary Sexual Behavior: Critical Issues in the 1970s*. Baltimore: Johns Hopkins University Press, 1973.

Index